CHARLES READE

A Study in Victorian Authorship

CHARLES READE

A Study in Victorian Authorship

by

WAYNE BURNS

BOOKMAN ASSOCIATES

New York

© 1961 by Wayne Burns

Library of Congress Catalog Card Number 61–7182

MANUFACTURED IN THE UNITED STATES OF AMERICA

TO MY MOTHER

Preface

SINCE THE PRESENT WORK does not fit into any of the usual categories, a few words of prefatory explanation may be in order. In the first place this is not a biography, although it includes several biographical chapters; neither is it literary history, although at least two chapters may be so designated; nor is it criticism, although many chapters are primarily critical. Because it fits none of these categories yet includes them all I have designated it a study in Victorian authorship—with as much emphasis on "Victorian" as on "authorship." For Reade was as Victorian as Martin Tupper, and to study his artistic aims and achievements is necessarily to study the Victorian ideals of authorship that he shared with his greater and lesser contemporaries—from Dickens to M. E. Braddon.

In the now famous Notebooks and Notecards Reade has left a unique record of his efforts to fulfill these ideals[1]—a record so voluminous that a definitive scholarly treatment of his life and work can hardly be attempted at this time. At least I have not attempted it—although I have, for the first time, made full use of both the Notebooks and Notecards, and in addition have studied the major collections of Reade manuscripts available in American libraries.[2] The rest of my manuscript materials I have derived primarily from Compton Reade's *Charles Reade A Memoir* (1887), Malcolm Elwin's *Charles Reade* (1931), and Léone Rives's, *Charles Reade Sa Vie, Ses Romans* (1940). The documents reproduced in the *Memoir* are of course basic to any study of Reade, as are those in Elwin's *Charles Reade,* and Rives's book reproduces much new biographical data—as much, apparently, as Reade's descendants care to make available.[3]

But despite my scholarly indebtedness to these earlier works, particularly in matters biographical, my aim is not to correct or supplement them. My aim is rather to offer another and radically different interpretation of Reade's artistic career. Elwin presents Reade as a novelist of genius whose once great reputation has been destroyed by the forces of respectability; Rives, whose criticism can hardly be taken seriously, presents him as "a great novelist" who is also "the father of the modern theatre."[4] From my own point of view, Reade's is a story of artistic defeat, essentially a tragic story even when it verges on farce; and I have therefore tried to present it as a Victorian tragedy: to show how Reade came to write the novels he wrote in the way he wrote them, how in all but one of these novels he sacrificed his limited but nevertheless genuine artistic gifts to the Victorian "Enemies of Promise," finally to be defeated by the very forces he sought to propitiate. Moreover the tragedy has a moral, and in my introductory and concluding chapters I have tried to bring out its implications: to show that Reade's defeat is not his alone, that it is in many ways the defeat of his greater and lesser contemporaries.

✓   ✓   ✓

Although the faults and shortcomings of the present work are entirely my own, I am indebted to friends and colleagues for advice and criticism. My greatest debt is to Professor Emerson Grant Sutcliffe—for his unselfishness in permitting me to make use of his own work on Reade, and for his continued help and encouragement. I am also much indebted to Professors Leon Howard, Jerome Beaty, and George Bluestone, for their kindness in reading and criticizing the entire work in manuscript, and to Professors Gwendolyn Needham, Porter Perrin, Edward E. Bostetter, Leonard Manheim, Irving Howe, and John Carter for their criticism of various chapters in manuscript.

For grants that have enabled me to carry out my research I wish to thank the Pacific Coast Committee for the Humanities, The Huntington Library, and the University of Washington. And for a liberal publication subsidy I wish to thank the Agnes Anderson Committee of the University of Washington.

Also I wish to thank the librarians and staffs of The London Library, The Huntington Library, The Yale University Library, the Pierpont Morgan Library, and the Library of the University of California in Los Angeles—not only for permitting me to quote from their Reade manuscripts but for their courtesy and helpfulness in making these materials available.

✓   ✓   ✓

Earlier versions of chapters one and nine of the present study appeared in *Literature and Psychology;* the latter part of chapter five (together with parts of chapter one) appeared in my "Charles Reade's *Christie Johnstone:* A Portrait of the Artist as a Young Pre-Raphaelite" in *From Jane Austen to Joseph Conrad,* ed. by Robert C. Rathburn and Martin Steinman, Jr. (University of Minnesota Press, 1958), pp. 208–221.

[8]

Contents

Introduction

CHARLES READE (1814–1884) is a neglected, almost a forgotten novelist. If he is remembered at all, it is for *The Cloister and the Hearth*. The rest of his novels are becoming mere titles, easily confused with the titles of other Victorian novels—as recently demonstrated by a Victorian scholar in his reference to "Kingsley's *Griffith Gaunt*."[1] That such a slip could find its way into print shows how far Reade has fallen from his Victorian eminence, which was as high if not higher than that of the novelists we now consider great. Indeed if Malcolm Elwin is correct, "When Dickens died, Reade automatically ascended his seat above the heads of contemporary novelists . . . in America, he had been considered for some years even the equal of Dickens."[2] Elwin is presumably speaking of Reade's popular reputation. Many of the more serious reviewers were hostile, on occasion derisive, although he did receive far more critical acclaim than has generally been recognized, not merely from capable but little known writers like Hain Friswell, but from some of the finest and best known critics of the time—including the young Henry James, who in his early reviews (1865) placed Reade in the foremost rank of English novelists, far above Trollope and the Kingsleys, even above George Eliot: "She has the microscopic observation, not a myriad of whose keen notations are worth a single one of those great sympathetic guesses with which a real master attacks the truth, and which, by their occasional occurrence in the stories of Mr. Charles Reade (the much abused "Griffith Gaunt" included), make him, to our mind, the most readable of living English novelists, and prove him a distant kinsman of Shakespeare."[3] Other prominent critics, notably Swinburne and W. D. Howells, seconded James's criticism, their main argument being that despite all his faults, "Reade was at his best, and that not very rarely, a truly great writer of a truly noble genius."[4] And they found him at his best in *Christie Johnstone*, *It Is Never Too Late To Mend*, *Hard Cash*, and *Griffith Gaunt* as well as in *The Cloister and the Hearth*.

Later critics, however, have tended to subscribe to Lewis Melville's opinion: that *The Cloister and the Hearth*, "as compared with his other fiction, is as gold to dross." [5] And in their passing references, as in their more formal criticism, these critics have placed *The Cloister and the Hearth* in the first rank, not merely of historical fiction, but of all fiction. Indeed for Kipling it represented the fulfillment of his own fictional ideals: "I dreamed for many years of building a veritable three-decker out of chosen and long-stored timber—teak, green-heart, and ten-year-old oak knees—each curve melting deliciously into the next that the sea might nowhere meet resistance or weakness; the whole suggesting motion even when, her great sails for the moment furled, she lay in some needed haven—a vessel ballasted on ingots of pure research and knowledge, roomy, fitted with delicate cabinet-work below-decks, painted, carved, gilt and wreathed the length of her, from her blazing stern-galleries outlined by bronzy palm-trunks, to her rampant figure-head—an East-Indianman worthy to lie alongside *The Cloister and the Hearth*." [6]

Thanks to these and similar praises, duly echoed by literary historians, *The Cloister and the Hearth,* has long been considered a literary classic. But whether it deserves this recognition is another question—a question that I myself, in an earlier essay, have answered negatively.[7] And while I still consider this criticism essentially correct, I can now see that my judgment of the novel, in relation to other Victorian novels, was unduly severe. For if *The Cloister and the Hearth* seldom rises above the level of moral melodrama it is nevertheless superior to Scott's *Antiquary,* and at least equal to *Henry Esmond,* which for all its technical perfection achieves the illuminative intensity that distinguishes a good novel from a "good story" in only a few of Beatrix' scenes. And those scenes are equalled, if not surpassed, by the scenes in *The Cloister and the Hearth* in which Reade explores the emotional consequences of Gerard's enforced celibacy.

Yet to acknowledge the few virtues and many virtuosities of *The Cloister and the Hearth* is not necessarily to set it apart from, or above, Reade's other novels. "Had Reade never written *The Cloister and the Hearth,*" Hugh Walpole has suggested, "there is no doubt that *Griffith Gaunt* . . . would be awarded a higher critical position. . . . In many ways indeed *Griffith Gaunt* is the best novel he ever wrote. . . ." [8] Concurring with this judgment, which is also that of Swinburne, W. L. Courtney, and numerous earlier critics, Malcolm Elwin has gone a step further, maintaining that *Griffith Gaunt* is not only Reade's best novel but a masterpiece in its own right, "far exceeding anything ever achieved by Dickens in loftiness of artistic design and unflagging dramatic fervor." The novel was killed, Reade's artistic reputation more or less destroyed, Elwin argues, because Reade was "in his aspirations far in advance of the ruck and vulgar herd of humanity . . . a novelist of genius had for the first time unmasked the battery of truth against the forces of Humbug, and middle-class respectability was alarmed into mass reprisals to punish his temerity. The success of respectability is reflected in Reade's reputation today; he is known as the author of a great medieval romance. . . . while *Griffith Gaunt,* one of the most important novels of its generation . . . is obtainable only with difficulty. . . . When he died . . . the press organs . . . played loud pedal about the greatness of *The Cloister and the Hearth,* discreetly ignored his other books, and encouraged the readily forgetful public to forget about them." [9]

Although certain of Elwin's statements are extravagant, to say the least, there is much to be said for Reade's better novels—*Griffith Gaunt* in particular—and beginning with chapter five of the present study I shall try to say it. My plan is to discuss each of Reade's major artistic efforts in turn, excepting only *The Cloister and the Hearth,* which I shall reserve for a brief critical postscript. Through this arrangement I hope to do critical justice to *The Cloister and the Hearth* without permitting it to overshadow the now forgotten novels. For I am convinced that in certain of their aspects *Christie Johnstone, It Is Never Too Late To Mend,* and *Hard Cash* possess considerable artistic merit, and that "the much abused *Griffith Gaunt*" will bear comparison with George Eliot at her mature best.

By stressing these genuine artistic achievements and overlooking fundamental artistic shortcomings it might even be possible to make out a case for a Readian revival—a more convincing case than has been made out for, say, Wilkie Collins. But to do so, I believe, would be to invoke concepts of historical relativism that are critically fallacious, and in large measure responsible for the critical confusion so prevalent in studies of Victorian fiction. My own critical standards, in any event, are those I have derived from such critics as Herbert Read, E. M. Forster, and R. P. Blackmur, and my intention is to apply them in all their rigor. In consequence my criticism may at times seem heartless, or worse still, foolish, especially when applied to passages that seem closer to the modern comic book than to serious fiction. Yet there are such passages in nearly every Victorian novel, regardless of its quality or pretensions, and in Reade's case quality often has little to do with pretensions: when he most closely anticipates "Dick Tracy" he may consciously be trying to emulate Homer and Shakespeare (not to mention Samuel Warren and Harriet Beecher Stowe). In short Reade was always, in his intentions, a serious novelist, and the final measure of his defeat is the distance that separates his artistic achievement from that of the great writers whose principles he constantly invoked.

But whatever the validity of my critical reconsiderations, this is not primarily a critical study. More significant than the fact of Reade's defeat is why he suffered it, and my ultimate aim, adumbrated in my title, is to explain the meaning and implications of his defeat in relation to the Victorian forces that, according to some critics, proved too much even for Dickens. In *Fiction and the Reading Public*, for example, Q. D. Leavis dismisses Dickens, along with Reade and the Kingsleys, as merely "popular" novelists: "Dickens stands primarily for a set of crude emotional exercises . . . his originality is confined to recapturing a child's outlook on the grown-up world . . . emotionally he is not only uneducated but immature. When he is supplying the *sine qua non* of the popular novel—the young lovers who have traditionally to be of good birth and breeding and their background of upper middle-class life—he does not merely fall back on conventional situation and character, like Scott, he produces them at the level of Sir Leicester Dedlock and Dr. Strong—the painful guesses of the uninformed and half-educated writing for the uninformed and half-educated. The eighteenth-century novelist's was a mature, discreet, well-balanced personality. Dickens is one with his readers; they enjoyed exercising their emotional responses, he laughed and cried aloud as he wrote. We miss equally in Reade and the Kingsleys the adult and critical sensibility of the older novelists, who wrote for the best, because it was the only, public." [10]

Although the conditions Leavis describes are crucial, her analysis of them is as simplistic as her criticism of Dickens. According to her concept of "adult and critical sensibility" there is no accounting for the qualitative distinctions that separate Dickens' super-realism (or fantasy) from Reade's matter-of-fact realism. If anything Reade should be the better novelist. For he was in many ways more adult, more aware, than Dickens, and was following essentially the same techniques in an effort to achieve what he believed were the same literary ends. Nor is the usual explanation—that Dickens was a genius, Reade not—wholly satisfactory. If Dickens was a genius, so in a more limited sense was Reade; for that matter, so were at least a dozen other Victorian novelists, many of whom, like Reade, failed to realize their genius in any but a few passages, or perhaps a single novel. And if all their defeats were due to personal limitations, why were they at times able to overcome those limitations? How, on this basis, can one account for Dickens' astonishing failure in *Nicholas Nickleby?* The isolated triumphs of lesser novelists such as Mrs. Gaskell and Charles Lever? These and like instances which might be cited suggest that the personal equation, though of first importance, is not decisive when considered apart from outside influences. In one sense Reade failed because he was Reade; in another sense, he failed because he was a Victorian and not, say, an Elizabethan; because he was subjected to pressures only two or three novelists of his generation were able to withstand.

In this connection Julian Symons (in his *Thomas Carlyle*) has observed that "we are gradually becoming accustomed to the idea that great literary fame could be achieved in the nineteenth century only at considerable risk of mental or physical unbalance. Dickens suppressed certain criminal tendencies, which emerged in his extraordinary public readings; Swinburne was a masochist to a pathological degree; Ruskin we believe to have been impotent, in spite of his gallant and interesting offer to give public proof to the contrary; Lewis Carroll liked to take photographs of little girls, but not of little boys, naked; Samuel Butler was a repressed homosexual, Oscar Wilde an open one." [11]

The main difficulty with this statement—a difficulty Symons corrects in his book on Dickens[12]—is that it presents as consequences what, in the case of Dickens at least, would seem to be causes. Certainly Dickens' genius was rooted in his "criminal tendencies"—so deeply rooted, as Edmund Wilson has shown, that these tendencies inform all his greatest work, from *Pickwick* to *Edwin Drood,* and are nowhere more evident than in *Great Expectations*, the novel that in my opinion marks the culmination of his artistic development. In this novel, which in many ways anticipates Kafka's *The Castle*, Dickens lays bare the reality of portièred Victorian life with the devastating power of a Swift or a Celine. He reveals through Pip and his aspirations the deadliness of a world in which surface sham (Miss Havisham) provides a ritualized disguise for ultimate fact (Jaggers)—a Kafkaesque world that prefigures Auden's poetic delineation of our own in "September, 1939":

> The lights must never go out,
> The music must always play,
> All the conventions conspire
> To make this fort assume
> The furniture of home;
> Lest we should see where we are,
> Lost in a haunted wood,
> Children afraid of the night
> Who have never been happy or good.

And Dickens gives fictional expression to this world—not through technique, or even technique informed with vision (Q. D. Leavis' "sensibility"), but through technique transformed and controlled by his own vision—the vision that he derived from the "rebel and criminal within him."

But if this be true, it may be objected, why did not those Victorian novelists who shared Dickens' rebellious and criminal tendencies also share his vision? The answer, of course, is that none of them fully shared Dickens' tendencies—although, as I have noted, Reade thought he did, and from the first set out to write as a Dickensian, in part at least modelling his first major fictional effort (*It Is Never Too Late To Mend*) after *Martin Chuzzlewit*. But, lacking Dickens' vision, he had only facts plus Dickensian structure and technique to rely upon, and so, with the exception of a few passages, his novel will bear comparison with only the weakest elements of *Martin Chuzzlewit*—its melodramatic double plot and stock Sensation techniques. These stock elements—the elements that Dickens transformed—Reade merely reproduced, as in his Australian chapters, which are as structurally indefensible as the American chapters of *Martin Chuzzlewit* would be if their structural deficiencies were not redeemed by Dickens' vision.

"A reader of the first few chapters of *Chuzzlewit*," James Wright has explained, "cannot find anything in the character or action of Pecksniff, or of anybody else in the novel, that might promise an inevitable trip to America. And yet, once the trip to America has been introduced, the reader can discover that Dickens is extending and amplifying, and finally in the person of Hannibal

Chollop, crystallizing the theme of dislocation between language and action which Pecksniff most dramatically exemplifies. . . . We need some kind of metaphor, for critical purposes, which will allow the monstrous characters their ultimate importance in Dickens' novels in general, and in *Martin Chuzzlewit* in particular. I suggest the Coleridgean image of a tree—an organism whose irregularity is part of its beauty, which begins, regularly enough, which branches out in directions which are simultaneously inevitable and unpredictable, and which finally bears on the branches the fruit which was the purpose of the tree's growth in the first place. On one branch—probably a lower one—we should find the face of Pecksniff, polished by the sunlight and yet rotten within; and on a higher branch we should find the green hard face of Hannibal Chollop. Chollop probably will never achieve ripeness; yet he is one of those accidental fruits whose insides have been rotted by worms even before in the due course of things he could achieve fulness. One could not have predicted the blossoming and hardening into existence of a Chollop by the mere survey of the rotten and blushing Pecksniff. But, depending on the same terrible and ungainly tree, they have a relation to each other which depends on their vitality—on their deriving from the same deep root of Dickens' imagination." [13]

For every other Victorian novelist, however, the problem of how to tap and control the deep roots of the imagination was a well nigh insuperable one—even when, as in Reade's case, the roots themselves were as deep and flourishing as those of another great Victorian, Thomas Carlyle. Sharing Carlyle's sadistic tendencies (as described by Julian Symons) Reade also shared Carlyle's vision—even as he opposed Carlyle's ideas. *The Cloister and the Hearth* is a fictional counterpart of *Past and Present;* and *Christie Johnstone, It Is Never Too Late To Mend,* and the factual *Heroes and Martyrs* also offer variations on Carlylean themes—variations that are at times as Carlylean in spirit as they are anti-Carlylean in idea.

But only at times. Reade could not, like Carlyle, give full and sustained artistic expression to his vision because he could not, like Carlyle, achieve positive control over the sadistic tendencies in which his imagination was rooted. I stress the word "positive" as well as the word "control" because by "positive control" I mean the power to "free" or "let go" or "release" as well as the power to curb or check or channel the imagination. In other words I mean what William Carlos Williams meant when, in addressing a group of young writers, he declared: "You must let yourself go—release it and be that transcendence (but in control by your technique which you have learned—like the voice of an opera singer) but inside that frame of reference you must *release* yourself to act." In developing the implications of this advice, Williams makes clear "what distresses can happen in the effort to let go! to release ourselves to the imagination." Moreover he explains what underlies these distresses, what makes it so difficult for the writer to let go: "It is because we are really afraid. We can be struck to the ground by a tardy realization of how we have been conditioned in our lives. The realization of it may be a terrific blow. In all our conscious lives we stick to what we call standards—to precedents—to those bulwarks against quicksands—so we say. Think of Rimbaud, etc. Then to reverse the process: where might we not land? What fences we put up in the past are now precisely our stumbling blocks. . . ."[14]

The Victorians were likewise afraid, almost to a man, and with even more reason. For they had to consider not only their own fears but also those of their editors, reviewers, readers—and yes, even their most liberal fellow writers. Dickens, for example, objected to defending *Griffith Gaunt* in court on the ground that he could not, speaking as a father and as an editor, condone certain passages in the novel. And yet Dickens was the creator of Quilp, whose lip-smacking passes at Little Nell might be included in Krafft-Ebing's *Psychopathia Sexualis*.

To identify Quilp in this way is not of course to question the artistic validity of his antics, which are as revealing as they are monstrous. Nor is it to question Dickens' own domestic arrangements. The truth is that his seeming hypocrisy or pruriency was neither hypocrisy nor pruriency: it was a form of Victorian naivete or double-think essential to his being a great Victorian novelist, since without this naivete he could never have presented Quilp and Little Nell as he did, could never have developed their relationship into what it finally is—a variation on the myth of beauty and the beast that exposes the Victorian purity it is meant to illustrate.

Similar discrepancies characterize the fiction of nearly every other great novelist of the period, and are perhaps most obvious in the work of Charlotte Bronte. Although her understanding of sexual relationships was far less conventional than Dickens', she too had her naive pieties and proprieties, and when she managed to give them positive expression, as in *The Professor,* her fiction is of a piece with *Fanny the Little Milliner.* But when she became fully engaged with her biographical materials, as in *Jane Eyre,* she wrote in a different vein altogether: she poured her deepest feelings into her writing, and with so much intensity that she transformed her Gothic story into a passionate quest for love and human fulfillment. Of course she retained the outward trappings of melodrama, as well as her Methodist morality and phraseology. These were the only words and forms of expression she knew. Yet at her best she gave her words an emphasis all her own—a personal accent that expresses, not what a Victorian Methodistical lady was supposed to feel, but what Charlotte Bronte felt she did feel. And it is those feelings, expressed in her differentiated language, which underlie the melodramatic surface of the novel and give it the poetic depth Virginia Woolf attributes to it in *The Common Reader.*[15]

Charlotte Bronte's best work (like that of Dickens) consequently represents the triumph of what Virginia Woolf has defined as the "unconscious artistic intention," what E. D. H. Johnson, in *The Alien Vision of Victorian Poetry,* has defined as "alien vision." And it can be demonstrated that, with the exception of George Eliot, nearly all the Victorian novelists who produced genuine art were "unconscious writers"—mainly because, given the conditions of Victorian authorship, there was no other way for them to let go their imaginations. The novelists' only hope, whether they realized it or not, was to break through their Victorian chains. And for most of them it could not very well be a conscious break through, since they did not realize they were in chains: they were under the illusion that they were free, that the formulas they accepted were true; that these formulas, given fictional trimmings, were not only true but beautiful. Thus deluded, nearly all the Victorian novelists were, on the conscious level, fictional counterfeiters. It was only when their unconscious awareness took over, as in *Jane Eyre* or *Great Expectations,* that they managed to give full expression to their imaginative powers.[16]

But Reade could not express his unconscious awareness through any of the usual forms of artistic indirection. The Brontes' poetry and Dickens' super-realism were alike beyond his reach—not so much because he lacked unconscious awareness as because he feared and mistrusted it, dubbing it "inner consciousness," "cobwebs," "a well of self-deception," and never missing an opportunity to hold it up to Baconian scorn. Indeed his fears, which were ultimately fears of self-revelation, went so deep that for some fifteen years after he set out to be a writer he could not write a single line. And when he did begin to write he seldom ventured beyond adaptation until he had worked out a Baconian system of documentation designed to supplant inner consciousness with outer facts.

The effect of such a system, fully carried out, was of course to deny the inner consciousness or imagination altogether by smothering it beneath a mass of facts—the way the Crystal Palace smothered it in life, the way Kean smothered it in his dramatic productions, or Frith in his Pre-Raphaelite paintings. And if Reade had been able to fulfill the demands of his Baconian system, his works, like those of Kean and Frith, would be of no more than historical interest. But the facts he collected by his Baconian method are not Baconian. They are not even systematic. They are Readian. And at times they reflect not only his ideals and rationalizations but his inner consciousness—the very inner consciousness he was trying to deny.

That Reade should free his imagination in this way—by first disguising himself as a Baconian writing machine then writing from Baconian reflections twice removed from reality—may seem strange indeed, particularly in view of the fact that he did much of his actual writing in a study "multiplied tenfold by great mirrors from floor to ceiling . . . [which] laid hold of the garden and flowers, and by double and treble reflection filled the room with nooks of verdure and color." [17] Such extreme applications of Hamlet's dictum (about holding the mirror up to nature) may seem to have more in common with a circus performance, or a visit to the "fun house" at an amusement park, than with a serious attempt to write. Yet Reade was perhaps the most serious of all the Victorian novelists, and in the succeeding chapters I shall attempt to do justice to the seeming strangeness of his efforts: to show them for what they are and what they reveal about the related efforts of his fellow Victorians.

Emotional Development:
A Victorian Son and Lover

1835.—Assist us merciful God in the settlement of our son Charles, and suffer neither his wishes nor our weakness to prevail in any line that may injure his soul and bring him to the grave in sorrow. Convert his soul, and make him a child of grace, and then direct his path, and guide us in all our ways with him. Correct every false view of life, and bring all our wishes into one point, the salvation of his soul!

—From the manuscript *Dear Mother*

✓   ✓   ✓

He was tall and stout, of a fine florid complexion, and with large wide-opened eyes, gentle and mild, as I think he himself used to say, "like those of a cow." His voice was rather husky, and gave one sometimes the idea that he was speaking with suppressed passion.

—Edward Marston

✓   ✓   ✓

One could not imagine his doing a mean or an ignoble thing. . . . But his indomitable pugnacity, his determination to resent every supposed offence, his intolerance of adverse criticism—even the most considerate and the most qualified—and his immense self-conceit, made enemies for him everywhere. . . . Where another author would have seen only some inferior person's want of appreciation, Charles Reade saw the deadly hand of some malignant assassin. He was as ready with his threats of an action for damages as a politician out West in the old days would have been with his cowhide.

—Justin McCarthy

✓   ✓   ✓

Charles Reade was a Victorian eccentric; indeed he was "so entirely odd in the ordinary relations of life" that Goldwin Smith and a number of others apparently considered him crazy.[1] Of course Reade had his defenders—those who tried to explain his oddities as the concomitants of genius—yet on occasion they too were perplexed: as for instance, the time the young W. B. Maxwell encountered an antelope in Reade's London home.[2] Reade's acquaintances were constantly subjected to minor shocks of this kind, plus others of a more serious nature, such as those which prompted Trollope (in his *Autobiography*) to say he looked upon Reade "as one endowed almost with genius but as one who has not been gifted with ordinary powers of reasoning." And Trollope, it should be noted, was trying to be friendly. The truth is, none of Reade's contemporaries, friendly or unfriendly, could fathom the depths of his Jekyll-Hyde duality. Confronted with so many seemingly disparate antics and ideas they were as baffled as Ellen Terry, who summed up his personality in a series of contradictory adjectives: "Dear, kind, unjust, generous, cautious, impulsive, passionate, gentle Charles Reade!"

Even now, in the light of recent scholarship and biography, Reade is still a shadowy figure. But it is possible to discern the lineaments of a man behind the mask of "odd violences, impetuosities, and generosities"—a man struggling for personal and literary expression. And if he ultimately failed in his literary struggle, he fought, and to a certain extent won, his battle for personal salvation. Although lonely and frustrated, continually at war with himself, his family, in fact all his surroundings—not for a year or a period of years, but from boyhood, into early middle age—he finally managed to overcome his difficulties, at the age of forty-two achieving his own Baconian version of "The Everlasting Yea" with the publication of his first great fictional success, appropriately entitled *It Is Never Too Late To Mend*. From this time onwards he was a new man, still lonely and frustrated and truculent, despite the love and companionship of Mrs. Seymour, but able to write out, and upon occasion act out, his own heroic vision of himself, and thus make his daydreams and fantasies come true. Reade's famous "Notebooks" reveal the precariousness as well as the artistic consequences of his Victorian compromise with reality. But that is another story which I shall take up later on. The first need is for a reinterpretation of what Reade later referred to as his "wasted youth."

II

Reade himself furnished the key to his emotional development. In later life, speaking as a famous writer, he was fond of declaring (with more percipience than he realized), "I owe the larger half of what I am to my mother, the rest to the accident of my father's grandfather having married the daughter of the village black-smith." Compton L. Reade, in his obituary article on Reade, and later in *Charles Reade A Memoir*,[3] denied the obvious implica-tions of this statement, maintaining that, despite Reade's insist-ence upon "Brains first, virility next, and ancestry in the back-ground . . ." he cherished "the knowledge that he was by descent a gentleman . . . and adhered beneath the surface to such old-world beliefs as religion and birth. His pen was so far *con amore* on the side of virtue that his readers—erroneously—may have imagined him a saint; and his passionate appeal to the people in one of his grandest dramatic scenes, no less than his habit of constituting his countrymen the real arbiters of every issue, includ-ing, as in the Staunton Case, life and death, may have conveyed the impression that his political sentiments were democratic. As a matter of fact, he was alike a believer in Christianity, and a Tory in his reverence of proprietary rights, albeit he recked little of the claims of creed, and less of those of royalty."

Of course there is some truth here. Reade was the youngest child of "John Reade, lord of the manors of Ipsden Huntercombe and Ipsden Bassett, and of half the manor of Checkenden in the county of Oxford, by Anna Maria, eldest daughter of Major John Scott-Waring M.P. . . ." Moreover, he was acutely aware of his ancestry, in his own autobiographical sketch "devoting about a tenth part of its entirety to his pedigree"; and his "almost romantic reverence for his ancestors extended beyond them, to their acreage and mansions. . . ." All this is undeniable: Reade did accept many of the ideas and attitudes which may be labelled "Tory," including a love for field sports, hunting in particular, which in later life he attempted to abjure as inconsistent with humanitarian principles. Yet he was never a Tory in the sense Compton Reade implies, not even as a boy. In playing a word game at Ipsden, presumably when he was about sixteen, he set forth his ideals in verse, and they are as Commercial and Benthamitic as they are tritely Tory:

> My desires are not grand,
> Funds and railway shares and land,
> Health, wit, money, quantum stuff.
> A beauteous spouse, and that's enough.
> Add good horses, a true friend,
> A happy life, and a good end.
> The rest I value a rope's end.[4]

While these verses are obviously intended to be playful, Reade's boyish references to funds and railway shares take an added point when viewed in relation to his own expectations. The youngest of eleven children, in a family more ancient than wealthy, he was further handicapped by his father's reluctance to give him any more financial help than was absolutely necessary. For instance, when it came to a decision as to whether or not he should go to Oxford, his father objected to the expense, saying he could go, but only provided he could obtain a scholarship. Undoubtedly in this, as in other instances, Reade's father was neither unkind nor ungenerous according to his own lights, which were those of a reasonably intelligent and well-meaning country squire. But Charles, though he showed no enthusiasm for Oxford, apparently felt the humiliation of his situation and treatment. In any case, he early developed a sense of alienation from his father and from the Tory life and values his father represented: "It was his boast through life that he was *par excellence* his mother's son, and a Scott-Waring rather than a Reade." This open repudiation of his father, implicit in his previously quoted acknowledgment of his mother and the village blacksmith, brings out the basic pattern of Reade's development: the rejection of the father and the Tory values of Ipsden in favor of the mother and a philosophy that would enable him to realize and justify his own conception of himself—a pattern that began in the nursery and continued through his entire life.

III

Very little is known about Reade's early childhood. He himself noted in his *Diary:* "I remember that when I was a little boy everybody noticed my extraordinary helplessness. My dear sister Julia noticed it particularly at Sandgate, seeing how feebly I got off the coach, like one that expected to be lifted down. Once I fell off a coach into a man's arms, as I was getting up." [5] In thus linking the memory of his "extraordinary helplessness" with the name of Julia, Reade lends credence to what the *Memoir* asserts to be the facts of his early childhood. From the cradle Charles was, it seems, Julia's special charge; then, as he began to grow up, she became his playmate and teacher as well as his nurse. In all these roles, aided and abetted by Mrs. Reade, Julia evidently responded to Charles's helplessness with extraordinary devotion—going so far, the *Memoir* declares, as to shelter "the fair-haired, rosy cheeked urchin with the large thoughtful eyes" from every consequence of his "temper" and "wilfulness." Until he was nine, therefore, the young Charles had as much protection and love as the most demanding child could wish for. Then Julia married and, in the words of Malcolm Elwin, "a small boy was left derelict."

The word "derelict" is well chosen. It might even be said, without benefit of Freud, that the nine year old Reade never quite recovered, that all his life he was to be searching for another Julia, a woman who could give him the unquestioning love and security he felt as a child. His later references to Julia, his never mentioning her name "except with some preface of endearment," the letter he wrote when she died—these and other supporting biographical facts, taken in conjunction with the characteristics of Julia Dodd and a whole line of his fictional heroines, point towards the interpretation I have suggested. And where the influence of Julia left off, that of his mother began. According to the *Memoir* "Charley" was always Mrs. Reade's prime favorite, and after Julia left, she apparently took over completely, causing Charles, already "a spoiled child if there ever was one," to seek in his relationship with her the answer to his developing conflicts with the outside world.

Of Mrs. Reade more later. It was at this most critical point in Reade's young life, just after Julia's marriage, that he was bundled off to a private school at Rose Hill run by a Mr. Slatter whom Reade later referred to as "Scourger." From the loving care of Julia and his mother to the prison-like discipline and beatings of Rose Hill was a transition like that which George Orwell later went through when his parents sent him to Crossgates. "Your home might be far from perfect," Orwell wrote, "but at least it was a place ruled by love rather than fear, where you did not have to be perpetually on your guard against the people surrounding you. At eight years old you were suddenly taken out of this warm nest and flung into a world of force and fraud and secrecy, like a gold fish into a tank full of pike. Against no matter what degree of bullying you had no redress . . ."[6] This was Reade's situation, made worse by the fact that Slatter was as much of a Squeers as the *Memoir* declared him to be—which is to say, he was literally a sadist, i.e., a man who beat the children in much the same way and for much the same reasons that Warden Hawes, in Reade's *Never Too Late To Mend*, beat the prisoners.[7] Possibly, as Malcolm Elwin has suggested, Slatter was no worse than many other nineteenth century schoolmasters, but that does not alter the effect of his treatment, for Reade seems to have had the same reaction to physical violence as the young George Augustus Sala, who so feared the treatment he was likely to receive in an English school that he talked his mother into letting him study in Paris.[8] For a number of reasons, however, Reade could not expect or request such leniency from his father. After all, his older brothers had literally passed through Slatter's hands without flinching, and in any case Mr. Reade did not believe in coddling. As a consequence Reade had no choice but to endure the rigors of Rose Hill for a period of almost five years. Yet as he endured in body he recoiled in spirit: the effect of Slatter's treatment, in so far as it can be ascertained, was to inflame rather than to curb his pride and sensitivity, causing him to feel more than ever alienated from the gentlemanly code he was expected to live by, more dependent on the love and tenderness and guidance of his mother.

Even if Mrs. Reade had been an ordinary woman, playing Gertrude to Reade's Hamlet, the situation was such that her influence would have been as powerful as the Oedipal ties that bound Reade to her. But Mrs. Reade was by no means ordinary. She was a mind and a force as well as a woman and a mother. While still a girl, the *Memoir* recounts, she entered into "the life of politics, society, the Court. . . . Haydn taught her music. . . . Sheridan epigram and repartee. . . . Her manner was perfect . . . her conversational powers so extraordinary as to have fascinated so superior a master of rhetoric as Samuel Wilberforce." Making due allowance for Compton L. Reade's own rhetoric, the facts still seem to indicate that the girl whom Grattan called his "Pretty Puritan" was a remarkably attractive and accomplished young lady, conversant with the best books and the best people in the best tradition of eighteenth century gentility. Why a woman so truly elegant, in Jane Austen's sense of the word *elegant*, should marry a somewhat boorish young Squire and bury herself at Ipsden is more than a little puzzling. Perhaps, as the *Memoir* suggests, it was a true love match. If so, love was much less than enough for Mrs. Reade, who was not long content to be a mere wife and mother. Soon after the marriage she began to transform Ipsden, first into a country seat of culture and refinement; later, after she herself had become imbued with new Evangelical faith, into a stronghold of militant Evangelicalism.

Reade grew up in this later Ipsden, in the midst of the rustic

[26]

court his mother had established. "At Ipsden House," in the words of the *Memoir*, "divines hummed like bees about a hive; Samuel Wilberforce was lately become curate of the neighboring parish of Checkenden, the Fabers were frequently there, and from Oxford came a little host of ecclesiastical dons, Plumptre, Macbride, Ellerton, and anybody who advocated Low-Church Doctrines." Upon occasion Mrs. Reade seems to have extended a welcome to many who were not Evangelical, drawing a hard and fast line only against "Puseyites." George Grote was a member of her circle, so perhaps the religious atmosphere took on a Benthamitic tinge at times. Nevertheless the prevailing atmosphere of the household was suffocatingly pietistic, with Reade's mother restlessly exhorting her children to follow the true faith, which she was at pains to interpret for them in aphoristic phrases such as the following, taken at random from the manuscript *Dear Mother:*

My hearts desire is that my children may be heirs to the Kingdom of God.

✦ ✦ ✦

I have my several trials. I am chastened by them. . . . I am more satisfied when I feel sorrow, than when my heart rejoices.

✦ ✦ ✦

The Love of the world is poison to the Christian.

✦ ✦ ✦

What is true religion? It consists in a real conformity to the Law and in a genuine compliance with the Gospel.

✦ ✦ ✦

She [Mrs. Reade's six-year-old daughter, Anna Maria] was my daily companion at 12 o'clock, and her father was wrapt in her. But both of us rejoiced when we found she had put off mortality for immortality.[9]

For her favorite son Mrs. Reade also had more specific words, the words I have quoted as an epigraph to the present chapter plus others I shall mention later on, all aimed directly at Reade, and designed to "convert his soul and make him a child of grace."

And while Reade could not respond quite as his mother wished, neither could he reject Evangelicalism outright, the way Edmund

Gosse and so many other eminent Victorians rejected it. His mother's hold on his mind and imagination was simply too powerful. What he did, as a boy and later as a man, was rather to interpret the doctrines to fit his own personal needs and aspirations—no great feat of rationalization, for Evangelicalism had its worldly side, and Mrs. Reade, for all her later piety, was inordinately ambitious for her children, particularly for Charles. She wanted him to be a success: to achieve greatness, "intellectual greatness," to become a bishop or something comparable. Needless to say, she also stressed polite accomplishments and gentlemanly conduct, much as Dr. Arnold stressed these ideals at Rugby. But her emphasis was different. Success was second only to Godliness, and Godliness, if not a means to success, certainly was in no way incompatible with it. Consequently she felt free to urge Charles on to the greatness that she, as a woman, and a woman married to Squire Reade, had never been permitted to achieve, that neither her husband nor her older sons had been able to achieve. Charles was her last hope, and in her anxiety to secure his triumph she consciously or unconsciously sought to mold his every feeling and thought, to make him into a male counterpart of herself, or more accurately, her own image of herself.

There is, of course, nothing unique about Mrs. Reade's efforts. Overly fond mothers often try to mold their sons in this way—with no very serious consequences, so long as the boy in question is finally able to break the Oedipal ties and develop his own individuality. This is part of the normal process of growing up. And if the young Charles had been less petted by Julia, less beaten by Mr. Slatter, less "spoiled" as "the baby of the family," he too might have been able to cope with his mother's domination. As it was, however, he needed the mother image she imposed almost as much as she needed to impose it—and he responded accordingly. So that, although he never surrendered unconditionally, he became his mother's son in a very special sense—how special can be seen (in part) by glancing through the following lines:

> One does not wish to see sentiment oozing out at every pore; but there is a bright look and a beaming eye that sets all life within afloat, and *that* pleases. Profession of all sorts is an emetic —but ice chills. . . .

Nothing annoys me so much as the loss of the English language in the literature of the day. There is Carlyle, with his abominable German phraseology—conceited divines, with their Frenchified sentences and compound words that make me throw the book down. What think you of Montgomery ending an octavo volume with 'How?' I like pithy and epigrammatic sentences, a little antithesis also, but only a little. . . .

Living in London, what is it? Cliques fashionable, cliques political, cliques religious, and clubs the exceptions.

Actually these bits of aphoristic wisdom are specimens of Mrs. Reade's conversation—yet in idea, attitude, even style, they can hardly be distinguished from Reade's own writing. Noting this closeness, the authors of the *Memoir* remarked that "his mother's brain was in many ways the replica of his own"—a statement that is entirely true if one recognizes that his mother's mind was the original, Reade's the replica.

These similarities suggest the ultimate consequences of the mother-son relationship. Until Charles left Ipsden, however, the Oedipal marks were not so immediately apparent: his letters, the account of his activities at school and at Ipsden given in the *Memoir*, the manuscript *Dear Mother*—all these sources, when pieced together, reveal a self-centered, precociously pompous boy of seventeen: not particularly brilliant or gifted, yet proud, ambitious, sensitive—so sensitive, if the *Memoir* is correct, that he preferred the company of women to that of boys or men. This was the young Reade of 1831, when he was preparing to go to Oxford. Up to this time his personal ideas and attitudes had been more or less acceptable to everyone around him. At home Julia and his mother had seen to that. And at school he had been partially protected by his older brother Compton. Except for the psychological shocks deriving from Slatter's treatment (and perhaps from his father's)[10] he had therefore escaped any flagrant violations of his acute sensitivity. Magdalen College and the world outside were not to be so indulgent.

IV

That Charles should go to Oxford (preparatory to becoming a bishop!) was Mrs. Reade's idea, opposed by both Charles and Mr. Reade: by Charles because he did not wish to take even a first step toward the Church; by Mr. Reade because he considered the expense too great. After considerable debate Mrs. Reade prevailed, as usual, although Mr. Reade did manage to qualify his compliance, making it contingent upon Reade's ability to secure a scholarship. And so, at the very outset, Reade was doubly forced, doubly humiliated. For his mother's wishes, coupled with his father's stipulation, obliged him to secure a scholarship in order to enter upon a course of study he disliked in order to prepare for a career he detested.

If Reade felt as much resentment as I have suggested—and Mrs. Reade's comments in *Dear Mother* indicate that he did—he nevertheless entered upon his Magdalen career auspiciously enough, winning a "demyship" by writing a brilliant English essay on the subject "How far is Ambition productive of Virtue." In the red-plush phraseology of the *Memoir:* "To a man, the other candidates . . . proceeded . . . to decry ambition as one of the devastating forces of humanity. Charles Reade, however, being himself wildly ambitous, was not so canting a hypocrite as to abuse a quality he admired intensely. He took pen and wrote *con brio,* yet judgmatically, his ideas. In barbarous days, he affirmed, when war is the only outlet for ambition, ambition showed to the greatest disadvantage as being pure selfishness. But . . . to the domain of learning and the arts these censures were quite inapplicable. Without ambition as a motive power . . . there would be no excellence, nothing but a dead level of mediocrity. Further, he argued that the sole aternative of ambition would be chaotic stagnation of all the mental faculties; and, in brief, his peroration was the warmest eulogium of the very quality which the other candidates had been gibbeting as the meanest of vices." Minus the rhetorical flourishes this would appear to be a fair summary of the essay. At least it sounds like Reade—as if he were repeating his mother's arguments, but with a peculiar vehemence that should perhaps have given his Magdalen examiners some clue to his make-up. Certainly if they had understood the attitudes underlying his expressed ideas— attitudes anathema to Magdalen—they would have been less ready to laud his honesty and talent, less willing to elect him Demy. But from Mills, a tutor, to Dr. Routh, the president of the College, they declared the essay a student masterpiece. "And thus, as it were, by acclamation," the *Memoir* concludes, "Charles Reade was elected Demy of Magdalen."

The prosaic fact is that Charles Reade matriculated on "26th July 1831." Soon afterwards Mrs. Reade accompanied Charles to Oxford, and once again, this time at the age of seventeen, a boy was left derelict. Mrs. Reade after returning to Ipsden, recorded her own feelings at parting: "I left my Charles in his solitude of College with an aching heart. Recollections pressed on me. How differently situated were my elder sons, cast into the wild world at seventeen or eighteen; and perhaps Oxford only seventeen miles off, as dangerous as India!" Mrs. Reade's fears were justified: Oxford was as dangerous as India, though not quite in the way she envisaged. Reade was never to take Tractarianism seriously—"Newman amused him, but only as a polished buffoon"— nor was he attracted to the society of "the purely betting and equine men." The dangers he encountered were of a different order altogether, the result of his personal conflict with Magdalen, at that time a notoriously backward college in "a University that still clung to the past with obstinate tenacity, and prided itself on keeping behind the material and intellectual movement of the age." [11] To Reade, fresh from the atmosphere of his mother's Ipsden, Magdalen was by contrast a sink of intellectual and moral decadence, peopled by monkish scholars and clicquish students whom he could not respect, or pretend to respect. It was not long, therefore, until his reactions became evident to his fellow students, inciting them to respond in kind. "His aversion to alcohol alone," Malcolm Elwin has observed, "was enough to offend those who were fond of the College port." And that was only the beginning: Reade's ways and values fitted so poorly with those of Magdalen that he was soon at odds with nearly everyone in the College, more particularly and most disastrously with the Demies of his own common room.

For the first time, it would seem, Reade experienced the overwhelming pressures of group antagonism. Magdalen was not Ipsden; the men of the common room would not honor his feelings of difference and superiority. Yet he could not comply, or even compromise with their demands for conformity: he was too sensitive, too proud, or, if one wishes, too "spoiled." He had no choice but to fight back. This is why their criticism, designed to put him in his place and make a man of him, had just the opposite effect. The more he was pressured, the more perversely he reacted, until, as Léone Rives points out, he began to cut a revolutionary figure, wearing long curls, a bright green coat with brass buttons, and in general conducting himself so strangely—what with his fiddle playing and dancing the double shuffle—that he came to be referred to as "Mad Charles." Of course he was not really mad, any more than William Morris was mad when the students at Marlborough declared him so. The loud clothes and eccentric behavior were an expression of defiance, his protest against what he felt to be the deadliness of Magdalen mediocrity.[12]

Much as Reade despised Magdalen, however, he could not break away. Perhaps he lacked the courage to defy his mother's wishes—wholly, that is; perhaps too he was coming to realize that the material independence he so wanted could best be secured through academic channels. At any rate, though he continued his protest, and in 1835 began "to make notes with a view to writing fiction," he still did enough prescribed work to maintain his standing in the College, knowing full well that once he had taken his B.A. his Demyship qualified him for a Fellowship. Then rather unexpectedly, in June, 1835, a Fellowship open to candidates born in Oxfordshire became vacant. The only difficulty was that Reade did not yet have his B.A., had not even planned to take his examinations that June. Nevertheless, with only three weeks preparation, he took his degree—a third in Greats—and a month later, on July 22, he was elected a probationary fellow.

At the age of twenty-one Reade thus secured a modest income for life, subject only to the requirements of the Fellowship, minimal save for the enforced celibacy. Moreover, in this same year, by virtue of some adept maneuvering, he won a Vinerian Scholarship in addition to his Fellowship. The Vinerian, it seems, was awarded by a vote of the Masters of Arts—a procedure which, in the ordinary course of events (i.e. with only the resident Masters voting), would have nullified Reade's chances altogether. But in this instance he was one too many for his detractors. Taking advantage of the technicalities that governed the voting, he enlisted the aid of his parents to wage a campaign such as Oxford had never before witnessed. On the day of the election (December 1, 1835)[13] nonresident Masters from miles around—friends and acquaintances recruited by the Reades—descended upon the University in such numbers as to elect Reade by a crushing majority.

Yet his feelings were still not assuaged. To add to the discomfiture of his Magdalen enemies he decided to attend the "solemn High Table Dinner" where, as he well knew, the men would be obliged to offer their congratulations. "The etiquette of the High Table" was scrupulously observed, the *Memoir* relates, until one man, less guarded than the rest, openly challenged Reade by saying he had displaced two better men than himself. To which Reade answered: "No, better scholars, not better men. The Vinerian is a law scholarship, and law is a practical sort of science. Now the way in which my canvas was organized and carried out was rather unusual, but it argues a talent of the practical kind superior to that of my competitors. The University in its wisdom has chosen right." If this account is reasonably accurate—and it seems to be—it shows that Reade's youthful powers of self-justification were quite remarkable. And to strengthen them still further there was always his mother, who on this occasion, in an effort to bolster Reade's confidence and urge him on to greater things, went so far as to express herself in verse:

> Vinerian Victor! lash thy steed
> And gallant ride the classic field,
> Silence the clamorous bevy:
> Let talents and thy worth declare
> You'll earn the laurels that you wear
> Though friendship gain'd the victory.
>
> Let pride and sloth, two foes of thine
> No more their selfish web entwine
> Around Vinerian Victor.
> Up, up, and with the golden shield
> Of principle, your weapons wield
> And slay your foes like Hector.
>
> Then rouse thee, Victor, rouse thee
> Shake off that ominous dozy:
> Bind that bright armour on.
> Let "Rome's Magnificence" charm thee
> Her pillars, columns, history,
> And gain the classic crown! [14]

The martial spirit of these verses Reade undoubtedly found congenial: by this time he too recognized the need for victory, and to achieve that end was quite prepared to slay his foes like an Evangelical Hector. But his goal was not the classic crown, could not be achieved through the Church. On this one point neither the exhortations nor the commands of his mother could change his mind, not even when they were put into the form of prayer, as in the lines from *Dear Mother* beginning "Assist us merciful God . . ." Reade's struggle, obliquely reflected in Mrs. Reade's comments, must have cost him agony, yet he maintained his dogged resistance without wavering—as though he somehow realized that surrender meant psychic death—until Mrs. Reade finally gave way.

V

Though more his own master after 1835, Reade's struggle for personal independence was far from ended. His victory over his mother was both limited and Pyrrhic, serving only to loosen, not to break, the ties that bound him. Moreover, his victories over Magdalen were in themselves restrictive. After rejecting a religious career, for which nearly all the Fellowships at Magdalen were reserved, his only possibility was to secure a lay Fellowship in either medicine or law. With Mrs. Reade's grudging consent (expressed in her comment "Law is a cold study for the inner soul of a Christian") he first chose law—to discover that there was only one Law Fellowship available. For a time, when he thought he had lost this Fellowship to a rival candidate (Richard Sewell, a Newdigate prizeman who later became a noted barrister) he gave up law and went to Edinburgh to study medicine—only to faint on his first sight of blood. At this point it looked as if he had no choice but to take Orders or renounce his Fellowship. With typical resourcefulness, however, he discovered a way out by appealing the Magdalen decision which had gone in favor of Sewell. In his own words: "The matter turned on the interpretation of a statute . . . I appealed to the Visitor. The Visitor directed the case to be heard before him. Neither side employed counsel. I was victorious, and won my first litigation out of eighteen, and retain my Fellowship to this day." A typical Readian statement, yet the Visitor, it must be noted, "was the Bishop of Winchester, Dr. Sumner, his mother's friend . . ." It was therefore with his mother's help— the whole idea of an appeal may have originated with her—that he once again conquered Magdalen, this time creating so much indignation that the College revoked its own statutes and permitted Dr. Sewell to retain his Fellowship as a layman.

The year following this episode must have been a purgatorial one for Reade, since as a probationary Fellow he had to remain in residence for some time—perhaps for a whole year, even though, if Elwin is correct, he was formally entered at Lincoln's Inn, on November 20, 1835. In any event when he was able to leave Magdalen for Lincoln's Inn, presumably in November 1836, he immediately found in London a freer, more congenial life. During his first year he "read in chambers with Samuel Warren," a novelist who had already achieved some reputation and was soon to become noted as the author of *Ten Thousand A Year*. And while it may be true, as the *Memoir* states, that "the two of a trade failed to agree," Reade's acquaintance with Warren almost certainly encouraged him in his own literary ambitions, if only in giving him a sense of what it meant to be a popular author. Then too there was the London theatre, opening up to Reade, familiar only with the touring companies that visited Oxford in the summer, a new and wonderful world of make-believe—a world so artfully presented that for a few hours of the twenty-four he could escape Magdalen, his mother, everything, and live his own heroic vision of himself. Finally there was London itself, with all the romance of its actuality—its people, activities, commerce. To all this he responded, finding himself at one with the restless modernity of London life. "Here," he wrote, "a man so clearly sees, by looking out of a window for 10 seconds, that if he dawdles he will be distanced, that he cannot help shaking himself."

But resolutions are one thing, actions another; held prisoner by his inner confusions he could not muster the psychic energy necessary to throw off his Magdalen lethargy. Furthermore, he was considerably handicapped by the restrictions attached to his Fellowship. Until he took his M.A., in April, 1838, and was granted formal permission to live in London, he was obliged to spend a part of every year at Magdalen, now so hateful to him that in order to make his rooms more bearable, he painted the walls green, the ceiling an intense blue—to imitate, he said, tropical vegetation and the sky of the Antilles. And when he was in London, there was his work at Lincoln's Inn, for which he had less and less enthusiasm. Although he spoke favorably of his law studies in a letter of November 12, 1836 (quoted by the *Memoir*) his guarded words suggest that he was probably trying to reassure his mother, whose ambitions for him were as grandiose as ever. Thwarted in her desire to see him a Bishop, she now looked forward to his becoming Chief-Justice. Knowing this, Reade could hardly write everything he thought. Certainly he could not tell her of his literary interests, for like so many strict Evangelicals she had come to look upon the theatre as little short of iniquitous, other forms of literary activity as at best frivolous. "Immortal beings," she declared, undoubtedly for Reade's special benefit, "should not flutter among the trifles of literature. What a field for thought and action are the realities of life, and the certainty of a future state."

Although Reade failed to respond to these admonitions in the way Mrs. Reade would have liked, she nevertheless continued to hope for the best, in the meantime giving him spiritual and financial support. In 1839, the *Memoir* points out, she "provided him with adequate funds for a tour of the continent"—a tour that is recorded in Reade's letters (printed at length in the *Memoir*) to his mother, his father, and William, the one brother he admitted to something approaching friendship. The letters to his mother and father, evidently written for the whole family, are uniformly trite and properly deferential, relieved only by a few individual touches, notably his account of Mlle. Mars's acting, which I shall discuss in another connection, and a revealing little postscript that requires no comment: "P.S.—In answer to something in your letter, I have not spent one farthing of your money in knick-knackeries, and I will not spend above one napoleon so during all my tour. 'Foi de Chevalier!'"

More interesting because less inhibited is his letter to William, in which he writes: "Of course I have been all along on the lookout for little traits of character, national and individual. . . ." This statement suggests he was carrying out his plan, presumably undertaken in 1835, of taking notes with a view to writing fiction. In any event his selection of traits and incidents reveals the preoccupation that was to dominate his "Notebooks" and nearly all of his writing: "There are in Paris four thundering slaughterhouses. . . . One of these I visited, and having to cross a moderate-sized river of blood and filth I showed signs of aversion, whereon my French conductor grinned from ear to ear and said: 'Monsieur, ce n'est pas propre!'" Again, apropos of his difficulties with spoken French, he wrote: "I once soared in conversation as high as what Aristotle calls a gnome, i.e. a sort of moral maxim sententiously expressed: e.g. a cab-driver was working his machine over the stones to take me to a neighboring village, and kept whipping his beast. Says I, 'Ne fatiguez pas votre cheval. Les chevaux sont les bons serviteurs de l'homme.' 'Bon,' says the Frenchman with a look of intense admiration, his eyes glistening, and (as they invariably do when anything bright strikes their minds from within or without) took his horse a flank that sounded like the crack of a pistol." Then a few sentences further along: "I went to the Morgue twice. There was a corpse there each time, the first had no marks, the second a number of little cuts round the left breast. . . ." And to this observation he appends an account of murders, particularly as practiced on the bridges of Paris. It is almost as if Reade spent his time shuttling between the slaughterhouse and the morgue, with side trips to the bridges, where he was constantly on the lookout for horsewhippings and throatcuttings. Actually, as the full context of the letter shows, he also noted a few non-violent French traits, e.g. the shortcomings of lower-class dancing, which he quite inexplicably attributed to the fact that "The French ladies are so very ill-made. . . ." But these observations are over-shadowed by his extraordinary interest in blood and violence.[15]

Beginning with the extreme sensitivity he showed at Mr. Slatter's there seems to be a straight psychological line extending through his experiences at medical school, where he fainted at the sight of blood, to the reactions apparent in these letters from Paris—a line that became broader and deeper in the years that followed, to emerge in his later life and writings as an obsessional form of humanitarianism that conforms to a pattern which has since come to be recognized as sadomasochistic. Not that Reade's feel-ings—or those of anyone else for that matter—can be fully explained by reference to a psychoanalytic pattern. Every man is unique, even in his typicality; and if one is to understand Reade's sadistic tendencies, it is necessary to see them in relation to the similar tendencies of Victorian writers and reformers from Tennyson to Lord Shaftesbury, many of whom, to all outward appearances, were as violently humanitarian as Reade. Where Reade's humani-tarianism differed (as further analysis will reveal) was in the quality of its bloodthirstiness; and this difference, most sensation-ally evident in the Notebooks, seems to derive from the sadistic tendencies already evident in these early reactions to blood and violence.

VI

During the years immediately following his European tour Reade was freer than ever before—and, it would seem, lonelier. In his restlessness, he was forever moving between London, Ips-den, and Scotland, with an occasional trip to Paris, and now and then, when necessity demanded, a brief stopover at Magdalen. "To avoid the trouble of packing up, carrying luggage, and form-ing plans," the Memoir relates, he kept "a complete outfit at all points of the compass." Thus when he felt too much alone in London (he had no close friends; only the squirrels, the prede-cessors of the antelope and numberless other pets, that ran loose in his Leicester Square lodging) he could turn to his mother and Ipsden. Or rather he could until his dealings in old violins precipitated an open break with his father. After that he took another trip to Paris, and for a considerable time omitted Ipsden from his nomadic itinerary, possibly supplanting it with more frequent trips to Scotland where, sometime between 1835 and 1839, he had met and fallen in love with a young fishwife, the prototype of Christie Johnstone.

According to Léone Rives, whose account of this episode substantiates what Elwin and others had surmised, there was probably a Scotch marriage, i.e., a kind of marriage oath before witnesses. At least Reade lived with this girl (whenever his circumstances and Mrs. Reade permitted) from 1838 or 1839 up to the time of her death in 1848, following the birth of a son who was christened Charles Liston and generally thought to be Reade's godson, until Reade, shortly before his death, recognized him as Charles Liston Reade. Beyond these few facts little is known about the relationship between Reade and his Christie, although, if one accepts Malcolm Elwin's autobiographical interpretation of *Christie Johnstone*, Mrs. Reade played a role similar to that of Mrs. Gatty in the novel, forcing Reade to treat Christie as a mistress, his son as a godson—as a means of preserving his Fellowship and as the price of retaining her own love and respect. That it happened this way is almost certain: Reade could hardly have kept his affair with Christie a secret from the family; indeed he probably met her on one of his many visits to his brother William, who lived at Crieff, in Perthshire. And if Mrs. Reade knew, she acted—doubtless with the same despatch she was to show a number of years later (1851) when her boy was thirty-seven years old, vice-president of Magdalen, and threatened by the charms of a famous actress, Mrs. Stirling, who had come to spend a week with him at Oxford. In Reade's own words (as recounted by John Coleman in his *Charles Reade as I Knew Him):*

Some good-natured friend wrote to Ipsden that the Vice-Chancellor of Magdalen had been seen trotting about with a play-actress, and next day, just as my fair friend and I were sitting down to lunch in my rooms, the Chatelaine of Ipsden descended upon us. She did not wait for any introduction. It was the first and only time I ever knew the Mater to forget herself.

I must do the other lady the justice to say *she* did not—indeed, she never acted so well on the stage as she did on that occasion.

"You are his mother, madam, and he is my friend," she said. "Don't trouble, sir; you are needed here, and I am not. I can find my way."

I drove home with mother that night, and next day (Sunday) we went to church together. When she said "forgive us our trespasses," she clasped my hand. I returned the clasp, and from that time forth the incident was closed.

Although Coleman is not always a trustworthy biographer, he did know Reade personally, and some of his information, rejected as unreliable by Malcolm Elwin, has been verified by more recent scholarship. In the present instance, if one discounts the awful sprightliness, Coleman's dramatization seems to be authentic—even to the final handclasp, which is psychologically in keeping with what is known of Reade, his mother, and the situation. Reade's own letters to and about Mrs. Stirling—one of which Percy Allen described as "too intimate and passionate for quotation"—show that Reade was in love with Mrs. Stirling, or thought he was; that despite a break in their relationship, probably accentuated if not caused by Mrs. Reade, he was thinking of Mrs. Stirling as well as Christie when he wrote the last chapter of *Christie Johnstone*. In a letter of 1852 to Mrs. Baylis, mostly devoted to Mrs. Stirling, he wrote: "C. J. concludes with a panegyric on Marriage (as I understand it). I describe it as Moses might the promised land, all the brighter because I have no hope of ever tasting it." [16]

By 1853, then, Reade was a confirmed though reluctant bachelor, ostensibly because of the technical celibacy required by his Fellowship, but also, it seems clear, because of his mother's feelings, and his own. In addition to Mrs. Reade's direct influence, there was Reade's own image of her, sufficient in itself to create a psychic block against any possible marriage, since the most perfect woman could hardly measure up to the more than human perfection of his Julia-mother ideal. For this reason he could love and wish to marry only those women who were unattainable—except as ideal wives, e.g. the married Mrs. Stirling, the dead as opposed to the living Christie. In the flesh these women were too much like "the charming, clever woman, beautiful as the dawn" whom he met at Durham (July 15, 1852)—only to discover, a few days later, that she was "madly in love with a man hideous as midnight, and not one idea in his skull." Such women, Reade comments, are like Miss Chaworth, who "utterly despised Lord Byron, and venerated a brainless boor, a snob, a beast, who leathered her with his riding whip. . . . She respected the Beast and despised the Man." Of all the weaknesses common to women, it was this attraction to the Beast and/or Blackguard—a trait he recorded in the

Notebooks under the heading "Calibani" [17]—that Reade found most disturbing. And so, within five days after meeting this real woman, beautiful as the dawn, he rejected her and once again turned to his ideal, this time as embodied in Peg Woffington, an eighteenth century actress whose portrait he had studied, and fallen in love with, during his evenings in the Garrick Club. On July 20, 1852 he confided to his *Diary:* "I am in love with Peg Woffington. She is dead, and can't sting. I love her. . . ."

VII

Ideals like Peg could not sting, but neither could they return Reade's love. Eventually he managed to find a livable compromise between the real and ideal in his relationship with Mrs. Seymour. But that was much later. During the years from 1838 to 1852 he had only his mother and Christie, neither of whom could give him the love and encouragement he so much needed. Whatever her virtues, Christie's position was such that she could only function as a mistress, and that for only a few weeks at a time. And Mrs. Reade, who was after all a mother not a wife, could only respond to Reade's psychic demands by denying his manhood—which, all unknowingly, is exactly what she did. Unwilling or unable to let him grow up and therefore away from her, she continued to regard him as her own wayward boy, to be coaxed or cajoled into accepting her will and her ideals as his own. To overcome his resistance—always, as she saw it, for his own good—she exerted all her motherly wiles, and with such effect that Reade either submitted or vacillated uneasily between rebellion and compliance. In 1845, for example, when the office of Dean of Arts at Magdalen fell to Reade's option, she insisted that he accept, for her sake as well as his own. At first Reade flatly refused, much as he needed the extra money which went with the office, on the ground that he could never live through another year in residence—only submitting, and then reluctantly, when his brother William agreed to share his rooms. So the struggle went on and on, with Reade torn between the demands of his mother's love and those of his own confused feelings and ambitions.

In this state of turmoil, and without any close friends to share his problems, Reade followed one vocation after another, in one place after another. Though called to the Bar in 1842, he never practised, seemingly because he could not settle down to the confining routine of legal work. He much preferred the life of a herring fisherman, or that of a dealer in violins and pictures, for these businesses, if they can be so designated, offered him excitement as well as a chance for quick gains. The bargaining, speculative side of commerce strongly appealed to Reade, as did the power that came with commercial success; indeed, if he had possessed more capital and been more fortunate in his business ventures, he might well have channeled his ambitions towards commercial rather than literary success. As it happened, however, he failed in every single venture, not disastrously but to the extent that he was repeatedly forced to apply for subsidies from his mother, who "permitted him to anticipate the sum he would . . . receive under her marriage settlement after death."

So it was that Reade's every effort during these years ended in frustration and continued dependence. As he failed in one undertaking after another, as he saw himself, after Christie's death, alone and defeated in the eyes of everyone but himself and his mother, his pride was at the breaking point. Unless he was to sink hopelessly into the life of an academic nonentity he had to write. That was, he believed, his sole remaining hope. Yet he had been trying since 1835, and the words simply would not come. All he could do was read and take notes and go to school to the theatre—mostly it seems, he went to the theatre, where he could laugh and cry with the hero at the same time he was initiating himself into the secrets of dramatic art—or so he believed. In any event, whether his wanderings led him to Paris, or London, or Edinburgh, evening always found him in or about some theatre. During one of his stays in Edinburgh, Coleman reports, he was so often in the front row of the pit, at the Theatre Royal and the Adelphi, that the company, noting his sailor-like walk and eccentric dress, christened him "The Mad Sailor." In Reade's own words, as recorded by Coleman, "I knew no one—not a living soul in Auld Reekie—save the actors and actresses, to whom I never spoke then, but whom I seem, after the lapse of all these years, to recall as the dear friends and companions of my lonely youth."

The phrasing may be Coleman's but the loneliness was Reade's, and it was all he could do to bear up under it. For the hours of gas-light and make believe were inevitably followed by a return to his own situation—and his own attempts to write. How deeply he felt his literary impotence, combined as it was with all his other frustrations, is evident in the bitterness of his later references to "wasted youth," all to the effect that he never lived until he began to write. In 1857, following his first great success with *It Is Never Too Late To Mend*, he noted: "A man of genius should take great care of his body. On his carcass depends his fate. The genius that breaks down at 35 dies despised. At 40 he dies just as he is beginning to weather mortification, insult and wrong, and jackasses may bray praise over his bones. If he can contrive to keep his body afoot till 80, he shall be honoured." The reference to "the genius that breaks down at 35" is especially significant. Reade himself was close to breaking down at that age (in the year 1849) when he was called home to attend his father who had become senile and was thought to be near death. The call, it seems, came from his mother, who wished to have Reade with her at the time, possibly to reconcile him to his father. If this was her plan, it worked out beautifully, for upon seeing his father in so pitiable a state Reade quickly lost all his old bitterness and became a dutiful son. To combat his father's recurrent fits of "morbid depression" Reade taught him to play whist, a game to which he responded with such enthusiasm that it "was played from morning till night, with intervals only for meals." While Reade was devoting himself to his father, Elwin explains, "he was enabled to spend the few hours of freedom which he contrived to snatch from the bondage of the whist table in tranquil reflection, no longer agitated by the itch to be out and about in search of the elusive inspiration to write, because his inactivity was a necessity. And, ironically, his resignation to delay brought him nearer to his goal than all his years of restlessness . . . it was probably in 1849, while his father was declining gradually in senile decay, that he began the first draft of *Christie Johnstone*."

That Reade thus began writing (and therefore, as he says elsewhere, "living") just when his father began dying follows from what is known of the conflict between father and son. Given only the few facts contained in the *Memoir* one does not have to be a Freudian to see how Reade was able to throw off some of his deepest fears and inhibitions through his father's death (October 24, 1849). Of course it was a complicated process: even after expiating his feelings of guilt over the sacrificial whist table, Reade was doubtless afflicted with all the feelings of contrition Malcolm Elwin suggests. But along with these feelings, perhaps in spite of them, there was also a sense of release—a release from what he rightly or wrongly felt to be the unloving side of the parental tyranny he had so long struggled against. Freed from this hostile father figure, he remained on with his mother at Ipsden, writing at least a part of the time, until the fall of 1850, when he at last felt equal to challenging the theatrical world with his first dramatic version of *Christie Johnstone*.

VIII

Reade's first efforts to place *Christie Johnstone* were heartening enough. Mrs. Stirling liked the play and submitted it to Tom Taylor. Before Taylor had time to consider it, however, Reade had once again permitted his mother to talk him into accepting still another college office. He was therefore vice-president of Magdalen, and bound to fulfill the demands of that office for almost a full year, when Mrs. Stirling returned his manuscript, along with a note from Taylor saying that "the play was full of strength" but "unfitted for the stage," and suggesting "he should make a novel of it." With his heart set on dramatic success, Reade was cruelly disappointed—so much so that, as Malcolm Elwin has explained, he became "distracted at the proposal of existing impotently for a whole year at Oxford . . . [and] penned the following hysterical epistle to Dr. Routh:

> Rev. and dear Sir, I have to throw myself on your compassion in making what I feel is an unusual request. I have all my life been subject to occasional depression of spirits. I cannot account for it; it comes like a cloud, and like a cloud it goes. But my solitary rooms are very unfavorable to me under such circumstances, and the best thing for me is a Family where I see many cheerful faces and hear good people who speak to me of God. Will you look kindly on a constitutional misfortune, and permit me to leave College for ten days or a fortnight . . . your dutiful servant, C. Reade, V.P.

This letter, quoted in full by Elwin, shows how precarious was Reade's psychological balance. The closer he approached his literary goals the more restive, even frantic, he became. Victimized by his own anxieties he began to see the theatrical world as a macrocosm of Magdalen—himself as a lone and persecuted genius At one point, his *Diary* reveals, he broke down so completely that he had to spend several months in a sanitarium:

> Ipsden House, Wallingford, May 7, 1852
> I am so ill in mind and body that I have resolved to go to Malvern.

Bellevue Hotel, Malvern.—What is more horrible than being alone in a strange place at an inn, and it raining?

Then the doctors are like Eastern princes. Dr. Gully, I am told, receives no visits after noon. So I am to take mine ease in mine inn till tomorrow. . . .

June 7, Malvern—I have now been a month in this place, and were I to call it a month stolen from my life, it would not be far from the truth.

It has been a month of *ennui* and utter collapse of bodily and mental power. Mine is a nature that requires some little amusement, and also the sound of some little human sentiment. Deprived of these for so many dreary days, solitary and cheerless, my mind is collapsing, and will go unless I save myself by flight. . . . I shall certainly run off one of these days. To Paris? Anywhere, and wash the taste of this Dead Sea out of my soul.

Such is the result of a month filched from my short life in this wretched place.

June 17.—Forty days, constant wind, so that I have not been able to sit one half-hour in the air. No acquaintance with a grain of feeling or brains, and I cannot stand dolts or fleshy statues.

Took what they call a lamp-bath the other day. I was to perspire. No such thing. Fainted instead. More refined, but less agreeable.

After leaving Malvern, Reade apparently went to Durham, to what may have been another sanitarium, where he was equally unhappy. And so the carousel started turning again: from Magdalen to Ipsden to Malvern to Durham to London to Paris . . . from the Ipsden drawing room to "hydros" to theatres and back again. Yet wherever Reade went, whatever he did, it was always the same—because he was always the same. His search for "cheerful faces . . . good people . . . human sentiment . . ." was in reality a search for his lost childhood, at home with his mother and his sister Julia. The boy was not just father to the man; emotionally he was the man. The death of his father, although it had given him the added freedom he needed to break through his writing block, led to a renewed understanding with his mother that bound him even more closely to her. And the rebuffs he received when he began to write served to reopen and deepen the psychic wounds he had suffered in his earlier conflicts with reality. On the threshold of authorship, at the age of thirty-eight, Reade was therefore as lonely and lost, as sensitive and egotistical and truculent, as when he alternately quailed and rebelled under the treatment he received from Mr. Slatter, his father, and Magdalen.

Intellectual Development[1]:

The One Road to Truth

EVERY ENGLISHMAN of the present day is by implication either a Benthamite or a Coleridgian; holds views of human affairs which can only be proved true on the principles either of Bentham or Coleridge.

—JOHN STUART MILL

✔   ✔   ✔

Lord Bacon was the saviour of the human intellect. He discouraged plausible conjecture, or *a priori* reasoning, and taught humble, close observation. Thereby he gave the key of the heavens to Newton, and the key of nature, and her forces, to the physical investigator, and the prying mechanic. Man began to cultivate the humble but wise faculty of observation; it grew by cultivation, and taught him how to wrestle with nature for her secrets, and extort them. There is scarcely a branch of useful learning, that method has not improved 500 percent. Of course, even since Lord Bacon, prejudice has in holes and corners, resisted observation: but the final result is sure. *A priori* reasoning bled people to death with the lancet for two centuries after Bacon: But Bacon has conquered the lancet. A handful of Jesuits will tell you that the historical query, whether one Bishop of Rome has contradicted another in faith, must not be learned from contemporary history, but evolved by internal thought a thousand years afterwards. Well, that mediaeval crotchet will go, and Bacon stay. And so it must be, sooner or later, with everything, copyright at common law—the national expediency of piracy—the infallibility of men with mitres—and *everything*. The world has tasted Bacon. It will never eat cobwebs again for long.

—CHARLES READE

✔   ✔   ✔

"A man born in 1810 . . . entered manhood with the ground rocking under his feet as it rocked in 1789. Paris had risen against the Bourbons; Bologna against the Pope; Poland against Russia; the Belgians against the Dutch. . . . At home forty years of Tory domination were ending in panic and dismay; Ireland, unappeased by Catholic Emancipation, was smouldering with rebellion; from Kent to Dorset the skies were alight with burning ricks." Thus G. M. Young characterizes the eighteen twenties and 'thirties. "At such a time," he continues, "a young man looking for some creed to steer by . . . might, with the Utilitarians, hold by the laws of political economy and the greatest happiness of the greatest number; he might simply believe in the Whigs, the Middle Classes, and the Reform Bill; or he might, with difficulty, still be a Tory. But atmosphere is more than creed and, whichever way his temperament led him, he found himself at every turn controlled, and animated, by the imponderable pressure of the Evangelical discipline and the almost universal faith in progress." [2]

Reade, who was born in 1814, entered upon manhood at the time and in the world Young describes. The difference is that he reacted to Evangelicalism, Benthanism, Whiggism, Toryism, not as Young's typical "young man," but as Charles Reade, the son of Mrs. Reade. He was not looking for a creed to steer by (his course was already set); rather he was looking for a creed that would justify his own course and enable him to follow it through—as he sought to implement his rebellion against his father, Magdalen . . . in fact all the forces that denied his ideals, that stood between him and personal success. To Reade these were the forces of evil, and he fought them with every means at his command, in every way he knew how, in his daydreams and actions as well as in his thoughts and writings. It was through these various efforts, acting and reacting upon one another within Reade's being and in relation to the outside world, that he developed his own philosophy—in the form of a unique composite of all the prevailing doctrines that could be made to serve his own emotional needs.

II

Reade's intellectual development—like that of his arch-enemy Carlyle—is therefore a dialectical extension of his emotional development. As early as his first encounter with the terrible Mr. Slatter, he had begun to rebel against the principles he was expected to live by. Yet his break with the Toryism of Ipsden and Magdalen, it has been shown, was never psychologically complete. Hence the schemes and daydreams, based on a combined form of Cinderella and Jack the Giant Killer myths, in which he rebelled against and finally conquered the very peoples and groups he pretended to despise. *The Bloomer,* one of his earliest short stories, begins thus: "Richard Courtenay . . . was the younger son of a good Devonshire family: his elder brother inherited four thousand a year,—he fifteen hundred pounds down, from the same relative, his father,—*vive l'Angleterre!* His fifteen hundred pounds wouldn't do in a genteel country like England: so he went to America and commerce. He died richer than the owner of Courtenay Court." [3] Reade's situation almost precisely, in all respects save one: Reade could not undertake any adventurous removals to America, or anywhere else that involved a long sea journey because—and this must be taken seriously—he was afraid of sea-sickness. [4] It was a rather convenient fear, of course, since it gave him an excuse for not doing what he could never have done anyway, though it is true that in later life, after he had achieved success and was free to visit America—to lecture, if he wished—he still refused, presumably because he could not face the prospect of even a smooth crossing. But whatever his own limitations or rationalizations, sea-sickness did not afflict his characters, and these he could send to the new worlds to seek and win their fortunes—just as Courtenay did. For in America talent and energy were rewarded, not stifled by an outmoded hierarchical system.

This is why John, Courtenay's son, who "was richer still by the same honorable means," came to adopt radical views, or rather superimposed these views on his innate Toryism:

> He was also a staunch republican: the unparalleled rise and grandeur of the United States might well recommend their institutions to any candid mind; and John Courtenay spent his leisure moments in taking the gloss off John Bull's hide. He was not so spiteful against him as some of those gentry who owe their cleverness to themselves, but their existence to Bull and forget it: his line was rather cool contempt. The old country was worn out and decayed; it was progressing like a crab instead of going ahead, etc.
>
> For all this, one fine day something seemed to crack inside John Courtenay's bosom when he saw an announcement . . . that Courtenay Court was in the market.
>
> He did not think such an advertisement would have interested him any more than consols ninety-six and a half—but it did.

This is Reade again. Although he too espoused "republican" ideas, [5] he was still drawn to "ancestral acres"; [6] more than that, his dreams of wealth and power were in large part motivated by the possibility of enjoying a triumph like Courtenay's, when he purchased Courtenay Court at auction:

. . . It was at thirty-eight thousand pounds. . . .

There was a pause. . . .

He [the auctioneer] now looked carefully all round the room: a long attenuated figure with a broad-brimmed hat on, standing by a distant window, met his eye, and as if to oblige him, now for the first time made a cool *nonchalant* bid by nodding his head—round went all the company on their heels . . .

Forty-two, three, four thousand, were reached—two country gentlemen bidders turned red and white—the pin [Courtenay's representative] bid on, rhythmically, at measured intervals, like a chaff-cutting machine, unconscious of opposition, indifferent to result. . . .

So Charles Reade, alias Courtenay, using his money as a modern general uses his mechanized troops, mowed down the chaff-like opposition with machine-like relentlessness.

With power once secure, however, the conquering hero was no longer relentless. He came "home" to find love and security, and to gain the respect of his neighbors:

John Courtenay came home: I omit the objections he took, *chemin faisant*, to things in the old country. They would fill a volume with just remonstrance.

He came to his own lodge-gate; the old man who opened it sung out—

'Oh! Master John, how like you be to Master Richard, surely.'

Courtenay was astonished: he found this old boy had been thinking of him all that way off for sixty years, ever since his birth transpired.

The old housekeeper welcomed him with tears in her eyes.

He dined in a room enriched with massive old carvings, he walked after dinner under his avenue of birches with silver stems of gigantic thickness and patriarchal age. The housekeeper put him in a bed his father had slept in when a boy.

Soon the country gentlemen made acquaintance with him. The strong idea of distributive justice he had brought from commerce, and his business habits, caused him to be consulted and valued.

It is a fact that after some months in Devonshire he developed a trait or two of Toryism, but they could not make him believe that nations are the property of kings, and countries their home farms. They did all they could think of to corrupt him.

They made him perforce a justice of the peace. He remonstrated and pooh-poohed, but was no sooner one than he infused fresh blood into the withered veins of justice in his district. He became a referee in all nice matters of rural equity. In short, his neighbors had all overcome any little prejudice, and had learned his value when—they lost him. . . .

The pattern is that of sentimental melodrama, but the desire for power and acceptance is Reade's own. In this (a typical form of his incessant daydreams) can be seen the intellectual consequences of his emotional rebellion—as it led him, in his alienation, to project wishes that could only be fulfilled through Benthamitic action.

III

In real life Reade could not be quite so adventurous: there was always his sea-sickness, for one thing. But within his own limitations and those enforced by his mother he tried to live his daydreams, sinking his energies and his money in one business venture after another, in an effort to win his fortune and thereby emulate the triumphs of his fictional heroes. That he failed in all these ventures, in some rather ignominiously, did not alter his belief in Commerce, or in his own ability to achieve commercial success. As always, he considered himself the victim of some group or another, whose stupidity or malignity prevented him from achieving the success his efforts warranted.

In his career as a violin merchant, for example, he encountered the disapproval of his entire family, culminating in his father's wrath when, according to the *Memoir*, he discovered that Reade had "thought fit to convert his bed-chamber into a fiddle-manu-factory," and in the process of testing his combinations of amber on the window sill, had streaked one side of the house with "different shades of brown in hideous patches." While this episode may be apocryphal, it is reasonably certain that Squire Reade looked upon his son's fiddle-trading as another hare-brained scheme which was, in addition to its other drawbacks, considerably be-neath the dignity of a Magdalen Fellow. And Magdalen may well have shared this view, for Reade was not only a trader, he was an itinerant one, who issued press advertisements such as the follow-ing, sent to Dr. Routh, President of Magdalen, by "an indignant London Tradesman":

'CREMORNE VIOLINS AND CHOICE PICTURES

Mr. Reade

the only importer of genuine Cremonese Instruments, and who has for years supplied the London Dealers, will be a few days;

[49]

Ten Days

At No. 9 Bridge Street, Birkenhead with a collection which Amateurs, Professors, and the Trade will find it their interest to visit.

Every instrument sold by this Party is sold with a full and specific guarantee. Mr. R, being accidentally possessed of several first-rate Pictures would gladly dispose of them on very moderate terms. They are 30 in number containing a Chef d'oeuvre by Sasse Ferrade, ditto by Greuze—a full sized Cuyp, ditto, Hobbima. A sketch Rembrant. Small picture Dietricy—a fine sketch three figures Etty Etc., Etc., Etc.

9 Bridge St. Birkenhead. 12 o'clock to 5
August 18, 1847 [7]

President Routh, whose notions of trade and tradesmen dated from Dr. Johnson's time, could hardly have approved of this advertisement, or for that matter any of Reade's business activities. But if he expressed his disapproval—and there is little doubt that he did—it was not sufficient to quell Reade's commercial ardor, which was at its height in 1847 and did not really abate until 1853, when he was well on his way towards becoming an established writer. Until that time, the *Memoir* explains (in a chapter entitled "Cremonaphilism") his "penchant for violins . . . amounted to an overpowering passion." By Reade's own admission he "ransacked Europe . . . invested thousands of pounds in the trade" to become "a great connoisseur . . . the first connoisseur in England." Nor is this just another extravagant Readian boast; his claims are fully borne out by the testimony of his colleagues and competitors in the trade, and by his letters to *The Pall Mall Gazette* entitled "Cremona Fiddles." Indeed, if Malcolm Elwin is correct, these letters "represent the classic authority in our language on the subject."

And he could have been as great a merchant as a connoisseur—or so Reade himself thought—had he not been plagued with difficulties and misfortunes. First, there were the Ipsden and Magdalen objections; then, on the material side, there was the death of his partner, plus the losses he sustained in Paris, when he was caught in the midst of the revolution of 1848, and forced to abandon "a score of valuable fiddles and some pictures, together with an extensive wardrobe. . . ." Finally, and most disastrously, he had to contend with import duties, applied in "a spirit of extortion." The climax to this struggle came when Reade, accused of fraudulently undervaluing a consignment of violins, first petitioned "the Honorable Board of Commissioners," then the "Lords of the Treasury."

In his petition to the Lords, after describing himself as "the only importing merchant in England . . . ," Reade addresses "Lord John Russell by name as a great patron of Commerce" to argue that "it is not only the fate of a single consignment, but of an entire though small branch of commerce. . . ." Continuing on in this vein for some ten thousand words, Reade berates the Customs Officer as "a Pseudo-Valuer . . . an ignorant Monomaniac . . . a mad babbler . . . a Superficial Smatterer upon a subject . . . twice as deep, delusive, and difficult as that of ancient paintings, and six times as delusive as any third business that exercises the critical powers of man. . . ." Like a true businessman, he then proceeds to argue that only those in the trade have sufficient knowledge to understand the unfairness of the Customs Regulations, particularly as enforced by uninformed Customs Officials. In the name of "truth and justice" he therefore begs that his consignment be valued by "the examination upon the oath of persons in the trade." Only in this way, he concludes, can justice be done, the trade saved:

My Lords, my fate is in your hands, and as God is my Judge, my commerce lives or perishes at a word from your lips.

I am the last Importer left—I can maintain my ground under the ten per cent. duty. No other man in England can: the best proof is, no other man attempts it as a Merchant. But once begin to tamper with that ten per cent. duty by over-valuation, once substitute by sleight-of-hand twenty-seven per cent., which in its honest English is what the Custom-House proposes to me in Thieves' Latin, and your Lordships, in point of fact, prohibit a patriotic Commerce.[8]

For all its earnest eloquence, this petition is a flagrant example of special pleading, tricked out in "free-enterprise" phrases. But Reade, of course, was too selfcentered to realize the fact. From his point of view, every word in the petition was Gospel truth, and if the Lords of the Treasury were not convinced, it was because they, like the Customs Officials, could not recognize truth, even when it was presented by Charles Reade.

IV

Thus it was that Reade lived his Courtenay-like daydreams, and gave them intellectual justification. On one level his petition is that of a thoroughgoing businessman: he is using the arguments of "free enterprise" to defend his business, and therefore his own and the nation's welfare, against the restraints of bad laws and worse officials. On another and deeper level, his petition is a defense of all his dreams and actions, against the prejudices and stupidities of a closed hierarchical system that stifled his abilities and talents, that would relegate him to a career befitting the prospects of a genteel younger son—a fate he could not and would not accept. The Customs House might drive him from the fiddle-trade, but if it did, he would find some other business, or some other way to win the fame and fortune which were rightfully his, by virtue of his superior talents. So Reade believed—thanks to his mother and his upbringing—with a faith that could tolerate neither opposition nor criticism. Since his superiority was beyond question, any denial of it was a denial of justice—to be corrected by any means at his disposal.

But this is to anticipate. For a time, as I have shown, his resistance did not go much beyond loud clothes and unconventional antics: he was an individualist without a philosophy, a rebel without a cause. Then at Oxford, or soon after he went to London, he came into contact with the world of commerce, to discover in its theory of free enterprise a philosophic rationalization which supported his rebellious individualism, which justified him in his conviction that he, as a man of energy and parts, should succeed to the limits of his abilities, unhampered by the restrictions he had encountered at home and at Magdalen. Fortified by these theories he could give free rein to his egotism, his lust for power and success, for what was good for him was good for the country and mankind in general—a belief so exactly suited to his own needs that he could not relinquish it, even when his attempts to live it led to one frustration after another. He could not change his mind, or his ways; nor could he change reality. Yet something had to give way. In the circumstances his only solution was to shift the scene of conflict, to erase the line separating recalcitrant reality from the submissive world of his daydreams—and that he did through his writing. The difficulties he could not overcome in his own person he transferred to his fiction, where they could be conquered by his fictional alter-ego, in the form of a series of heroes who follow the pattern set by the hero of *The Bloomer*. His very last novel recounts the Horatio Alger story of a poor but honest and able man of business who eventually wins his way to fame and fortune—though, and here Reade's vestigeal Toryism comes to the surface again, it finally turns out that the hero is, in the best tradition of Adelphi melodrama, the son of a gentleman, not a workman. In one guise or another this same character—dubbed the "Resourceful Hero" by W. L. Courtney—appears in every single novel. "He is not," Courtney adds, "a Carlylean hero; he has some regard for human life, and he is usually an affectionate, warm-hearted Christian. But wherever he is and whatever problem besets him, he is sure to come through it triumphantly. . . ." [9] And, one should add, he is sure to come through it by means of his own power and ingenuity. The formula never changes—because Reade himself never changed. The individualism he expressed in his Petition to the Treasury is the same individualism he expressed, more fully and of course "triumphantly," through his Resourceful Heroes. In other words, it is an extension of his youthful revolt, redirected towards socially acceptable ends—as defined by the followers of Ricardo and Adam Smith.

v

In seeking to justify his personal revolt Reade was thus led to accept the laissez-faire theories that underlay revolutionary Benthamism. Moreover, in developing these theories into a personal philosophy, he adopted a number of key Benthamitic ideas. His dislike for Oxford, it has been noted, was motivated by more than personal pique. In part it was a protest against the intellectual deadness of the place. Oxford's quiescent traditionalism he found stultifying, its resurgent Medievalism comical—or terrifying. His remarks about Newman indicate that he would have liked to dismiss Puseyism (along with the social, political, and artistic doctrines that accompanied it) as more amusing than dangerous. But at Oxford this was impossible: he simply could not dismiss a movement that had swallowed up his closest friend at Magdalen[10] and was threatening to reduce the whole of England to the barbarism of the Middle Ages. He therefore reacted against everything Medieval, and with so much intensity that he was drawn towards those Benthamitic thinkers who were furthest removed from the Medievalists, who had, on the positive side, evolved a "Modernist" philosophy congenial to his own needs and attitudes.

Eventually Reade went directly to the writings of Bentham

and the Mills and to those of the philosopher he revered above all others, Francis Bacon. But in the beginning, it would seem, he absorbed his Modernism from the Benthamitic ideas that were generally current, possibly supplemented by reading in popular books of the time, e.g., G. R. Porter's *The Progress of the Nation* (1836) or Andrew Ure's *The Philosophy of Manufactures* (1835). Ure, the man whom Marx parodied as "the Pindar of Manufactures," [11] declares in his Preface that "the present" is distinguished from every preceding age by "an universal ardor of enterprise in arts and manufactures." Nations no longer fight with guns, he continues, but with factory implements. War has been replaced by the bloodless but still formidable strife of trade: "To impair the resources of a rival at home, by underselling his wares abroad, is the new belligerent system, in pursuance of which every nerve and sinew of the people are put upon the strain." Developing these points, Ure goes on to show that this new type warfare, which leads to plenty and "progress," demands new heroes with new outlooks. "Great Britain," he concludes, "may certainly continue to uphold her envied supremacy, sustained by her coal, iron, capital, and skill, if, acting on the Baconian axiom 'Knowledge is Power,' she shall diligently promote moral and professional culture among all ranks of her productive population."

By 1838, the year he entered upon his business career, Reade actively shared these views, though in his own expression of them he was less nationalistic, more Christian, particularly in his emphasis on bloodlessness. Trade was in many respects warlike, but not to the point of physical violence—and that, to Reade, was the crucial difference which distinguished the barbarism of the past from the humanitarianism of the present. In one of his fictional attacks upon Carlyle—presented in the form of a debate over the relative merits of Ancient vs. Modern civilization—the Readian hero explains:

> The earnest men of former ages are not extinct in this. . . . Whenever a scaffold is erected outside a prison-door, if you are earnest in pursuit of truth, and can put up with disgusting objects, you shall see a relic of ancient manners hung.
> There still exist, in parts of America, rivers on whose banks are earnest men, who shall take your scalp, the wife's of your bosom, and the innocent child's of her bosom.
> In England we are as earnest as ever in pursuit of heaven, and of innocent worldly advantages. If, when the consideration

of life and death interposes, we appear less earnest in pursuit of comparative trifles, such as kingdoms or dogmas, it is because, cooler in action we are more earnest in thought—because reason, experience, and conscience are things that check the unscrupulousness or beastly earnestness of man.

Moreover, he who has the sense to see that questions have three sides, is no longer so intellectually as well as morally degraded as to be able to cut every throat that utters an opinion contrary to his own.[12]

There is no mistaking the nature or intent of these Modernist arguments: Carlyle's Medievalism was to Reade what Hitler's Nazism was to the liberals of the nineteen-thirties, and he reacted accordingly. In addition to the anti-Carlylean attacks scattered throughout his non-fictional writings, two of his best known novels (*Christie Johnstone*, and *The Cloister and the Hearth*) are in the nature of anti-Carlylean polemics—the main plot of *Christie Johnstone* turning on the conflict between the good of Readian Modernism and the evil of Carlylean Medievalism. Although Viscount Ipsden, the Resourceful Hero of the novel, is outwardly a "dilettante" (Reade calls him that, in overt defiance of Carlyle) beneath the surface are more sterling qualities. Consequently when the need for action arises, he throws off his lethargy, proves himself a Modern "hero," and puts Carlyle's minion to rout.

The message is clear enough, yet Reade was still not content. To make absolutely certain his readers understood, he appended an explanatory note in which he referred to Carlylism as "a cant that was flourishing like a peony," and within the novel itself added whole pages of direct anti-Carlylean argument—as in the following commentary on Lady Barbara and the Carlylean buffoon who had misled her:

Antiquity, they agreed, was the time when the world was old, its hair grey, its head wise. Every one that said 'Lord, Lord,' two hundred years ago, was a Christian. There were no earnest men now; Williams, the missionary, who lived and died for the gospel, was not earnest in religion; but Cromwell, who packed a jury, and so murdered his prisoner,—Cromwell, in whose mouth was heaven, and in his heart temporal sovereignty, was the pattern of earnest religion, or, at all events, second in sincerity to Mahomet alone, in the absence of details respecting Satan, of whom we know only that his mouth is a Scripture concordance, and his hands the hands of Mr. Carlyle's saints.

> Then they went back a century or two, and were eloquent about the great antique heart, and the beauty of an age whose samples were Abbot Sampson and Joan of Arc . . .

Lord Ipsden, the Readian hero, puts up with as much of this Carlylean cant as he can stand; then exposes and denounces it for what it is:

> He suggested 'That five hundred years added to a world's life made it just five hundred years older, not younger; and if older, grayer; and if grayer, wiser.
>
> 'Of Abbot Sampson,' said he, 'whom I confess both a great and a good man, his author, who with all his talent belongs to the class muddle-head, tells us, that when he had been two years in authority his red hair had turned gray, fighting against the spirit of his age; how the deuce, then, could he be a sample of the spirit of his age?
>
> 'Joan of Arc was burnt by acclamation of her age, and is admired by our age. Which fact identifies an age most with a heroine, to give her your heart, or to give her a blazing fagot and death?
>
> 'Abbot Sampson and Joan of Arc,' concluded he, 'prove no more in favor of their age, and no less against it, than Lot does for or against Sodom. Lot was in Sodom, but not of it; and so were Sampson and Joan in, but not of, the villanous times they lived in.
>
> 'The very best text-book of true religion is the New Testament, and I gather from it, that the man who forgives his enemies whilst their axe descends on his head, however poor a creature he may be in other respects, is a better Christian than the man who has the God of Mercy forever on his lips, and whose hands are swift to shed blood. . . .
>
> 'If the phrase "earnest man" means man imitating the beasts that are deaf to reason, it is to be hoped that civilization and Christianity will really extinguish the whole race for the benefit of the earth.' [13]

In these passages Reade violates his fictional character—actually if not technically—to carry his denunciation to the point of frenzied abuse. Seemingly he could not discuss Carlyle's "beastly earnestness" without conjuring up visions that became his own King Charles's head. At such times he could not think, he could only cry "beast" and point to the blood-stained hands . . . "the hands of Mr. Carlyle's saints." Reacting with such horror to the consequences of Carlyle's doctrines, he could hardly view the doctrines themselves with equanimity, especially since they embodied in more extreme form the patriarchal authoritarianism that, to his way of thinking, had nearly wrecked his life. Hence the intensity of his reaction, causing him to reject everything Carlylean as a rationalization of Carlyle's beastly earnestness.

VI

On the positive side Reade's total rejection of Carlyle pushed him further towards Benthamism. Whereas Carlyle, along with other Medievalists appealed to authority, in the form of right or might, Reade's final appeal, as in the above passage, was to "reason." And by reason, his other writings show, he meant that which can be proved true by "scientific method." In line with John Stuart Mill's statement—that "every Englishman of the present day is by implication either a Benthamite or a Coleridgian. . . ." Reade established a clear-cut distinction between the two modes of searching truth. "One method," he explains in "The Rights and Wrongs of Authors," [14] is by "*a priori* reasoning, and was the method of the Greek sophists, and medieval schoolmen . . . the other is by observation, and evidence, and is the method of Lord Bacon and his pupils. . . . To test the systems take any period of 400 years before Lord Bacon, and estimate the progress of the world in knowledge and useful discoveries. Then take the 250 years after Lord Bacon. . . ." Reade then goes on to illustrate, at some length, how Baconian induction has conquered *a priori* and transcendental thinking (elsewhere referred to as "Cephalomancy") [15] and thereby enlightened the world. "Lord Bacon," he concludes, "was the saviour of the human intellect . . . he gave the key of the heavens to Newton, and the key of nature, and her forces, to the physical investigator, and the prying mechanic. . . ."

These lines recall a passage in Macaulay's essay on Bacon, the one in which Macaulay, paraphrasing Cowley's poem, compares Bacon to Moses standing on Mount Pisgah. There are other parallels too, and while most of them are of no great significance in themselves they do suggest that Reade was acquainted with the Baconian method by 1837, the year Macaulay's essay appeared in the *Edinburgh Review*. And there are other facts, mainly biographical, which suggest that Reade's acquaintance with the method goes back still further, to the early years of his personal rebellion against Ipsden and Oxford. At that time a young rebel in search of a creed could hardly avoid Bacon, for his writings were almost as much admired and vilified in the eighteen-thirties as Freud's in the nineteen-thirties. Basil Montagu's sixteen volume edition of Bacon's works, which appeared in the years between 1825 and 1834, gave rise to innumerable essays and reviews—among others, Macaulay's. Then, in addition to such Baconian studies as those listed by Fowler in his *Bacon's Novum Organum* there was De Maistre's *Examen de la Philosophie de Bacon* (1836)—an Ultramontane attack upon Bacon's inductive philosophy that set the pattern for similar though less violent attacks by Newman and the Tractarians.[16] Stimulated by these studies and the controversies that centered around them Reade may well have gone straight to Montagu's edition, there to discover the answers to his intellectual problems. Or—and this seems more likely—he could have become generally acquainted with inductive method through his reading at Oxford and Lincoln's Inn,[17] never realizing that the method could form the basis for divergent philosophies until he encountered the writings of those contemporary thinkers who were attempting to renovate the *Novum Organum,* notably Whewell and John Stuart Mill. Whewell's *History of the Inductive Sciences* appeared in 1837, his *Philosophy of the Inductive Sciences* in 1840, to be followed three years later by Mill's epoch-making *System of Logic.* These works brought out the philosophic implications of Baconian as well as later versions of scientific method, and Reade was undoubtedly influenced by them—though not in the way or to the extent Lewis F. Haines has argued in his article on "Reade, Mill, and Zola." [18] Reade did not derive his theories of induction from Mill, did not become "an ardent believer in latter-day English empiricism, as elucidated in Mill's *Logic.*" Indeed the ultimate effect of the *Logic* was to send Reade scurrying back to Bacon. Like Harriet Martineau's Mr. Atkinson—another eccentric Baconian—he dismissed Mill's theories of induction to return to those embodied in the *Novum Organum.*

Throughout his works, fictional and non-fictional alike, he constantly eulogizes Baconian or Solomonian, never Mill's revised principles of induction. "Nothing in man is an inch deep," he proclaims in *The Eighth Commandment,* "but knowledge painfully acquired, partly by personal observation, partly from the testimony of other eye-witnesses. Nothing in man is a foot *deep,* but knowledge acquired by the science of sciences, statistic. That science, sneered at by buzzards, is *'the soi-disant Baconian principle'* worked by a vast machinery of eyes and hands. It is what I call Solomon (a) + Argus + Briareus." [19] Reade time and again reiterated these principles, most clearly perhaps in *The Coming Man,* a series of letters contributed to *Harper's Weekly* in which he tries to prove, on Baconian principles, that man is by nature "either-handed." In the course of his argument he once again pillories the ancients. Then, after exposing their method of false reasoning, still practiced by Cephalomants, he finally explains the only true one, which is "Statistics Collected by men without a theory . . . all the investigations up to date have been on too trumpery a scale, and in the hands of theorists, which is fatal. . . . Medicine is mere Fiction when ever the theorist is allowed to collect the facts. . . ." [20] And what holds true for medicine, Reade made clear, holds true for morality, politics, art—in fact everything save religion.

With such principles Mill took direct issue. "Bacon's greatest merit," he pointed out, "cannot consist, as we are so often told that it did, in exploding the vicious method pursued by the ancients, of flying to the highest generalizations for it, and deducing the middle principles from them, since this is neither a vicious nor an exploded method, but the universally accredited method of modern science, and that to which it owes its greatest triumphs." [21] Mill here points to the primary weakness of the Baconian method. In other passages in the *Logic* he goes still further, analyzing the method at length to show the limits of its usefulness, the danger of trying to apply it in the wholesale manner Reade was attempting. For instance he had nothing but scorn for those Baconians who would apply the method to political subjects: "The vulgar notion that the safe methods on political subjects are those of Baconian induction—that the true guide is not general reasoning, but specific experience—will one day be quoted as among the most unequivocal marks of a low state of the speculative faculties in any age in which it is accredited." In short Mill considered Baconian induction outmoded, its practitioners men who "know nothing whatever of the methods of physical investigation beyond a few precepts which they continue to parrot after Bacon, being entirely unaware that Bacon's conception of scientific inquiry has done its work, and that science has now advanced into a higher stage." [22]

Nearly all the philosophers of the day—from George Henry Lewes to Augustus De Morgan—conceded the validity of Mill's criticism; also the fact that, on the positive side, his principles of induction corrected and refined those of Bacon. But not Reade.[23] He could not accept the implications of Mill's revised theories, particularly when, as in the *Logic,* those theories committed him to a philosophic system that held nothing sacred, not even religious beliefs, that carried the scientific method all the way through to its logical conclusions. Despite all his philosophic blustering, Reade was not, like Mill, engaged in a philosophic quest for truth; rather he was searching for a means of retaining and defending his own needs and beliefs, and for this purpose the Baconian method—at least in the form he came to understand and apply it—was much preferable to Mill's. It gave him a scientific method without obliging him to use it scientifically or even consistently. In other words, it gave him a weapon, a means of rationalization, which he could use to substantiate and piece together an empirical philosophy that included everything from his "either-handed" to his religious notions.

VII

Reade's first need for the Baconian method was in connection with his Evangelical beliefs. Although his revolt carried him a long way towards Benthamism, he never went so far as to become a free thinker. Indifferent if not hostile to all forms of doctrinal severity he nevertheless accepted the main essentials of his mother's Evangelical creed. So long as he remained her son he could not do otherwise. Yet neither could he surrender his Benthamitic ideas: they were his intellectual stay against the injustices and evils that constantly threatened him. Seemingly his dilemma was that of his intellectual contemporaries, forced to choose between the conflicting truths of science and religion. But there was a way to avoid such a choice altogether, and Reade of course found it, thanks first to the Baconian method, secondly to the fact that the doctrines of Benthamism were in many respects hardly distinguishable from those of the Evangelicals.

As A. V. Dicey long ago pointed out (in his *Law and Opinion in England*): "Benthamism and Evangelicalism represented the development in widely different spheres of the same fundamental principle, namely, the principle of individualism. The appeal of the Evangelicals to personal religion corresponds with the appeal of Benthamite Liberals to individual energy. Indifference to the authority of the Church is the counterpart of indifference to the authoritative teaching or guidance of the State or of society. . . . The theology, again, which insisted upon personal responsibility, and treated each man as himself bound to work out his own salvation, had an obvious affinity to the political philosophy which regards men almost exclusively as separate individuals, and made it the aim of law to secure for every person freedom to work out his own happiness. . . ." After further clarifying and developing these points, Dicey goes on to show how both groups relied on the principle of utility, how in their actual teachings they appealed to much the same feelings: "Evangelical teachers and philosophic Radicals urged their disciples, though in very different ways, to lead better and nobler lives; they appealed, as regards matters of national concern, to the public spirit and to the humanity of Englishmen; they excited among all whom they could influence the hatred of palpable injustice, and felt themselves, and kindled among others, a special abhorrence for that kind of oppression which manifestly increased human suffering."

Drawn together by all these likenesses and affinities the two groups formed a united front in matters of social reform. "Wesley on his deathbed wrote to encourage Wilberforce in his 'glorious enterprise, in opposing that execrable villainy [the slave trade], which is the scandal of religion, of England, and of human nature,' whilst Bentham in a later year wrote to express his sympathy with the exertions of Wilberforce, 'in behalf of the race of innocents, whose lot it has hitherto been to be made the subject-matter of depradation, for the purpose of being treated worse than the authors of such crimes are treated for those crimes in other places.'" And the followers of Bentham and Wilberforce took up where their masters left off: they united to condemn the same social evils—slavery, prison abuses, etc.—in terms so nearly alike that, paraphrasing Dicey, even the moral tone of Benthamism was akin to that of Evangelicalism.

Close as the two groups were, however, their beliefs never actually merged, not even in matters of social reform, where their common attitude towards cruelty and injustice brought them closest together. The Benthamites were Radicals as well as free-thinkers; to the Evangelicals their individualism must have appeared democratic and atheistic. The Evangelicals, on the other hand, were for the most part Tories, and "men of ardent faith." In the last analysis, as Dicey himself admitted, the difference between Benthamism and Evangelicalism "is nothing less than the gulf which severs religion from secularism." [24] In part Reade was aware of this primary difference, and its implications. But as a good Baconian he was no whit daunted. "For certain it is," according to Bacon, "that God worketh nothing in Nature but by second causes . . . but when a man passeth on farther, and seeth the dependence of causes and the works of providence, then . . . he will easily believe that the highest link of nature's chain must needs be tied to the foot of Jupiter's chair . . . therefore, let no man . . . think or maintain that a man can search too far or be too well studied in the book of God's word or in the book of God's works, divinity or philosophy, but rather let men endeavor an endless progress or proficience in both; only let men beware . . . that they do not unwisely mingle these learnings together." [25] By following this solution, which Bertrand Russell has descrbed as "the doctrine of double truth," Reade was able to retain as many of his Benthamitic ideas as were compatible with his Evangelical faith. Which meant, in practice, that he retained any belief he chose. For, as I have shown, the two modes of thought had much in common, and where they differed fundamentally—as in matters of politics or theology—Reade could always use the Baconian method to validate the idea that suited his fancy.

VIII

A number of other discernible elements went into the intellectual melange that was Reade's philosophy, and if this were a definitive study of his intellectual development they would have to be taken into direct account: notably the "democratic," "romantic," and "heroic" aspects of his individualism; also perhaps his views on medicine, feminism, etc. But these more unique aspects of his thought usually spring directly from his emotional prejudices. In so far as he gives them intellectual substance they can ordinarily be explained by reference to the basic elements of his philosophy, which may be summarized under four main heads: 1) *laissez-faire* individualism 2) a form of Modernism that accepted machinery, science, and all the "progress" of the Nineteenth Century 3) Baconian Method, to be applied to all "God's works" as distinguished from "God's words" 4) Tory-Evangelical Christianity, with emphasis on philanthropy.

This summary reflects the basic contradictions that underlie Reade's thought, contradictions that he himself compounded by his disregard for intellectual consistency. Although his individualist and Modernist beliefs were essentially Benthamitic, he was by no means a thoroughgoing Benthamite. Like Macaulay and so many others, he fully approved of certain Benthamitic doctrines but rejected the system as a whole. Yet if he was not a Benthamite, neither was he anything else.[26] His Evangelical like his Tory beliefs were more spiritual than doctrinal, and his Baconianism was for the most part centered in Bacon's method, which as often as not he applied according to Solomonian (i.e., Readian) rather than Baconian principles. In short he accepted no ready-made philosophy, and was neither original nor systematic in his own thinking. The personal philosophy which he brought to fiction was made up of scraps from the ragbag of Evangelicalism, Toryism, and Benthamism, patched up by the Baconian method to clothe the emotional nakedness of a proud, lonely, and thwarted egotist—a Benthamitic rebel who was yet a son of Mrs. Reade and Tory-Evangelical Ipsden.

Despite its obvious limitations, this philosophy served Reade the man rather well, providing him with an ideal means for evading those aspects of reality which threatened his precarious emotional balance. All he had to do, when confronted with a real problem, was to translate it into a Baconian one, then use the Baconian method to secure the right Benthamitic or Evangelical answer. With these answers—which invested his boyish daydreams with the maturity and objectivity of a Parliamentary Bluebook—Reade could sublimate all his personal difficulties, secure in the knowledge that his motives were as pure, his ideas as noble, as those of Solomon himself; that he was in fact what he conceived himself to be in fancy: a latter-day Solomon carrying the light of God and the Baconian method to the dark places of the Victorian world.

Self delusion cannot be carried much further without becoming psychopathic. Stripped of his philosophic disguise, the latter-day Solomon can be recognized as a rebellious son of Ipsden trying to hide from himself as well as from outside reality. Indeed if one looks closely enough the word of God he carried can be recognized as the words of Mrs. Reade, the light of the Baconian method as an ideational reflection of his own prepossessions, the dark places of the world as surface manifestations of the still darker abysses of his own psyche. But Reade of course was blissfully unaware of these discrepancies. He could not recognize them because, from his Baconian point of view, they could not exist. After all, facts equalled reality, and his own vision of himself and the world was a matter of fact.

So it was that Reade translated his genuine if eccentric feelings and perceptions into systematized Baconian delusions. For Reade the man these delusions were perhaps advantageous, but for Reade the novelist, the next few chapters will show, they were little short of disastrous. A writer can be an escapist, can even live a total lie, so long as he knows he is living it, and can somehow see through and beyond it. For in this case he is fooling the world, not himself. What he can never do, without radically impairing his artistic vision, is to live a lie and not know he is living it; for then he cannot see beyond his own delusions, which will, in his eyes, take on the characteristics of the true and beautiful. When this happens, as it did with Reade, the novelist is forced to write under an almost insuperable handicap. His ability to overcome it will in large measure depend, again as it did with Reade, on the adequacy of his fictional theories and techniques.

Artistic Development 1835–1849:

"Fourteen Years a Student"

IF YOU WANT to find out who the people are who know nothing whatever, even by hearsay, of the progress of the literature of their own time—who have caught no chance vestige of any one of the ideas which are floating about before their very eyes—who are, to all social intents and purposes, as far behind the age they live in as any people out of a lunatic asylum can be—go to a theatre, and be very careful, in doing so, to pick out the most popular performance of the day.

—WILKIE COLLINS

✔   ✔   ✔

Romance, if I am not mistaken, is destined shortly to undergo an important change. Modified by the German and French writers—by Hoffman, Tieck, Hugo, Dumas, Balzac, and Paul Lacroix (*le Bibliophile Jacob*)—the structure, commenced in our own land by Horace Walpole, Monk Lewis, Mrs. Radcliffe, and Maturin, but left imperfect and inharmonious, requires, now that the rubbish, which choked up its approach, is removed, only the hand of the skilful architect to its entire renovation and perfection. I have not included the great name of Walter Scott in this list. . . . But I cannot help echoing the wish of the French aspirant [Victor Hugo], that we may yet see the only romance, which could surpass the creations of our, as yet, unrivalled novelist;—"*le Roman à la fois, drame et épopée; pittoresque mais poétique; réel, mais idéal; vrai, mais grand; qui enchâssera Walter Scott dans Homère!*"

The novelist is precisely in the position of the dramatist. He has, or should have, his stage, his machinery, his actors. His representation should address itself as vividly to the reader's mental retina, as the theatrical exhibition to the spectator. The writer, who is ignorant of dramatic situation and its effects, is unacquainted with the principles of his art, which require all the adjuncts and essentials of the scenic prosopopœia. "*Imaginez*," says M. de Balzac, "*un conte sans intérêt de drame, sans émotion lyrique, sans couleurs nuances, sans logique exacte. Il sera pâle, extravagant, et faux. Il n'existera plus.*" The romance, constructed according to the rigid rules of art, will, beyond doubt, eventually, if not immediately, find its way to the stage.—It is a drama, with descriptions to supply the place of scenery.

—HARRISON AINSWORTH[1]

✔   ✔   ✔

1835 was a year of action and decision for Reade. In that year, it will be recalled, he took his A.B., won two scholarships, and freed himself from the necessity of entering the Church. For the son of Mrs. Reade these were notable victories, and they encouraged him to carry his resistance to the prescriptions of Ipsden and Oxford still further—by setting out to be a writer. Although he could not announce his decision openly—his fear of his mother's censure was still too great—he was apparently acting upon it even before he left Oxford for Lincoln's Inn. "In the year 1835," he relates in his autobiographical sketch (ironically entitled "Reade's Luck"): "I began to make notes with a view to writing fiction, but, fixing my mind on its masterpieces in all languages and all recorded times, I thought so highly of that great and difficult art that for fourteen years I never ventured to offer my crude sketches to the public."

"Fiction," as Reade seems to be using the word here, undoubtedly means drama or drama and novel, for he immediately goes on to say: "I began at last, and wrote several dramas, not one of which any manager would read; but theatrical England at this time was a mere province of France. Observing which, I crept into the theatre at last with a French translation. From that I went to better things, and wrote several plays alone, and in conjunction with my friend Mr. T. Taylor, but though my talent, whatever it may be, is rather for the drama than the novel, I was, after a hard fight, literally driven into the novel by bad laws and corrupt practices." Reade is here taking much the same position as Wilkie Collins, another dramatist manqué. "If I had been a Frenchman," Collins declares in his "Memorandum," "all the stories I have written . . . would have been told in the dramatic form . . . if I know anything of my faculty it is a dramatic one." [2] The difference is that Reade was more certain of his "faculty," and made a great deal more of it, maintaining his interest in the theatre, and continuing to write what he called "great dramas" up to the very end of his career. And finally, when he summed up his career in writing his own epitaph, he placed the word "Dramatist" before the word "Novelist."

II

Legend has it that Reade became enamoured of the stage during his undergraduate days; further, that he completed his play *Peregrine Pickle* before he left Oxford for Lincoln's Inn. Coleman, adding to this legend, suggests that Reade went so far as to submit the play to Macready, who summarily rejected it. Although Coleman's additions may be spurious, it seems that Reade's interest in the theatre was highly developed by 1835, needing only the stimulus of London life and the London theatre to bring it to full intensity. In any event Reade was, from 1836 onwards, so wholly enamoured of the theatre that he might well have devoted his whole life to it—perhaps to become a literate Vincent Crummles— had it not been for the restraining influence of his mother, who had long since forgotten her youthful acquaintance with Sheridan, and looked upon all things theatrical as a threat to religion and morality. But Mrs. Reade's disapproval merely checked Reade's theatrical ambitions; it was not sufficient to destroy them. During these years nothing could keep Reade away from the theatre: his loneliness was too intense, his need for theatrical make-believe too great. For him, as for his fictional hero, Mr. Vane, the green room was a "magic chamber," the stage "a scene of enchantment" where he could live and love while he was learning the craft that would bring him fame and success.[3]

With these aims and needs Reade went to play after play, night after night; and he found the kind of enchantment he wanted—in the theatres of Paris as well as in those of London and Edinburgh. In Paris there was the romantic drama of Hugo and his followers, the "severe young men" who had seen Bonaparte and refused "to be the train-bearers of outworn superstition." According to Hugo's "Preface" to *Cromwell*, (generally regarded as a charter for the romantic movement in France) "The poet of the modern world is not Racine (the classicist) but Shakespeare or Molière; for the object of modern art is not beauty but life; and that which gives us the keenest sense of life is not solely the beautiful, but the *characteristic*, even though that be ugly, odious or deformed. A multitude of figures, quantity of details, a sense of the scene, an impression of time and place startling in their exactitude, a realization of all that is individual, peculiar to a moment and a person; in fact an insistence on local color, on every exactest detail of Nature and truth, are not only permissible in drama, but necessary. . . ."[4] These critical views anticipate Reade's own, in everything from Hugo's emphasis on "exactest detail" to his admiration for Molière and Shakespeare, the two playwrights whom Reade too placed above all others, Molière for his comedies, Shakespeare for his tragedies. The one point to which Reade would have demurred (Hugo's frank acceptance of the "deformed") he was quite willing to accept under another name, for his own humanitarian interests, as revealed in his fascination for the exactest detail of the Paris slaughterhouses and morgues, corresponded to Hugo's interest in the "ugly, odious or deformed," as represented in the scenes of flagellation, torture, and bloodshed that constantly recur in his plays. How fully Reade accepted these plays—blood and all—is evidenced by his translation of *Angelo,* and by his encomiums in *The Eighth Commandment* proclaiming "*Lucrezia Borgia, Angelo, Le Roi s'amuse, Ruy Blas, Hernani, Marie Tudor,* etc. great world-wide plays." [5]

By any but mid-nineteenth century standards such an estimate is of course extravagant. Hugo's poetic plays, modern critics have shown, can still be taken seriously, but his prose dramas, such as *Angelo, Lucrezia Borgia,* and *Marie Tudor,* are by common critical consent the "naked melodramas" J. Brander Matthews declared them to be when he noted that "to read them straight through is almost as good as a course in toxicology. The dagger is abused as frequently as the bowl. To call the death roll of all the *dramatis personae* who die by the sword or the axe would be as tedious as unprofitable." [6] As for the other French dramatists whom Reade admired and adapted (e.g. Maquet, Scribe, Legouvé) they were but men of talent producing a marketable commodity, the sole virtues of their plays being those Shaw acknowledged in his "Preface" to *Three Plays by Brieux.* From Reade's point of view, however, these writers were the successors to Molière and Shakespeare, and it was his constant aim to emulate their dramatic achievements.

III

Of his English contemporaries, Reade had no such high opinion. "The French dramatists," he asserted, "are writers . . . *as a class* . . ." whereas "the English playwrights, *as a class,* and exceptis excepiendis, are scribblers." [7] Nevertheless he went to school to all forms of the English drama, and he learned his lessons well, particularly those embodied in the ubiquitous melodrama of his day. "During the period from 1800 to 1850," Allardyce Nicoll has explained, melodrama "may be classed in three main divisions: the romantic, the supernatural, and the domestic; and we may consider this dramatic form as a whole to have developed from one division to another." [8] The domestic melodrama, he adds, "may be regarded as a kind of reaction to the earlier types . . . although in essence it is but the enunciation by illegitimacy of the realistic tendency which ever accompanies romanticism. . . . On the one side . . . the gloomy castles, the ruined abbeys; on the other, the dingy cottage, the slum tenement, the poverty-stricken alleys." According to Nicoll, then, Reade was primarily exposed to a form of melodrama which shared all the characteristics common to the genre, but which emphasized social realism and social purpose. Humanitarianism was spiced with sentiment, and used as a justification for realistic scenes of blood and violence—as in Brooks's *The Creole* (1847) "a direct appeal to the audience in favor of the anti-slavery campaign . . . planned as a concrete example of the slave-trade." [9]

Of course the realism of these plays was far from subtle. The theatres were large, the audiences uncritical;[10] for these and other reasons the plays were written to secure broad effects, mainly through the bodily and facial contortions of the actors, who were apparently expected to register "some two-score emotions" in a conventional manner. When portraying "rage," *The Actors' Hand-Book* explains, "the neck is stretched out, the head forward, often nodding, and shaken in a menacing manner against the object of the passion . . . the mouth open, and drawn on each side towards the ears, showing the teeth in a gnashing posture; the feet often stamping; the right arm frequently thrown out and menacing, with the clenched fist shaken. . . ." [11] And another handbook, Gustave Garcia's *The Actors' Art*, carries "rage" still further, demanding that "the veins of the neck and temple swell . . . the eyes become fiery and roll in their orbits. The hands contract violently, the mouth foams, the teeth grind fiercely. . . . The stride is long, heavy, and irregular. We stamp the ground with our feet; we tear our hair . . . we smash everything we get in our hands—in short, an enraged person offers the dismal spectacle of a man who has lost all control over himself." "Dignity," on the other hand, was not so strenuous: "The attitude and action appropriate to this sentiment would be these: the head and body must be erect, the walk rather slow, the steps long and regular, the toes slightly turned outward . . . at times one of the hands will be placed high on the breast, under the coat or waistcoat. . . . The face assumes a kind, although serious, expression. Dignity in its manifestation suggests great regularity of features. The higher our station in life is, the more dignity we observe in all our actions. . . ." For "Pride," which immediately follows "Dignity," Garcia specifies similar actions, "only with the addition of marks of affectation . . . the toes extremely turned out." [12]

And when the actors' hair was sufficiently torn, when their toes would not turn out any farther, the dramatist would switch off the dialogue entirely, and turn to the italics and capitals of stage direction—a tactic that was especially useful in securing a strong "curtain," such as the following, which is the *finale* to Moncrieff's *The Scamps of London* (1843):

CHARLOTTE *has rushed to* BOB—LOUISA *to* HERBERT—*and* ELIZA, *encouraged by her Father, to* FRANK. *A desperate Combat then takes place between* POLICE, *headed by* FOGG—*and* ONION, BRINDLE, *and* SCAMPS, *headed by* DEVEREUX—*the* POLICE *hastening to secure them—pistols are fired—cutlasses crossed, 'till* ONION *and* SCAMPS *are conquered by the* POLICE; *and* DEVEREUX *receives a pistol shot from* FOGG, *who has wrested it from him in the struggle, when levelled at his own head, and, in self-defence, has lodged the contents of it in* DEVEREUX's *body, it stretches him lifeless on the ground— with his last breath he makes a motion as if imploring pardon.* FOGG *regards him with great agitation, then turns away, as if in forgiveness, and raises his eyes to heaven in grateful thanks—he then sinks into his daughter's arms, who leaves* HERBERT *to support him.* SHABNER *has sneaked off in the confusion—Parties form Tableau, and Curtain falls.*[13]

In this scene Devereux would have died and been forgiven according to the "Handbook." The realism would have been in the actual shooting, sword play, etc., and in the costuming and stage scenery. From the beginning melodramatists had striven for realistic staging and stage effect, apparently taking their cue from Pixérécourt (1773–1844), the generally acknowledged father of melodrama, who had, in his role as manager-author, gone to ridiculous lengths to guarantee the factual accuracy of his stage productions. "With all his jigs at hand to stamp it into Gothic patterns," M. W. Disher has explained, "Pixérécourt could make melodrama out of any romance of fact and fiction." [14] The more unlikely his materials the greater his energy in consulting learned works of history, ethnology, archeology—works which he used to secure scenic authenticity for everything from a Babylonian ballet to the dialogue of savage cannibals.

At this time, paraphrasing Reade himself, theatrical England was a mere province of France; consequently it was not long before English writers and stage managers were adapting Pixérécourt's stage techniques, along with his plays. In the beginning, it would seem, the English efforts along these lines were rather crude, consisting mainly of louder stage thunder and more dazzling stage lightning, plus real horses, monkeys, dogs. Reynolds's *The Caravan* (1803) saved Drury Lane from disaster, "not by reason of its character or its wit, but because a real dog, Carlos, after a good deal of coaxing, was persuaded nightly to rescue a heroine from a tank of water." [15] Another dog with almost the same name will appear in Reade's work; also a remarkable bird. . . . But these and other similarities will have to be discussed in a later chapter. The point here is that Reade, with his special fondness for animals, was much taken with this form of zoological realism, which is perhaps best represented by Osbaldistone's production of *Thalaba the Destroyer* (Covent Garden, 1836) featuring "real Burmah bulls, elephants, ostriches . . . from the Surrey Zoological Gardens." [16]

With the advent of Madame Vestris, however, this type of circus-realism was no longer sufficient in itself. Her aim, following Pixérécourt, was to make every aspect of the *mise-en-scene* "true to the life," and by the standards of the day she was eminently successful, achieving realistic effects never before seen upon the English stage. The first scene of *The Court Beauties*, for instance, "was the Mall in St. James's Park, beautifully reproduced from a print of the period of the play. The effect of this scene was much heightened by our making use of a passage, fully one hundred feet in length, which led from the back of the stage to Craven Buildings, and by which the Mall was represented going away into perspective, with wonderful appearance of reality." To complete this scene there were "singing birds . . . scrupulously correct costumes of the reign of Charles II . . . moreover the King was accompanied . . . by a number of King Charles's spaniels . . . twelve in all . . . one couple of them alone—named respectively 'Nell Gwynne' and 'Old Noll'—cost no less a sum than seventy pounds. . . ." [17] For a number of reasons—mainly that of expense— Mrs. Vestris could not be quite so meticulous or so elaborate in her routine melodramatic productions; nevertheless she still managed to fill them with spectacular effects, e.g. in one scene of *A Chain of Events* (adapted by G. H. Lewes from *Les Dames de la Halle*) "a ship with all hands on board was seen to toss in the waves, turn first one side and then the other to the audience, and then sink, leaving the victims struggling in the waves." [18] Though few staged it as effectively as Mrs. Vestris, this sort of meretricious actualism was common dramatic fare during the 'thirties and 'forties, and Reade, along with almost everyone else concerned, seems to have accepted it as a new and superior form of dramatic realism.

IV

The comedy of the period was if anything more banal than the melodrama. For the most part it consisted of burlettas, extravaganzas, farces—all or nearly all subliterary in character. And the more pretentious comedies were little better.[19] Yet Reade declared Lytton's *Money* "a dramatic masterpiece," Douglas Jerrold's comedies "as witty as Congreve's"; moreover, he had similar words of praise "for lighter but able writers" such as Albert Smith, Shirley Brooks, and John Oxenford.[20] Seemingly Reade was wholly taken in by these dramatists, and by the stagecraft they employed to give their stock pieces an air of wit and freshness—the same stagecraft, by the way, that was being used by the melodramatists. Ernest Bradlee Watson makes this point quite clear in his analysis of Boucicault's *London Assurance* (1841). Its effect, Watson shows, was more Vestris' than Boucicault's. In fact its chief if not its only merit, considered as a play, was that it lent itself to Vestris' method of staging—so admirably that the reviewer for Thomas' *Theatrical Observer* found it "impossible adequately to convey an idea of its superlative grandeur . . . the Squire's house, opening on to a green lawn, the drawing-room so magnificently furnished, with the most costly articles of decoration—not stage properties, but *bona fide* realities—were such as were never before seen beyond the pale of fashionable life, and could only have been imitated by one used to that society." [21]

"The Squire's house," from the drawing room to the green lawns, might pass for a stage version of Ipsden. It is easy enough to understand why the middle classes of Thackeray's London thrilled to such *bona fide* realities; also why Reade, although he had grown up with these realities and was never a snob, shared the general enthusiasm. For Mrs. Vestris' Ipsden, in contrast to the real one, was an ideal home inhabited by ideal characters, e.g., there was a genial squire on the lawn rather than a grim visaged father muttering over the varnished-splotched paint underneath Reade's bedroom window. In short the stage Ipsden provided a realistic variant of his own daydreams—and for Reade that made it a great comedy by a great writer. How thoroughly he studied this play, along with the thousands of other comedies and melodramas that employed the same techniques, may be gauged by the fact that, years later, when he and Boucicault collaborated on *Foul Play*, the two were as one in their conception of fictional structure and technique.

V

By 1825, it is generally agreed, "melodrama had wellnigh vanquished the enfeebled armies of the tragic muse." Of the "legitimate" plays that were written and produced few possessed any dramatic merit, and those few (exemplified by Knowles's *Virginius*, Talfourd's *Ion* and Lytton's *Richelieu*) were all melodramatic in tendency. "The interest and force of *Virginius*," one contemporary noted, "consists in . . . the domestic feeling . . . the scene is the Forum, but the sentiments those of the 'Bedford Arms.'" And the same might be said for all the "legitimate" plays of this period. The sparks of life they contained were struck from the clashing blades and flintlocks that guaranteed the virtue of English maidens on the Surrey side. In so far as Reade was influenced by these plays—and *Richelieu*, for instance, he considered a "masterpiece"—their ultimate effect was to confirm him in his melodramatic propensities.

For his final confirmation, however, he turned to the playwright that he—along with almost every other Victorian—considered the greatest dramatist of them all, viz. Shakespeare. Not, of course, the Shakespeare one now sees on the stage, not even the Shakespeare one now sees in the movies, but the Shakespeare of the mid-Victorian stage, the Shakespeare Henry James described in his review of M. E. Braddon's *Aurora Floyd*. "Crime has always been a theme for dramatic poets," James observes, "but with the old poets its dramatic interest lay in the fact that it compromised the criminal's moral repose. Whence else is the interest of *Orestes* and *Macbeth?* With Mr. Collins and Miss Braddon (our modern Euripedes and Shakespeare) the interest of crime is in the fact that it compromises the criminal's personal safety . . . the nearer the criminal and the detective are brought home to the reader, the more lively his 'sensation' . . . and it is through their skill in the choice of these circumstances—their thorough-going realism—that Mr. Collins and Miss Braddon have become famous. In like manner, it is by the thorough-going realism of modern actors that the works of the most poetic of poets have been made to furnish precedent for sensational writers. There are no *circumstances* in 'Macbeth,' as you read it; but as you see it played by Mr. Charles Kean or Mr. Booth it is nothing but circumstances. And we may here remark, in parentheses, that if the actors of a past generation—Garrick and Mrs. Siddons—left with their contemporaries so profound a conviction of their *greatness,* it is probably because, like the great dramatists they interpreted, they were ideal and poetic; because their effort was not to impress but to express." [23]

One may question James's reading of *Macbeth;* also his notions of "the ideal and poetic," but not his analysis of the "circumstances in the acted versions of *Macbeth."* From the time of Macready onwards the leading mid-Victorian actors, almost to a man, practiced the type of realism James describes (the realism of *The Actors' Hand-Book* naturalized after the fashions G. H. Lewes set forth in his *On Actors and the Art of Acting*); and this melodramatic realism undoubtedly furnished precedent for the writers and would be writers of the time—for the young Charles Reade as well as for the young Wilkie Collins. Nor was the realism of the actors in the legitimate drama all that served as a precedent. Charles Kean went beyond Mrs. Vestris, in fact beyond any of his predecessors, legitimate or illegitimate, in his realistic stage settings; moreover, he combined this stage realism with moral purpose, in just the proportions that had proved successful in humanitarian melodrama. So that Reade the apprentice saw much the same type of play—whether it was billed as Shakespeare's *Macbeth* or Pocock's *The Miller and his Men.*[24]

Of course Reade's knowledge of the drama was not limited to the plays that were being presented on the stage. His references in *The Eighth Commandment* indicate that he knew as much about the drama as any man in England. But knowledge, as everyone knows, does not always lead to understanding. The inimitable Boucicault was learned too in a way. "Without any real culture, and without having the least critical faculty," Augustin Filon remarked, "Boucicault had read everything about the theatre—read everything and remembered everything, good, bad, and indifferent, from *Phormio* to the *Auberge des Adrets.* He knew by heart all the *croix de ma mère* of modern melodrama, and from his mass of reminiscences he concocted his . . . plays. . . ." [25] With a few qualifications this description applies directly to Reade, for despite his background and education he was at one with Boucicault in his addiction to the *"croix de ma mère."* Whatever plays he read, it

[74]

would seem, he read according to the light provided by the theatre of his day—a light that inevitably blurred all but melodramatic distinctions, that turned Shakespeare's tragedies, *Hamlet* included, into "philosophical melodramas." The term is Reade's own, and he apparently used it to designate the highest form of dramatic literature. Shakespeare, he wrote in *The Eighth Commandment,* "at last rose to that in which he has never been approached, the philosophical melodrama." [26]

The implications of this and similar statements cannot be mistaken. To Reade's mind the great dramas of the past, as they took shape from the printed page, were indistinguishable from those he saw nightly on the stage. For this reason his reading could not, or at least did not, appreciably deepen his understanding of dramatic art; it merely extended and confirmed the lessons he had already learned in the theatres of London, Paris, and Edinburgh—the lessons he was soon to embody in his own dramatic writing, nowhere more revealingly than in *The King's Rival* (1854), an historical play in which Nell Gwynne is presented, not as a Restoration whore, but as a realistic Dickensian prostitute.

VI

Although Reade's was primarily a dramatic apprenticeship, he also studied non-dramatic fiction of many types, fixing his mind, as he said, on "masterpieces in all languages and all recorded times. . . ." For the son of Mrs. Reade the most influential masterpieces necessarily included those of "the sacred historians," which for fictional purposes he placed alongside the writings of Homer and Virgil. Years later, in *Bible Characters,* he explained that "character-painting is much attempted by certain writers of fictitious narrative . . . but they do not evolve characters by simple narration. They clog the story with a hundred little essays on the character of each character. They keep putting their heads from behind the show, and openly analyzing their pale creations, and dissecting them, and eking them out with comments, and microscoping their poodles into lions. These are the easy expedients of feeble art. They succeed with contemporaries. . . . But it would be paying this false method . . . too great a compliment to compare its fruits with the characters that are self-evolved in the sacred writers, and, indeed, in Homer and Virgil. . . ." [27] This criticism—one of Reade's many thrusts at Thackeray, George Eliot, and domestic and psychological novelists in general—obviously represents a certain amount of rationalization. After all it was to Reade's advantage to answer his critics by citing as his models works and authors of accepted greatness. Still there is no denying that his notions of "plot," "character," (and if Swinburne is correct, "style") do conform in a general way to those of Homer and the biblical writers.

It is also quite possible that Reade derived his ideas of proportion and brevity from the biblical narratives. "The Book of Jonah," he noted, "is in forty-eight verses, or one thousand three hundred and twenty-eight English words. Now, take one thousand three hundred and twenty-eight words in our current narratives: how far do they carry you? Why, ten to one, you get to nothing at all but chatter, chatter, chatter. Even in those close models, *Robinson Crusoe,* the *Vicar of Wakefield, Candide, Rasselas,* one thousand three hundred and twenty-eight words do not carry the reader far; yet in the one thousand three hundred and twenty-eight words of Jonah you have a wealth of incident, and all the dialogue to carry on the grand and varied action. . . ." After repeating "one thousand three hundred and twenty-eight words" twice more, Reade concludes that "only hot-pressed narratives live forever . . . it is condensation that declares the master." And to "condensation" he later adds "proportion": "Only the great artists of the pen," he explains, "hit upon the perfect proportions of dialogue and narrative. With nineteen story-tellers out of twenty there is a weary excess of dialogue. . . . In Job the dialogue is excessive. . . . In the Apocrypha 'Judith' and 'Tobit' are literally massacred by verbosity and bungling; not so, however, in 'Susannah and the Elders'—that is a masterpiece as far as it goes." [28] To borrow a phrase from Hemingway, these are the words of an "old pro"; yet the critical ideas they represent are those Reade brought to fiction in 1850, and it would seem that he derived them, in part at least, from his study of the sacred writings.

Undoubtedly Reade's apprentice reading also embraced the fictional masterpieces of the Middle Ages and Renaissance—though it is impossible to say, on the basis of the slender evidence available, just what he did learn from Boccaccio, Rabelais, Cervantes. Whatever their influence it is thickly overlaid with that of later novelists. Likewise conjectural, although there is more evidence to go on, is the nature of his indebtedness to eighteenth century fiction. At one time or another he spoke favorably of Lesage, Defoe, Johnson, Smollett—in fact nearly all of the better known eighteenth century novelists—and it may be that he was influenced by their novels in the way Elwin and others have suggested. On the other hand he could have learned the same lessons from later and lesser known writers who were closer to his own ways of feeling and thinking. As for Edmund Ahlers' more detailed attributions of influence (in his *Charles Reades Romane und ihr Verhältnis zu ihren literarischen Vorbildern*) they too are open to serious question, even those in which he points to specific borrowings. The fact that a writer borrows from a given author is not in itself proof of significant influence. Reade, further analysis will show, was just as happy to steal from Mr. Selby as from Mr. Smollett, and Mr. Selby's influence, it need hardly be argued, was of no consequence whatsoever.

If one may judge by Reade's later comments he owed more to Goldsmith and Voltaire than to Defoe or Fielding, or any other novelist of the period, with the possible exception of Smollett. Defoe's novels he considered "stupid," save only *Robinson Crusoe*[29] Fielding he found undramatic, at times obscene. At least he dismissed Fielding's plays as slavish imitations of Molière, filled out with "ordure of profaneness and obscenity."[30] In fiction as in his travels, it would seem, Reade was more interested in blood than in sex. Hence the appeal of Smollett's humanitarian sentiments and Voltaire's Baconian-humanitarian ideas. "Next to Voltaire," Reade declared, "Oliver Goldsmith . . . was the greatest genius in Europe." And in his direct references to Voltaire he proclaimed him "le roi Voltaire," a great thinker and writer and a still greater man: "When the Family Calas were about to be executed unjustly, with the consent of all the lawyers and statesmen in France, one man in a nation saw the error, and fought for the innocent, and saved them; and that one wise man, in a nation of fools, was a writer of fiction." [31] In other words Voltaire was a modern Solomon of the pen, and therefore the ultimate "Resourceful Hero." At one time, the notebooks reveal, Reade planned to write a play with Voltaire as hero. And while he never completed the actual writing of the play, probably because he realized that it could never be produced as long as Voltaire was considered a dangerous revolutionary, he could and did act out a larger version of the play in his own life and writings, with himself as the Voltairean hero.

Reade's debt to Voltaire and eighteenth century fiction was therefore more spiritual than technical. He admired the realism of Lesage, Smollett, and John Gay as well as the craftsmanship of those close models, *Robinson Crusoe,* the *Vicar of Wakefield, Candide, Rasselas.* It is also quite possible that he was influenced to a lesser degree by the novelists Edmund Ahlers has suggested—from Richardson to William Godwin.[32] But for his final lessons in the art of fiction he turned to more recent novelists, mainly to those of his own day.

VII

In his *Dickens, Reade and Collins: Sensation Novelists,* W. C. Phillips has traced the development of "Sensation Fiction" from its earliest beginnings. His study shows how Byron and Scott, by rationalizing and rendering more credible the characteristically supernatural melodrama of Walpole and the Terrorists, helped to establish "the sensation tradition"; how Dickens, Reade, and Collins, working in this tradition, developed the formulas that Collins made explicit in his "Preface" to *Basil.* "Believing that the novel and the play are twin sisters in the family of fiction," Collins wrote, "and that one is drama narrated as the other is drama acted and that all the deep . . . strong emotions that the playwriter is privileged to excite, the novel writer is privileged to excite also, I have not thought it necessary . . . to adhere to everyday realities only. . . ." To which Phillips adds: "If for Collins's word *drama* we read *melodrama* we have roughly what our trio meant by the parallel, and can understand why they were fond of describing their own novels as dramatic." [33]

All this is generally true: Reade knew Byron and Scott as well as the lesser Gothicists and realists of the early Nineteenth Century—from Peacock to Monk Lewis to Maria Edgeworth—and he probably learned a great deal from these writers. Yet if he (together with Dickens and Collins) was a thoroughgoing sensationalist, so were a good many others. W. H. Ainsworth, in his "Preface" to *Rookwood* (quoted at the beginning of this chapter) stated every single one of Collins's points as early as 1836. And literally scores of other novelists went as far or further than Ainsworth in their sensationalism. Dickens, Reade, and Collins were neither so unique nor so close a trio as Phillips implies. To the extent that they differed from their fellow sensationalists, they differed individually, not as a group; and if one is to understand Reade's theories and practices it is necessary to recognize his apprenticeship as his own, not as that of two other novelists. For instance, Reade almost certainly learned a great deal more from Scott than Phillips has recognized, since Scott was a master of the documentary techniques Reade was later to make his own. "Another thing in my favor," Scott noted in his *Journal,* "is that my contemporaries steal too openly. Mr. Smith has inserted in *Brambletye House* whole pages from Defoe's *Fire and Plague of London.*

> 'Steal! foh! a fico for the phrase—
> Convey, the wise it call!'

When *I convey* an incident or so, I am at as much pains to avoid detection as if the offense could be indicted at the 'Old Bailey.'[34]

Though at times Reade's "conveyed" incidents read more like Smith's than Scott's, the fault cannot be attributed to lack of study, for Reade was fully acquainted with Scott's techniques as well as those of his more creative followers—notably those evolved by Victor Hugo, whose novels were as much to Reade's liking as the plays, and for much the same reasons. As a melodramatist turned novelist, Hugo made the most sensational use of Scott's techniques, and in such a way as to embody them in exactly the type of novel that Reade considered the highest form of fictional art—the "romance" that Hugo himself defined in *Litterature et Philosophie Mélées: "le Roman à la fois, drame et épopée; pittoresque mais poétique; réel mais idéal; vrai, mais grand; qui enchâssera Walter Scott dans Homère!"*

These words anticipate Reade's fictional aims and ideals—almost to the letter; just as Hugo's melodramatic techniques anticipate his fictional practices. Yet—and this is crucial—Hugo's theories and techniques also anticipate those of Eugene Sue and Dumas *père* in France, Harrison Ainsworth and G. P. R. James in England. In the hands of these writers, as one can immediately see, merely by glancing through their novels, Hugo's high-sounding phrases led to *bas-romantisme* of a piece with that which was being presented on the stage. Even Balzac succumbed in part to this melodramatic clap-trap, and Reade, already so stage-struck that he mistook limelight for daylight, was completely victimized: he not only accepted run-of-the-mill horrors and heroics, he accepted them at the level of *Rookwood* and *Les Mystères de Paris.* Actually he seems to have preferred this more exciting and sadistic level. His perspective was not that of a well-adjusted Magdalen don in search of literary verities; it was that of a neurotic younger son, a rebellious Baconian who was addicted to humanitarian violence and

[79]

to the theatre of his time, and who was, moreover, a would-be writer with his eye on the literary stock market, where *Valentine Vox* was being quoted at a higher figure than Thackeray's *Catherine*. The fuss Reade made about studying only "masterpieces" is therefore highly misleading when applied to the novels of his own day, since he tended to define a "masterpiece" as a best-seller that combined sensation with social purpose. *Uncle Tom's Cabin*, for example, he proclaimed one of the greatest novels of the century, noting that it was "written with red ink and the biceps muscle." [35]

Uncle Tom's Cabin is relevant here, even though it properly belongs to a later period of Reade's apprenticeship, because it typifies the novels Reade most admired. While the point cannot be proved until the wilderness of popular Victorian fiction has been fully explored, it seems safe to say that Reade owed as much (if not more) to the best-selling but now forgotten novelists of the 'thirties and 'forties—to Theodore Hook, Henry Cockton, Charles Rowcroft, Samuel Warren, *et al*—than to the better known writers (e.g. Lytton and Disraeli) who have been considered his immediate models. Indeed he probably owed more to Samuel Warren than to any other novelist of the period. During his first year at Lincoln's Inn—the very year he decided to become a writer—he studied law and shared an apartment with Warren, who was already on the way to becoming a famous novelist. Warren's personal example, it has already been suggested, may well have encouraged Reade to avow his literary ambitions, but whether it did or not, he knew and was profoundly influenced by Warren's writings—more especially by their documentary realism. In *Passages from the Diary of a Late Physician* (published in 1837, after having appeared serially in *Blackwood's*) Warren drew upon his medical knowledge to present a series of what would now be called psychiatric case histories—in his "Preface" maintaining that he wrote as a scientist, not as a mere novelist, that his case histories therefore presented unadulterated facts as instances of "the real practical working of virtues and vices."

For the most part there is nothing new or startling in these statements, which are cast in the conventional prefatory mode established by Defoe. Where Warren went beyond earlier realists was in the pretentiousness of his claims to scientific validity, and in his use of those claims to justify the inclusion *ad nauseum* of gory suicides, duels, etc.—all presented after the manner of Krafft-Ebing, with "gruesome anecdotes of body-snatching the only comic relief."

Such episodes Reade must have found almost as edifying as his later visits to the Parisian morgues and slaughterhouses (if indeed his visits were not in part motivated by the *Diary*), for to his Baconian way of thinking everything in the *Diary* was factual, and therefore true. And since it was also well written, by "sensation" standards, it was not only true but beautiful. Hence his admiration for the book, which was certainly not lessened by the fact that it became a bestseller, and made Warren famous as both a writer and a humanitarian—precisely the reputation that he was striving to win for himself during these years.

Warren's next bestseller (*Ten Thousand a Year*, 1841) was more conventional than the *Diary*, at least in its outward form, which was that of a picaresque novel of social purpose. Yet in spite of this fact, or perhaps because of it, he once again insisted on the utilitarian character of his work, this time drawing upon his experience as a lawyer, since the novel was an exposé of the legal system. In his "Preface" he argued that the novel, though written in fictional form, was not for "mere novel-readers"; rather, he explained, it was for persons of "sober, independent, and experienced judgment." In other words it was for those who could distinguish between fanciful fiction and a serious novel based on experience and fact. In part, of course, this was a selling argument, designed to overcome the still strong prejudice against novel-reading. Basically, however, it was an honest statement of intention—even though its effect was to reduce fictional art to a form of humanitarian journalism that justified the inclusion of one humanitarian horror after another. But this Warren could not see. Confronted with any such objections, he would have answered that he was but following in the footsteps of the greatest writers, from Homer to Shakespeare. For as Warren understood them they too had piled horror upon horror, and with less justification, since their horrors were at times merely literary, and without the sanctions of science and social purpose.

Misguided as they are, Warren's notions of realism add up to a close anticipation of Reade's, most obviously in their emphasis on science, fact, and morality. In developing his theories of "the matter-of-fact-romance," later analysis will show, Reade appropriated the whole of Warren's realistic-moral strategy, even that aspect of it which demanded that the writer make a scientific study of every problem touched upon in his fiction. Moreover, Reade thoroughly admired the deftness with which Warren transmuted his facts into fiction—so much that he copied many of Warren's specific techniques, and in "The Sham Sample Swindle," writing in answer to an article in *The Quarterly Review*, he proclaimed Warren a greater novelist than Defoe: "Defoe wrote several stupid stories and one masterpiece *(Robinson Crusoe)*; Warren wrote several powerful stories and one foolish rhapsody *(The Lily and the Bee)*; yet here, in the name of science (for criticism is science, or it is nothing) is Warren defined by his exceptional failure, and Defoe by his exceptional success. . . . (N.B. The dead are apt to get the sunny side of this swindle, and the living the windy side.)" [36] In thus praising Warren and "the living" at the expense of Defoe and "the dead," Reade was indirectly praising himself, for he must have known how closely his own sensational techniques approximated those of Warren. Yet however much he praised and followed Warren, there was only one novelist whom he called "master"—and that was his "good friend and Master, Dickens."

VIII

In *The Eighth Commandment* Reade openly declared himself a follower of Dickens. "Mr. Dickens," he wrote, "has a school, and in that school are some good men . . . nearly twenty-five years ago, Dickens changed the face of the English novel, sharpened our sight, widened our sympathies, and coloured everyone of us more or less. . . ." [37] Again, in "The Rights and Wrongs of Authors," he spoke to the same effect, though more specifically: "Now, the class 'authors' may be said to rain sympathy. That class has produced the great Apostle of Sympathy in this age; and many of us writers follow in his steps, though we cannot keep up with his stride. . . ." [38] To Reade, Dickens was first and foremost "the great Apostle . . ." just as Voltaire was the great Apostle of the preceding age. Consequently, in proclaiming himself a Dickensian, he was proclaiming little more than a desire to emulate Dickens' humanitarianism. True, he also recognized that Dickens had "changed the face of the English novel," that he "was just as capable of renovating the stage, and raising it, and enlarging its sphere, its mind, its eye, its heart, its form." [39] Considered in context, however, these words (even including the word "form") imply that, in so far as he understood Dickens' art, he understood it as conventional "sensation" enriched by humanitarian sympathy—after the manner of *Oliver Twist*, which he believed to be a great novel that Dickens, given the opportunity, could have made into a great play. In short Reade admired those aspects of Dickens' art which were indistinguishable from those of Boucicault's plays and Warren's novels. The proof is that his own novels and plays contain only casual traces of Dickens' personal influence. Where they parallel Dickens, they nearly always parallel Warren, or Boucicault, or some other minor sensationalist, oftentimes more closely than they parallel Dickens, whose originality, as expressed in everything from his "humor" to his use of what George Orwell has described as "irrelevant detail," was antipathetic to Reade's notions of "brevity" and "proportion." Reade may have been "coloured" by Dickens, but not in the sense he himself believed, for the only colours that stuck were those of a conventionally humanitarian and melodramatic hue—the blacks and blues and the blood reds that were the trademarks of the entire "sensation" school.

The truth is, Reade was never, at any time in his career, a thoroughgoing follower of Dickens. Had he been such a follower he would never have acknowledged the fact. He was too egotistical, and above all, too anxious to avoid comparisons that might tell against his own work. As it was, however, he knew that his stripped-down melodrama was the opposite of Dickens', and he undoubtedly hoped that any comparisons would raise his own work at the expense of the Master's. Not that he wished to drag Dickens down. What he really wanted was to pull himself up; and since Dickens' work stood far above everyone else's, he had everything to gain and little to lose by stressing his Dickensian allegiances.

This is not to impugn Reade's sincerity; it is merely to state what his life and writings bear out, viz. that he was too self-centered to become the follower or disciple of any living writer, too anxious for personal security and success to strike out on his own. Instead of following Dickens, or Warren, or Hugo, he lumped them together with literally hundreds of other "sensation" writers—and followed them indiscriminately. He was on the lookout for good things and did not care where he found them. Presumably he learned more from certain writers than others—more from Dickens say, than from Mrs. Trollope—yet his seeming indebtedness to any given writer may in reality extend to a dozen others. For example, he seems to have derived his more extreme realistic concepts from Warren, yet there is no way of telling how much he learned from other and still more obscure novelists and writers, some of whom may have gone as far (or possibly even further) than Warren in their "factual realism." Myron Brightfield, in his

Theodore Hook, has listed a number of titles that indicate the growing popularity of fiction based on fact during the first quarter of the century. Among these are Mrs. Pilkington's *Characteristic Incidents Drawn from Real Life* . . . (1810), M. A. Grant's *Tales Founded Upon Facts* (1820) etc., etc.[40] Such novels appear more frequently after 1825, to become a literary staple in the 'forties and 'fifties, e.g., Henry Cockton's *The Steward* (1850) is subtitled "A Romance of Real Life." Furthermore, one continually encounters such titles as *Recollections of a Policeman* (1852), and usually, as in this book, the "Preface" contains some such statement as the following: "The record of 'hair-breadth 'scapes,' which follow, is another verification of the old saying 'Truth is stranger than fiction.'" [41] Although most of these books are sub-literary, that would not have deterred Reade in the slightest. Unless his early reading habits were more discriminating than those of his maturity—and there is no reason to believe that they were—he was as much steeped in the Newgate aspects of current fiction and journalism as in the corresponding aspects of the Victorian theatre.

IX

The ultimate effect of Reade's study of the novel was therefore to reinforce and amplify the melodramatic lessons he had learned through his study of the drama. Despite his allusions to the great fictional writers of the past and present—from Homer through Dickens—he was not their pupil, any more than he was Shakespeare's. Although he studied and absorbed certain features of their stylistic and structural techniques, what he primarily admired in these writers was what they had in common with the Warrens and the Boucicaults, or on a still lower level, the writers of transpontine melodrama and Newgate shockers. The primary distinctions that the young Henry James later recognized—the distinctions between Shakespeare's *Macbeth* and Charles Kean's, between *Orestes* and such a novel as *Aurora Floyd*—were totally lost upon the young Reade. Although he too had studied *Macbeth* and *Orestes,* along with innumerable other "masterpieces in all languages and all recorded times," his knowledge of these masterpieces was so conditioned by the stage and fiction of his time that he could recognize only their melodramatic highlights. The more subtle aspects of their art he dismissed as domestic, or psychological, or otherwise misguided. As a consequence he was always studying the same type of play or novel, whether it was written by Shakespeare or

Moncrieff, Homer or Henry Cockton; moreover, his studies always pointed towards the same literary conclusions: that a great play consists of conventional melodrama enriched with Dickensian sentiment, Voltairean purpose, and Hugolian realism; that a great novel is essentially the same type of play narrated with biblical brevity and directness.

The basic theories Reade brought to his own writing (in 1850) were therefore not very different from those that Hugo and Ainsworth had set forth some fifteen years earlier, that Dickens and Warren and Collins, as well as the lesser sensation writers eventually came to defend and practice. For Dickens, further analysis will reveal, these melodramatic theories worked reasonably well, despite their obvious shortcomings; but for Reade, as for so many others, they were not only inadequate but positively crippling. Instead of curbing his escapist tendencies, and forcing him to cope with reality, they actually enabled him to retreat still further from himself and the outside world—by providing him with an aesthetic rationale that fitted with and substantiated his Baconian rationalizations. If Reade's philosophy was a Baconian patchwork designed to cover his emotional nakedness, his aesthetic was a still heavier cloak, borrowed from Mrs. Vestris' wardrobe, and tailored to fit the fictional fashions of the 'fifties.

Yet Reade was still not content. Doubly wrapped as he was, he still felt naked and therefore vulnerable. Like Dostoevski's character in *The Double,* he could now and then see himself as himself; and that was disastrous, for even these fleeting glimpses tended to destroy his *idea* of himself and reality—the *idea* that he was trying so desperately to live and to write. The solution, of course, was to carry the disguise (or, as Reade saw it, the "realism") still further—to the point where in fiction (as in life) the mask became the person, the *idea* the Baconian reality. At least this is what he attempted when he finally began to write. Working from the theories he had evolved during his apprenticeship, he drew upon everything from Parliamentary oratory to Pre-Raphaelite painting to develop a new and more extreme form of documentary realism—at what cost to his art the succeeding chapters will show.

CHAPTER IV

Artistic Development 1849–1852:
Melodrama With a Difference

I MYSELF had glorious hopes I now look back on with bitter melancholy. . . .
If, by a miracle, a genuine dramatist got a play played, then piracy punished
him in another way. The price was not a remuneration, but a punishment, of
labour and skill. I saved a first-class theatre from bankruptcy, with a drama
[Gold]. I received only £110; and the last ten pounds I had to county-court
the manager for; gratitude is too good a thing to waste on that ethereal
vapour, yclept an author. For "Masks and Faces," a comedy which has survived a thousand French pieces, and more, Mr. Taylor and I received £150.
In France, it would have been £4,000. For "Two Loves and a Life," a
drama that has been played throughout Anglo-Saxony, and is played to this
day, we received £100. In France it would have been worth £5,000.

—CHARLES READE

✓   ✓   ✓

The local color, the sensation, the craft of the melodrama, and to make
all these doubly sure, the extreme activity of mechanician and scene-shifter,
made up the Boucicault drama . . . which contributed powerfully to that
new dramatic era. It was realistic for its times, and the more attractive because it was sensationally realistic. . . . Here was realism without its sting,
its pessimistic afterthought; here was humor true to the life the audience
knew; here were wit, song, and endless thrills. Almost by mathematical cal-
culation, the proportions had been adjusted to the popular psychology of
the middle of the nineteenth century.

—ERNEST BRADLEE WATSON[1]

✓   ✓   ✓

Reade's first love was the theatre; his first serious writings, it
has been pointed out, were plays. Then came the rebuffs, and
the consequent feelings of persecution that made him "so ill in
body and mind" that he sought medical sanctuary in the sanitariums of Malvern and Durham. Yet he continued to write, even
while he was in the sanitariums. Once he had gained the power
of placing one word after another on the page he permitted

nothing to stand in the way of his literary ambitions—not even his mother's opposition or his own pride. When he failed to gain a hearing for his own plays, "not one of which," in his own words, "any manager would read," he put them aside temporarily, and, as he said, "crept into the theatre at last with a French translation."[2]

"Crept" is an appropriate word, for the translation he refers to is *The Ladies' Battle* ("First performed at the Royal Olympic Theatre, on Wednesday, May 7th, 1851.") which he himself described in his "Preface" as "a condensed version of a comedy [*Bataille de Dames*] by Messrs. Scribe and Legouvé with some trifling changes intended to give a little more reality to the interest."[3] The nature of these trifling changes is perhaps best exemplified by the realistic touches with which he ended another of his adaptations from the French, viz. *The Lost Husband* ("First performed at the Strand Theatre, Monday, April 26, 1852."):

LORAIN *utters a piercing cry, trips up* JEAN MARIE, *snatches a musket, and darting to the other end of the apartment, falls on his knee as on his guard—All the* GENS-D'ARMES, *from their several positions, level their pieces at him.*

LOR.   I could kill any one of you—but what should I gain? There is nothing for me but the galleys or death! I know the galleys, and I choose ——

Fires the musket against his own person—is blown into the air—the gun falls in another direction—The WOMEN *scream, a dead silence succeeds—Long pause.**

COM.   (*gravely, but not loud*) Recover arms!

Makes signs to MEN *to come between the object and the* WOMEN'*s sight—A line is formed, behind which glimpses only are seen of the* MEN *lifting* LORAIN, *and carrying him out.*

FRANCES *clasps* MAURICE, *and shudders—*ROBERT *runs to look.*

GEN.   Leonard, don't let the boy go there.

FRA.   Yes! let him look upon the end of talent and dishonesty! Ah! Maurice, you are saved!

Curtain

How seriously Reade took these directions, particularly the starred item referring to the suicide, is brought out by his added footnote: "For directions how this is done, apply to the Author."[4] Apparently he had learned or devised some realistic trick whereby the force of a bullet at close range could be shown to be that of a direct blow—the same trick, it would seem, that has been employed in some of Hollywood's more pretentious "Westerns," e.g., the scene in *Shane* in which the villainous gun-fighter literally blasts the Texas squatter into the mud.

That Reade was so adept at this type of stage realism is not surprising, in view of his fourteen years apprenticeship. And he himself felt that his apprenticeship had taught him a great deal more: that he was an authority on everything from stage setting to acting. Although *The Ladies' Battle* was his first acted play, and presumably his first direct contact with the theatre, he did not hesitate to exert his full authorial rights, and so imperiously that he usurped the functions of stage-manager, director, and actors. Yet—and this is a good measure of his ego—he felt genuine surprise and disappointment when he encountered resistance. "How ludicrous is the *amour-propre* of English actors . . ." he noted in his *Diary*, "And their notion that no author knows the meaning of his own words! A play of mine loses so enormously when not rehearsed by me that I fear I shall always torment them for the sake of my own credit. What a difference there was in 'Ladies' Battle' brought out at a second-rate theatre under my rehearsal and at a first-rate theatre under Leigh Murray's. . . ." [5]

Moreover, Reade was equally brash in his "Preface" to the printed version of *The Ladies' Battle*, using his praises of Mrs. Stirling as a means of chiding both the audience and the critics for their failure to appreciate Mrs. Stirling's efforts (and, by implication, his own). "The 'Countess' is so much better acted than on the French stage," he argued, "that it merits particular notice. . . . The soliloquy in Act I is one of the longest that, in a Comedy, has been risked in a Female Comedian's hands (in England) for some years. It is, however, perfectly safe with this lady. Each change of passion in it is marked by her with truth and vigour. The irresolute inspection of the mirror, the ejaculation, and still more the look that precedes it, are fine strokes of art. It is more than a change of expression; a new face, radiant with beauty and hope, glides into the place of one clouded with misgivings. These things escape a vulgar audience, and vulgar critics, for an obvious reason: they are the great feats of acting. . . . This point was taken in Paris, as far as the voice, which is nearly half the business, but at the French theatre in London it is entirely missed. . . . Generally she [Mrs. Stirling] gives the part the reality that belongs to it, and *acts* it with equal power and grace, instead of walking, gliding, or dancing through it." [6]

In tone and manner, Reade's assertiveness resembles Shaw's.

The crucial distinction, of course, is that Shaw was an original dramatist trying to defend a new dramatic form, whereas Reade was merely adapting the formulas that constituted the well-made play. His "trifling changes" were trifling indeed—trumpery realistic tricks designed to heighten already sensational effects. As for Mrs. Stirling's acting, it may possibly have raised the play somewhat above the usual level, but if it did, the credit is hers, not Reade's, since the text he provided her is at best a workmanlike rendering of the Scribe and Legouvé original. And little more can be said for his other adaptations that were staged in 1851–1852: *Angelo* (from Hugo's *Angelo*), *A Village Tale* (from George Sand's *Claudie*), and *The Lost Husband* (from Bourgeois' *La Dame de la Halle*). In these plays, as in *The Ladies' Battle*, he followed the conventional melodramatic practices of the day, and without achieving any marks of distinction, save perhaps in his emphasis on realistic stage effects. Donald Hutchins MacMahon's final remark on *A Village Tale*—that it "must have been solely impressive because of its . . . realistic effects"—applies with even greater force to the lurid melodrama of *Angelo* and *The Lost Husband*.[7]

II

Reade's first original play to be acted, *Masks and Faces* (first performed at the Haymarket Theatre, November 20, 1852), was written in collaboration with Tom Taylor, another barrister and Master of Arts turned playwright. Reade, it will be recalled, fell in love with Peg Woffington when he first saw her picture at the Garrick Club. Then he soon afterwards fancied a resemblance between Peg, his ideal love, and Mrs. Stirling, who was, for the moment, the living embodiment of that ideal. Ergo—the idea for *Masks and Faces*, a play about Peg Woffington with Mrs. Stirling to play the heroine. This was in the summer of 1851. Why Reade, who was so frantically on the make, did not write the play himself, instead of inviting Tom Taylor's collaboration, is not quite clear. Perhaps he felt that he could trade upon Taylor's name and reputation as well as upon his demonstrated theatrical skill. (At this time Taylor was a famous dramatist, Reade still a nonentity.) But whatever Reade's motives Taylor promptly agreed to a collaboration, Mrs. Stirling agreed to play the heroine, and within a short time Ben Webster agreed to produce their work at the Haymarket. The only remaining problem was to write the play.

From first to last there were differences and troubles without end. Taylor was almost as irritable and pugnacious as Reade; and to complicate matters still further, Mrs. Stirling and Webster had to be consulted at every turn. For these and other reasons the play was not so much written as manufactured, the process being something like that which Reade himself describes in his *Diary*, though, as usual, allowances must be made for his efforts at self-dramatization, his tendency to see and present himself as the "Resourceful Hero" of every action in which he is involved:

June 7 [1852]— . . . My *collaborateur*, Taylor, has written a new *dénouement*, and without submitting it to me has read it to the Haymarket Company. This has hurt my *amour propre*, and a nobler feeling of creative paternity. . . . What is the history of this play? I wrote a certain scene in which Triplet, whose broad outlines I then and there drew, figured; and another personation scene containing Peg Woffington, Colley Cibber, James Quin. I showed these to Taylor as scenes. He liked these two characters, and we agreed to write a comedy.

I began. I wrote the greater part of Act I., and sketched situations of second act, viz., the company assembled in Mr. Vane's house, and Mrs. Vane's sudden appearance, Mrs. Vane's kindness to Triplet—a mere sketch; and in Triplet's house the first picture scene almost as it stands now; and I wrote a little of a third act. Well, Taylor came down to me, added to my first act, filled up the chinks, got Vane into a better position, and made the first act an act.

I think it lay idle six months. He then went to work and treated the rest in the same way. So that at this period he was author of two thirds of the play, so far as sentences went. He was satisfied with it, and read it to Mrs. Stirling, who turned her back on him and said plump, 'It won't do.' Full stop for a month or two. Then he wrote to me, and I took the bull by the horns. Flung Act I. into the fire and wrote a new act, dashing at once into the main story. I took his cold stage creation, Pomander, and put alcohol into him, and, on the plan of the great French dramatists, I made the plot work by a constant close battle between a man and a woman. I then took in hand Act II., and slashed through Taylor's verboseness, losing none of his beauties, and he has some pretty things in that act. Then I came to Act III., where I found my own picture-scene wanted little alteration. Then, with the help of a speech or two of Mabel's as sweet as honey (Taylor's), I softened Woffington so that she cried in the frame, and Mabel found her out. Then I offered the MS. to Taylor. He did not like the fence-

and-rail prepared for him, and he said, 'You reconcile the two women, and I'll go on.' Well, I did so, and I was not sorry to stop, for I was working in a high key, and did not see my way to sustain it through a mist of stagy manœuvres that I saw ahead. However, while at Paris I did actually finish the play on thin paper, and sent it to my *collaborateur*.

Taylor did not like my *dénouement*. He altered it, and read his to Webster, who did not like it. He has altered it again, and so the matter stands.[8]

A few days later—June 10, to be exact—Reade "consented to let 'Masks and Faces' be brought out altered to please Webster, who is not so good a writer as an actor." Another blow to his *amour propre,* and there were still others to come. According to Tom Taylor's brother, Arnold Taylor, whose account of the collaboration contradicts Reade's at every turn, it was Tom Taylor, not Reade, who put the play into final form: "Very much to Charles Reade's vexation, and contrary to all his ideas and wishes the play was cut down by my brother to two acts, and worked by him into the shape in which it was finally acted at the Haymarket." [9] During these final revisions, if Coleman's version of the collaboraton can be trusted, Taylor became so high-handed that Reade eventually gave up altogether and went off in a huff—to Ipsden and his mother (and later to Malvern and Durham); whereupon Taylor, with the aid and advice of Mrs. Stirling and Webster, slapped the play together willy-nilly without even bothering to secure Reade's approval. Upon his return to London Reade was therefore confronted with a *fait accompli:* the play was on the eve of production, and there was nothing he could do but await the result.

Though hurt and angry, Reade was also expectant. After all the play—*his* play—was to be played. Then the fateful night came. In Reade's own words, as reported by Coleman: "Webster was a bit loose in the text (he always is!); then that infernal 'Zumerzetshire' dialect was against him, but he *can* act; and as for La Stirling, she carried everything before her like wildfire, and the curtain fell upon a scene of unbounded enthusiasm. I forgot all about the alterations and the rows, and ramped round in a transport of delght, embraced my faithless Peggy in sight of all Israel, hugged Taylor and Webster, and then, for the first time in my life, was called for, and Taylor led me before the curtain, and the house 'rose at us,' and I cried for joy. . . . In years to come, I had, as you know, my triumphs, but this was the first time

I tasted blood, and the cheers of the crowded and delighted pit lifted me into seventh heaven." [10]

The response of the pit is easy enough to understand, since, as G. H. Lewes pointed out, in his review in the *Leader,* the play "has the elements of eternal success—character, emotion. . . . Laughter and tears of sympathy alternate through the varying scene; bright, ingenious dialogue, playing like lambent flame, stimulates the intellect; and homely pathos, homely mirth, kind hearts and loving voices gently touch the various chords of emotion." [11] Although Lewes' words sound as if they belonged in the lyrics of a popular song, such as "Kind Hearts and Gentle People," they are peculiarly apt in that the play is an unmitigated tear jerker: a sentimentalized embodiment of Reade's own sentimental yearnings (expressed directly in his letter to Dr. Routh) for "cheerful faces . . . good people . . . human sentiment." While the play also deals with the problems of impoverished though genteel writers and painters, they too are sentimentalized, and fitted into stock situations. The closest approach to wit is to be found in the satire visited upon two hapless art critics, Soaper and Snarl, who are made to appear complete boobs when Peg Woffington sticks her face through the portrait they are criticizing, and they proceed to point out how unlike "nature" it is. This scene, like certain of the domestic scenes, titillates and to a certain extent exercises the mind and emotions—though always along lines that avoid doubt and lead to renewed faith in accepted ideas and beliefs. Thus the exposure and consequent humiliation of Soaper and Snarl is nicely designed to flatter the collective ego of the audience—to show that the man in the street is a better judge of art than the "high-falutin" critics.

That Lewes could still praise the play as he did—maintaining that "the bright, ingenious dialogue, playing like lambent flame . . . stimulates the intellect . . ."—would seem to be more of a tribute to Mrs. Stirling than to the play itself. Accepting at face value the encomiums showered upon her performance, one may concede that her acting may have brightened up the dialogue considerably. Nevertheless it still seems impossible that she or anyone else could have made the Reade-Taylor lines stimulating to a man of Lewes' intellect—unless that intellect, like Reade's, lost its usual perceptiveness when exposed to limelight, and became like that of nearly everyone else connected with the theatre of the time, i.e. a Victorian counterpart of the soap-opera mentality now engendered by Hollywood. Matthew Arnold or any critic who had not come under the spell of the theatre could have revealed the "kind hearts and gentle voices" for the sentimental counterfeit that they were, could have shown that the play, as a play, was beyond literary redemption. But Reade would not have listened, or if he had listened, he would not have understood. He would have considered their criticism as meaningless and "high-falutin" as that of Soaper and Snarl. If the play had shortcomings—and he seems to have recognized that it did—they were, from his point of view, mainly attributable to the process of composition and production, which had drained off his "creative alcohol" and prevented him from exercising the realistic techniques he was developing in connection with his work on *Gold* (first performed at the Drury Lane Theatre, January 10, 1853).

III

Notable as they were, Reade's efforts to secure realistic stage effects in his adaptations and in *Masks and Faces* had gone little beyond the practices established by Mrs. Vestris. To go further he needed a subject that would lend itself to realistic treatment, one that he could develop on his own, without help and its consequent restrictions. For some time, it appears, he had been on the lookout for such a subject. Then, in August of 1852, at the time when he was most discouraged over his collaboration with Taylor, when, in his own words, he felt "purposeless, hopeless, languid . . ." he found just the dramatic material for which he had been searching—in the form of a factual autobiography dealing with prisons and gold-diggings.

Working from this autobiography, which gave him the outlines of a plot, he immediately set to work. The theories he brought to the actual writing, his *Diary* reveals, were those he had evolved during his years of apprenticeship, supplemented by his own dramatic experiences, and by his acquaintance with the newer forms of realism that were being developed by Charles Kean and the Pre-Raphaelites. As early as 1847, his printed advertisements show, Reade had begun to deal in paintings as well as violins; by 1850 he was writing to the famous art collector, Mr. Joseph Gillott, and, with his usual bumptiousness, telling him how to improve certain paintings in his collection:

1. There is a woman stooping in rather an absurd attitude with

her hand touching her foot. Insert at her foot a rose which I could do so that Etty could not tell it from Etty and put a curtain in her left hand, and the absurdity vanishes. We have a woman stealing from behind a curtain, and picking up a *gage d'amour* which one has thrown at her feet . . .

2. Diana waiting for Endymion. Paint out her night cap. Confine her hair by a band glittering in the moonlight, and let this band be surmounted by a crescent as in the picture you sold Mr. Hart . . .[12]

Diana in her nightcap is at least more interesting than a Victorian Diana with "a band glittering in the moonlight . . . surmounted by a crescent." In this, as in the first picture, Reade's suggested improvements are of a piece with those he visited upon his dramatic adaptations.

Yet however foolish the suggestions themselves may appear they were entirely in line with the prevailing standards of the day, as epitomized in the works of William Powell Frith, R. A., whose paintings invariably provided conventionalized reflections in which, to quote Sir Philip Hendy, "middle-class people could admire themselves at their ease."[13] And "middle-class," in Hendy's sense of the word, included the Royal Family. Queen Victoria purchased *Life at the Seaside* in 1854; in the following year "Frith was presented to the Queen's husband at the request of the Prince Consort, who even went to the trouble of suggesting some of the alterations . . . to *Derby Day* . . . the most popular of all his works . . . now in the national collection. . . ." It is the essence of Frith's art, Hendy explains, that there should be no disturbing emotions: "There is no room for passion . . . for sensuousness . . . if there is drama, then it should be melodrama, not too close to reality—as in *A Stagecoach Adventure in 1750, a scene from Roderick Random*."[14] Viewing life in this way—as a series of domestic, melodramatic scenes—Frith could not interpret it, no matter how much time and skill he expended on his paintings. The most he could do was to dress up his Tupperish conceptions in realistic trappings. Yet he performed this feat so well, with "such remarkable solidity . . . and competence" as to rival the Pre-Raphaelites. In 1856, Ruskin praised *Many Happy Returns of the Day* as "a taking picture, much, it seems to me, above Mr. Frith's former standard. Note the advancing Pre-Raphaelitism in the wreath of flowers round the child's head. One is only sorry to see any fair little child having too many and too kind friends, and in so great a danger of being toasted, toyed and wreathed into selfishness and misery." [15]

Ruskin's observation—including those on child-care—are sound as far as they go. Where he fell short was in his failure to see that the Pre-Raphaelites were almost as much given to the practice of toasting, toying, and wreathing their subjects as Frith himself. Millais' *Sir Isumbras Crossing the Ford,* for instance, the painting that Reade later purchased and hung in his drawing room, is every bit as sentimental as anything of Frith's. It was Reade's boast, in speaking of the painting, that "he could write a three-volume novel on it, and have sentiment enough to spare. . . ." And he could have found as much spare sentiment in Millais' *Ophelia, The Blind Girl, The Race-Meeting, Retribution, A Flood,* or for that matter, any number of other Pre-Raphaelite paintings, e.g., Holman Hunt's *The Awakened Conscience,* Ford Madox Brown's *Work,* D. G. Rossetti's *Found.* From the beginning, Holman Hunt explained, "we set ourselves to illustrate themes which we conscientiously persuaded ourselves to be connected with the pathetic, the honest, the laudable, the sublime aspects of humanity. . . . Take Millais as a fair exponent of our purpose. . . . His *Blind Girl* is a heart felt appeal to commiseration. *The Rescuing Fireman* provokes expansive recognition of the divine in unpretentious humanity. Rossetti's early designs were pronouncedly religious. . . . These pictures by my two companions . . . prove that our purpose had not only a newness in its outer form, but also took up in more extended aspiration the principle exemplifying that 'Art is Love. . . .'" [16]

Hunt's sincerity is beyond question. Elsewhere he points out that the Pre-Raphaelites "were following the example of the poets of the early Victorian age . . . in an effort to purge [their] art of what was in the nature of bathos, affected in sentiment, and unworthy according to wholesome English tradition. . . ." [17] Unfortunately, however, the models they chose were themselves given to sentiment that was none the less sentimental for being "wholesome." For these and other reasons there is little to choose between Pre-Raphaelite wholesomeness, as represented by *The Rescuing Fireman,* and Frith's bathos, as represented in *Derby Day.* The main difference is that the Pre-Raphaelites expressed their bathos more realistically, by means of a method that guaranteed its factual accuracy, and therefore, they thought, its truth to nature. Influenced by current trends in philosophy, science, and the arts, and more especially by recent developments in photography, "they fitted real people and real backgrounds to imaginary scenes or vice versa, painting these imaginary scenes from nature with the most scrupulous fidelity of detail and pure and vivid colour. . . . There was no limit to the pains taken to secure accuracy. At Ewell in Surrey, obliging countrymen shot water rats for Millais and held down sheep for Hunt to copy with the requisite care; and the strawberries in the young aristocrat's hand in Millais' *The Woodman's Daughter* cost five and sixpence at Covent Garden." [18]

Needless to say the realistic strawberries do not alter the Frith-like character of "The Woodman's Daughter." Like so much Pre-Raphaelite detail they merely serve as a new and more distracting form of ornamentation, encouraging the viewer to what D. S. R. Welland has defined as "a piece-by-piece approach to the picture." [19] In some of their paintings, however, the early Pre-Raphaelites (wittingly or unwittingly) carried their method considerably further, to a point where their realism tended to overwhelm their conventional idealism. And it was these paintings which most infuriated right-thinking Victorians. Millais' *Christ in the House of his Parents* Dickens considered lacking in "all Post-Raphael ideas, all religious aspirations, all elevating thoughts; all tender, awful, sorrowful, ennobling, sacred, graceful, or beautiful associations. . . . You behold the interior of a carpenter's shop. In the foreground . . . is a hideous, wry-necked, blubbering red-headed boy, in a bed-gown [Christ]; who appears to have received a poke in the hand, from the stick of another boy with whom he has been playing in an adjacent gutter. . . ." [20] Continuing in this vein, Dickens runs through Millais' entire group of characters, concluding with the carpenters, who "might be undressed in any hospital where dirty drunkards, in a high state of varicose veins, are received. Their very toes have walked out of St. Giles's." And this after Millais had gone to the trouble of securing a working carpenter as his model, so that the muscles—and presumably the toes as well—would be right. The only part of the carpenter that was not authentic was his head, and that Millais had modelled after his own father. Yet Dickens, if he knew these facts, was not at all impressed by them—any more than he was impressed with Millais' "faithful portraiture of [wood] shavings, or the skilful colouring of drapery. . . ." To admire such virtuosities, he maintained, was to give "greater weight to mere handicraft, than to . . .

considerations of common reverence or decency; which absurd principle in the event of a skilful painter of the figure becoming a very little more perverted in his taste . . . might place Her Gracious Majesty in a very painful position, one of these fine Private View Days." This, the low point of Dickens' style, is the high point of his rhetoric—though he prolongs his denunciation for three more pages, stressing the retrogressive implications of Pre-Raphaelite Medievalism, and encouraging them to "amalgamate with the Pre-Newtonian, Pre-Gower, and Pre-Chaucer . . . Brotherhoods . . . in a high festival to be called the Convocation of Eternal Boobies."

That Dickens, who considered himself a realist, could become so incensed by this painting, shows how far his own realism was permeated with Victorian idealism. Like the admirers of Frith, he insisted that art be "informed with mind and sentiment." It was the business of the painter as well as the writer, he believed, to express the "ideal" through the "real," i.e. "to show to all, that in all familiar things, even in those which are repellent on the surface, there is Romance enough, if we will find it out. . . ." By the "ideal" he therefore meant what Frith meant by the term, what G. F. Watts expressed in his hopelessly noble portraits of the Victorian great, what Millais and the other Pre-Raphaelites came to express in their paintings of fallen women and rescuing firemen. Hunt's *The Awakened Conscience*, it may be recalled, was directly inspired by Dickens' Little Emily.

Sharing Dickens' concept of the real and ideal, Reade likewise deplored the Medievalist tendencies of the P. R. B.; also their "want of mind and taste." In *Christie Johnstone*, the "Resourceful Hero," Lord Ipsden, "cooled down Charles Gatty, Esq.," the young Pre-Raphaelite painter of the novel, with a few well-chosen words:

'You, sir,' he went on, 'appear to hang on the skirts of a certain clique, who handle the brush well, but draw ill, and look at nature through the spectacles of certain ignorant painters who spoiled canvas four hundred years ago.'

'Go no farther in that direction.

'Those boys, like all quacks, have one great truth which they disfigure with more than one falsehood.

'Hold fast their truth, which is a truth the world has always possessed, though its practice has been confined to the honest and laborious few.

'Eschew their want of mind and taste.

'Shrink with horror from that profane *culte de laideur,* that "love of the lop-sided," they have recovered from the foul receptacles of decayed art.'

He reminded him further, that 'Art is not imitation, but illusion; that a plumber and glazier of our day and a mediæval painter are more alike than any two representatives of general styles that can be found; and for the same reason, namely, that with each of these, art is in its infancy; these two sets of bunglers have not learned how to produce the illusions of art.'

Of course this is Charles Reade speaking, albeit not very originally, e.g., the last paragraph probably came from *The Times's* answer to Ruskin's letter in defence of the P. R. B.[21]

But Reade, unlike Dickens and the journalistic critics, was not wholly opposed to the Brotherhood. If he could not accept their entire aim and doctrines, he did accept the "one great truth" which Gatty and "those boys" held so dear, namely, their "truth to nature"; furthermore, he recognized that Pre-Raphaelite method, informed with "mind and taste," offered him and every other Dickensian a convenient means of securing this "truth"—a means whereby they could express the "Romance of familiar things," and give this "Romance" the authenticity of actual fact. "I will just premise," he said, "that there is, *me judice,* but one road to truth in literature, or any human thing, viz. the method of the Naturalist and the Jurist . . ." a statement wholly in keeping with the scientism of the Pre-Raphaelites. For however much they hankered after the Middle Ages, they too were revolting against established authority and transcendental thinking—and they were revolting in the name of Science and Truth. Consequently their method was as scientific and as Baconian as even Reade could wish—a point F. G. Stephens (alias John Seward) makes clear in "The Purpose and Tendency of Early Italian Art" *(The Germ,* 1850). Moreover, their method, as elucidated by Stephens, harnessed science to morality: "If this adherence to fact, to experiment and not to theory . . . had added so much to the knowledge of man in science, why may it not greatly assist the moral purpose of the Arts?" The Pre-Raphaelite answer to this rhetorical question is to be found in their realistic techniques, and the paintings they produced with them, such as *Work, Found, The Blind Girl, The Order of Release, Pizarro Seizing the Inca of Peru.* And Reade (as I have indicated in a separate essay, "Pre-Raphaelitism in Charles Reade's Early Fiction") was not slow to adapt their method (and more especially their research techniques) to his own literary purposes, seeking thereby to achieve the truth and success in literature that Millais had begun to enjoy in painting, that Charles Kean, by adapting Pre-Raphaelite techniques to the stage, had already achieved in his dramatic productions.

IV

Along with Pre-Raphaelitism in art, perhaps in part a result of it, a similar movement was taking place on the English stage. This movement in the theatre was not radically new—its earlier manifestations have already been described—but about 1850 it underwent an intensification so marked that it may be considered as something apart from the old. The leader of this movement was Charles Kean, and his primary aim was to secure the utmost fidelity to "Nature" (i.e. actuality) in the staging of all types of plays—from Shakespeare to melodrama. To this end, he adopted a naturalistic method approximating that of the Pre-Raphaelites. The Vestris-type realism was no longer sufficient: every word, every gesture, every costume had to be factually correct, and correct in every single particular. His *King John*, for instance, represented years of antiquarian research, and he was equally meticulous in his staging of melodramas, going so far as to preface them with scholarly disquisitions (attached to the playbills) in which he reviewed his sources and researches. In his "Preface" to *Pizarro* he noted that the success which had attended his production of *Sardanapalus* (based on the researches of Layard and Botta) had encouraged him to "select the well-known drama of *Pizarro*, for the purpose of exemplifying the customs, ceremonies, and religion of Peru at the time of the Spanish invasion. . . ." To prove the accuracy of his production he subsequently lists his various sources (e.g., "the Indian airs introduced into the music are founded on melodies published in Rivero and Tschudi's work on 'Peruvian Antiquities . . .'"); then, after showing how he has used these sources, he goes on to discuss the changes he has made in the play, for the specific purpose of adapting it "to the purposes of historical illustration," justifying his tactics by concluding that "the present age demands that all dramatic representations must of necessity be accompanied by a certain selection of scenery, dresses, and music. The public voice has justified me in deciding that *truth* in these matters is preferable to *inaccuracy*." [22]

ARTISTIC DEVELOPMENT 1849-1852

According to these pronouncements "truth" was truth to "fact"—not ordinary facts, it is to be noted, but exciting and exotic ones; moreover, the productions themselves reveal that Kean arranged and dressed up his facts in a manner calculated to create sentimentality, suspense, wonder, awe, and fear—in short the ultimate in every form of "sensation." To cite only one example, the "conflagration of the palace and city" which closed the fifth act of *Sardanapalus* was so realistic that "Many of the audience . . . sat in mingled admiration and terror. On the first night, an old half-pay colonel, in the stalls, was overheard by his neighbor saying to himself, 'Oh! hang it! this is too much. Kean is going beyond the mark this time—he will certainly burn the theatre down. . . . There'll be a rush to the doors in a moment, and lives may be lost; but I shall keep my seat, come what may, until they are all out.'"[23] Nor was the half-pay colonel the only one who was frightened: the insurance companies "took the alarm, and sent their officers to make a strict investigation."[24]

The beauty of such effects, from Kean's point of view, lay in their documentary truth. That they were also sensational and successful merely proved that *truth* was stranger and more profitable than *inaccuracy*. "Hence I conclude," he wrote in his "Preface" to *Pizarro*, "that when an appropriate opportunity is embraced of blending instruction with amusement, when the mind may be informed while the eye is gratified, the drama is not likely to lose or be degraded by the attempted association." Perhaps Kean really believed his own arguments; perhaps he was sincere when he maintained that his theories and method offered a sure means of regenerating the "national drama of the country."[25] Still, it is to be noted that he never once permitted his regard for truth to interfere with stock methods of stage appeal. The Pre-Raphaelites, whatever their shortcomings, had braved public disapproval in their attempts at naturalistic expression; Kean, on the other hand, was always the opportunist, always the showman—a Barnum and Bailey Baconian posing as the saviour of the legitimate drama.

The partisans of Samuel Phelps challenged Kean's pretensions, maintaining that "the painter, the tailor, and the upholsterer are Mr. Kean's interpreters of Shakespeare. . . ."[26] Yet with few exceptions both the critics and the theatrical public accepted Kean at his own estimate—as a daring innovator whose productions initiated "a revolution in literary and dramatic taste"—a true and beautiful and comfortable "revolution" that made Shakespeare's plays as entertaining and instructive as the works of M. E. Braddon and Wilkie Collins. With his Baconian and Pre-Raphaelite and Dickensian beliefs, Reade was bound to share these views. More than that he was bound to recognize in Kean's method and techniques features that could be incorporated into his own dramatic writing, for Kean was not just reproducing plays, he was rewriting them, i.e., he was utilizing his researches to vary and fill out and upholster otherwise routine plots. And that, Reade came to believe, was the essence of dramatic authorship.

From the beginning his main difficulty had lain in the realm of what he called "invention," by which he meant the ability to work out original plots, characters, and situations. Until he wrote *Gold* the most he could do was to "adapt," or what amounted to much the same thing, the way he and Taylor worked it out, "collaborate." For a time, it appears, he tried to convince himself that he preferred collaboration to creation. "I only wish," he noted in his *Diary* (June 10, 1852), "I could reduce collaboration to a science. . . . I could write twelve halves of three-act plays in a year, writing only between breakfast and luncheon; but I could not write six plays without hurting my brain." Perhaps he really was afraid of hurting his brain—these lines were written at Malvern, where he was trying to regain his emotional balance—yet for all their ingenuousness his remarks also represent a considerable amount of rationalization. His greatest ambition, the *Diary* reveals, was to write a dramatic hit, and to write it himself, so that he alone would receive the plaudits of the critics and the crowd. Moreover, he wanted to vindicate his creative powers, to himself and to the world. In his own words *(Diary* Sept. 27 [1852]): "I want to show people that, though I adapt French pieces, I can *invent* too, if I choose to take the trouble. And it *is* a trouble to me I confess."

For Reade this was a considerable admission; and he could hardly have stated it so openly if he had not already overcome his "trouble"—thanks mainly to Kean, whose production had showed him how documentation might be substituted for imagination, and used to expand routine melodramas into great and successful plays, e.g., *Pizarro, Sardanapalus,* and Boucicault's *The Corsican Brothers.*[27] "The year 1852," Watson has pointed out, "marked the complete break between the Boucicault of *London Assurance* . . . and the Boucicault of sensation, sentimentality, and intense realism. In that year at the Princess's he enjoyed the immense popularity of *The*

Corsican Brothers. . . ." While this is essentially correct, the break Watson speaks of is not so much in the play itself (which differs little from Boucicault's other plays) as in the mode of production. The "intense realism," and the consequent popularity, can be traced directly to Kean, whose documentary techniques apparently gave Boucicault's melodrama something of the realistic vividness he had imparted to his Shakespearean productions.

The example of *The Corsican Brothers* was not lost upon Reade. Nor, with his knowledge of the theatre, was he likely to mistake the reasons for its success. Kean's innovations showed him that he had been right all along—that documented plays could be more true as well as more sensational and successful than those written from "inner consciousness." And for this type of dramatic composition he felt himself to be uniquely well qualified. To Boucicault and nearly all the other dramatists of the time documentation was but a fashionable literary device; to Reade, as to the Pre-Raphaelites, it was the Baconian key to all knowledge, and all the arts. Furthermore, in adapting this key to his own writing, he could draw upon all the lessons he had learned as an apprentice, and later as a translator and collaborator; all the knowledge he had gained from his study of the arts, including a direct acquaintance with the Pre-Raphaelite techniques Kean had modified and transferred to the stage. As early as 1850, speaking through the Pre-Raphaelite hero of *Christie Johnstone,* he had looked forward to *"Pictures . . . that shall refresh men's inner souls, and help their hearts against the artificial world, and charm the fiend away, like David's harp! The world, after centuries of lies, will give nature and truth a trial. What a paradise art will be when truths instead of lies, shall be told on paper, on marble, on canvas, and on the boards."* [28] Again, in the *Diary* (Durham, August 3, [1852]), he had noted: "Wait till I get to London, and organize a little society of painters, actors, and writers, all lovers of truth, and sworn to stand or fall together. Why not a Truth Company as well as a Gala Company?—*l'un vaut bien l'autre.* Now I think of it, there is, I believe, a company and a steam-engine for everything but truth."

A paradise of art via steam engine! Reade's metaphors are peculiarly apt. His further entries in the *Diary* show that he really was in search of a company, or better still, a literary steam engine, i.e., a device or devices whereby he could secure the truths and write the plays that he could not invent, without hurting his brain. Hence his adaptations, his collaboration with Taylor, his efforts to attach himself to Mrs. Stirling and other famous actresses. In discussing Reade's later association with Ellen Terry, Edward Gordon Craig noted that he was always on the look-out "for a good actress to play parts in his plays, and thus make them successful." [29] And, for the same reason, he was equally anxious to secure good stage-managers, costumiers, and scene painters. When a play of his failed, invariably it was the fault of the cast, or the management, or, as in the case of *Dora* (adapted from Tennyson) the scene painter, who, according to Reade, painted a corn-field so blatantly unnatural "that when the farmer of the play pointed to his acres of golden grain . . . the audience was convulsed." Although *Dora* is one of Reade's later plays, he wrote *Gold* (November, 1852), *The Courier of Lyons* (1854) and *The First Printer* (1856) in much the same way. In fact he wrote all three of these plays expressly for Kean, who actually produced the last two.

V

Since he intended *Gold* for Kean, the main thing, he thought, was to capitalize on the documentary potential of his materials. And that is what he did, calling upon the knowledge he had gained from Warren *et al*, and supplementing it with the newer techniques he had derived from the Pre-Raphaelites and from Kean himself. When first confronted with imprisonment for debt the Pre-Raphaelite hero of *Christie Johnstone* had been more than a little distressed: "Then," as Reade explains, "he took a turn, and began to fall into the artistic, or true view of matters. . . . 'Look here, Christie,' said he, 'I am sick of conventional assassins, humbugging models, with dirty beards, that knit their brows, and try to look murder; they never murdered so much as a tomcat: I always go in for the real thing, and here I shall find it. . . . I shall find the accessories of a picture I have in my head. . . .'" [30] Emulating his own hero, Reade also went to prison for his accessories. On August 10, 1852, he noted in his *Diary:*

I have sketched the plot of an original drama; I am studying for it a little. One of my characters is to be a thief. I have the *entrée* of Durham Gaol, and I am studying thieves. I have got lots of their letters, and one or two autobiographies from the chaplain. But the other subject, the gold-diggings, makes me very uneasy. I feel my lack of facts at every turn. On the subject I wish I had some one I could consult; but it is utter solitude here. I have no friend, no acquaintance that knows

Sound	from	Noise
Bombast	from	Sublime
Beauty	from	the Beast
Smell	from	Stink
	or	
H	from	H.

In part Reade may here be reacting against "the charming, clever woman, beautiful as the dawn" whom he mentioned in his *Diary* (Durham, July 15). By this time she had deserted him for the beast she was to marry, and Reade apparently felt lost without the encouragement and sympathy, and, if Coleman is correct, the literary help she had given him. It was she, Coleman avers, who suggested that a thief in Durham Gaol, one Jennins, would "make a capital central figure for a popular drama" having to do with Australia: "Australia!—diggers, loafers, riots, gold discovery, natives! I can see it all!" To which Reade supposedly replied: "So can I . . . and I *did* see it, and began to churn the incidents up day and night. Then Jacky began to dawn on me! . . ."[31]

While there may be some truth in this account (which is, for Coleman, quite specific and circumstantial) it appears exaggerated in the light of the *Diary*. Reade's idea for a play dealing with the gold-fields almost certainly grew out of his idea for a play dealing with prisons—the one idea leading to the other when he discovered the fresh material on gold-fields contained in the autobiography given him by the chaplain of Durham Gaol. After all, the gold-diggings were sensationally topical at this time (August, 1852), and a dramatist of Reade's proclivities hardly required the aid of a provincial Egeria to recognize the theatrical possibilities of Australian documentation. The assistance he desired was of a different character altogether. He already had the outlines of a play; the problem was to fill them in—not with literary imaginings, but with facts, and more facts, ideally those drawn from the accounts of prospectors and diggers fresh from the gold-fields. But time was short, and since it was difficult to secure first-hand reports, Reade apparently did the next best thing and turned to the library—there to find (in the flood of newspaper, magazine, and book-length journalistic accounts of the diggings) just the facts he had been looking for, and in such abundance that within a month and a half he was congratulating himself (*Diary*, September 27,

1852, Magdalen College, Oxford) on the near completion of *Gold:* "Have nearly finished a great original play, a drama in four acts, containing the matter and characters that go to a five-act piece. I suppose I must go to London to push it. Mem.–Not to let it go out of my hands. Not to trust it in any theatre, because there are plenty of blackguards about, and any fool could write a play that would go down upon this subject."

Reade's worst fears were soon realized. On October 23 *The Illustrated London News* reviewed "a new piece [at the Surrey] entitled 'Off to the Diggins' . . . in which the diggers are shown at work, with all the picturesque accompaniments of dingy linen, spades, pickaxes, cradles and lynch-law weaponry. . . ." To be thus anticipated, just when he felt himself on the verge of success, was almost more than Reade could bear. On the day "Off to the Diggins" was reviewed (and declared a success) he cast up his account with literature in a form that even the authors of the *Memoir* recognize "as being a little hysterical":

Oct. 23, London.–Charles Reade in account with literature–

Dr.		s.	d.	Cr.
Pens, Paper, Ink, Copying,	11	11	0	0
Brains,	4000	0	0	
	4011	11	0	

List of my unacted plays: 1. 'The Way Things Turn.' 2. 'Peregrine Pickle.' 3. 'Marguerite.' 4. 'Honor before Title.' 5. 'Masks and Faces.' 6. 'Gold.' 7. 'Nance Oldfield.' 8. 'The Dangerous Path.' 9. 'The Hypochondriac.' 10. 'Fish, Flesh, and Good Red Herring.' 11. 'Rachel the Reaper.' I don't remember the rest. I am a little soured, and no wonder.

At just this moment, however, he was lifted up by new hope. In his own words: "Just had a civil note from Kean, inviting me to read my drama to him. This is the first bright speck in my present destiny." Even this one bright speck was soon to disappear. Kean refused the play. But Reade, buoyed up by the success of *Masks and Faces*, continued to submit *Gold* to one manager after another until it was eventually produced by E. T. Smith at Drury Lane on the tenth of the following January.

VI

Gold was a near failure the first night. *The Times* (January 11, 1853) declared it "a mixture of domestic rural sorrow and out-

landish villainy, which if it did not belong to the genus Transpontine, at all events looked more like that genus than any other."
The most the reviewer could say for the play was that "the scene
of the 'diggins' in Australia, with all the mechanism of 'cradles,'
the chymistry of testing, and instances of the rude administration
of justice in a lawless state of society, furnishes a living picture of
a region which now engrosses the attention of every class of the
community, and those who care little for the piece, may go to
see this particular scene, as they would go to one of the numerous
dioramas of the day." From first to last this criticism is entirely
just, measured against serious literary standards. Yet to Reade it
must have appeared senseless, even vicious. Had he not studied the
lessons of the masters for fifteen long years? Had he not practiced
their lessons in his own adaptations and collaborations? Had he
not brought these lessons to the writing of *Gold?* Had he not
written it according to the highest standards—those of Shakespeare,
and more recently Boucicault? Where was the difference between
his plays and theirs? Had he not combined purpose with facts,
after the manner of Hugo, to produce the truth of great art, i.e. the
truth of documentary realism?

To all these questions one is forced to give an affirmative
answer—if one adopts Reade's point-of-view. The play does contain social purpose, for instance. MacMahon has noted a number
of passages;[32] and there are others, such as the following:

ROB. Well, young lady, work is rewarded in California—here it is
snubbed. This very morning, I heard one of your clod-hoppers
say, "The Squire is a good gentleman—he often gives me a day's
work."—*Gives* me a day's work! I should think it was the clod-
hopper gave the gentleman the day's work, and the gentleman
gave him a shilling, and made five by it.
WILL. (*scratches his head*)
ROB. Ay—try and rake that idea into your upper soil, Sandford
No. 2.—And that is the reason I invite my friend George to rake
his muscle, wind, pluck, backbone, and self out of this miserable
country, and come where the best man has a chance to win.[33]

At first glance these lines may seem to strike a rather serious note
of social protest. And to a certain extent they do—the same note
that had already appeared in *Propria Quae Maribus*, that will re-
appear in all the early novels, most notably in *Peg Woffington*. But
this note is of little real significance in the play, since Reade forces
it into harmony with the conventional patterns of humanitarian

melodrama—with the lily-white virtue of the poor but resourceful hero finding its reward in the form of a blushing heroine and a literal pot of gold. In other words Reade's moral-social purpose was like Dickens' or Boucicault's, and therefore, he thought, like Shakespeare's. He once described Shakespeare's tragedies as "philosophic melodrama" and later, in his "Preface" to *Hard Cash*, he distinguished between his own works and those of lesser Sensationalists by maintaining that his were "idead," like Shakespeare's, and taught moral and social lessons, again like Shakespeare's, by virtue of their truth to nature, their factual realism.

Other dramatists might be more inventive, more clever, but *Gold*, Reade believed, was more true—because more factual. While he was writing the play he noted in his *Diary:* "I ought to make a great hit with my drama 'Gold.' The very first work on modern Judaism I took up showed me just what I had calculated on in coming here [Magdalen], that the Jews are a people of whom we know nothing, and who know nothing about the Christian religion. Here is one of those rich veins with which a hit is to be made. If I had the patience to read, I could write the subject, I know, when I had the facts. . . ." And he did write it, presumably from the facts, which he combined with other facts about the diggings, to produce such scenes as the following, in which Mr. Levi, a true Jew, exposes a true hoax, and nearly precipitates a true riot (much like a factual one William Howitt described in his *Land, Labor, and Gold*). As the scene opens Jem, a digger, is trying to sell Mr. Levi a handful of what appears to be gold-dust:

LEVI. Whence had you this?

JEM. Out of the ground!

LEVI. False!

JEM. What do you mean by false? I saw a man lift a lot out of one hole, gave him thirty pounds, and washed this out the very first washing.

LEVI. You have been made a scoff and a jest—this dust is from Birmingham, and neither Australian or natural.

ROB. The man planted it for you.

JEM. Keep it—keep it—till I come back—I'll find him.

Exit

ROB. What is it, Mr. Levi?

LEVI. It is prepared by one who knows the metals. Here is brass ormolu, and, I think, some gilt platinum to give it weight.

ROB. Heigh, lads! here's a new dodge. Brummagen planted on us so far off. That is hard!

MEN *are collecting with angry faces.* NOISE *heard. Re-enter* JEM, *dragging in* WALKER.

JEM.   Justice—justice—and Lynch Law! [34]

Another true episode is that in which George, the hero, reveals "the wonder of the world" to his friend Robinson:

Scene II—*A narrow Rocky Pass—Heap of quartz stones* L.H. *Enter* GEORGE, *running,* L.H.

GEO.   How slow he is! Come on!
ROB.   (*without*) How much farther?
GEO.   No farther—here!

Enter ROBINSON, L.H.

ROB.   Well?
GEO.   D'ye see that broad vein of quartz in the rock? That is the home of the gold. Those lumps of quartz have all rolled out from there.
ROB.   Did you bring me here to tell me that?
GEO.   That and something else!
ROB.   (*whispering*) Found something?
GEO.   Yes!
ROB.   Where?
GEO.   In sight. I haven't moved it from where I saw it.
ROB.   Hold your tongue, and let me find it. It is not on this heap—too many men have sat down there. (*peers about*)
GEO.   Tom! 'tis the mind find [sic] things—not the eye; a hundred black shepherds have sat there, but they left *this* for a Berkshire farmer.
ROB.   Why—Gracious heavens! Can this be? You take away my breath. It can't be gold—gold it is! You have found the wonder of the world.
GEO.   What is it worth—five hundred pounds?
ROB.   Five hundred!—don't ask me what it is worth—how shall we get it home? They'd murder us like rats, if they saw it. There, there!—Now fling it down—throw stones upon it. Ah! George, George! it is too great a find—it will get us into trouble. (*takes out revolver*) Those thieves are upon us, and my revolver is not loaded. [35]

This scene typifies the action of the entire play, which consists of just such factual episodes, connected up by just such melodramatic devices (drawn revolvers, etc.), and acted out against just such factual settings as those exemplified in the following stage directions, designed to give a realistic picture of the "Summer Hill Creek Diggings by the River McQuarrie":

> *The Sun begins to rise, and displays the following scene (which ought to be a very remarkable one)—A high bank L.H.—A high bank or cliff R.C., with rocks running all round stage—Low ground, and rocks beyond, C.—The River McQuarrie winding in a valley, along the banks of which are seen countless tents of every colour, size, shape, &c.—The whole extent of stage, and also rocks occupied by the* DIGGERS, *&c., who at the beginning of this change gradually awake, take up tools, and proceed to work in groups.*
>
> *Enter* NATHEN *from tent—he places a rough table and the paraphernalia of a gold assayer and purchaser for* LEVI, *who enters and seats himself at table.*
>
> *Music,* subdued, but rising with the opening prospect—at last breaks into "Hail, smiling Morn!"[36]

To which Reade added a long explanatory footnote:

> All the beautiful concomitants of that great event in Nature—Sunrise—must be attended to. Undistinguishable sounds in the distance—sparkles of dew here and there. Men seen to draw open tents and issue forth to work. Men enter at intervals—one with a tool over his shoulder, another wheeling a barrow, &c. The important part of this scene is the River in perspective—the rest ad libitum. A good effect is produced at L.H. by Children in the background, intended to represent men in the distance; but Children should not be placed in centre and foreground, or the other effect is lost. The more gradually the light breaks, the better; all that is required is that the music and the light should be progressive, and the pantomime varied by several entries. Do not let them begin to work too soon,—you will find the audience very patient, if the music is good and the business rational.—C.R.[37]

These directions are unique, even for the mid-nineteenth century. Reade knew exactly what theatrical effects he wanted, and he knew exactly how to achieve them; moreover, he knew how to combine these effects with action and dialogue—to produce a spine-tingling yet purposeful finale. As the final scene opens, the hero and Robinson and their new-found ally, Jem, are once again faced with disaster:

> JEM. *(entering)* Did you call, Tom?
> ROB. Hallo! our tent has been broken into!
> JEM. Mercy on us!
> ROB. They have cleared us out!

JEM.   I'm sorry for it.

ROB.   They have taken my very boots that cost me fifty shilling.

Re-enter ROBINSON, *staggering under* CARLO, *stuffed—puts it down, dashes back, and re-appears with small iron box open.*

—But they left the dog.

JEM.   The dog?

ROB.   Yes—they hadn't the sense to take Carlo. Carlo saved our lives when he was a dog, and our gold since he has been furniture. D'ye see this, ye thieves? *(tapping dog)*

March, *"God save the Queen," and tramp of feet heard in the distance.*

—And d'ye hear that, ye rascals?—d'ye know the meaning of the agreeable little melody.

MEN.   *(all listen)*

ROB.   I'll tell you. It means God, and the Queen, and Law—it means justice for the rich—*(taps* CARLO*)*—as well as the poor—it means man instead of serpent, shark, and tiger—and peace and comfort instead of knife, and revolver, and lawless law.

Enter CLERK, CAPTAIN, *and* SOLDIERS, *marching—*GEORGE *between them* [presumably with his nugget]—SOLDIERS *come down to front of stage.*

CAPT.   Halt!—front!

CLERK.   *(to* GEORGE*)*   You are a digger—read that. *(gives him proclamation)*

GEO.   *(reads proclamation)*   "In the Queen's name!" *(Chord)* "Forasmuch as it has been represented to me, Governor of Sydney, that, by deeds of rapine and violence, the gains of honest labour are rendered insecure to her Majesty's subjects, we have therefore sent a force of soldiers to maintain order and good rule, according to law. *(joyous murmur)* All good citizens and honest men of all nations are invited to co-operate with the Government, in their own interest, and that of all human society,—to protect person and property—to guard inviolate the sacred fruits of industry, and the laws of great Britain and her Colonies throughout the world. God save the Queen!"

SOLDIERS *present arms—The National Anthem is played with the whole power of the band—Every person waving caps, &c., and shouting—As the Act Drop begins to descend,* ROBINSON *and* JEM *touch spring in dog, and gold dust pours out into box—*ROBINSON *shakes his fist at* BLACK WILL *and* THIEVES.—

TABLEAU
END OF ACT THE FOURTH[38]

All this seems baldly clear, yet Reade, in an effort to exploit every possible effect, again added supplementary footnotes:

* To produce the Dramatist's effect, the proclamation must be sustained with occasional chords, all through until the word "world"; and the words "God save the Queen" must be played with an increase of power. The reader must go lightly over the words at first, and begin to give them a rising importance at the word "order," and so till the end. The crowd of people for whose sake the proclamation is issued and read, must be taught to utter expressions of interest rising gradually in power during the reading of the proclamation. In other words, all parties concerned—the musicians, the speaker, and the actors—must work together upon the great principle of climax. This attended to, the act drop will fall with effect.

** Let the gold-dust in this instance be metal, and plenty of it—so that, the dog being held high, it may descend in a regular shower, and attract the eye. C.R.[39]

VII

Gold, it should now be clear, follows the time-tried formulas of "humanitarian melodrama." Reade was not trying to alter these formulas, which he believed to be those of Shakespeare and all the great dramatists of the past; rather he was trying to revivify them, to breathe into them a measure of Shakespearean life and truth and purpose. And he was trying to do this by means of his factual researches. Hence his inclusion of realistic gold-nuggets, dew-drops, etc., arranged according to "the great principle of climax." For, if facts equal truth in drama, and drama is conceived of as "purposeful sensation," there is no aesthetic limit to the number or kind of sensational facts that may be included. The more the better, so long as they are "true," and lend themselves to a good cause or purpose, and do not violate the stock responses of the theatrical audience. In actual practice, therefore, Reade's theories enabled him (as in *Gold*) to draw upon every melodramatic device known to the trade—and yet still maintain (and believe) that he was following the path that led to dramatic truth and art. Indeed he was convinced that, in *Gold*, he had approached the summits of dramatic achievement, that it was, in its essentials, a great play, akin if not equal to Shakespeare's.

Reade's self-criticism reflects his usual egotism, plus what he described as "nobler feelings of paternity." *Gold* was his first original play to reach the stage, and it simply had to be good. Nevertheless his estimate was not wholly subjective. After a slow start the play eventually became a theatrical success. And if the critics still considered it transpontine, they came to have a far different and much higher regard for *Two Loves and a Life* (1854) and *The King's Rival* (1854), both written in collaboration with Taylor. In fact a number of critics came to look upon Reade and Taylor as the ablest dramatists of the day. William Bodham Donne, writing in *The Quarterly Review* (June, 1854), even went so far as to declare that their plays pointed the way towards the regeneration of English drama: "That dramas under few obligations, beyond the skill displayed in their plot and dialogue, to our ingenious neighbors [the French], can attain popularity, has been proved by the success of Messrs. Taylor and Reade's plays. . . . 'Masks and Faces,' and 'The King's Rival' . . . are exceptional instances of merit, and . . . encourage the hope of a restoration of a national drama. . . ." [40]

If Donne, along with George Henry Lewes and others, could find exceptional merit in these collaborations (which are slicker than *Gold* but not otherwise better) Reade cannot be too severely censured for seconding their opinions, and extending them to include his own plays—above all, *Gold*. Consequently, when he felt obliged to turn from the theatre to fiction, he saw no reason why *Gold*, his first great play, should not form the basis for his first great novel, since, as he saw the play, it embodied the dramatic precepts of Shakespeare and Molière, Kean and Boucicault—precepts which, to his way of thinking, were essentially at one with the fictional precepts of Homer and Virgil, Defoe and Scott, Hugo and Dickens.

This is not to excuse Reade's creative limitations; nor is it to condone his critical rationalizations. It is merely to indicate the extent to which his dramatic shortcomings were those of the Victorian theatre. True, he compounded those shortcomings with his Baconian ideas, and his Keanian and Pre-Raphaelite techniques, but he did so in a sincere if misguided effort to combine truth and purpose with sensation, after the manner of Shakespeare. And his plays, ridiculous as they may now appear, compare favorably with those of Boucicault, Lytton, or any of the other dramatists of the time.

CHAPTER V

Fictional Beginnings:

Peg Woffington and *Christie Johnstone*

CHARLES READE was of a better theatre than Charles Dickens, but he was of the theatre; and you seem to be reading a dramatization of his novels, rather than the novels themselves. Yet they are ingenious, brilliant, witty, and abound in true suggestions of femininity. . . . Dickens created a new school, or rather he characterized every young writer of his generation; and in a less measure Thackeray did the like. But Reade had no imitators and left none, though in certain things he was cleverer than either of these betters of his. He knew women better than they, and he could paint their manners, if not their minds, better than both his betters put together.

Why should I say his betters? If I do I am again controverting my prime position that the highest type of novelist is he who can most winningly impart the sense of womanhood. Charles Reade could do this beyond Dickens and beyond Thackeray; and so let the fact praise him as it may.

—W. D. HOWELLS—*Heroines of Fiction*

✶ ✶ ✶

A few months ago I was at the old home, and I read that book [*Christie Johnstone*] again, after not looking at it for more than thirty years; and I read it with amazement at its prevailing artistic vulgarity, its prevailing aesthetic error shot here and there with gleams of light, and of the truth that Reade himself was always dimly groping for. The book is written throughout on the verge of realism, with divinations and conjectures across its border, and with lapses into the fool's paradise of romanticism, and an apparent content with its inanity and impossibility. But then it was brilliantly new and surprising; it seemed to be the last word that could be said for the truth in fiction; and it had a spell that held us like an anaesthetic. . . .

—W. D. HOWELLS—*My Literary Passions*

✶ ✶ ✶

Reade's first love was the theatre; fiction he looked upon as a lesser form of the drama. In later years he constantly maintained—and believed—that he, like Dickens before him, had been

[113]

driven from the theatre by corrupt practices and bad laws. Yet the biographical facts show that before he was driven, he went; that he wrote *Peg Woffington* (his fictional version of *Masks and Faces*) before the play itself was completed; that in the years following, when he was presumably dedicating himself to *Gold* and further collaborations with Taylor, he wrote a number of short stories, all of *Christie Johnstone,* and parts of *It Is Never Too Late To Mend.* The explanation would seem to be that, much as he loved the drama, he loved success even more, and with the fictional triumphs of Dickens and lesser would-be dramatists constantly before him, he could hardly fail to see the advantages of following their lead, particularly when, as in May of 1852, he found himself at loggerheads with Tom Taylor over the denouement of *Masks and Faces.* If they could not agree, why then he would do the next best thing and rewrite the entire play as a novel. And so, without so much as a "by your leave" from Taylor, he proceeded to turn *their* first play into *his* first novel.

Taylor, naturally enough, was more than a little upset when he discovered what was happening, and "remonstrated with Reade on the line he had taken;"[1] whereupon Reade, in an effort to meet his objections, prefaced the novel with the following dedication:

To
T. TAYLOR, Esq.,
My friend, and coadjutor in the comedy of
"MASKS AND FACES,"
To whom the reader owes much of the best matter
in this tale:
And to the memory of Margaret Woffington,
Falsely *summed up* until today.
This
"Dramatic Story"
is inscribed by
Charles Reade.

This is a rather lame acknowledgment, considering how closely the novel follows the play, yet Reade, with his peculiar notions of *meum* and *teum*, could not recognize any further obligations. So far as he was concerned the play was his own because the idea for it was his own, and he therefore felt free to novelize it under his own name. Later, when one of his readers questioned "the precise connection between the story and the play," Reade justified his authorship in a letter to the *Athenaeum* (Jan. 15, 1853). Admitting that *Masks and Faces* was written and produced before *Peg Woffington*, he went on to explain that he wrote the novel for three reasons: "First I was unwilling to lose altogether some matter which we had condemned as unfit for our dramatic purpose; secondly the exigencies of the stage had, in my opinion, somewhat disturbed the natural current of our story; thirdly, it is my fate to love this dead heroine, and I wished to make her known in literature and to persons who do not frequent the theatres." While these are good reasons, and true, as far as they go, they were written for public consumption, after the novel was published.

Reade's *Diary* tells a somewhat different story. On May 7, when he first began to work on *Peg Woffington*, he complained of being "ill in body and mind," and this illness, the entry of June 7 shows, was the result of his continued frustrations, exacerbated by his inability to get on with the actual writing of the novel: "Malvern. . . . I came here to work! What have I done. I have written in these thirty days ten pages of a novel; I have lost health, time, and digestion. But it serves me right! I knew beforehand I could not write a novel in a dungeon. . . . Such is the result of a month filched from my short life in this wretched place." Although Reade could not throw off his feelings of depression, even after he had quitted Malvern for Durham, he nevertheless continued to write, and by July 20 was progressing more rapidly: "I have written three copy-books of 'Peg Woffington,' a novel. I hope to make a decent three-volume novel of it; but whether any one will publish it is another question. If not now, perhaps in three years' time. Literature no doubt is a close borough." At this point, it seems clear, Reade had in mind a three-volume novel; then on August 3 he noted in his *Diary:*

> I have finished my novel, 'Peg Woffington;' I don't know whether it is good or not. I wish to Heaven I had a housekeeper like Molière. No man can judge his own work. I hope now to work out my *forte,* criticism. But how purposeless, hopeless, and languid I feel. On the other hand, I know that if I don't do something soon, some still more ignorant ape will fly the subject before the public, and take the bread out of my mouth. It is horrible how an idea never occurs to a single person, always to three. It is a feature of the day.

This last entry, coming just two weeks after the preceding one, would seem to indicate that, soon after July 20, he completely changed his plans for *Peg Woffington:* that he gave up the idea of making it a three-volume novel, and finished it off willy-nilly by piecing together direct transcripts from *Masks and Faces.* Possibly he found his materials too meager for a "decent three-volume novel," or possibly he really did have a critical project in mind. The most likely explanation, however, is that he had already hit upon the idea for *Gold*—he had "sketched the plot" by August 10—and simply decided to get the novel out of the way in a hurry so that he could devote himself entirely to his new play.

In any case the completed novel is little more than a narrative version of *Masks and Faces,* filled out with odds and ends left over from the play. In line with his Baconian and Pre-Raphaelite notions, Reade's aim in the play had been to present a Keanian (i.e. "true-to-the-life") picture of Peg Woffington and the mid-eighteenth century stage—an aim which he had apparently carried out, to the extent of gathering together a considerable body of documentary materials, only to have Taylor object to their inclusion, at least in the bulk and in the manner Reade envisaged. So much may be inferred from his letter to the *Athenaeum.* In writing the novel, however, he was free to incorporate as many facts as he saw fit—and this he did, going to such extremes that one critic described the novel as "more than half a memoir." Certain incidents he took directly from his sources—as, for example, the story that Peg once dressed as a man to win the affection of a girl with whom her lover had become infatuated. Many of his characters (e.g., Clive, Quin, Cibber) and the episodes in which they appear are also factual (or only slightly altered to fit the dramatic action), as are many of the descriptive passages in the novel,[2] e.g., Rich, a famous theatrical manager of the time, is quoted by Augustin Daly as saying that Peg "was as majestic as Juno, as lovely as Venus, and as fresh and charming as Hebe"—a description that Reade (in his role as narrator) reproduces in a more clipped style: "She was Juno, Psyche, Hebe, by turns, and for aught we know at will."[3]

It was the inclusion of such factual details, Reade felt, that made his novel a truth instead of a lie.[4] When, in his dedication, he declared "Margaret Woffington falsely 'summed-up' until today" he was affirming the factual and therefore the artistic truth of his novel,[5] as contrasted with those previous accounts of Peg's life which had shown her to be more (or less) womanly than was considered proper by Victorian standards. Reade could hardly deny Peg's improprieties—they were too obvious—but as he presented them in the novel they were the result, not of her propensities, but of her immoral surroundings. At heart, her later conversion proved, she was all sweetness and moral light: what she really wanted was to become a Victorian wife and mother, and when that privilege was denied her, she abandoned the stage to become a devout Christian (a pre-Wesleyan Evangelical) who spent her life knitting socks for the poor—her final development thus showing her to be an eighteenth century prevision of Mrs. Reade. Reade stresses this aspect of Peg's character throughout the novel, and in his epilogue goes so far in his moralizing that he appears to be writing directly to and for his mother—in an effort to prove that her morality is his own, that whatever the subject matter of his novel it is in reality a tribute to the ideals that she herself believes in and embodies.

By using his facts and moral observations in this way Reade further sentimentalized the dramatic action he had taken over from the already sentimental *Masks and Faces*. Yet a number of critics, impressed by the technical skill of his narrative transcriptions, have argued that the novel is among Reade's best, e.g., Wilbur L. Cross, in his *Development of the English Novel*, declared it "a delightful episode in the history of the stage, and from the artistic point of view solely . . . the most perfect novel as a whole Reade wrote." [6] What this means, apparently, is that the novel retains the structure as well as the tearful charm of the original play. And so it does, to a large extent, but these features are less palatable in cold print than on the stage; in any case they are insufficient to redeem the stock sentimentality of the central action, the banality of the Soaper and Snarl episodes. So that, even if one admits structural and technical virtues, the novel, as novel, hardly deserves serious consideration.

Its prime importance—apart from what it reveals about Reade's personal situation—is in relation to his technical development. His willingness to upholster *Masks and Faces* and call it a novel shows that in practice as well as in theory he accepted without reservation the Sensational view of fiction enunciated by Harrison Ainsworth, viz. that the novel "is a drama, with descriptions to supply the place of scenery." In fact Reade went even further, for he understood "drama" to mean Kean's type of melodrama, with documentation to supply the place of imagination. That he fell short of these ideals in his actual writing, his documentary techniques not going much beyond those established by Scott, merely indicates that he had not as yet learned how to exploit the full potential of his Keanian and Pre-Raphaelite concepts. But the novel shows that he was learning, that he was developing techniques which would enable him to reduce the art of fiction to an exercise in Baconian induction.

II

The final pages of *Peg Woffington* are filled with references which seldom occur in Reade's or any other Victorian novels. At one point he speaks of "this dirty little world"; at another, in speaking of Triplet's death, he says: "And I, who laugh at him, would leave this world today, to be with him; for I am tossing at sea—he is in port." Moreover these remarks, so unlike Reade's usual bumptiousness, set the tone of the entire epilogue, which is filled with "dust and ashes," the worthlessness of life on this earth, and the brightness of eternity. When Reade wrote these lines he was apparently entertaining thoughts of suicide; in any event he wrote the greater part of the novel, the *Diary* shows, while he was undergoing medical treatment at Malvern and Durham. And he remained in a state of depression for months afterwards, despite the favorable reception accorded *Masks and Faces* and *Gold* and *Peg Woffington*. Seemingly he had waited so long that when he gained a modicum of recognition it was no longer enough. He could not remain content with a few pounds and a few critical nods; he had to win a real success that would permit him to act out his daydreams, that would enable him to become the hero as Baconian novelist and thus a writer-saviour of the Nineteenth Century. These were the boyhood dreams that, Candide-like, he still cherished, and the closer he came to their seeming realization, the more frantic became his efforts.

He began work on *Gold*, it will be recalled, before he completed *Peg Woffington*, and in December of 1852, while he was still deeply involved with *Gold* and his other dramatic activities, he began work on his second novel *Christie Johnstone*. The speed with which he completed this novel, the existence of an earlier play by the same name—these and other biographical facts, together with the form of the novel itself (in his own words: "a dramatic story, novel by courtesy") suggest that it was another adaptation. Yet he himself, in a postscript to the published novel, offered a quite different explanation:

> This story was written three years ago, and one or two topics in it are not treated exactly as they would be if written by the same hand to-day. But if the author had retouched those pages with his colors of 1853, he would (he thinks) have destroyed the only merit they have, viz., that of containing genuine contemporaneous verdicts upon a cant that was flourishing like a peony, and a truth that was struggling for bare life, in the year of truth 1850.
>
> He prefers to deal fairly with the public, and, with this explanation and apology, to lay at its feet a faulty but genuine piece of work.

Taken at face value, Reade's words can have only one meaning: that he wrote the novel in 1850 and published it in substantially the same form in 1853, avoiding revision in order to retain the genuineness of its "contemporaneous verdicts." But this meaning fails to square with the known facts. Prior to 1853 he always refers to *Christie Johnstone* as a play; in fact he became quite incensed when (early in 1851) Taylor suggested that he turn it into a novel. The most likely explanation of his postscript would therefore seem to be that in speaking of "this story" he was referring to *Christie Johnstone* in its dramatic form, or possibly to an unfinished narrative draft dating from 1851 or later. In either case, his postscript is disingenuous, if not dishonest, though not of course by his own peculiar standards, which permitted him to say one thing and mean another so long as by doing so he could justify his own shortcomings—in this instance his failure to revise the dated elements of social purpose he had taken over from the play.

This, the most likely explanation of the postscript, is entirely in line with Reade's usual tactics. Were it not for keeping the record straight, however, there would be no need to insist on the point because, regardless of which came first, the novel or the play, he wrote the novel according to the same formulas he had used in writing *Peg Woffington*. In short, if he was not transcribing and filling out a dramatic original, he wrote as if he was; for the completed novel, though looser in structure than *Peg Woffington*, is still a play written in narrative form, i.e., a series of melodramatic scenes filled with social purpose and linked up by a stagey double plot. In the opening chapter Lord Ipsden, cultured and intelligent, but lackadaisical and bored, is refused by Lady Barbara (a disciple of Carlyle); whereupon he lapses into even greater listlessness than before. At this point an eccentric doctor advises him to acquaint himself with the "lower classes." Following this advice, Ipsden goes to Scotland, does his duty by the lower classes, and becomes something of a Baconian hero when he effects a daring rescue in a storm at sea. In the meantime, Lady Barbara appears in Scotland, becomes disillusioned by the un-heroic actions of her Carlylean suitor, and eventually learns the true worth of a modern man—nay, a modern hero! They live happily ever after. That is one plot. The other centers around Christie Johnstone, a beautiful, intelligent, and talented Scottish fish-wife, and Charles Gatty, a weak but well meaning and gifted English painter imbued with Pre-Raphaelite ideas and ideals. They fall in love, and marriage is in the offing, even though Gatty is penniless and as yet unsuccessful in his work, until Gatty's mother appears on the scene. She dissuades him, and does not relent until Christie saves him from drowning. They also live happily ever after. The two plots are rather mechanically joined by bringing Ipsden into contact with Gatty, Christie, and the lower classes.

For the expression of Reade's "genuine contemporaneous ver-dicts," which merely demanded a certain amount of slanted melo-dramatic action, reinforced by his own preaching, this double plot proved reasonably adequate; but for the expression of the titular theme (clearly a fictional version of his own Scotch marriage) its melodramatic grooves were far too arbitrary and divisive.[7] To give his autobiographical experiences artistic meaning he was, at the very least, obliged to dramatize them in such a way as to bring out their essential implications, perhaps by having Ipsden (rep-resenting the real Charles Reade) fall in love with the Christie of the novel (representing the real Christie) to battle out the question of marriage with a fictional Mrs. Ipsden (representing the real Mrs. Reade). But this or any similar alternative would have forced Reade into soul-searchings that he could ill afford, especially where his mother was concerned. It was simpler and more reassur-ing to look into the heart of the theatre and theatrical fiction, where doubts were resolved as they should be—in line with his own daydreams.

This helps to explain why, in the novel itself, he so flagrantly dissipated the artistic potential of his autobiographical materials, scattering them over two plots and using his structure to separate out or eliminate those elements which could not be brought into conformity with his dual purpose. While Ipsden, as his name suggests, is a self-portrait, and Christie represents his Scotch wife, Reade does not permit them any such intimacy as that which led to their real life struggles with Mrs. Reade. In the novel he leaves Ipsden motherless and separates him from Christie by means of the double plot, permitting them to meet only after he has provided them with suitable mates chosen primarily to illustrate his artistic and social theories. True, Reade includes a mother-son conflict (between Charles Gatty and his mother over Christie) that approximates certain features of his own personal experience, but he presents this conflict so melodramatically that (with the exception of a few scenes, to be discussed presently) it degenerates into a transpontine version of *The Silver Cord*—with Mrs. Gatty, a former servant of the Ipsdens who had married a greengrocer and developed delusions of social grandeur, poisoning her son's mind against that common fishwife, and never relenting until Christie, "in front of three thousand spectators," snatches Gatty from a watery grave.

As this dénouement suggests, the entire Christie plot is a projection of Reade's wishes and daydreams expressed through his own variations upon the usual Sensation formulas. The stress he places upon Christie's Amazonian proportions (e.g., her "grand corporeal tract," her "leg with a noble swell"), the way he lauds her man-like abilities in everything from trading to fishing, the reversal of the man-woman roles in the final rescue—these and related features of his presentation tie in with his real-life interest in the androgynous and help to explain his admiration for the beautiful yet physically powerful women he constantly reproduced in his novels. It is almost as if, sensing the female component in his own make-up ("my heart is womanish"), he realized that he was too weak, too Gatty-like, to break with his mother, that if he were to marry, the woman would have to play the man and carry him off—the way Christie carried off her Gatty.

But this is a biographical, not a literary interpretation. In the novel itself, Reade's first concern—in line with his own beliefs, techniques, and anxieties—was to render his individual variations conventionally pure. Christie's "grand corporeal tract" he was at pains to present as so much Victorian womanhood, Gatty's female helplessness as a Victorian version of the artistic temperament. And for the most part he succeeded, thereby sacrificing the artistic potential of his genuine but aberrant perceptions to his own and his reader's ideals.

III

So far as Reade knew, however, the novel was conceptually as well as structurally sound. The only shortcomings he could recognize (*Diary* June 17, 1853) were shortcomings in executive technique: "Busy correcting proofs of 'Christie Johnstone.' Fear there is an excess of dialogue in it. I think I ought to throw some of that into narrative. Mrs. Seymour thinks there is too much criticism in it. I have no doubt there is. These are defects to me which judgment cannot correct. I lack the true oil of Fiction, and I fear she will have to inspire me, as well as reform me. The drowned fisherman's scene was admired by Kinglake and by Tennyson; but I feel how much more a thorough-bred narrator would have made of it." For Reade these remarks are unusually sanguine: they indicate that he had at long last found his Egeria, plus a certain amount of outside praise from the right quarters; also that he felt he was on the way to greater things—if only he could improve his narrative technique and pour "the true oil of Fiction" over his other defects.

Just how he proposed to do this he explained at some length in a typically Readian document—an "Auto-criticism" designed to present "the author's candid notion of what an honest critic would say were he disposed to avoid the minimum alike of praise and blame. . . ."[8] In the guise of "honest critic" Reade begins thus:

"CHRISTIE JOHNSTONE
"A Dramatic Story
The origin of this title appears to be the quantity of pure dialogue in the work.
To those effects in which the drama shines the volume before us makes less pretension than three novels out of four.

Once again the stress on excessive dialogue, to the exclusion of other and more flagrantly melodramatic effects. And his further criticism follows along the same lines. "The author of 'Christie Johnstone,'" he points out, "has not the art of mixing his materials. Hence the compound, with some exceptions is dry and lumpy. This is to be the more regretted as the materials themselves are decidedly good. . . ." What the author needs, he goes on to explain, is "A supple and changeable style . . . but above all, some warmth of imagination: this it is which clothes incidents with those glowing details that make them vivid and interesting. . . !"

While it may seem that Reade is here probing a bit deeper, his words are deceptive unless one bears in mind his addiction to Sensation. For example, in criticizing "the drowned fisherman's scene," he implies that the episode, though made up of good materials, is not handled so as to bring out all possible sentiment and suspense. Yet in point of fact the scene consists of nothing but sentimentality and suspense, culminating in Christie's daring triumph over the village strong man and alcoholic, when she prevents him, by moral and physical force, from entering that den of iniquity, the local pub—thereby saving him "fra the puir mon's enemy, the enemy o'mankind, the cursed, cursed, drink."

If this were an isolated example of Reade's self-criticism, it might be excused on the ground that he had been temporarily misled by Kinglake and Tennyson, who apparently admired Christie's Cambyses' vein. But Reade was equally well pleased with other and even more questionable aspects of the novel—including its impossible climactic action, which he recounts at length, and with undisguised satisfaction:

All Newhaven is watching a swimmer, who, it appears, is in the habit of going out to the roads and back. One spirit, quicker than the rest, compares the time, the tide, and other circumstances, and doubts the swimmer's safety. This is Christie, who throws off her listlessness, and with her brother darts down to the pier, and goes out in a boat amidst the jeers of the others; before, however, she has made her first tack, the whole town has come to her opinion, and it is in front of three thousand spectators that she with difficulty and dexterity saves her lover without discovering his identity, which her brother, who hates him, is anxious to conceal from her.

The feat has been seen by Lord Ipsden and Lady Barbara from the shore; and Mrs. Gatty, the artist's mother, who had learned in the heat of the business that it was her son, has fainted and been carried to Christie Johnstone's house.

Thus a dramatic close is prepared.

Reade's final "thus" underlines what is all too clear: that in the novel as in the play he resorted to the crudest kind of stage directions as a means of working out his melodramatic plot. In the words of Professor E. G. Sutcliffe: "Christie moves forward on stage waves while a well drilled mob shouts encouragement and applause from the front." [9]

IV

The social purpose of the novel Reade also considered good in itself. As "honest critic" he congratulates himself on having a "quick eye for all that is good and clever in the lower classes," on having expressed his observations "covertly and not without plausibility . . ." and on having shown "forbearance" in his arguments. "They who hold his sentiment," he says of himself, "seldom let us go to bed till they have told us that corduroy is virtue, and broadcloth and soap are vice: and we are in some terror lest through hearing this too often we may end our career by believing it." Nevertheless, after stressing all these virtues (plus numerous others), he once again reverts to the author's lack of narrative skill—a lack which he seeks to remedy by having the author "associate himself with one of our authoresses. . . . The pair would produce a novel considerably above the average: something we should read with pleasure and lay aside with delight. . . ." This suggestion harks back to his earlier statements about dramatic collaboration, and his never-ending doubts concerning his powers of invention. The difference is that in his dramatic collaborations he looked to Tom Taylor, a writer of some skill and sophistication, whereas the authoresses he apparently had in mind were of the type now represented in *Queens of the Circulating Library*.

V

However one views this auto-criticism—as a *jeu d'esprit* or as a serious piece of self-analysis—it shows how inadequate, even simple-minded, were Reade's conceptions of narrative art and the creative process, how inept were his specific criticisms and suggested improvements. On the analytic side, all he could do was to measure his own performance, in a most superficial way, against the most naïve Sensation standards. Of his more crucial shortcomings he showed little if any awareness—and that was usually misguided, e.g., his remarks on "warmth of imagination" and "the true oil of Fiction"—though seemingly perceptive—actually tend to reduce imagination to the oil that lubricates the gears of his creaking stage machinery.

Indeed he was so committed to Sensation mechanics that he could neither recognize nor appreciate the more creative aspects of his work—not even those qualities in his realistic presentation of Christie which W. D. Howells praised so highly, and which still hold up remarkably well, in comparison with similar presentations of Dickens and Thackeray. Less timid in sexual matters than these novelists (or for that matter any other novelist of the time) Reade took advantage of the stage traditions governing the treatment of comic and low-life characters to introduce his heroine as a woman of physical as well as moral substance. In the opening scenes, he uncorsets her, literally as well as metaphorically; and if his performance is a trifle self-conscious, not to say bumptious, he at least does not fall into the inverted pornography that too often characterizes such Victorian efforts, most flagrantly perhaps in Thackeray's presentation of Amelia on the eve of Waterloo, when (posing as George) he enters the novel and Amelia's bedroom to give the reader a strip-tease version of his Victorian ideal: "The purple eyelids were fringed and closed, and one round arm, smooth and white, lay outside of the coverlet. Good God! how pure she was. . . ." After this "one round arm," the "noble swell" of Christie's leg appears refreshingly physical—though, as has been pointed out, Reade's ideals of womanhood ultimately obliged him to reduce Christie's physical beauties to the attributes of an ideal pastoral type.

Equally realistic at times, despite the prevailing theatricality of Reade's presentation, are Christie's actions and words—as, for instance, when Ipsden tries to purchase herring from her:

"What is the price?
At this question the poetry died out of Christie Johnstone's face, she gave her companion a rapid look, indiscernible by male eye, and answered,—
"Three a penny sirr; they are no plenty the day," added she, in smooth tones that carried conviction.
(Little liar, they were selling six a penny everywhere.)[10]

Although Reade's interpolated observations may be irritating, Christie's words are realistic enough in themselves—as are those of the widow Rutherford, one of the lesser characters, when Ipsden mentions her troubles:

"Oh! ye need na vex yourself for an auld wife's tears; tears are a blessin', lad, I shall assure ye. Mony's the time I hae prayed for

them, and could na hae them. Sit ye doon! sit ye doon! I'll no let
ye gang fra my door till I hae thankit ye—but gie me time, gie
me time. I canna greet a' the days of the week." [11]

But this anglicized Scots dialect, however brilliant in itself, in no
wise strengthens or deepens the dramatic action: for the most part,
as the above quotation illustrates, it merely imparts a realistic
Scots flavor to the otherwise stock sentiments and reactions of the
dramatis personae.

Likewise brilliant, though even more stagey, are the stylistic
touches through which Reade now and again twists the words and
actions of his otherwise conventional characters into meaningful
juxtaposition. The widow Rutherford stands upon "the high ground
of her low estate"; Ipsden's conversations with Saunders (a comic
counterpart of Dickens' Littimer) are on occasion satirically
succinct:

"Saunders! do you know what Dr. Aberford means by the lower
classes?"
"Perfectly, my lord."
"Are there any about here?"
"I am sorry to say they are everywhere, my lord."
"Get me some" (cigarette).[12]

Saunders, one of the most successful minor characters, not only
talks like a literary annual, he has a three volume novel in the
press: ". . . one of those cerberus-leviathans of fiction, so common
now; incredible as folio to future ages." [13] All too often, however,
these passages of "realism, with divinations and conjectures across
its borders," are merely incidental or ornamental. And even when
they are functional, as in the treatment of Saunders, their sophisticated effects too often eclipse or negate the artless responses
demanded by the narrative action.

The most notable exceptions are the directly autobiographical
scenes, particularly those centering in the Christie-Gatty-Mrs.
Gatty relationship. While these scenes too are basically melodramatic, they are enriched by realistic elements—presumably taken
directly from Reade's own experience—which make for an intensity
analogous to that which Dreiser and Farrell sometimes achieve in
their painfully actualistic scenes. Mrs. Gatty's nagging is strikingly
effective in this respect, not only in substance and psychology but
in style. Of course it must be recognized that she is not an indi-

vidualized mother. She cannot be compared with such a character as, say, Mrs. Bede of *Adam Bede,* despite a number of superficial resemblances between the two. Mrs. Gatty is rather an Oedipal villainess (a stage version of the relentlessly possessive mother who alternately pets and lacerates her son into masochistic submission) and her self-righteous platitudes and stratagems would be simply irritating, were they not at times so close, in their theatricality, to the Oedipal reality—the climactic scene being that in which Mrs. Gatty, using her platitudes like a priest his catechism, forces Gatty to break with Christie:

"Look at me, Charles; at your mother."

"Yes, mother," said he nervously.

"You must part with her, or kill me."

He started from his seat and began to flutter up and down the room. Poor excitable creature! "Part with her!" cried he; "I shall never be a painter if I do. . . . What is an artist without love? How is he to bear up against his disappointments from within, his mortification from without? the great ideas he has and cannot grasp, and all the forms of ignorance that sting him, from stupid insensibility down to clever, shallow criticism?"

.   .   .   .

The old woman paused to let his eloquence evaporate.

The pause chilled him; then gently and slowly, but emphatically, she spoke to him thus:—

"Who has kept you on her small means ever since you were ten years and seven months old?"

"You should know, mother, dear mother."

"Answer me, Charles."

"My mother."

"Who has pinched herself in every earthly thing, to make you an immortal painter, and, above all, a gentleman?"

"My mother."

"Who forgave you the little faults of youth, before you could ask pardon?"

"My mother. O mother, I ask pardon now for all the trouble I ever gave the best, the dearest, the tenderest of mothers."

"Who will go home to Newcastle a broken-hearted woman, with the one hope gone that has kept her up in poverty and sorrow so many weary years, if this goes on?"

"Nobody, I hope."

"Yes, Charles: your mother."

"O, mother; you have been always my best friend."

"And am this day."

"Do not be my worst enemy now: it is for me to obey you, but it is for you to think well before you drive me to despair."

And the poor womanish heart leaned his head on the table, and began to sorrow over his hard fate.

Mrs. Gatty soothed him. "It need not be done all in a moment. It must be done kindly but firmly. I will give you as much time as you like." [14]

The melodramatic intensity of this scene, deriving from the calculated deftness with which Mrs. Gatty wields her pieties, is genuinely expressive. It reveals the features behind the veil of Victorian motherhood, and if the features bear a marked resemblance to Mrs. Reade's, they are still so powerful in their Oedipal grossness that they serve to define not merely Gatty's predicament, and Reade's, but that of nearly all the other Victorian sons and lovers.

VI

But one scene can hardly redeem an entire novel, not even when the novel, in certain of its aspects, compares favorably with those of Thackeray and Dickens. For what avail technical virtues and virtuosities when they are used not to explore but to evade the very realities they are pretending to interpret. Reade could not, as one of his critics advised, express what was in "his own heart": there was too much locked up in it—feelings that he could not contemplate, much less write, without calling into question nearly all the rationalizations on which his emotional balance depended. And this was particularly true where his feelings for his mother were concerned. If he now and then became aware of what it meant to be her son—a querulous, loveless, middle-aged bachelor—he never permitted that awareness to develop into full realization. He could not acknowledge his condition, or its primary cause, even to himself; as for putting such a mother-son relationship directly into fiction, that was, for Reade, literally unthinkable, and therefore unimaginable. For what he could not think, in good round Baconian terms, he dismissed as "cobwebs" spun from "the depths of a penny a liner's inner consciousness."

This is why he could not invent. There was nothing wrong with his imagination. He simply refused to use it through fear of self-revelation, then justified his refusal on principle, maintaining that he wanted truth: the truth of Bacon that was also the truth of Shakespeare and Homer—though it is to be noted that this truth resembles nothing so much as his own grandiose daydreams and their literary counterparts, the "true" romances of Harrison Ainsworth and Samuel Warren. In short he was so caught up in the squirrel cage of his own emotional confusions that it was only in those rare moments when he managed to escape from his notions of self and art that he could, in any creative sense of the word, "write." At other times the most he could do, in fiction as in life, was to fall back upon the time-tried formulas that reproduced his own heroic vision of himself and the world, varying the formulas, as in *Christie Johnstone,* with autobiographical touches, and filling in their outlines with anti-Carlylean and Pre-Raphaelite purpose.

The autobiographical passages, it is true, suggest that, if he had been willing to carry his treatment of the Gatty-Mrs. Gatty-Christie relationships a few steps further, he might conceivably have broken through the stock patterns he had carried over from the original play—perhaps to express poetically or fantastically, after the manner of Dickens or the Brontes, what he could not possibly express openly. But Reade could not see this, nor did he want to see it. He had no use whatsoever for Dickensian fantasy or any other form of indirection which derived from "inner consciousness." He wanted the direct, purposeful truth, and up to a point, the auto-criticism reveals, he thought he had achieved it in *Christie Johnstone.*

CHAPTER VI

The Beginnings of the Great System:

Gold in Fictional Disguise

THE BOOK WAS "Uncle Tom," a story which discusses the largest human topic that ever can arise; for the human race is bisected into black and white. Nowadays a huge subject greatly treated receives justice from the public, and "Uncle Tom" is written in many places with art, in all with red ink and with the biceps muscle.

Great by theme, and great by skill, and greater by the writer's soul, honestly flung into its pages, "Uncle Tom," to the surprise of many that twaddle traditional phrases in reviews and magazines about the art of fiction, and to the surprise of no man who knows anything about the art of fiction, was all the rage. . . .

—CHARLES READE—*It Is Never Too Late To Mend*

✓   ✓   ✓

June 20, 1853—The plan I propose to myself in writing stories will, I see, cost me undeniable labor. I propose never to guess where I can know . . . My story must cross the water to Australia, and plunge after that into a gold mine. To be consistent with myself, I ought to cross-examine at the very least a dozen men that have farmed, dug, or robbed in that land. If I can get hold of two or three that have really been in it, I think I could win the public ear by these means. Failing these I must read books and letters, and do the best I can. Such is the mechanism of a novel by Charles Reade. . . . If I can work the above great system, there is enough of me to make one of the writers of the day; without it, No, No.

—CHARLES READE—*Diary*

✓   ✓   ✓

Reade had high hopes for *Christie Johnstone*—even higher hopes than for *Peg Woffington*—and when, despite favorable reviews, it failed to catch the public fancy, he was forced to reconsider his efforts and prospects. He knew that, in writing *Christie* and *Peg* he had strained his powers of invention to the utmost; moreover, he knew that in the process, he had, in a sense, written himself out; that his future efforts, so long as he followed along the same lines, would be as brief and thin—and therefore as un-successful—as his first two novels. It was this prospect which drove him frantic. He was almost forty, and if he was going to become "one of the writers of the day" it had to be soon. He could not afford another *succès d'estime;* his next novel had to be a "hit." Hence the desperateness of his efforts to find a subject and to improve his narrative techniques—through collaboration or any other means that would enable him "to command the popular ear."

It was at this point, while he was still casting about for a popular subject, that he received the full impact of *Uncle Tom's Cabin.* Upon its first appearance this novel was so widely read that, in Reade's own words, "Not to have read it was like not to have read 'The Times' for a week." [1] And this was only the begin-ning. "Within the twelve months of its first appearance," accord-ing to Sampson Low, "no less than eighteen different houses in London were engaged in supplying the demand that had set in. The total number of editions was forty . . . the aggregate number circulated in Great Britain and her colonies exceeded one million and a half. It was read everywhere, by all classes of people. . . . The pity, distress, and soulfelt indignation in which it had been written, were by it transferred to the minds and consciences of its readers, and the antagonism it everywhere engendered, threw the social life . . . into angry effervescence through all its strata." [2] Furthermore the dramatic adaptations were almost as successful as the novel itself. "During 1852," Winton Tolles has noted, "every suburban theatre, as well as the Olympic and the Adelphi in the West End, produced a version of the American novel." [3] In fact the Adelphi version, which was prepared by Mark Lemon and Tom Taylor, was produced on November 29, 1853, just nine days after *Masks and Faces.*

Reade's comments leave no doubt that he too was mightily impressed. *Uncle Tom* was, he declared, "great by theme, and great by skill, and greater still by a writer's soul honestly flung into its pages . . ." which were "written in many places with art, in all with red ink and with the biceps muscle." In other words *Uncle Tom* embodied Reade's own fictional ideas, in everything from its "soul" to its "success." And when Mrs. Stowe published *A Key to Uncle Tom's Cabin,* frankly proclaiming the factual basis of the novel, he was quick to see that the greatness of *Uncle Tom* was a greatness that he himself might duplicate—and without resorting to collaboration, or straining his mind in a vain effort to invent. For *The Key* showed him that Mrs. Stowe's powers of imagination were as feeble as his own, that the greatness of *Uncle Tom* derived not from her inner consciousness, but from her mass of Baconian facts, which she had treated in accordance with his own theories of purposeful documentation. He too had flung his "soul" (by which he apparently meant "soulfelt indignation") into the anti-Carlylean passages of *Christie Johnstone;* and Mrs. Stowe's example showed him that he must go still further in this direction: to treat a bigger and more immediate "theme," with more "skill," by means of more "facts," derived from a more thorough and systematic application of his own Baconian and Keanian and Pre-Raphaelite theories. In this way he could fill three volumes with the blood-red ink of his humanitarian "purpose"—or "soul"—and thus duplicate the greatness, and perhaps the success of *Uncle Tom.*

And that, it would appear, is what Reade set out to do. He found a subject comparable to Mrs. Stowe's in the unused sections of his play *Gold:* "Mem: If I ever write a novel on '*Gold,*' introduce a Jew and a learned Divine (Chaplain of Tom Robinson's gaol)." Then using Mrs. Stowe's *Key* as a model—in fact he later wrote *A Key to It Is Never Too Late To Mend,* obviously patterned after Mrs. Stowe's[4]—he formulated his own theory of documentation, which he set down in outline form in his *Diary:*

> June 20.—The plan I propose to myself in writing stories will, I see, cost me undeniable labor. I propose never to guess where I can know. For instance, Tom Robinson is in gaol. I have therefore been to Oxford Gaol and visited every inch, and shall do the same at Reading. Having also collected material in Durham Gaol, whatever I write about Tom Robinson's gaol will therefore carry (I hope) a physical exterior of truth. . . .
>
> One of my characters is a Jew—an Oriental Jew. It will be his fate to fall into argument not only with Susan Merton, but with the Chaplain of my gaol. It will be my business to show what is in the head and in the heart of a modern Jew. This entails the reading of at least eight considerable volumes; but those eight volumes read will make my Jew a Truth, please God, instead of a Lie.
>
> My story must cross the water to Australia, and plunge after that into a gold mine. To be consistent with myself, I ought to cross-examine at the very least a dozen men that have farmed, dug,

or robbed in that land. . . . Such is the mechanism of a novel by Charles Reade. . . .

Much has been made of this statement, on the ground that it marks a turning-point in Reade's career. Actually, however, it is not so much a turning-point as a culmination. Reade, it has been shown, had been moving towards such a "system" of documentation since the earliest years of his apprenticeship, had in fact made considerable use of documentary techniques in his early plays and novels. And with the example of Kean, the Pre-Raphaelites, and Mrs. Stowe immediately before him, to prove that facts not imagination provided the key to greatness and success, he saw no reason why he should not develop the full potential of their techniques. If facts equalled truth, then, the more facts the better, and the way to achieve ultimate truth, in literature as in other matters, was through a systematic application of the Baconian method. Hence his "great system," which is his *Novum Organum* for the writing of stories.

II

About this system, as system, Reade had no doubts whatsoever. The only question in his mind was whether or not he was equal to its demands. After formulating his new plans *(Diary,* June 20) he declared: "I know my system is right; but unfortunately there are few men so little fitted as myself to work this system. A great capacity for labor is the first essential. Now I have a singularly small capacity for acquisitive labor. A patient, indomitable spirit the second. Here I fail miserably. A stout heart the third. My heart is womanish. A vast memory the fourth. My memory is not worth a dump. Now, I know exactly what I am worth. If I can work the above great system, there is enough of me to make one of the writers of the day; without it, No, No."

For Reade this is a remarkably accurate self-estimate. Eventually, as the Notebooks testify, he so far overcame these limitations that his labors in connection with the system, even the most tedious, became a downright joy. But not in the beginning. In a letter to Mrs. Baylis, after expressing his fear that *Christie Johnstone* would be "no fatter a volume than *Peg Woff* . . . ," he went on to say: "My two vols. will be a much heavier blow—at least I think so—but Lord, if you knew the trouble and bother of writing a solid work upon my present plan, i.e., verifying everything I say or describe! To write my two vols. I must read twenty, and hunt up men as well as books." [5] Reade apparently continued in this mood, doing very little work, until his visit to Reading Gaol (*Diary* July 8, 10, 17), which stirred his sense of the odd ("There was one gaol-bird reading Hebrew") and the "awful" ("Went to hear the assize sermon and see the judges. Awful to behold. Going to the criminal court tomorrow. . . ."). At this point Reade was certainly not forcing himself. Yet as soon as he had completed his investigation at Reading (July 17) and was faced with the necessity of completing his more tedious researches, he once again reverted to his old listlessness and self-commiseration: "It doesn't become me to complain of others. Look at myself. Can't write 'Never Too Late To Mend,' . . . ."

In fact Reade accomplished so little during the summer—apart from the data he collected at Reading—that on August 22 he felt obliged to restate his plans and renew his resolutions:

> Aug. 22, London.—Tom Taylor has made me over his chambers. They are in a healthier part than Covent Garden, and I feel as if I could set to work. My plans: I will work hard at my tale of 'Gold,' whether under that title or another. I will hunt up two men who have lived in Australia, and are very communicative; from them I will get real warm facts. I will visit all the London prisons, and get warm facts from them for the Robinson business. . . . I will play steadily for hits. I will not be worse than the public—or not too much so. I will write better than 'Christie Johnstone.' The story there is dry and husky. I will live moderately. I will take decisive measures for being out of bed at eight.

While it seems unlikely that Reade lived up to his final resolution, he did live moderately, as always; and, with lapses and grumblings, he did continue his researches, which were considerably simplified, on the prison side, by the appearance of an article in the *Times* (September 12, 1853) on atrocities in Birmingham Gaol.

III

In the meantime Reade had already begun work on the novel itself, presumably on the early domestic chapters, set in Berkshire, since he no doubt felt that in these chapters he could dispense with the system, and write from personal knowledge. As the son of Squire and Mrs. Reade, he had grown up among the Berkshire farm-folk, and since then, through his frequent visits to Ipsden, had developed a first-hand knowledge of their habits, ways, and manners of speech.

Confident in this knowledge, he lost no time in setting about the actual writing. On June 21, the day after he first outlined his great system, he noted in his *Diary:* "Today I sat out upon the lawn and scribbled for six hours. . . ." And he continued to scribble, the *Diary* reveals, even while he was conducting his investigations at Reading Gaol; indeed he wrote one passage so powerful that he himself was overcome by it—a reaction which he duly recorded in the *Diary* (July 10), following his remarks on the assize sermon and the criminal court: "I made myself cry to-day writing a bit of my story, 'Never Too Late To Mend.' Is that a good sign? Laura Seymour says I have pathos. I suspect I shall be the only one to snivel."

Although it is impossible to be certain—there are so many tearful bits—the one Reade was almost certainly referring to is that in which George, the hero, departs for Australia. In brief the situation is this: George, an upright and independent yet poor young farmer, has been forced into debt by Meadows, the villain, who is of course trying to win George's sweetheart, by fair means or foul. George has worked hard to pay off the mortgage, but to no avail, and as a last resort has decided to seek his fortune in Australia, leaving his sweetheart, Susan, at the mercy of the villainous Meadows, save for what protection George's brother, William, can give her. (William too had been in love with Susan, though he now looked upon her with a "purified heart"—achieved when George, sensing his errant feelings, took him on a long walk to their mother's grave.) As the scene opens, George is on the point of departing, and the whole neighborhood has gathered to see him off:

"And now," faltered George, "I feel strong enough to go, and I'll go."

He looked round at all the familiar objects he was leaving, as if to bid them farewell. . . .

"Good-by little village church, where I went to church man and boy; good-by churchyard where my mother lies; there will be no church-bells, Susan, where I am going; no Sunday bells to remind me of my soul and home. . . . God help me! Oh, God help me! What *shall* I do? what *shall* I do?" And the stout heart gave way, and George Fielding covered his face with his hands, and burst out sobbing and crying.

[135]

Susan flung her arms round his neck—"O George, my pride is all gone; don't go, don't think to go; have pity on us both, and don't go." And she clung to him—her bonnet fallen off, her hair dishevelled—and they sobbed and wept in one another's arms.

Meadows writhed with the jealous anguish this sad sight gave him, and at that moment he could have cursed the whole creation. He tried to fly, but he was rooted to the spot. He leaned sick as death against the palings.

George and Susan cried together, and then they wiped one another's eyes like simple country folk with one pocket-handkerchief; and then they kissed one another in turn, and made each other's tears flow fast again; and again wiped one another's eyes with one handkerchief.

Meadows gripped the palings convulsively—hell was in his heart.

"Poor souls, God help them!" said William to himself in his purified heart. . . .

George was the first to recover himself. "Shame upon me!" he cried; he drew Susan to his bosom, and pressed a long, burning kiss upon her brow.

And now all felt the wrench was coming. George, with a wild half-terrified look, signalled William to come to him.

"Help me, Will! you see I have no more manhood than a girl."

Susan instinctively trembled. George once more pressed his lips to her, as if they would grow there. William took her hand. She trembled more and more.

"Take my hand; take your brother's hand, my poor lass," said he.

She trembled violently; and then George gave a cry that seemed to tear his heart, and darted from them in a moment.

Poor Susan uttered more than one despairing scream, and stretched out both her hands for George. He did not see her, for he dared not look back.

"Bob, loose the dog," muttered William hastily, in a broken voice.

The dog was loosed, and ran after George, who, he thought, was only going for a walk. Susan was sinking pale and helpless, upon her brother's bosom.

"Pray, sister," said gentle William; "pray, sister, as I must."

A faint shiver was all the answer; her senses had almost left her.

When George was a little way up the hill, something ran suddenly against his legs—he started—it was Carlo. He turned, and lifted up his hands to heaven; and William could see that George was blessing him for this. Carlo was more than a dog to poor George at that cruel moment. Soon after that, George and Carlo reached the crown of the hill. George's figure stood alone a moment between them and the sky. He was seen to take his hat off, and raise his hands once more to heaven, whilst he looked down upon all he loved and left; and then he turned his sorrowful face again towards that distant land—and they saw him no more.[6]

And this, it must be understood, is a cut version; in its entirety the scene is drawn out to twice this length, while George listens to the church-bells, says good-bye to his aged father, etc., etc. That Reade could put together such an assortment of transpontine cliches, then weep over them, is not too surprising, not even when one comes to realize that he took the entire scene directly from his play *Gold*. After all, the cliches were none the worse for being repeated, since to Reade they represented one phase of his never-ending daydream of lamented departure and triumphant return, first expressed fictionally in *Propria Quae Maribus*. Nor is it surprising that, in form, the scene follows *Gold* line for line, word for word—with only the most trifling and obvious exceptions, such as the omission of "Act-Drop" at the end. He considered *Gold* a great drama, and in so far as he could use it without change, he did so, just as he had used *Masks and Faces* in writing *Peg Woffington*.

The first three chapters of the novel, which introduce the leading characters and establish the main lines of the plot, are little more than a direct transcription of *Gold*, Act I, filled out with cancelled materials from the original manuscript of his play, e.g., in one scene (not included in the printed play) Robinson, the thief, has just been handcuffed, and is being taken to jail, when two children appear:

Just then a little boy and girl, who had been peering about mighty curious, took courage, and approached hand in hand. The girl was the speaker, as a matter of course;

"*Farmer Fielding*," said she, courtesying, a mode of reverence which was instantly copied by the boy, "*we are come to see the thief; they say you have caught one—oh, dear!* (and her bright little countenance was overcast) *I couldn't have told it from a man!*"

The words italicized are taken verbatim from Reade's original manuscript (Act I, pt. 2, p. 12),[7] indicating that he merely transcribed the dialogue, then added a few words of descriptive commentary designed to give the reader a picture of how the action might take place on the stage.

One can only wonder why this episode, with its stagey cuteness, was not included in the play as printed and acted. At least it would have been more excusable on the stage—as would a number of the other cancelled bits from the manuscript that he stuffed directly into the novel, e.g., the solid page of dialogue between Meadows and Merton (*NTLTM*, pp. 10-11); likewise the long rhetorical exchanges between Levi and Meadows which lead up to Levi's melodramatic curse. Levi's references to Samson, David and Goliath, and the oppressors of the Jews, again taken verbatim from the manuscript, not only double the length of the corresponding speech in the printed play but also inflate the rhetoric to the point of absurdity—though Reade declared "that the whole thing was like epic poetry," and, drawing upon the manuscript once again, inflated "the respectable western brute's answer" to like proportions: *"What! you quote Scripture, eh? I thought you did not believe in that. Hear t'other side. Abraham and Lot couldn't live in the same place, because they both kept sheep, and we can't, because we fleece 'em. So Abraham gave Lot warning as I give it you. And as for dying on my premises, if you like to hang yourself before next Lady-day I give you leave,* but after Lady-day no more Jewish dogs shall die in my house nor be buried *for manure* in my garden." The words italicized (which are those taken directly from the manuscript but not included in the printed play) tend to confirm what the previous quotations have suggested: that the effect of Reade's additions from the manuscript is to make the novel even more flagrantly melodramatic than the printed play.

Certainly there can be no doubt as to this effect when, as was his common practice, Reade further enhanced his additions with poetically descriptive commentaries such as the following, which is intended to delineate Levi's reaction to Meadows' speech (quoted above): "Black lightning poured from the old Jew's eyes, and his pent-up wrath burst like lava from an angry mountain." Levi duly vents his epic wrath in a curse; then, in the midst of the actual cursing, just after Levi has said, "I spit upon ye, and I curse ye. Be accursed!" Reade breaks in with another of his poetic similes: "And flinging up his hands like St. Paul at Lystra he rose to double his height, and towered at his insulter with a sudden Eastern fury. . . ." The metaphorical language, reminiscent of *The Actors' Hand-Book*, is clearly intended to picture Levi as he appeared on the stage, or, more accurately, the

way Reade would have liked to see him appear on the stage—
if only he had been able to find a stage-manager and actors willing
to carry out his instructions to the letter. These passages, in fact
the entire first three chapters, may therefore be described as his
ideal version of *Gold* Act I—in so far as he could embody this ideal
version in words. Everything belonging to Surrey melodrama is
there—with Reade shouting poetry as well as directions from the
wings, and now and then descending into the pit to make sure
that the audience is seeing, and, what is more, appreciating, all
the fine things taking place on his fictional stage. For the reader,
who in Reade's fictional scheme is the audience, there is consequently no escape from the rant and fustian: in reading the play
one can, within limits, visualize actions and scenes in the light of
his own imagination, but in reading the novel that is simply not
possible, since Reade is always there to prod and to point, and,
most disturbing of all, to magnify his already magniloquent
language.

IV

Reade did not copy *Gold* quite so closely in the remaining
chapters of the domestic section. For one thing he was obliged to
extend the action of the play (through the introduction of new
characters and scenes) in order to prepare the way for his new
section on prisons. Yet these new extensions are so like the old
borrowings that they have little if any significance—except as they
show that, contrary to the views expressed by a number of critics,
the shortcomings in this section of the novel cannot be attributed
to his reliance on the play. Whether Reade was copying *Gold* or
creating a new chapter expressly for the novel he still wrote in the
same way—invoking the epic tradition, after the manner of Fielding, to justify his emphasis on action, as presented through dramatic techniques, in contrast to the modern emphasis on character, as presented through microscopic techniques. "The people
of our tale," he acknowledged, "were like men walking together
in a coppice; they had but glimpses of each others minds." The
one exception was Isaac Levi, to whom the motives of the other
characters "were a little human chart, spread out flat before
him. . . ."[8] And that is necessarily the way they appear in the
novel, since Levi is Reade's dramatic spokesman, and the only
motives he can perceive are those which tend to complicate the
action and build up suspense.

Yet Reade also intended that Levi's revelations should cut deeper. This is why he was at such pains to endow Levi with an Eastern version of his own wisdom: "For near half a century Isaac Levi had read that marvellous page of nature written on black, white, and red parchments, and called "Man . . . ," and his reading had taught him "that the heads of human tribes differ more than their hearts . . . passions and the heart he had found intelligible, and much the same from Indus to the Pole. . . ." As a consequence "he penetrated more than one disguise of manner . . . above all his intelligence bored like a centre-bit into the deep-heart of his enemy Meadows," [9] there to discover the source of his weakness and consequent villainy, viz., his passion for Susan, which causes him to writhe with Othello-like jealousy, and resort to Iago-like machinations in his efforts to win her, by "fair means or foul." Thus Reade (via Levi and dramatic action) sought to duplicate in fiction the mode of characterization that, as he understood it, was the mode of the greatest writers from Homer through Shakespeare. And by his own standards he succeeded. If his depths of "the passions and the heart" turned out, quite conveniently, to be much the same as those which prevailed on the melodramatic stage, that was because the passions and the heart were much the same, not only from Indus to the Pole, but from Shakespeare to Boucicault. As for the melodramatic coloring which resulted from this dramatic mode of characterization—Levi's "black, white, and red"—such coloring was, to Reade's way of thinking, the essence of art. Since Meadows was a black-hearted villain in his passion for Susan, the blacker he could be painted the better.

Reade's main concern in the novel was consequently to heighten his already melodramatic colors—to make Meadows' double-dyed villainy still blacker, Susan's double distilled purity still whiter. To this end he drew upon every rhetorical device known to the trade, including, in the case of Susan, a chapter-length sermon on "trouble" which typifies his efforts to bolster up his dramatic action through editorial comment:

CHAPTER IV

'The world is full of trouble.'
While we are young we do not see how true this ancient homely saying is.

[140]

A uniquely hopeless beginning, yet the lines which follow strike a different note: "That wonderful dramatic prologue, the first chapter of Job, is but a great condensation of the sorrows that fall like hail upon many a mortal house. Job's black day, like the day of the poetic prophets—the true *sacri vates* of the ancient world— is a type of a year—a bitter, human year." [10] In contrast to the emptiness of the biblical references quoted earlier, these lines, deriving from Reade's own black days, express genuine feeling with a directness that is at least rhetorically effective. Yet however genuine the expression it remains isolated and autobiographical; the minute Reade begins to connect Job's sorrows with those of George Fielding and Susan Merton he perforce begins to sentimentalize them, and his language once again becomes Tupperishly poetic: "It is terrible how quickly a human landscape all gilded meadow, silver river, and blue sky can cloud and darken." [11]

Reade continued on in this vein, comparing George to an oak tree buffetted by an "impalpable antagonist" (viz., the wind), and in general trying, with every rhetorical device he could muster, to give some sense of poignancy and significance to the plight of his hero and heroine, "two loving hearts . . . torn bleeding asunder." But he would not, he made it clear, resort to the microscopic techniques that certain novelists employed. When Susan finally "crept away . . . to her own room" he drew back: "What she suffered in that room the first month after George's departure I could detail perhaps as well as any man living; but I will not; there is a degree of anguish one shrinks from intruding upon too familiarly in person: and even on paper the microscope should spare sometimes these beatings of the bared heart." It was enough, he explained, to indicate her state "by and by . . . after time, and religion, and good habits had begun to struggle . . . against the tide of sorrow." [12] This is another example of Reade's extraordinary powers of rationalization. To detail "the beatings of the bared heart," Susan's or any other character's, he would have had to bare his own—and that, as *Christie Johnstone* revealed, he could not do. Hence his paranoiac bravado, his elaborately self-righteous appeals to religion and good habits, designed to show that, in eschewing close analysis, he was not covering up his own weakness but acting upon the highest moral-aesthetic principles—as exemplified in his concluding lines. "Let us," he admonished, "draw gently back and leave her, for she is bowed to the earth—fallen on her knees, her head buried in the curtains of her bed; dark, faint, and leaden, on the borders of despair—a word often lightly used through ignorance. Heaven keep us all from a single hour here or hereafter of the thing the word stands for; and Heaven comfort all true and loving hearts that read me, when their turn shall come to drain the bitter cup like Susan Merton."

Of course Reade could cite all kinds of precedent for concluding his sermon in this way. In line with their theory that the novel was but a play cast in narrative form the Sensation novelists relied heavily on such rhetorically embroidered stage pictures, often using them, as in the present instance, to provide a touching finale corresponding to a dramatic curtain. Nor was this merely a Sensation practice. In ending a chapter of *The Caxtons*, subtitled "A Family Story" Bulwer Lytton's appeals to the reader are if anything less excusable. "Happy those who are strange to that indescribable silent bustle which the sick-room at times presents . . ." he observes, after which he lists, with proper rhetorical embellishments, everything from ". . . the dark blood flowing—flowing . . ." to the "lull of the low whispers, the incoherent voice of the sufferer—babbling, perhaps, of green fields . . . while your hearts are breaking. . . ." Then, after listing every cliche connected with the sick room, he makes a simple request of the reader: "Picture all this . . ." followed by more cliches apropos of the patient's promised recovery, ending with "your gushing tears, your low 'Thank God! thank God!'" Thackeray too, despite his parody of the Sensation novelists, was given to the same practice; in fact Reade's stage picture is in some respects similar to Thackeray's more elaborate picture of Becky, after Rawdon has returned from prison to find her with Lord Steyne; furthermore, the similarity extends to Thackeray's moral commentary, with its appeal to Heaven and his readers' "true and loving hearts." But these likenesses in no sense vindicate Reade. Judged by serious literary standards such finales are indefensible—whether written by Lytton, Thackeray, or Reade—for the very good reason that, like modern soap opera, they seek to substitute the reader's experience (conceived as stock responses) for the writer's art.

And the same criticism applies to every aspect of this section, which may be finally described as *Gold*, plus cancelled passages from the original manuscript of the play, plus narrative additions designed to picture the dramatic action as on a stage, and still other narrative additions—usually cast in the form of commentary—designed to throw a moral-aesthetic halo around the pictures presented.

V

In writing the Australian section (also based on *Gold*) Reade followed a similar mode of composition—to which, in keeping with his original plans for the novel, he superadded the documentation of his "great system." One of Reade's earliest efforts to apply the system, as system, it would appear, was in connection with Levi, the Resourceful Hero of both the domestic and Australian sections of the novel: "June 14, 1853, Magd. Coll. . . . The very first work on modern Judaism I took up showed me just what I had calculated on in coming here, that the Jews are a people of whom we know nothing, and who know nothing about the Christian religion. Here is one of those rich veins with which a hit is to be made. If I had but the patience to read, I could write the subject I know, when I had the facts." Despite the tentativeness of this statement, Reade was in the process of committing himself to the system, and when he took the final step, in his statement of June 20, he reiterated his plans for Levi with his usual positiveness: "One of my characters is a Jew—an Oriental Jew. . . . It will be my business to show what is in the head and in the heart of a modern Jew. This entails the reading of at least eight considerable volumes; but those eight volumes will make my Jew a Truth, please God, instead of a Lie."

By implication these entries deny the Levi of *Gold*. Reade writes as if he had forgotten about his dramatic Jew, as if he intended to create the Oriental Jew of the novel from the whole cloth of his "eight considerable volumes." But if that was his intention he quickly abandoned it to fall back upon his routine methods of adaptation, transferring the Levi of *Gold* directly to the novel, and using the "eight considerable volumes" (or however many he read) only to provide corrections in detail, e.g., the Levi of the play is called "old sixty per cent," the Levi of the novel "old thirty per cent." Apart from such piddling details, there is no change, merely extension plus rhetorical inflation, which, as previous quotation has shown, tends to make the Levi of the novel more flagrantly melodramatic than his stage counterpart.

It is only fair to add, however, that at least one modern commentator has expressed a contradictory opinion. Montagu Frank Modder, in his *The Jew in the Literature of England* (1939), not only praises Reade's documentary realism (comparing it to Zola's) but also points out that his presentation of the Jewish moneylender is "free from the sort of unpleasant caricature that makes so many portraits of the Jew repulsive." According to Modder: "Isaac Levi's righteousness in business transactions, his active benevolence towards those whom he can serve without hurting his own interests, the grave and lofty tones of his rebukes to foolish wrong-doing, his faith in the destinies of his people—all these aptly combine to make him more real than any of the superb heroes of Disraeli. Keenly resentful of injury, astute, able and patient, the Jewish money-lender follows his long-cherished revenge with terrible ingenuity and persistency; and yet, at the end of the narrative, we see that Isaac Levi can be softened towards a fallen foe who asks of him justice tempered with mercy. In the final scene, there is a certain grandeur, a sort of scriptural majesty about Isaac Levi. . . . The effect of Charles Reade's novel is in the direction of fair and just judgment of the people to which Isaac Levi belongs." [13] This final statement is true enough, as are Modder's other sociological observations; but in his criticism he has separated content from form, fact from expression, and as a consequence has mistaken aims and methods for accomplishments. Although Reade, turning the Shylock tradition upside down, has made his Jew a hero, instead of a villain like Fagin, this reversal merely serves to make Levi a pleasant rather than an unpleasant caricature—a distinction that has little if anything to do with truth or realism. Levi's sentiments at the end of the novel (when he removes his curse) may be fine, as sentiments, but the scene itself is arrant melodrama—of a piece with the scene (previously quoted) in which he does the cursing.

Reade also applied the great system in creating Jacky, the Australian aborigine, and since Jacky does not appear in *Gold* (except as one of several "Australian Blacks") it would seem that, in this one instance, he constructed his character entirely from fact—without reference to a dramatic original. Perhaps, among his "some thirty books" on Australia, he found an account of a particular aborigine which provided him with a factual original, though, in the light of the available evidence, it seems more likely that he pieced together his own composite from factual odds and ends such as those included in G. C. Mundy's *Our Antipodes*.[14] "The swimming had been good," Mundy relates (I, 386-7), "until November, 1849, when a school of sharks appeared . . . early in December a poor man swimming near the Fig-tree was attacked by a huge shark so near the bathing place that another person repeatedly struck the fish with a boat-hook, thereby forcing it to release its victim. . . ." Continuing his discussion of sharks (I, 390) Mundy adds: "A smart blow a few inches above the snout is more instantly fatal than the deepest stab"—an explanation which he enlarges upon a bit later, in describing the tiger shark: "His broad back is spotted over with Leopard-like marks; the belly is of yellowish white . . . neither lance nor gaff will penetrate his tough hide, but a blow on the head with an axe proves instantly fatal." And on the very next page (I, 392-3), though in another connection, he introduces "a Black spearing the rock-cod and groper. . . . The figure of this man poised motionless on a pedestal of rock, with his spear ready to strike, the waves dashing up to his feet, was a subject for a bronze statue."

From these facts, as brought together by Mundy, Reade may well have derived the idea for the scene in which he introduces Jacky.[15] The scene opens with George Fielding on shore, lost in the admiration of "a single savage . . . his lithe sinewy form . . . the grace and rapidity with which he urged his gossamer bark along." Following this picture, which corresponds to Mundy's statuesque portrait of the noble savage, Reade turns to heavy-handed theatrical slapstick: "a mosquito flew into blackee's nortrils, which were much larger and more inviting—to a gnat—than ours. The aboriginal sneezed, and over went the ancestral boat." Then, reverting to his original mood and point-of-view, he gives a full account of the noble savage's encounter with the sea-tiger, which would have been fatal but for George Fielding, who "darted up a little bed of rock elevated about a yard above the shore," and "with one foot advanced and his arm high in the air," proceeded to stone the monster—to no avail until the shark, having momentarily lost sight of its prey, "reared his huge head out of the water a moment to look forth; then George Fielding, grinding his teeth with fury, flung his heavy stone with tremendous force at the creature's cruel eye. The heavy stone missed the eye by an inch or two, but it struck the fish on the nose and teeth with a force that would have felled a bullock. 'Greesh!' went the sea-tiger's flesh and teeth, and the blood squirted in a circle.

Down went the shark like a lump of lead, literally felled by the crashing stroke."

With the exception of the slapstick every single point in the scene corresponds to Mundy's facts. Yet Reade has so selected and compressed and arranged and embroidered the facts (which in Mundy are disparate, and scattered through seven pages) that the scene itself is totally incredible. Through a series of like scenes (every action involving Jacky is curious, comic or sensational) Reade builds up a composite character who is alternately a noble savage and a comic black. Loyal, courageous, and, in his own element at least, intelligent, Jacky nevertheless lacks the white man's sense and sensibility, which makes him, when confronted with the white man's values and ways of life, stupid to the point of being comical—as evidenced by his dislike for work, his belief in his own Gods, and, more specifically, his actions after George Fielding's departure. Left alone on the farm, he forgets all that George has taught him, and with his fellow tribesmen reduces everything about the farm to a shambles: "They slept on the lee side of the house, warmed at night by the chairs and tables, etc., which they lighted . . ." until "one fine morning, without the slightest warning, whir-r-r they all went off to the woods, Jacky and all, and never returned. . . ." [16]

No doubt Reade could cite factual precedent for Jacky's ineptness and final return to the woods, just as he could for Jacky's battle with the shark and other such remarkable adventures, e.g., one of the most unlikely incidents in the entire novel, the discovery of the huge gold nugget, is a close rendering of the account which appeared in a Bathurst newspaper and was reprinted in a number of books on Australia. But such examples in no sense justify Reade's Baconian pretensions, since a glance through his possible sources will show that he chose only the most sensational facts, and combined them, not according to their consistency or typicality (as revealed by such authorities as T. L. Mitchell and John Edward Eyre)[17] but according to the popular conception of a black savage which prevailed on the English stage. The textual evidence on this point, clear enough in the novel, cannot be mistaken in the play he later wrote from the novel, for in the play (*It's Never Too Late To Mend*, 1865) Jacky not only acts like a stage darky with a boomerang, he actually speaks a dialect resembling that of the Southern Negro.

Reade's aborigine is therefore as lurid a caricature as his Jew—

and for essentially the same reasons. So long as he accommodated his facts to his melodramatic preconceptions, it mattered little whether he began with the facts, as in creating Jacky, or merely added the facts to a character he had taken over from *Gold*, as in creating Levi. The final result was the same in both instances, viz., conventionalized stage types togged out in factually correct dress and manners.

Nor can Reade be excused on the ground that he intended Jacky and Levi to be vehicles of Sensation and nothing more. As they appear in the novel, that is all they are, but that is not the way he intended them to appear—nor is it the way he thought they did appear. As he saw his Jew and aborigine they completely vindicated his documentary system: indeed they were so true and original that they would live for all time. In the novel, after concluding his sketch of Jacky, he asseverates: "In a few years the Australian savage will breathe only in these pages." And years later, when Boucicault (in a letter) advised him to eliminate Jacky and the Jew from his play *It's Never Too Late To Mend*, he wrote on the envelope: "Aha! old Fox, they will outlive thee and me." [18]

VI

Little need be said of the minor characters in this section, since with a few insignificant exceptions Reade transferred them bodily from *Gold* and upholstered them in the same way he did Levi. A typical example is Jem, a nebulous "tough" in the play whom Reade enlarged to fictional proportions through the addition of factual details appropriate to an Australian outlaw. Reade's prime object, it would seem, was to establish Jem as a realistic criminal type who could act as Crawley's agent in crime, and thus put into effect the villainous plans of Meadows on which (following *Gold*) the entire action turns. And up to a point Reade succeeded, not only with Jem, but with his other minor characters. Though still *dramatis personae*, the realism of their outward characteristics at times gives them the appearance of being types endemic to "the diggings," and therefore capable of the otherwise inexplicable robberies, etc. which, again following *Gold*, the plot demands that they perform.

Apart from their plot functions, however, these characters have little if any significance: they are but figures in the scenic tableaux that Reade transferred directly from *Gold* to the novel, then

enlarged by means of the great system—as in the following description of sunrise at the diggings: ". . . the pinnacles of rock glowed
burnished gold—nature that had crept from gloom to pallor, burst
from pallor to light and life and burning color—the great sun's
forehead came with one gallant stride into the sky—and it was
day." [19] To this poetic description, taken verbatim from his stage
directions in *Gold* (p. 33), Reade added a long series of phono-
graphic reproductions of bird songs cribbed from William Howitt's
Land, Labour, and Gold, e.g., Howitt describes a thrush that seems
to say, "'Where's your bacca-box, your box, your box?' And then
this cry as rapidly changes into a jovial, rollicking note of 'Gy-
roc-de-doc, roc-de-doc; cheboc! cheboc!'"—a description which
Reade, in the novel, reproduces almost word for word: "Where
is your bacca-box! your box! your box! then before anyone could
answer, in a tone that said devil may care where the box is or anything else, gyroc de doc! gyroc de doc! roc de doc! cheboc
cheboc! . . ." [20]

It was through such factual details as this that Reade hoped
to validate his picture of life in Australia—and Howitt, he later
acknowledged, provided him with an ideal source:

> . . . To avoid describing Hyde Park, and calling it Australia, I read
> some thirty books about that country; but yours was infinitely the
> best. In reading you I found I was in the hands of a man who
> had really been there, and had seen things with his own eyes, and
> judged them with his own judgement, and, rarer art still, could
> paint them to the life. Your vivid scenes took hold of me; and your
> colours are the charm of many of my best pages. I could not tell
> you all my obligations; but some of them I can. You restored my
> faith in nature. A pack of noodles had been out there, and came
> home, and told us the air had no perfume, and the birds no song.
> The real fact is, that there have not yet been in Australia two
> centuries of poets to tell people what to hear and what to smell.
> You extinguished that piece of cant. You smelt the land like cow-
> slips ninety miles off; and you not only heard the birds, but
> described the song and note of each with a precision of detail
> that were invaluable. That passage of yours was a nugget.
> I made use of it in a full description of the rising sun; and it
> is, to my fancy, the light of my whole picture. I had from you,
> too, the snow-storm,—the flakes as large as the palm of your hand,
> and the great branches of trees rent from the stems with reports
> like cannon, by the weight of superincumbent snow.
> Then, in the details of digging, it was you who told me the

furtive diggers were discovered by the stream coming down dis-coloured.

Item—the diggers steeped in cold water from the waist down-wards, yet steaming with perspiration from the waist upwards. Two out of three comic advertisements in the mine are also from you.

Adde huc—the thunder of the cradles, the bottles sown broad-cast over the land, with other happy touches of the sort, and one divinely felicitous phrase,—"the sentences measled with oaths and indelicate expressions." In short, I have taken from you far more than I could have taken with decency if our two works had not been heterogeneous. As it is, I hope you are too candid and too good-natured to grudge me, who can never hope to see that wonderful land, a few colours from your palette. A traveller with a painter's eye is a rarity. He must make up his mind to teach the artists of the pen as well as the public. . . .

To conclude: I wish, my dear Sir, I could make you some return by sending all my readers to your two rich volumes. I can assure them the pearls I have strung from them on my string are sur-rounded by hundreds of others of equal intrinsic value.[21]

This statement, one of the few in which Reade acknowledged his full debt to a given book, indicates that he appropriated Howitt's words as well as his facts, tacked them onto the scenes and stage settings he had transferred from *Gold,* then furbished and adorned the resultant mélange with his own rhetoric. And he apparently exploited his other Australian sources in a similar manner—though in a few instances he created wholly new scenes (not found in *Gold*) in order to extend the range of his factual detail. In the play, for example, George Fielding's experiences as a shepherd are necessarily left to the imagination; in the novel they are presented in all their particulars—including a step by step account of George's experiences when his sheep contract the scab that is technically correct down to the last detail. In fact the only difference between Reade's account of the disease and that of Peter Cunningham (in *Two Years in New South Wales*) lies in their seeming disagreement over the type of "dip" that should be used as a cure.[22]

VII

The extremes to which Reade carried this type of documenta-tion are most readily apparent in his letters to his American pub lisher, James T. Fields, expressing concern over the factual correctness of the illustrations. In one letter he describes the "colored wood-cut required for Book 8 . . . a pinch of gold dust (taken from nature) lying on a portion of an old knife. The blue of the knife to form a background to the gold-dust . . ."—to which he adds the following directions:

> N.B. There is but one way to do this: and Messrs. Ticknor & Field will perhaps oblige me by purchasing a pinch of Californian Gold as it comes from the mine and an old Knife. *broad blade* a small pruning knife. And putting these under the artist's eye and insisting on an *exact*
> representation—
> I think this would require only two blocks
> I send herewith a figure and
> landscape printed in colors by means of several blocks. to show what can be done in this way
> To comprehend the importance of this [apparently?] childish illustration study the verbal context by means of which the effect is prepared.[23]

Nor is this the limit of his Pre-Raphaelite thoroughness. In another letter, concerning a vignette for the domestic section, he is even more explicit in his directions, and explains why they must be carried out to the last minute detail:

> 193 Piccadilly
> Nov. 2
> [1855]
> In Book A₃ Susan Merton there is a space left for a vignette, about which I am anxious, and will try to explain what I want—
> This is the situation
> George Fielding & Susan Merton are acknowledged lovers
> William Fielding G's brother loves her secretly, as he thinks, but in point of fact George knows it—
> George is going to Australia, after having quarrelled with his brother and he wishes to make a strong appeal to his Brother's heart—
> He says 'Come with me William" and takes him vide MS across the yard—down the lane etc.—to the Church-yard. He takes him to their mother's grave.
> Now the way grandmama has always done this sort of thing is by diluting the draughtsman's work with the writers. Thus "Then they come to a rustic tombstone on which was engraved these words

. . . .
. . . .
. . . .

This is the way to miss an effect but I want to produce one. So
I write   They came to *this*.
         Here . . . .
        Fields

. . . . . .
. . . . . .
. . . . . .

Here the visible takes up the tale. The writer lets the other artist
speak for him and for himself—
     But then the artist of the pencil to whom I confide thus much
of my work must not fall beneath me. He must draw in the same
Key I have been writing in. I want an artist who instead of sitting
in a room and imagining a lie will take the trouble to go into a
churchyard and have the humility and the wisdom to copy something he sees there. I want a tombstone that has been up twenty
years—it should I think be drawn at a distance of 8 to 10 paces.
No Church or yew tree I *think* to distract the readers eye from
the single point I want to make.
N.B. The *letters must be as legible* as the rest of "Susan Merton"
I think there is a quarter edition of Gil-blas in which are one or
two of these little skilful vignettes illustrating a single point. These
might be of use so far as giving a general idea. [See illustration six].
     I enclose Saunder's work merely for the sake *of the words.* I
shall feel much obliged if you will examine the M.S. observe what
I want done—and watch over this effect Parentally—I will answer
for the effect if it is done my way—and being a bright effect
which is only to be got in one way I am a little anxious—
A line on this point or a sketch should there be time would oblige.
                  Yours very sincerely
                  Charles Reade

     Considering that Ticknor and Fields were trying to print ahead
of the English publisher, Reade's Pre-Raphaelite specifications
were, to say the least, wholly impracticable. Nevertheless he continued to insist: a few weeks after his request for the woodcut
done from *real* California gold-dust he wrote: "I am surprised
at one thing; that you have never communicated with me about the
wood-cuts." And when Fields still failed to respond Reade became
even more insistent (July 20): "I cannot help feeling some anxiety
about your wood-cuts; and this anxiety is increased by your silence
which leads me to fear I have not succeeded in showing you the

importance of those effects I aim at by them. These are no vulgar illustrations: they are not done upon the common plan of illustrations. *They take the place of the text and the reader reads them as well as views them.* The more important is it that they be finely executed and above all true. However at present I can only repeat what I have said to you before that it will be worth your while to look closely into the matter and reject all inaccurate or feeble representations of tombstones, and knives with gold dust on them."

These letters leave no doubt as to the genuineness of Reade's anxiety, or the sincerity of his Pre-Raphaelite arguments. He firmly believed that, by separating the draftsman's work from the writer's, he was initiating a new principle. And in a sense he was—though the principle amounted to little more than an adaptation of the Keanian stage practice of having a character manipulate a real prop, or point to a bit of realistic stage scenery—a practice which he had already exploited to the full in his own plays, a notable example being his stage directions for the finale of *Gold*: "As the Act Drop begins to descend, Robinson and Jem touch spring in dog, and gold dust pours out into box. . . . Let the gold-dust in this instance be metal, and plenty of it—so that, the dog being held high, it may descend in a regular shower, and attract the eye. . . ." In these directions Reade was clearly aiming towards a direct pictorial representation of the real that would be as sensational in its actuality as in its truth. And that was exactly what he sought in his colored woodcut of the knife and nuggets—in so far as the pencil could approximate the actuality of stage props. This is why he was so uncompromising in his demands for Pre-Raphaelite accuracy, why in his last letter to Fields concerning the wood-cut he wrote: "If you can't do the digger's knife and gold so that a digger seeing them should acknowledge the likeness cut out the whole passage 'Would you know etc.' Cut it all—Your public will never miss it and besides it ends a volume *with* us, so that a coup is required but it will come in the heart of your second volume where no coup is required. . . ."

Confronted with this ultimatum, Fields apparently tried to meet Reade's demands. At any rate the passage in question does appear in the first American edition, along with a woodcut that appears to be a reasonably accurate representation of "the digger's knife and gold" that Reade had in mind. The passage itself consists of two paragraphs of rhetorical questions, beginning, "Would you know why that wolvish yell of triumph?" proceeding through "Would you see what sight so electrified those gloating eyes and panting bosoms?" and concluding with "Would you behold this great discovery the same in appearance and magnitude as it met the eyes of the first discoverers, picked with a knife from the bottom of a calabash. . . . Then turn your eyes hither, for here it is." And here it is indeed, as, from the blankness of the white page, a huge knife blade with realistic gold nuggets lying on it is literally thrust out at the reader.

Whether or not this woodcut provided the coup Reade intended, a chapter-volume ending as sensationally realistic as the final Act-Drop of *Gold*, its effect is much like that of his own word pictures, in which he also employed the great system to enhance and extend the realistic scenic effects of his original play. Consequently the Pre-Raphaelitism of the woodcuts is of a piece with every other aspect of these Australian chapters, which may be summarily described as a fictional reproduction of *Gold*, plus factual upholstering.

VIII

Although Reade himself was pleased with these chapters, and felt that they vindicated his system—witness his self-congratulation in his letter to Howitt—Henry James is the only critic of note who has singled out this section of the novel for special praise. Reviewing Henry Kingsley's *The Hillyars and the Burtons* in 1865, James observed: "It is one of those rudimentary truths which cannot be too often repeated, that to write a novel it is not necessary to have been a traveller, an adventurer, a sightseer; it is simply necessary to be an artist. Mr. Kingsley's descriptions of Australia are very pretty; but they are not half so good as those of Mr. Charles Reade, who, as far as we know, has never visited the country. We mean that they do not give the reader that vivid impression of a particular place which the genius of Mr. Reade contrives to produce." [24] James's point—that it is simply necessary to be an artist—may be generally true, but it is not well taken in the present instance, since for the most part Reade's art consisted in cribbing the descriptions of Howitt, Mundy, *et al* and fitting them onto the theatrical backdrops he had taken over from *Gold*—as in his description of sunrise at the diggings. If James derived a vivid impression of a particular place from this description, the place was not Australia, but a Drury Lane version of that country.

Even so there is no denying the validity of James's comparative judgment. Reade's treatment of Australia is more vivid than Kingsley's; indeed it can be argued that his chapters are more vivid than those of Howitt, Bulwer, or any of the other mid-Victorian novelists who wrote on Australia—all of whom, according to Susanne Howe (in her *Novels of Empire*), were striving for like realistic effects by means of similar documentary techniques. But Reade's superior vividness only makes his chapters better melodrama, not better fiction. In the words of Susanne Howe: "A rapid preview of Bulwer, Kingsley, Trollope, and Reade in Australia, suggests Roy Rogers and his horse Trigger, the charms of Tom Mix or even William S. Hart. They are lively and exciting and well informed . . . have done their homework, as it were, on the Australian scene . . . but they are external and sometimes 'literary.' "[25]

It Is Never Too Late To Mend:
"The Immortal Part of the Work"

WHO IS SO SICK of "Susan Merton" as I am? But I am a writer. I *cannot scribble.* A 3 vol. Novel is a great Epic. I hope never to write another and this one must not lower me. . . .
— CHARLES READE (in an undated letter to James T. Fields)

✦   ✦   ✦

My new novel is an original and important work but both its originality and its importance moral and fictional are unconnected or slightly connected with Susan Merton. The scenes in which she figures are the stale and conventional part of the work. The soul of it are the scenes in which a bad man is despaired of and tortured by fools, and after-wards not despaired of by a wise and good man but encouraged, softened, converted. These psychological scenes and the melodramatic scenes that follow in which the thief's understanding is convinced as well as his heart are the immortal part of the work. The rest dozens of men and women on both sides the water could have written and better than I have done them—I stand therefore on my ace of spades and not on my nine of hearts and the title of the work is "Its Never Too late to Mend."
— CHARLES READE (in an undated letter to James T. Fields)

✦   ✦   ✦

Those black facts [concerning Birmingham Gaol] have been before the public before ever I handled them; they have been told, and tolerably well told, by many chroniclers. But it is my business, and my art, and my duty, to make you ladies and gentlemen *realize* things, which the chronicler presents to you in his dim, and cold, and shadowy way; and so they pass over your mind like idle wind.
This you sometimes call 'being harrowed,' but ask yourselves two questions:
(1) Do you think you are harrowed one tenth part as much as I have been; as I could harrow you?
(2) I, one tenth part as much as Josephs, who died under the harrow?

[155]

I have answered your questions broadly. I will do better; I will put it in your power to test that part of my story, if you think it worth while, and it is well worth while.

I will send you, as soon as I can lay my hand on it, a Blue Book, containing the results of a Royal Commission held upon a certain gaol three years ago. Here you will see my darker facts, and many more deposed to an oath.

Meantime, if you or any of your friends file *The Times,* look it over from the 6th to the 16th September, 1853.

—CHARLES READE (in a letter to an unidentified reader, Jan. 7, 1857)[1]

✓ ✓ ✓

In a letter to *The Times* (August 26, 1871) Reade wrote: "A noble passage in *The Times* of September 7 or 8, 1853, touched my heart, inflamed my imagination, and was the germ of my first important work."[2] Taken literally—the way it has so often been taken—this statement implies that Reade had never thought of prisons or prison reform as a subject for a novel before September 7 or 8 (actually September 12) when he encountered the noble passage in *The Times* detailing the atrocities in Birmingham Gaol. But this is not the way Reade intended the statement, or at least it is not the way, in all honesty, he should have intended it, for the *Diary* shows that he had begun his prison researches in 1852, in connection with his play *Gold,* "August 10,—I have sketched the plot of an original drama; I am studying for it a little. One of my characters is to be a thief. I have the *entrée* of Durham Gaol, and I am studying thieves. I have got lots of their letters, and one or two autobiographies from the chaplain. But the other subject, the gold-diggings, makes me very uneasy. I feel my lack of facts at every turn. . . ."

At this juncture Reade was seemingly on the point of dropping "the other subject, the gold-diggings," in favor of his first subject, prisons. Why he followed the opposite procedure is not clear. Perhaps he felt that his Australian facts, though meager, were more immediately topical and better suited to Keanian methods of staging. In any case he did not abandon his prison investigations until he had "personally inspected many gaols, and discovered terrible things; a cap of torture and infection in one northern gaol . . . in a southern gaol the prisoners were wakened several times at night, and their reason shaken thereby. In another gaol I found an old man sinking visibly to his grave under the system; nobody doubted it, nobody cared. In another, the chaplain, though a great enthusiast, let out that a woman had been put into the 'black hole' by the gaoler against his advice, and taken out a lunatic, and was still a lunatic, and the visiting justices had treated the case with levity. . . ." [3]

These "terrible things" seemed all the more terrible to Reade because of *Uncle Tom's Cabin*. The conditions of slaves had been likened to that of prisoners by philanthropists and novelists from Shaftesbury to Mrs. Trollope, [4] and Reade, with the example of *Uncle Tom* before him, was quick to see how readily he could exploit that likeness in a novel based on *Gold*—by sending the thief of the play to prison, and thus reintroducing the prison theme he had originally intended to include in the play: "June 14 . . . Mem. If ever I write a novel on 'Gold,' introduce . . . a learned Divine (Chaplain of Tom Robinson's gaol). . . ."

Reade's plans for documenting the new prison section indicate that at this time he envisaged it as a realistic protest against the cruelties of prisons, cast in the traditional picaresque mode of Smollett and Fielding, but enlivened and made more sensationally realistic through the application of the great system, after the manner of Mrs. Stowe (as revealed in "The Key to Uncle Tom's Cabin"). By June 20, the *Diary* reveals, he had already "been to Oxford Gaol and visited every inch . . ." and was planning to "do the same at Reading"—a plan which he carried out with due thoroughness (July 10-17), even extending his researches to the prison chapel, where, in his own words, he "heard and saw a parson drone the liturgy, and hum a common-place dry-as-dust discourse to two hundred great culprits and beginners. Most of those men's lives have been full of stirring and thrilling adventures. They are now by the mighty force of a system arrested in their course, and for two whole hours to-day were chained under a pump, which ought to pump words of fire into their souls; but this pump of a parson could not do his small share . . . he droned away as if he had been in a country parish church. He attacked the difficult souls with a buzz of conventional commonplaces, that have come down from book of sermons to book of sermons for the last century; but never in that century knocked at the door of a man in passing—nor ever will. . . ."

Though characteristically Readian in tone the substance of this indictment suggests that Reade, following his new system, had been consulting books as well as men, and was viewing "'the

Reading system"—with its unique emphasis on religious instruction—from the perspective provided by Hepworth Dixon, in the chapter he devoted to Reading Gaol in his *The London Prisons* (1850). Certainly Reade studied Dixon's chapter later, if not at this time, for in describing his fictional prison, modelled after Reading, he borrowed Dixon's phrases as well as his observations, and in his fictional indictment of "the silent and solitary system as practised at Reading and other County Gaols," he reiterated every single one of Dixon's charges, along with a number of his specific examples.[5]

Of the other books Reade apparently consulted at this time, J. Field's *Field on Prison Discipline* (1848) and Joseph Kingsmill's *Chapters on Prisons and Prisoners* (Second Edition, 1852) are among the most significant. Indeed it would seem that these books, along with Dixon's, provided Reade with dramatic and stylistic as well as factual and philosophic models. *The London Standard,* in reviewing Kingsmill's book pointed out that "from Gay and Fielding to Dickens, various writers of fiction have given us glimpses of the race of thieves, but the creations of these writers are imaginary, and therefore subject to exaggerations; Mr. Kingsmill, however, gives us reality, which far exceeds anything that has ever yet been presented in fictitious narrative."[6] In other words Kingsmill's was just the reality that Reade was striving to reproduce in fiction, and he did not scruple to incorporate its effects, as well as its facts, in everything from the treatment of scenic details to the characterization of Parson Eden, the Resourceful Hero of this section.

II

In the light of these borrowings it would appear that Reade had worked out his titular thesis and completed a draft of the prison section long before the appearance of the articles on the Birmingham atrocities. At least it is certain that he had worked out two of his three main characters. Robinson, the thief of *Gold* who exemplifies the titular thesis of the novel, he derived from the "one or two autobiographies" he secured in August, 1852, from the chaplain of Durham Prison. In his Preface to "The Autobiography of a Thief" (published separately in 1857 but originally intended for inclusion in the novel) he dedicated "this strange but true story of Robinson . . . to such as will deign to accept this clew to my method in writing. . . . I feign probabilities; I record improbabilities: the former are conjectures, the latter truths: mixed they make a thing not so true as gospel nor so false as history; viz. fiction. . . . Add then this autobiography to his character as drawn by me in the novel, and you possess the whole portrait: and now it will be for you to judge whether for once we have taken a character that exists on a large scale in nature, and added it to fiction, or here too, have printed a shadow, and called it a man." [7]

While the fallacy inherent in this theory of imitation is no doubt obvious enough, it should be noted, in Reade's defense, that he was consciously abjuring the techniques of Trollope and the domestic novelists (whose works he dismissed as "chronicles of small beer") in an effort to create epic characters equal to what he conceived to be his epic theme. "A 3 vol. novel," he wrote his publisher, "is a great prose epic," and in the novel itself he time and again invoked the epic tradition to justify his methods and techniques, as in his anti-Carlylean paean to the Nineteenth Century, in which, after announcing that he cannot sing the song of gold because he is "neither Lamartine nor Hugo nor Walter Scott," he goes on to proclaim that the present age "is a giant compared with the past, and full of mighty materials for any great pen in prose or verse":

God has been bountiful to the human race in this age. Most bountiful to poets; most bountiful to all of us who have a spark of nobleness in ourselves, and so can see and revere at sight the truly grand and noble (any snob can do this after it has been settled two hundred years by other minds that he is to do it). He has given us warlike heroes more than we can count, far less honor as they deserve; and valor as full of variety as courage in the Iliad is monotonous, except when it takes to its heels.

He has given us one hero, a better man than Hector or Achilles. For Hector ran away from a single man; this hero was never known to run away at all. Achilles was a better egotist than soldier; wounded in his personal vanity he revenged himself, not on the man who had wronged him,—prudence forbade,—but on the army, and on his country. This antique hero sulked; my hero, deprived of the highest command, retained a higher still—the command that places the great of heart above all petty personal feeling. He was a soldier, and could not look from his tent on battle and not plunge into it. What true soldier ever could? He was not a Greek, but a

Frenchman, and could not love himself better than his country; above all, he was not Achilles but Canrobert.

He has given us to see Nineveh disinterred by an English hero.

He has given us to see the north-west passage forced, and winter bearded on his everlasting throne by another. (Is it the hero's fault if self and snowdrop-singing poetasters cannot see this feat with the eyes of Camoens?)

He has given us to see Titans enslaved by man; steam harnessed to our carriages and ships; galvanism tamed into an alphabet—a gamut, and its metal harp-strings stretched across the earth *malgré* mountains and the sea, and so men's minds defying the twin monsters Time and Space; and now, gold revealed in the east and west at once, and so mankind now first in earnest peopling the enormous globe. Yet old women and children of the pen say this is a bad, a small, a lifeless, an unpoetic age: and they are not mistaken. For they lie.

As only tooth-stoppers, retailers of conventional phrases, links in the great cuckoo-chain, universal pill-venders. Satan, and ancient book-sellers' ancient nameless hacks can lie, they lie.

It is they who are *small-eyed*. Now, as heretofore, weaklings cannot rise high enough to take a bird's-eye view of their own age, and calculate its dimensions. . . .

My little friends aged nineteen and downwards—fourscore and upwards—who have been lending your ears to the stale little cant of every age as chanted in this one by Buffo-Bombastes and other foaming-at-the-pen old women of both sexes,—take, by way of antidote to all that poisonous soul-withering drivel, ten honest words.

I say before heaven and earth that the man who could grasp the facts of this day and do an immortal writer's duty by them, i.e., so paint them as a later age will be content to engrave them, would be the greatest writer ever lived: such is the force, weight, and number of the grand topics that lie this day on the world's face. I say that he who has eyes to see may now see greater and far more poetic things than human eyes have seen since our Lord and His apostles and His miracles left the earth.

It is very hard to write a good book or a good play, or to invent a good picture and having invented paint it. But it always was hard, except to those—to whom it was impossible. Bunglers will not mend matters by blackening the great canvases they can't paint on, nor the impotent become males by detraction.

"Justice!"

When we write a story or sing a poem of the great nineteenth century, there is but one fear—not that our theme will be beneath

Charles Reade

Courtesy of Princeton University Library

"MERCIFUL HEAVENS! IT IS MY DARLING."—THE FINALE OF A RECENT MYSTERIOUS DISAPPEARANCE—A LOVER WHO HAS QUARRELED WITH HIS SWEETHEART DISCOVERS HER BODY TIED TO A PIER IN THE NORTH RIVER—SEE PAGE 123.

"Merciful Heavens!   It is my Darling"

From the Notebook labelled "Pictura Novella 1873"
Courtesy of The London Library

"THINKING OF HOME."

"THINKING OF HOME."

O SAD, sweet eyes that send afar
 Their loving, longing gaze,
Fixed on yon fair and bright home-star—
 Star of undying rays?

O heart and soul that fondly yearn
 For dear ones o'er the sea;
O youthful cheeks that sadly turn—
 May this your story be?

"Gone are the faces so loving and kind,
 Gone are the hills and the valleys I know:
Far from my dear ones, I never can find
 Hearts like to thine, ever gentle and true.
O for my warm, sunny skies once again,
 O for the land where my feet loved to roam!
Long have I wandered, in tears and in pain,
 Evermore dreaming and thinking of home.

.... the faces that look into mine,
.... me seems the blue of the skies;
.... bosoms that lovingly shine,
Look not so fair as our own, to me eyes!
O, how my heart, like a bird, longs to go,
 Winging its way o'er the white, weary foam!
Day-time and night-time, each hour that I know,
 Fondly I'm dreaming and thinking of home!

"Home is the sigh of my lone, saddened breast,
 Home is the wish and the hope of my life;
Home is my balm, and my joy, and my rest,
 Home is my refuge from world-weary strife.
Watching the clouds at the dawn's early gray,
 Watching the stars in the night's ...... run-done,
Far from the land of my people I stray,
 Evermore dreaming and thinking of home!"

Gerald C—

"Boy's Beauty"

From the Notebook labelled "1872 & 1873 Classificanda"
Courtesy of The London Library

THE STORY OF THE MURDER AS RELATED BY LITTLE HELEN FUCHS.—ANDREAS FUCHS STRIKING WM. W. SIMONS THE DEATH-BLOW WITH THE HATCHET, IN THE KITCHEN OF THE MURDERER'S RESIDENCE, AT 26 NORTH THIRD STREET, WILLIAMSBURG, L. I.

Altitude Fascination.

JUMPING from points of elevation is a fashion of suicide. To stand on an elevated site exercises a singular fascination over some people, leading them to jump into the air. It causes others to await and tremble with fear. Last Summer I talked with the guardian of the steeple of the Cathedral at Strasburg on this subject, and he informed me that few visitors were free from the feeling of fright on reaching the first terrace, which is of great altitude, and that it was so pronounced as to generally prevent them going any higher. Sometimes the women fainted. I confess I was not free from a vague dread in looking out over the immense reach of landscape which this view takes in, although there was absolutely no danger.

THE IMPLEMENTS USED BY THE MURDERER IN MUTILATING THE VICTIM'S CORPSE.

the terrace being securely guarded by strong iron rails.

This man of the upper air—the guardian or guide—informed me that the Summer before an Englishman had fainted, but, determined to overcome his fright, he continued to ascend every day for a week until he could look out in the direction of the Black Forest, from the lantern, with equanimity. During the Summer a man had jumped into the air through altitude fascination. He was probably dealt before reaching the ground, on account of the immense height from which he hurled himself.

Formerly the Vendôme Column was the scene of so many deaths of this kind that a decree was issued to prevent visitors from ascending it unless accompanied by a guardian.

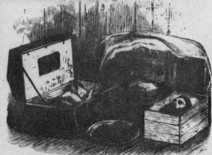

THE REMAINS OF MR. SIMONS PACKED IN VARIOUS VESSELS, AS SEEN AT THE MORGUE OF THE EASTERN DISTRICT.

SCENE IN FRONT OF THE UNDERTAKER'S SHOP, 297 FOURTH ST., THE MORGUE OF THE EASTERN DISTRICT.

It was the Tarpeian Rock of Paris. Such number have killed themselves from the fascination of altitude, that elevated places must be recognized as dangerous for certain people. The whose self-killing is premeditated of course are comprised therein.

Story of Dejazet.

MLLE. DEJAZET was one evening on her way to theatre, when, passing a corner of the Rue St. Honoré, she heard, issuing from the area of a cellar, the words of one of her best songs, "La Lisette." "Mon Dieu!" she exclaimed, "I did not believe it possible that my 'Lisette' could sound so dreadful. What would ce cher Beranger say?" And, in her impetuous way, she stepped

THE ACT OF MUTILATION.

carriage, and, descending the area steps, found herself face to face with six inebriated workmen to whom she said, in a pathetic voice:

"Mes enfants, how could you sing Beranger's 'Lisette' in such a manner?"

"Bah!" said one, less drunk than the rest, "it is Dejazet."

"Yes," she replied, "it is Dejazet, who has come to implore you not so to mutilate the song she loves best."

They regarded her stolidly while she seated self and sang "La Lisette." Silence was served throughout, and the noisy throng sobered by the magic of Dejazet's voice.

"Never," said Dejazet, "had I a greater triumph than that evening, and it was with difficulty I escaped from their enthusiasm."

THE APPALLING STORY OF THE SEVERED HEAD.—THE MURDER OF WM. W. SIMONS BY ANDREAS FUCHS.—SEE FRONT P.

"The Appalling Story of the Severed Head"

From the Notebook labelled "Pictura Novella"
Courtesy of The London Library

THE GREAT STRIKE.—THE SIXTH MARYLAND REGIMENT FIGHTING ITS WAY THROUGH BALTIMORE.—FROM A PHOTOGRAPH BY D. BENDANN.—[SEE PAGE 626.]

The dirty Oligarchy Crushed

by the Republican

"The Dirty Oligarchy Crushed by the Republic"

From the Notebook labelled "Classificanda 1876"
Courtesy of the London Library
This is the illustration described in Chapter XI (p. 282)

"Realistic Tombstone"

Vignette (presumably as executed by Saunders) intended for IT IS NEVER TOO LATE TO MEND *and enclosed with the letter to Fields quoted in Chapter VI (pp. 150-51).*
Courtesy of The Henry E. Huntington Library

Manuscript of "Hard Cash"

From the first page of the manuscript of HARD CASH
Courtesy of The Pierpont Morgan Library

Vita Eremitica et Monastica

Personalia

Ire is a Swine, one of the grete Seven
Abhominable unto the God of Heven
and to himself. it is destruction. chase

Take for his example Angelus Gualdensis, who
hid himself entirely in his cell but through
a little window blessed his visitor unseen and
gave them salutary advice for by these
vile hermits must try to assist those who
come for ghostly counsel.

Sits on a mossy trunk at commencement of
his eremitical career and many little
creatures never before remarked come forth and
play, and get bolder as soon as they see it is
not a Butler.

Studies for his model Aventine tempore Clovis
Digby 711 1 spirit of Solitude. 2 contempt of Vain
glory 3 care of Souls 4 assistance captives, 5
Alms to the poor 6 to be kind to animals.

Gathers acorns for the squirrels.

Deepens the stream. ups and downs of his
How is this my soul hath it, up and courage's soul
down like the sea Not so the Constant souls that
before me climb steadily to God by ladder of fasting, prayer
solitude whose rounds be fasting & prayer.

Angelorum amici et animalium hospes

At the cave of Guthlac
the birds and fishes of the
mere used to flock and swarm
to him. Wasps, tits, two
ravens came and perched upon
his arms, knees, breast
he used to place a straw in this
in his cell where he worked the
birds to build. and they did
the nest and built on that foundation

Hugh of Lincoln when
a Hermit found the Key to
animals, and after he became
Bishop of Lincoln little birds used
to sit on his hands and feed
freely. Also a wild swan
in the marshes used softly round
him, eat out of his hand. and
use to predict his return 713. 24th
survived the Saint many years, but
became savage again

St Columba received wounded
heron at Iona and feed
till they had strength to go again

St Columban in the forest
of Luxeuil squirrel etc

Albert of Sienna, used to
save hares from the hunters

S. Fructuosus. Apex et archive
precium ex Anichorita
sweet pretty story of the Stag
doe he saved its gratitude
and affection. Slain by down
perverso furiae his principle
rantis immundio vir cui
offern cum a visibor corpore et
anima liberavit, cujus offensam
ibidspine remisit.

Cum vir Sanctus prosper mira
cula a multis videretur
nec posset in quiete et silentio
permanere. Septum profunda
deserta penetrabat ibi per multos
manens, a deus due quietatis,
et inventis, charmeum clearinge
rumque arcum ope, sepium
ad Monasterium redierebatur.
Vita Patrum Occidentis
p. 275. Col 1 & 2 p...

---

us, but we miles below it; that we shall lack the comprehensive vision a man must have from heaven to catch the historical, the poetic, the lasting features, of the Titan events that stride so swiftly past IN THIS GIGANTIC AGE.[8]

With such poetic stories to write—and despite his rhetorical modesty, Reade believed he was writing them—there was no time for George Eliot's type of character analysis, which in any case "microscoped poodles into lions." The best if not the only way to create a fictional lion, or thief, was to copy an actual one, employing the techniques of "character painting used by the old epic and dramatic writers" to transfer the thief of the factual autobiography first to *Gold,* then to the novel.

But in fashioning Robinson in this way Reade was not really copying an actual thief; he was copying the actual thief's self-portrait, in which the actual thief presents himself, not as an individual man, but as a type of outlaw common to Newgate and Dickensian fiction. Like Bulwer Lytton's Paul Clifford he is so brave, sensitive, and talented that he could, and presumably would, have succeeded in any type of honest endeavor—had he not been led into a life of crime as a result of personal misfortunes and adverse circumstances. And like Mrs. Gaskell's John Barton and Kingsley's Alton Locke, he is finally led back to the path of bourgeois righteousness, after much suffering and many struggles, by virtuous friends and Christian eloquence. In short the factual thief of the autobiography is himself a literary type, and in transferring him to the novel Reade merely reproduced, from fact, a character he could just as easily have copied directly from any one of a dozen novels.

As for the touches that Reade himself added, in fitting the thief of the autobiography into the novel, they are of no positive consequence, except in so far as he endows Robinson with his own sensitivity to the tortures of the solitary and silent system. Robinson's climactic hours in "the black hole," for example, represent a convincing account of the terrors a sensitive man might experience in his efforts to cope with utter darkness and isolation.[9] Even here, however, Robinson's reactions are more typical than individual; and in many instances they are not merely typical, but crudely theatrical, as in the scene in which he is deterred from reverting to a life of crime by accidentally discovering, at just the right moment, one of Parson Eden's tracts, "The Wages of

Sin Are Death." As the scene opens, it is night, and Robinson, who is about to take part in a "house-breaking," has decided to have a look at one of a series of supposedly pornographic pamphlets he has just purchased:

> . . . He knelt down and took off his hat, and put his dark lantern inside it before he ventured to move the slide; then undid the paper, and, putting it into the hat, threw the concentrated rays on the contents, and peered in to examine them. Now the various little pamphlets had been displaced by mephisto, and the first words that met the thief's eye, in large letters on the back of a tract, were these: 'THE WAGES OF SIN ARE DEATH.'
>
> Thomas Robinson looked at these words with a stupid gaze. At first he did not realize all that lay in them. He did not open the tract: he gazed benumbed at the words, and they glared at him like the eyes of green fire when we come in the dark on some tiger-cat crouching in his lair.
>
> Oh, that I were a painter, and could make you see what cannot be described! the features of this strange incident that sounds so small and was so great. The black night, the hat, the renegade peering under it in the wall's deep shadows to read something trashy, and the half-open lantern shooting its little strip of intense fire, and the grim words springing out in a moment from the dark face of night and dazzling the renegade's eyes and chilling his heart: 'THE WAGES OF SIN ARE DEATH.' [10]

That Reade could declare Robinson's reactions to be those of a "man," the scene itself (along with those that follow) "true to nature . . . the immortal part of the work," [11] shows how naïvely and completely he identified nature and truth with his Dickensian preconceptions.

III

Along with his epic thief, Reade created an epic hero in Parson Eden (first referred to as "the chaplain of Tom Robinson's gaol") who is in all but name an idealized self-portrait and therefore the ultimate Resourceful Hero of the novel. Parson Eden's goodness is difficult to describe; to find anyone to compare with him one must turn to such paragons as Squire Allworthy, John Jarndyce, or Tom Newcome, and even these characters are inferior in that they are *merely* good. In addition to his perfect goodness, which is completely selfless and of course sexless, Eden is blessed with the intelligence of a Newton, the eloquence of a Whitefield . . .

and when the occasion demands he is also an expert wrestler, a pupil of Bendigo. His one seeming weakness—a tendency to sicken at the sight of blood and torture—is not really a weakness at all, it turns out, but a necessary concomitant of his sensitivity. Indeed he is so much the perfect hero that Swinburne, ordinarily so indulgent to Reade's heroes, was obliged to dismiss him as "that athletico-seraphic chaplain . . . Prince Rodolphe (of the *Mystères de Paris*) in Anglican orders." [12]

As in the case of Robinson, however, there is the matter of Reade's intention. He was not trying to create a commonplace parson, like George Eliot's Mr. Irwine; he was trying to create a modern hero who was also a modern saint. *Christie Johnstone* he had intended as, in part, a votive offering to his mother, and it would appear that in Eden, he was endeavoring to present her with the ideal parson she had intended him to be—a Christian clergyman who would represent God and Bacon and Progress, in contrast and opposition to the "infernal little disciples of Carlyle."

IV

As yet, however, Reade's sources had not provided him with a Carlylean hero whom he could cast in the role of villain. Nor was he content with the documentary evidence he had thus far collected. To duplicate the art and purpose of *Uncle Tom* he knew that he had to have more sensational facts, and as late as August 22, 1853, he was still resolving to find them: "I will visit all the London prisons, and get warm facts for the prison business. . . ." [13] A few weeks later, however, the articles on the Birmingham atrocities appeared (*Times*, September 6-16) to provide the ultimate answer to his Baconian prayers. For the articles were more than warm, they laid bare the workings of a nineteenth century Buchenwald, and in doing so provided leads towards the exposure of still further atrocities—leads that he immediately followed up. In his own words: "I studied the two extra-ordinary Bluebooks, viz., the Royal Commissioners' Report on Birmingham Gaol, and also on Leicester Gaol. . . . Then I conversed with one of the Royal Commissioners, and he told me the horrors of Leicester Gaol had so affected one of the Commissioners that it had made him seriously ill for more than a month. Enlightened by all these studies . . . I did what the anonymous Press had done on a vast scale . . . I struck a blow in defense of outraged law and outraged humanity.

But unlike the Press, to whom the prison rules are unknown, I did *not* confound the system with all its abuses; on the contrary, I conducted the case thus: I placed before the reader not one government official, but two—the gaoler eternally breaking *the prison rules,* and the chaplain eternally appealing to the prison rules. At last, after inflicting many miseries by repeated breaches of the prison rules, the gaoler does a poor boy to death; and then I bring in a third government official, who dismisses the gaoler." [14]

Reade's statement shows how neatly he fitted his new facts to his old thesis through a slight extension of his old epic framework. He did not, like his master Dickens, challenge the prevailing theories of penology which in America were presented under the aegis of the "Pennsylvania System," and in England, with slight modifications, were known as "the silent and solitary system." [15] Later, in his notebooks and in two of his novels, he condemned "the system" roundly, but at this time, following Dixon, he accepted it with minor reservations, basing his entire case on Dixon's key distinction between the system and its abuses. In one of his Notebooks he pasted in a printed copy of the "Rules relating to the conduct and treatment of prisoners in the County Gaol and House of Correction at Reading," and beneath these rules he wrote: "These are the Prison rules I used in writing 'It is never too late to mend.' They were repeatedly broken in the gaols whose abuses I explored. . . . I attacked the abuses but not the theory of those gaols. . . ." [16]

By thus taking his stand behind the system, Reade gained a number of advantages—not the least of which was a ready-made factual villain in the person of Lieutenant Austin, the warden responsible for the Birmingham atrocities. The one difficulty, from a reformist point of view, was that Austin had already been tried, dismissed, and held up to public scorn. But that did not deter Reade. He was looking for an excuse to harrow his readers—after the manner of *Uncle Tom*—and in Austin he had found his Simon Legree.

He therefore transferred the factual Austin directly to the novel, then proceeded to vilify him as that Carlylean demon of cruelty, that "lurid specimen of barbarism," that "black ray of the narrow, self-deceiving bloody past . . . earnest Hawes." [17] At times—the few times he tried to probe the whys and wherefores of Hawes's cruelties—Reade showed considerable insight. He recognized that "this unhappy dolt Hawes . . . must still, like his prisoners and the rest of us, have some excitement to keep him from going dead. What more natural than that such a nature should find its excitement in tormenting, and that by degrees this excitement should become first a habit, then a need? Growth is the nature of habit, not of one sort or another but of all—even of unnatural habit. Gin grows on a man—tobacco grows on a man—blood grows on a man." [18] But Reade the philanthropist was too close to Hawes the sadist to recognize the implications of his own analysis—either as it applied to Hawes or to himself. In any case his aim was not to understand Hawes, but to expose him as a nineteenth century Himmler—a monster so monstrous that he, Charles Reade (alias Charles Eden), could hound and beat and destroy him in the name of "outraged law and humanity." And in pursuing this aim he believed that he was writing in the epic tradition, that he was emulating Milton as well as Dickens and Mrs. Stowe. Hence his efforts to liken Hawes to Nero, Pharaoh, the inquisitors, and Carlyle's Great Men, and thus establish him as a modern Satan at war with a modern Christ for the souls of modern Christians as represented by Robinson, the human Adam.

v

The discrepancy between Reade's epic design and melodramatic treatment is evident as early as the first few pages of the prison section in which Reade presents a picture of the entire gaol—a factual reproduction based in part on Dixon's elaborate description of Reading Gaol, but with added rhetorical touches intended to show the evil lurking beneath the order and cleanliness.[19] Into this gaol—seemingly a model of its kind—Reade introduces Robinson and through him unveils the rigors of "the silent and separate system" as enforced by Hawes—rigors that soon reduce the intelligent and sensitive but misguided Robinson to a vicious animal, ready to strike back against and, if possible, kill his tormentor.

Then, just at the moment that Robinson is about to commit murder, and the other prisoners are for various reasons also at the breaking point, Parson Eden enters upon the scene. In contrast to his predecessor, Chaplain Jones, a well-meaning but in Reade's own terminology a "commonplace man," [20] Eden sets about his new duties with all the zeal and acumen of Charles Reade himself. In one of his sermons to the prisoners "he suddenly opens his arms, wth wonderful grace and warmth and energy," and speaks to them as only he can: "My poor wandering sheep, come—come

[165]

back to the heavenly fold! Let me gather you as a hen gathers her chickens under her wing. You are my anxiety, my terror—be my joy, my consolation here, and hereafter the brightest jewel in my crown." In this strain, according to Reade, Eden soared higher than earth-clogged wings can follow: "Gracious words of entreaty and encouragement gushed from him in a crystal stream with looks and tones of more than mortal charity. Men might well doubt was this a man, or was it Christianity speaking? Christianity, born in a stable, was she there, illuminating a gaol?" [21]

At this point the reader may be tempted to interrupt Reade's Christ metaphor—which he carries on through another half page—with the type of witticism visited upon Dickens' Wopsle. Yet there is a certain amount of Readian logic in this seeming rhetorical madness, for Eden's Christlike love gives him the Godlike right to hate—and he hates cruelty, which is the subject of his next sermon:

"No crime is so thoroughly without excuse as this. Other crimes have sometimes an adequate temptation, this never. The path to other crimes is down-hill; to cruelty is up-hill. In the very act, Nature, who is on the side of some crimes, cries out within us against this monstrous sin. The blood of our victim flowing from our blows, its groans and sighs and pallor, stay the uplifted arm and appeal to the furious heart. Wonderful they should ever appeal in vain . . . God has written his abhorrence of this monstrous sin in letters of fire and blood on every page of history."

Here he ransacked history, and gave them some thirty remarkable instances of human cruelty, and of its being punished in kind so strangely, and with such an exactness of retribution, that the finger of God seemed visible writing on the world—"God hates cruelty."

At the end of his examples he instanced two that happened under his own eye—a favorite custom of this preacher.

"A man was tried in London for cruelty to animals; he was acquitted by a legal flaw, though the evidence was clear against him. This man returned homeward triumphant. The train in which he sat was drawn up by the side of a station. An express-train passed on the up-line at full speed. At the moment of passing, the fly-wheel of the engine broke; a large fragment was driven into the air, and fell upon the stationary train: it burst through one of the carriages, and killed a man upon the spot. That man was seated between two other men, neither of whom received the slightest injury. The man so singled out was the cruel man who had evaded man's justice, but could not escape His hand who created the beasts as well as man, and who abhors all men who are cruel to any creature He has formed." [22]

Nor does Eden stop here. He continues on for some four more pages, and when it seems that even he has exhausted his powers of Biblical rhetoric, he works himself up into a hell-fire and damnation finale: "Tremble, ye cruel, God hates ye!" And so, by making God a humanitarian with sadistic propensities, in support of his cruelty-hating Christ, Reade secured every possible sanction for expressing his own "abhorrence of cruelty" in "letters of fire and blood."

VI

The struggle between Eden and Hawes is therefore grotesquely unequal from the start. Eden finds a copy of the prison rules, mentioned earlier, and then proceeds to prove, point by point, that practically every single punishment employed by Hawes is illegal and must be stopped. Any prison official who so much as tampers with a prisoner's diet is, he declares, "a felon," and he, Charles Francis Eden, will proceed against any such official "by the dog-whip of the criminal law, by the gibbet of the public press, and by every weapon that wit and honesty have ever found to scourge cruelty . . . since civilization dawned upon the earth." [23] And Eden carries out this threat to the letter. In fact he works himself into such a frenzy—just by recounting Hawes's cruelties—that he steps forth in his own person to revoke Justice Coleridge's decision in the Austin Case:

I revoke that sentence [of Justice Coleridge] with all the blunders on which it was founded. Instead of becoming, as other judicial proceedings do, a precedent for future judges, I condemn it to be a beacon they shall avoid. It shall lie among the decisions of lawyers, but it shall never mix with them. It shall stand alone in all its oblique pity, its straightforward cruelty, and absurdity; and no judge shall dare copy it while I am alive; for if he does, I swear to him by the God that made me, that all I have yet said is to what I will print of *him*, as a lady's riding whip to a thresher's flail. I promise him, on my honour as a writer and no hireling, that I will buy a sheet of paper as big as a barn-door, and nail him to it by his name as we nail a pole-cat by the throat. I will take him by one ear to Calcutta, and from Calcutta to Sydney; and by the other from London via Liverpool to New York and

Boston. The sun shall never set upon his gibbet, and when his
bones are rotten his shame shall live— Ay! though he was thirty
years upon the bench. Posterity shall know little about his name,
and *feel* nothing about it but this—that it is the name of a muddle-
head who gained and merited my loathing, my horror and my scorn.

The civilized races, and I their temporary representative revoke
that sentence from the rising to the setting sun in every land where
the English tongue is spoken.[24]

The indignation expressed in this passage borders so closely on
the psychopathic that it not only fails of its intended effect but
reflects back upon Reade himself.[25] And other passages in which
Eden anathematizes Hawes have a similar effect. Eden's humanitarianism is but Hawes's sadism, plus moral sanctions, and the moral
sanctions are in themselves rationalizations.

VII

Although, for strategic reasons, Reade does not challenge the
system directly in the novel, he can and does criticize the system
and its workings indirectly—by making Eden ill, and then permitting him to air his notions in the form of a dream: "But one day
it so happened that he was light-headed and greatly excited, holding a conversation [with an imaginary companion] . . . The
enthusiast was building a prison in the air. A prison with a farm,
a school, and a manufactory attached. Here were combined the
good points of every system, and others of his own . . . there
shall be both separation and silence for those whose moral case
it suits—for all, perhaps, at first—but not for all always. Away
with your Morrisons's pill-system, your childish monotony of moral
treatment in cases varying and sometimes opposed." Continuing
in this vein Eden outlines a theory of prison reform quite advanced
for the time—although he is careful to point out that "systems
avail less than supposed . . . all depends on your men, not your
machinery." For this reason, he argues, old-fashioned gaolers and
turnkeys and visiting justices must go. "As they were in the days
of Fielding so they are in the days of light, and as they are now
so will they remain until they are swept away from the face of the
soil. . . ." Then, after these "men of the past" have been swept
away, they must be replaced by men of light—as in Eden's Utopian
dream: "Now we have really a governor and warders instead of
jailers and turnkeys. The nation has discovered these are high
offices, not mean ones. . . . Our officers are men picked out of

all England for intelligence and humanity. . . . Our jail is one of the nation's eyes; it is a school, thank Heaven, it is not a dungeon." [26]

Yet even in such a Utopian prison, manned by such model officials, there was still the need for outside surveillance. For no matter how intelligent or humane the officials might be there was always the possibility of their becoming enmeshed in red tape. As a final safeguard he therefore insisted that all prisons be kept open for public inspection—to enable the people, under the guidance of zealots like himself, to keep the prison under constant surveillance. "Justice," Reade constantly reiterated, "is the daughter of publicity." [27]

In designating the people, in the guise of "public opinion," the final arbiter in matters relating to prisons (as well as in all matters social, political, and literary) Reade doubtless thought that he was being republican if not democratic—in line with his own Benthamitic beliefs and in opposition to the authoritarian doctrines of his *bête noir,* Carlyle. Yet it should be obvious that he too subscribed to a form of hero-worship. His final appeal is not to the people as such (elsewhere, in a statement reminiscent of Bumble's remarks on the law, he says flatly: "the public is an ass") but only to the people as informed and guided by "modern" heroes. And while it can of course be argued that Reade's heroes are liberal, intelligent leaders, not medieval despots, and therefore not authoritarian in the Carlylean sense at all, this is to overlook the spirit of their words and actions. For if Eden ordinarily speaks the language of Bacon, the Mills and the Evangelical pulpit (rather than that of Fichte, Cromwell, and Carlyle's captains of industry) he speaks this language with a peculiarly Readian accent that is much closer to Carlyle than to, say, Mill, or even Arnold. Eden seldom if ever speaks as Eden; it is always as the representative of God, humanity, law and order, the government, the Home Office . . . and he invariably invokes the power of these concepts and institutions in an effort to crush anyone who opposes him— from Hawes, to the gaolers, to the Visiting Justices, to Justice Coleridge.

VIII

Reade, it need hardly be added, saw nothing ludicrous in presenting his Christ as an authoritarian representative of the Home Office. Nor did he see anything reprehensible about using his

Christ to gibbet an actual prison official (Lieutenant Austin) who
had already been tried and punished. Reade's argument, which
anticipates the morality now exemplified in the work of Mickey
Spillane, was that Lieutenant Austin had not suffered enough,
that, consequently, he had to be tried and sentenced again—
this time by the public, with the Christlike Eden as prosecuting
attorney and Reade himself as judge.

Having thus reduced his epic structure to a sadistic formula
Reade could exploit to the full the blackness of his black facts—
as he did in the scene in which Hawes and the gaolers amuse
themselves by stuffing salt down the throat of a half-witted prisoner who has been confined in the punishment jacket for hours
and is already crazed with fear, pain, and thirst. *The Times's* comment on the factual counterpart of this scene—that it "eclipses any
scene in *Uncle Tom's Cabin,* those in which Legree figures not
excluded"—applies with equal force to Reade's fictional treatment,
which in this and similar instances eclipses Dickens (as well as
Stowe) in its sheer sadistic intensity, and can hardly be matched
outside the pages that Marcus Clarke (in his *For the Term of His
Natural Life*) modelled after Reade. Indeed it was one of the
factual scenes taken directly from the novel—in which a boy
named Josephs faints after being confined in the punishment
jacket—that very nearly precipitated a riot when Reade later
produced the play *It's Never Too Late to Mend.*[29]

Dramatically, however, these scenes are open to the same
criticism that Samuel Warren levels against the "frightful scenes"
in *Uncle Tom's Cabin* when he declares that "one might as well
describe, in detail, the slaughter of an ox by the slaughterer and
his two assistants." [30] Warren's implication, of course, is that the
slaughterer cannot be held morally responsible for his slaughter.
And neither can Hawes. The facts reveal that Lieutenant Austin
was more sick than satanic, more of a Bumble than a Pharaoh,
and Reade's Baconian dramatization of the facts conveys the same
impression—an impression that his rhetoric and invective fail to
alter. Hawes remains Hawes, and in gibbeting him as he does
Eden tends to negate the very humanitarianism Reade is trying
to enforce; just as, to cite a comparable but inferior modern
example, Laura Hobson's treatment of the anti-semites tends to
negate the avowed purpose of *Gentleman's Agreement,* by showing
the anti-anti-semites to be as authoritarian and as bloodthirsty as
the anti-semites.

The most telling prison scenes—in terms of Reade's avowed intentions—are therefore those scenes (previously described) in which Eden plays little if any part, in which Reade draws directly upon his black facts to show the prisoners alone and helpless, the victims of a dolt who is himself the victim of a system. Yet even these scenes, which, in themselves, are at least as compelling as the comparable scenes in *For the Term of his Natural Life*, or those in James Jones's *From Here to Eternity*, actually come to very little in the context of the novel. For when Reade (in the person of Christ-like Eden) assumes the role of father to the prisoners, he immediately reduces the prisoners, along with Hawes, to the pattern of his own sadistic phantasy—a pattern in which he anticipates Freud's "A Child is being Beaten" with his own "A Prisoner is being Beaten."

But of course Reade did not know that he had negated his humanitarian as well as his epic intentions, that in his efforts to emulate Milton and Mrs. Stowe he had anticipated Mickey Spillane and Laura Hobson—as well as Freud's case histories. To him Eden's feelings of obsessive tenderness for the prisoners—the sadistic feelings that compel him to torment their tormentor—were neither obsessive nor sadistic. They were the feelings of humane men and women everywhere, and in giving them fictional expression, in harrowing his readers as he himself had been harrowed by his factual investigations, he believed that he had, at long last, done justice to the teachings of his master—that he had, in fact, vindicated both himself and his great system.

CHAPTER VIII

The System Systematized

So FAR, the room was romantic; but there was a prosaic corner to shock those who fancy that fiction is the spontaneous overflow of a poetic fountain fed by nature only. Between the fireplace and the window, and within a foot or two of the wall, stood a gigantic writing-table, with the signs of hard labor on it, and of severe system. Three plated buckets, each containing three pints, full of letters to be answered, other letters to be pasted into a classified guard-book, loose notes to be pasted into various books and classified (for this writer used to sneer at the learned men who say, "I will *look among my papers for it*"; he held that every written scrap ought either to be burned or pasted into a classified guard-book, where it could be found by consulting the index); five things like bankers' bill-books, into whose several compartments MS. notes and newspaper cuttings were thrown, as a preliminary towards classification in books.

Underneath the table was a formidable array of notebooks, standing upright, and labelled on their backs. There were about twenty large folios of classified facts, ideas, and pictures; for the very woodcuts were all indexed and classified on the plan of a tradesman's ledger; there was also the receipt-book of the year, treated on the same plan. Receipts on a file would not do for this romantic creature; if a tradesman brought a bill, he must be able to turn to that tradesman's name in a book, and prove in a moment whether it had been paid or not. Then there was a collection of solid quartos, and of smaller folio guard-books called Indexes. There was "Index rerum et journalium," "Index rerum et librorum," "Index rerum et hominum," and a lot more; indeed, so many that, by way of climax, there was a fat folio ledger entitled "Index ad Indices."

By the side of the table were six or seven thick pasteboard cards, each about the size of a large portfolio, and on these the author's notes and extracts were collected from all his repertories into something like a focus for a present purpose. He was writing a novel based on facts. Facts, incidents, living dialogue, pictures, reflections, situations, were all on these cards to choose from, and arranged in headed columns; and some portions of the work he was writing on this basis of imagination and drudgery lay on the table in two forms, his own writing and his secretary's copy thereof, the latter corrected for the press. This copy was half margin, and so provided for additions and improvements, but for one addition there were ten excisions, great and small.

—CHARLES READE, *A Terrible Temptation*

✦ ✦ ✦

Reade completed his final revisions of *Never Too Late To Mend* in July of 1856. But he still could not let go of the work: he continued to fuss and fidget over the text, bemoaning printers' errors and in general making life miserable for his American publisher, the long suffering Fields. On July 29, by way of apology and justification he wrote Fields: "I am afraid I have tried your patience hard with the three-volume novel, but you must consider that while you have been kept waiting the work has been growing in importance, and believe me that great successes are not to be achieved without Time and Labor. It would never have done for me to produce three mediocre volumes. As it is I think I can promise you a success in the U.S. In this country it is doubtful, I shock their prejudices so—poor dear souls. . . ."

In this last statement Reade is already beginning to prepare himself for possible failure—even as he hopes against hope for the "great success." And his anxiety increased, the letters to Fields show, as the date of publication approached: "Never Too Late To Mend now out here August 8 though not as yet public . . . send me over two copies one of which I will return to you with my final corrections . . ."—after which he goes on to explain that by the time he receives the two copies "a jury of my friends will have sat upon the book at my special request and suggested what elisions I can make with advantage. I feel myself that the prison business is too long." By August 11, however, he had reverted to his more optimistic view, and wrote to assure Fields that "the Book will certainly succeed in the United States. . . . It's success in England will I think be slow but sure." And, in the same letter, he repeats his earlier request: that Fields collect for him "every critique that comes out."

To relieve his mounting anxiety Reade apparently hurried off to Brighton, there to await the issue—which by August 16 he felt was clear. In a tone of guarded optimism he wrote Fields: "I am happy to tell you that the success of the work is already placed beyond doubt: but whether it will be a lasting success only time will show. However Bentley is already talking about a second edition. . . ." By way of concrete evidence he also included a dated list of the reviews he had read, as follows:

Aug. 9 *Daily News*
         Press
         Athenaeum

Aug. 16   *Spectator*
          Saturday Review   3 columns each
Aug. 15   *Critic*

"The Press," he noted, "is unfavorable—the others are considerably warmer than to any former work of mine." And by September
24, the date of his next letter to Fields, the book had apparently
begun to make its way with the public. In Reade's words: "I am
happy to inform you that the title is as successful as I expected—
letters have been written in the journals under the signature "It is
never too late" and many public allusions show the title has hit
I cannot tell you what *measure of success* the *book* has for I don't
know. But it is a success, and they have really made a cut into a
second edition."

From October through December and on into 1857 the sales
as well as the reputation of the book rose steadily. While there
were, to be sure, a number of dissenting critics—notably Goldwin
Smith and Fitzjames Stephen[1]—their criticism seemingly had little
effect on the popularity of the book, which was being praised
and purchased by everyone from shopkeepers (Q. D. Leavis'
"new . . . naïve reading public")[2] to writers and philanthropists.
Nathaniel Hawthorne thought so highly of the novel that he read
it aloud to his family,[3] and on January 12, 1857, Caroline Fox
noted in her diary: "Reading 'Never Too Late To Mend,' one of
the weightiest events of late. Oh those prison scenes! How they
haunt one! How they recall those despairing women's eyes I met
in the model gaol at Belfast!"[4]

Though not personally acquainted with Caroline Fox, Reade
heard or read like encomiums. And how he loved them! Almost as
much as he loved the sales figures from Bentley—which he considered the ultimate test of fictional art. On December 9 he
wrote Fields: "We have sold two Editions at 30s. 22/9 to the
trade. And the demand continues, Bentley hopes another small
edition at the heavy price then some thousands at 10s and eventually a larger at 5s." And in another undated letter, presumably
written a few weeks later, he announced: "Bentley has just published a cheap edition. . . . He sold 2,700 copies the first two
days and orders come in fast. . . ."[5]

II

Thus at the age of forty-three Reade had at long last written
a hit, and could henceforth count himself "one of the writers of

the day." In one sense this success came none too soon, and was all to the good. In fact it is doubtful that he could have accepted the failure of the novel and still continued to write. In another sense, however, the success of the novel was unfortunate in that it tended to confirm his megalomaniacal notions of himself and his writing. Always before his self-justification had contained within it a note of uncertainty, indicating that, for all his bluster, he could see that two and two make four, even though he could not always afford to admit it. But as the sales of the novel increased that note disappeared—and with it his last tenuous hold on reality, at least in those areas in which his ideal ego was involved. He firmly believed that he was the writer-saviour of the Nineteenth Century, that he, like Shakespeare before him, had been vindicated by "coal heavers and prentices"—over the protests and despite the machinations of publishers' and reviewers' cliques such as those which "puffed" the works of George Eliot.[6]

And when he could not blame cliques—as for instance, when the American sales of the novel did not measure up to his expectations—he immediately turned on Fields. "Don't talk to me of 4000 copies of such a book as 'Never Too Late,' please . . ." he wrote on April 9, and on April 30 he openly challenged Fields' statement of sales: "I am not satisfied with your statement about 'Never Too Late To Mend' nor with the manner of it. . . . I must not be told the sale of my books declines the moment I happen to have an interest in their sale. Such statements repeated will be sure to end our connection. . . ." Nor was he appeased by Fields's explanations. He refused to believe (June 2) that "the greatest work of fiction of modern times does not sell so well as the average of feeble novels on your side the water . . ." and on July 21 he repeated his charge of dishonesty in an even more direct and offensive manner: "I have certain information from three good sources that "Never Too Late To Mend" was a great success from the first. . . ."

Furthermore Reade demanded—at the very time he was making these charges—that Fields accept his eccentric plan for the publication of a new novel he was writing—to be entitled *White Lies:* "Oblige me by consenting at once to this arrangement. It comes from a man who has never yet made a mistake or miscalculated the public. Answer by return mail and be surprised at nothing that may happen—if you decline." Fields did not decline, although Reade, making good his paranoiac demands, was already considering other offers when Fields's offer arrived. And then Reade was not content with the terms—even though he himself had dictated them. On July 6 he wrote: "Harper gives a large sum of money to Thackeray for early sheets of a serial not quite £1500 I believe. . . . You have a fairer start than Thackeray gives Messrs. Harper and I have taken so much pains and been at so much expense to get you an advantage which is quite as well worth £1500 as Mr. Thackeray's early sheets that I am naturally surprised at the carelessness and want of zeal you seem to show in dealing with a property at once *so valuable* and *so delicate*. . . . 'White Lies' is by far the most powerful story I have yet printed and it will sell like fire in the U.S. I should not wonder if it sold quite as well as Mr. Thackeray's serial. I tell you this that you may not fancy I am writing beneath my mark, because I happen to be writing in 'The London Journal' quite the contrary I assure you. It shall be my best story out and out." [7]

Critical self-delusion cannot be carried much further. *White Lies* is at best a vapid adaptation of an undistinguished French play (Auguste Maquet's *Le Château Grantier*) filled out with the usual Readian embellishments. Later, after his appropriations from Maquet had been exposed, and the novel itself had proved such an unmitigated failure in its serial run that it "well nigh swamped The London Journal," he tried to repudiate his work as pot-boiling: "I sat down to write a pack of fibs . . . one or two honest fellows came about me, animated with a friendly warmth, to bid for the coming fibs. I bled them." But this is another instance of Reade's convenient forgetfulness. In his correspondence with Fields he repeatedly described *White Lies* as "my best story," and as late as November 1857 and January 1858, after its failure as a serial, declared that he still "had faith in the story and its ultimate success in the U.S. . . . There are signs of great popularity. In the states there are no petty jealousies conspiring against my success. . . ."

III

Although jealousy had little if anything to do with it, Reade was by this time encountering serious opposition (which he attributed to jealousy) from editors and publishers as well as from other writers and critics. In his disagreements with his English publisher Bentley—over Bentley's cheap edition of *Christie Johnstone* and later *Peg Woffington*—Reade was morally if not legally in the right. "The cheap English Edition," he wrote Fields (March

12, 1857), "has been dishonestly brought out in spite of an understanding between Bentley and myself." And the facts of the case, as set forth in the ensuing court actions, seem to bear out this contention.

The publishers themselves, however, viewed the case in a different light. They considered Reade's actions a revolutionary attack upon their time-honored practices, and reacted accordingly; indeed there are indications that Reade was by 1858 the victim of a publishers' boycott. And when, quoting Elwin, "Reade sought to evade their lock-out by publishing on his own account, they still had a card to play. Mr. C. E. Mudie refused to receive a copy of *Cream* . . . comprising the *Autobiography of a Thief* and . . . *Jack of all Trades* into his library . . ." alleging, in a letter to the press, that the *Autobiography of a Thief* seemed to him "of less than average ability, quite unworthy of Mr. Reade's high reputation, or of a place in any select library . . ." adding that if Reade would "write anything like his old delicate and sparkling freshness of style and feeling," he would "cheerfully give a good round sum for the first edition." [8]

In this instance Reade was not without his supporters, even among those he had dubbed "criticasters." *The Critic,* which published Mudie's letter, went on to comment: "We know that Mr. Reade's last work is rather unpopular with 'the trade,' not so much on account of its inferiority to *Christie Johnstone* as from the fact that Mr. Reade has taken the independent course of publishing the work on his own account." [9]

While this interpretation is no doubt correct, and perhaps helped to salve Reade's wounded pride, it did not cause Mudie to alter his decision. And in the meantime Reade's megalomaniacal schemes and machinations had led him into still another and in some respects even more disastrous battle over French copyright. He himself struck the first blow when, soon after the publication of *Never Too Late To Mend,* he purchased the English rights to *Les Pauvres de Paris,* a play by Brisebarre and Nus, then advertised his own English version of the play in *The Times,* announcing that he would "restrain by injunction any other version or imitation." His avowed object was "to try a great question of international good faith . . . for the benefit of literature and humanity," [10] and if in the process he also benefited Charles Reade, by securing what amounted to monopoly rights for his own translation, that to his way of thinking was quite compatible with his more ideal aim. For literature was a trade, writers tradesmen, and they could only do their best work when, like other trades-men, they were secure in their property rights, and bought rather than stole the works of other writers. "In my novel, 'It Is Never Too Late To Mend,' the thief's conversion is finally settled by his becoming a proprietor. This was true to nature, I assure you. If property will unbohemianize a thief, it will certainly unbohemian-ize artists. [11]

Coming from Reade such arguments appeared grossly hypo-critical, for as his criticasters were quick to observe, he too had stolen from the French, and in several instances had passed off the stolen work as his own—one of the most flagrant examples being his current novel *White Lies*. Quoting from Reade's own account of these charges (included in *The Eighth Commandment*): "A pseudonymuncule, writing under the sham signature of M. P. says . . . that my novel, 'White Lies,' *is in dialogue and incident a translation from a drama called 'Château Grantier,' filled up into three volumes with the moral reflections of the distinguished appropriator*, etc. Now the above statement having obtained a large currency, perhaps it may be as well to compare it with the truth." The truth, as Reade goes on to present it, is that "all the author's reflections together . . . may be six pages . . . com-pare this with the impression this liar has sought to create. . . ." [12] While Reade's count is doubtless correct, it is based on his own lawyer-like definition of what constitutes the "author's reflections," and is consequently a manifest evasion of the original charge, which is substantially correct. If anyone was a liar it was not the pseudonymuncule but Reade.

Also evasive are his efforts to vindicate himself scientifically: "Let us apply for once in a way scientific criticism. The test I propose is one, the value and severity of which will strike every man who knows the A B C of that science. . . . On its first appear-ance in the 'London Journal' 'White Lies' was illustrated by Mr. Gilbert. I don't know Mr. Gilbert . . . held no communica-tion with him. Proof-sheets were no doubt submitted to him by the publisher, and he selected for his pencil what his experience told him were the most dramatic and telling incidents. I put the inventor's name opposite each of these situations selected by Mr. Gilbert." [13] This test obviously worked to Reade's advantage, since his additions almost invariably took the form of "telling situa-tions" made to order for the illustrator's pencil. Yet even if one accepts the test at face value its results (seventeen or eighteen to four in favor of Reade) by no means exonerate Reade from the charge of plagiarism; they merely indicate that he stole less than had been implied. In his own words: "The plagiarism, you see, is small, the invention large by comparison." [14]

That Reade should go to such lengths to arrive at such a lame defense may appear foolish. The point is, however, that he was not trying to defend himself against the charge of plagiarism, but against the charge of theft, which was, in his vocabulary, something quite different. "By the word 'appropriator,'" he argued, "it was intended to convey that I have *stolen* French ideas (as my detractors do, and those they praise) instead of *buying* them like an honest trader." [15] In other words plagiarism was not stealing so long as one paid for what one plagiarized. It therefore followed, since he had paid Maquet £40 for *Château Grantier,* and added touches of his own devising, that he was perfectly justified in presenting the finished work as his own.

To Reade there was nothing curious or inconsistent in such a mode of reasoning; in fact he was genuinely at a loss to understand why his contemporaries should be so unreasonable—why, in addition to their charges against *White Lies,* they should point out that his early short stories (republished by Bentley in 1857 in a volume entitled *The Course of True Love Never Did Run Smooth*) were plagiarisms, implying "that their origin, instead of being doubly notorious, was a discreditable mystery; and that French talent was selling me, instead of being sold by my personal reputation. . . . By the light of 'It Is Never Too Late To Mend' Mr. Bentley, I hear, sold twenty-five thousand copies in a few months. . . ." [16]

So Reade argued, first in letters to the Press, and when his critics still persisted, in *The Eighth Commandment.* This book, which Reade himself described (in a letter to Fields, Nov. 3, 1859) as "a mixture of argument, scientific criticism not worded in jargon but telling English and *personal narrative,*" presents the case of Reade versus the literary world of his time, with Reade conducting his own defense, much as he did in the actual case of Reade vs. Bentley, and in the fictional case of Eden vs. Hawes. This is not to suggest that he was consciously adapting fictional techniques to non-fictional writing, or vice versa; the truth is, he could think in no other terms in matters involving his *amour propre.* The world, like the stage, was a courtroom in which he, the virtuous Solomonian, was constantly obliged to plead his case against cruelty and stupidity and villainy in the hope that the people, the final judge, would be able to recognize his wisdom and virtue. "Do not allow my good friend to resign his own excellent judgment to that of mediocre *writers*," he wrote Mrs. Fields (July 24, 1860). "Your housemaid will give you a better opinion of any work of mine than those men can."

And so, in the book itself, Reade belabored his criticasters with everything from erudition to indignation—expressing the latter with so much heat that, on the advice of Fields, he made a number of last minute revisions. "The most important," he wrote Fields (July 15, 1860), is "the alteration of 12 chapter. . . . Dirty Dixon would certainly have an action of libel against me on the original text . . . and as the English courts always favor the press in these cases I should have no chance of justice, besides being laughed at for nothing." It would be interesting to see the deleted passages since those he retained are fiery enough in themselves. From first to last he argued his case with paranoiac sincerity and brilliance, finally to demonstrate that his attackers were "skunks . . . a cabal of bookseller's hacks," that he "alone represented the honor of the nation in matters of dramatic copyright." [17]

IV

Reade's self-justification cost him dear—in time and energy as well as money. On the final page of *The Eighth Commandment* he noted: "It costs me at least £1000 to write such a book as this, the sale of which will not pay its expenses." Moreover, the vindication he sought through the courts was, in terms of hard cash, even more costly. "Being engaged in one or two lawsuits for the benefit of literature and humanity," he wrote Fields (Nov. 19, 1857), "I am bleeding like a bullock and shall receive with gratitude any sums, however small, you may find owing me. . . ." And this, as subsequent letters show, was only the beginning: to help defray the expenses of Reade vs. Conquest (over the dramatic rights to *Never Too Late To Mend*) he was obliged to apply to Ticknor (via Fields) for an advance amounting to an outright loan (Nov. 20, 1860)—even though, in an effort to cut down his own expenses, he had buried himself at Oxford, where he was "writing and spending about £1 per week."

Reade's poverty, which was not less bitter for being genteel, helps to explain why, following the publication of *Never Too Late*

To Mend, he temporarily abandoned "the great system" in favor of hasty adaptations and reprints, why his one piece of original writing, *Love Me Little, Love Me Long* (1859) was not a complete novel at all, but a fragment. "It will be in fact the first half of a 3 vol. novel," Reade wrote Fields. "But being in itself a complete story inasmuch as it ends with my Heroine's marriage after the usual troubles it will be published here by itself. . . . If you wish absolutely to secure this work you can do so by offering me £250 for it by return mail." Not a very strong recommendation; nor did Reade intend it to be. *Love Me Little, Love Me Long* was frankly a pot-boiler, written to defray his legal and publishing expenses while he made good his return to "the great system."

For by this time Reade himself was beginning to realize the seriousness of his predicament. He had used up the literary capital accruing from his first great success, and unless he could duplicate that success, and soon, the cabal might succeed in dismissing him as a one-novel novelist, like Samuel Warren, and thus drive him out of literature altogether. But if Reade was disturbed by these considerations, he was not so frantic as in his earlier crises. As early as January 8, 1858, he had spoken of "the necessity of writing *something great,*" and by something great, he of course meant another novel embodying the great system. "A man who steps out of the beaten track in every way," he wrote Mrs. Seymour, "must expect greater difficulties than other people. The question whether I can overcome them or not is not settled. When I produce another 'Never Too Late,' and the Cabal succeed in burking it, then I will give in. Not before!" [18]

v

In writing *A Good Fight,* his first version of *The Cloister and the Hearth,* Reade therefore applied the system in the spirit and after the manner he had followed in writing his prison epic—save for the fact that his historical subject rendered him entirely dependent on books, and consequently involved him in even more tedious research. "You may well be surprised," he wrote Fields, "that I am so long over 'Good Fight,' but the fact is it is not the writing but the reading which makes me slow. It may perhaps give you an idea of the system on which I write fiction if I jot down the list of books I have read, skimmed or studied to write this little misery." The list itself, which runs to 79 titles and ends with "etc. etc.," was designed to impress Fields and reaffirm his own faith in the system. [19] Immediately following the list he observes: "Yet forsooth all novel writing is to be called 'light literature. I should like to put my saddle on a criticaster: you would soon see the saddle on the ground with donkey pancake under it." Then, apropos of his own writing problems, he goes on to explain: "This system wasted on an old world story has kept you and me apart some months, which I regret, but then I hope your turn will come to benefit by it: for surely this *must be* the right method. Any way I shall apply the same diligence and research to the subject of our own day I am preparing for you, that I have expended, perhaps wasted on a medieval tale. Luckily a great part of the research is already done."

At this point Reade evidently held little hope for *The Cloister and the Hearth*. His main concern was for "the subject of our own day," and his statement "a great part of the research is already done" (presumably a reference to the materials he had collected on asylums in 1858, while working on the Fletcher Case) would seem to indicate that he had finally begun to extend and develop his mode of documentation to its full Baconian potential. In writing *Never Too Late To Mend*, his first "matter-of-fact romance," he had gathered his facts as he went along, in order to document specific aspects or phases of the novel. And he followed essentially the same procedure in writing *The Cloister and the Hearth*—his one technical innovation being the introduction of the now famous Notecards. "Alas, indeed," he wrote Mrs. Seymour, "Stuck! That is to say, I found such a wealth of materials about hermits in Magdalen College that I have filled three of those gigantic cards." But the cards, though helpful, did not solve his most difficult problem—how to combine research with writing. "Now my poor little head seems constructed on so narrow a basis," he continued, in his letter to Mrs. Seymour, "that whenever the ardor of research is on, the ardor of writing is extinct." [20]

VI

Discounting his researches in the Fletcher Case, which were to some extent adventitious, Reade's first attempt to develop a systematized collection of Notebooks seems to date from January 8, 1858, and has to do with the American theme he adumbrated in *Never Too Late To Mend*. "If I was in America," he wrote Fields, "what a romance I could write without a particle of exaggeration. Even from this side of the water if I could only get to read a thousand of your newspapers I think I could do something. I wish you would try and get hold of a lot cheap and send me over as goods and debit me. . . ." For one reason or another this plan did not work out too well: perhaps Fields did not prove to be a very enterprising collector, or perhaps the shipping expenses were greater than Reade anticipated. In any event he turned from Mr. to Mrs. Fields when, on July 24, 1860, he sought to initiate a more systematic plan: "Among your friends and mine is there anyone who has leisure and charity to make extracts of American papers under certain heads for me and send them me in a bushel basket once a quarter?" [21] In answer to this request Mrs. Fields bravely volunteered her own services: she had made extracts for Reade earlier, to his entire satisfaction, and was apparently willing to devote a few hours to the process once again; in fact she even went so far as to send along a number of extracts with her letter. But Reade, in acknowledging the kindness of her offer (Sept. 6, 1860), made it clear that he was no longer interested in a limited number of extracts, that he was in deadly earnest about the bushel basket: "I did not mean you to be the victim of my newspaper cutting propensities. There are idle people in the world, to whom even this sort of thing may look like doing something. And there are poor people who might like to do this easy work for a little money. Now I, on my side, would be very glad to invest a few dollars per annum in this way. These things have a value to *me* which you can hardly conceive; only I want them en masse."

Perhaps Reade did receive extracts and clippings *en masse,* but if so, he did not enter them *en masse,* as was his practice in later Notebooks; for the only extant Notebook devoted to America is the one now in the Parrish Collection labelled Americana, and it consists almost entirely of notes and anecdotes (in Reade's own hand) having to do with slavery. A few of the notes (there are no clippings whatsoever) are but brief references that seem to be copies of newspaper extracts. On page 1, for instance, Reade notes:

Colleges

Negro Blood not admitted

to them.

Why?

And again on p. 4, under the heading "Negrocide":

> *Mulatto girl . . — mulattos delicate*
> *Religious mistress. frailty, order*
> *her 190 lashes and then sent to the*
> *plantation on a horse — corpse arrived*
> *on the horse* tantum religio potuit.

This last entry connects up with and may in part provide the basis for the entries on the immediately succeeding pages, in which Reade seems to be crystallizing his facts into dialogue and characters:

> *Mrs. Merryweather at the ball*
> *beautiful. softened light in her*
> *once.*
>
> *Mrs. M. There is a strong feeling*
> *[about?] you and [would?] it not*
> *be as well to*
>
> *No. I will live it down or die.*
> *Isn't she beautiful?*
>
> *Yes. . . but. She is a murderess*
> *Ah . . but it was only a negro . .*
> *and she is very pretty.*
>
> *I will break the ice. and ask . . .*
> *her to dance*
>
> *Well if you will do that I will*
> *follow. —*
> .   .   .   .
>
> *Mrs. Merryweather*
> *You have not been quick enough*
>
> *Oh Mistress. You. don't know*
> *this work*
>
> *What do you . . .*
>
> *There that is enough —. . . [trip?]*
> *the bell. Send for the overseer.*
> *. . . No Jerry shall whip her.*
>
> *The Machine*
>
> *quadrilaterals: —*

[184]

feet tied together
arms extended —

Mrs. Merryweather. out of window.
jeweled hand. lay on. lay on! —
overseer. — lay on harder
drew her up. —. found her dead —
Mrs. M. goes to whip her again.
          — dead.

. . . .

                    hurt
Oh. I didn't mean to kill her . .
Cut her down directly and bury her.
Make a bonfire of her clothes.

Yet if you met her . . she would
fascinate — you —

Zealot objects to her. soft. hand
like a piece of cotton. . —
like a cat.

Messenger sent to arrest her:
how they managed

Jerry . . .
sugar coated pill
cursed with power, and beauty.[22]

Needless to say this is a classic example of sadistic fantasy. And Reade treats similarly another group of characters and incidents having to do with slavery under the headings "Incidents" and "Miscellaneous." As Professor Sutcliffe has observed: "These entries may well be early notes for the novel on which Reade requested Mark Twain's assistance in 1872" [23]—in which case Reade applied to the wrong novelist. Mrs. Stowe would have been a more logical choice, or even Sacher-Masoch, for the notes themselves have little more to do with America than his earlier descriptions of Parisian morgues and slaughterhouses had to do with Paris. The explanation would seem to be that Reade found the same excitement in the newspaper accounts of American slavery that he had found in the accounts of Birmingham prison, and that this excitement caused him to lose sight of his Baconian objectives in the Notebook, which are evident only in matters of outward format.

VII

In the meantime, however, Reade had begun work on at least one other Notebook, labelled "Digest," and to make certain that he developed it and others he had in mind according to plan he set down on page one a "Memoranda Agenda" consisting of some nineteen points, the most revealing of which are as follows:

1. Plagiarize from Ephemerales "Times" in particular
3. Make pictures disgorge for the benefit of Tales and Plays, Capital idea. ditto didactic passages and characters in didactic works
4. Study pictures largely for stage effects.
8. Practice Excision on Musical Composers as on Dramatic. Handel like Shakespeare. wants the Scissors.
11. Apply the modes of Physical investigation to letters. Learn what are the modes. Statistics too are gathered. How carry out the great principle. Microscope. Telescope. Glass Hive.
13. Having wasted too many years to be learned I must use cunning. Think of some way to make young active fellows run and collect materials for me. Think of A Machinery. Government though not very brainful produces books. Briareus like; why might not I, and lick the rough cub into shape. Thus start the conception. Learn the sources by Watt's Bibliotheca, Mr. Donne, Bandinel etc. Then put my hacks on, *leaving gaps:* so that they may not see the whole design, and steal the capital idea. German hacks good for this. University hacks ditto. Pay them well and keep them dark.
14. Cultivate the foreigner's eye
Get every book intelligent Foreigners have written upon England or London and write a story and try to view familiar things with a stranger's eye. There is a book by a Frenchman date 1812 recently a good book on London by a German. Make inquiries for more . . .
15. Get Alphabetical Box for loose notes
16. Collect Plays with a good Master Idea
17. Mem. It is necessary to command an anonymous defence. start a magazine & hold a property in it. The just the plain-speaker just judge.
18. Collect minutiae of Desolation, Decay, and many other things
19. Dramatize Haliburton's Apothegms vide Sam Slick & his other works. A fund of wisdom under his fun. English can't see this: could not see Sydney Smith's Wisdom. All this in an article "Merry and wise." [24]

With the possible exception of numbers 8, 14, 17, and 19, which have to do with plans for specific books or projects, there is nothing new in any of these statements. They merely represent a further extension and systematization of the Baconian principles that he enunciated as early as 1852, and that he had practised in all his writing through the intervening years. The most significant change is in the tone of the statements, the greater complacency with which Reade covertly acknowledges the feebleness of his imagination and openly elaborates his plagiaristic schemes. Already one of the writers of the day without benefit of a fully developed fictional Instauratio, there was no limit to what he might achieve with it.

Primarily, then, Reade envisaged the Notebooks as "a steam engine for truth"—a Baconian steam engine on which he, provided he was a good engineer, could ride to the heights of literary greatness that only a few writers, and those the very greatest, had been able to reach by their own unaided powers. And when he was not riding the machine to literary greatness he could guide it into other, and as he conceived them, broader areas of human experience—finally to solve all, or nearly all, the world's problems. The magic, he acknowledged, was in the machine, but he, as engineer, was both the builder and operator of the machine, which should therefore stand as a monument to his own greatness. Hence the number and variety of the Notebooks devoted to *personalia:* some given almost entirely to manuscripts and reprints of his own works, others to clippings critical and biographical, and still others to biographical materials he had himself collected. Hence too the bulk and variety of the entries in these notebooks, ranging from the address of his tailor to guarded comments on his abstemiousness, and all designed to validate his magniloquent conception of himself as the writer-saviour of the Nineteenth Century.

To do justice to his self-image Reade from the very first directed his more strictly Baconian Notebooks to all sorts of grandiose schemes—non-fictional as well as fictional. In the "Digest" alone, as Professor Sutcliffe has pointed out, his "projects include not only novels and plays, but (1) a legal handbook for the man in the street; (2) a 'nova scientia'—a cosmopolitan survey of good and bad national practices; (3) collections of short stories and anecdotes; (4) a book on social abuses." [25] Nor is this the end. Entries and statements in other Notebooks dating from this time show that he projected a *Medicina Laici,* and, less definitely, books on the Bible, advertising, food adulteration, and a host of other subjects.

Although he failed to complete any of these projects, at least in the terms outlined, his manner of stating and restating his plans—as in his initial discussion of the legal handbook ("Digest," p. 39)—leaves no doubt as to the seriousness of his intentions: "A gigantic success might be atchieved [sic] by a law-book that should tell people what the judgment of the Court will be. . . . If this is used ridicule must be averted thus. I cannot be called a lawyer save by an extravagant stretch of courtesy. This is not a lawyer imposing his science on letters pedantically, it is a lay-man who has looked at the fences which the great balancers of proof have found it necessary to guard the judgment." [26]

And on page 40 of the same Notebook, under "Titles," he propounds at length his plans for a "Nova scientia":

The Wisdom of Nations

Collect and compare all the bits of wisdom in barbarous and civilized lands. Dwarf Quarto for the sake of the comparisons. N.B. Compton Reade solicitor says that whenever a statute is passed on an old subject every preceding statute ought to be repealed. The reasons.

N.B. This great work might be given to the world professedly inchoate and the plan shown the men of all Nations might be invited to contribute facts

better be done in numbers

This Book is the first stone of an Edifice too great for any one man to build. Receipt for making a statesman.

Each nation has its wisdom & its folly, and is wiser than other nations in some points, sillier in others. clings to them equally. Could one man by the industry of a single life compile the strong & weak points of the several Nations in one view he would be "The Father of all Statesmen." Yankee phrase.

Occasional glimpses of this method in the acts of governments sending over to Paris for this sort of information previous to legislating. They have often fingered the idea but they couldna haud it.

Plan of this great work

3 books 1 Large text 1 small 1 notes Query? whether English statutes ought not to be written in the Anglo Saxon element[27]

The beauty of this plan, from Reade's point of view, lay in its

imposing hugeness, which not only excused him from thinking it
through but also permitted him to indulge his pedantic interest
in all sorts of out of the way and insignificant facts—on the ground
that these facts provided the Solomonian foundations for "the
Wisdom of Nations." But of course the facts he collected are in
no sense Solomonian; they are invariably Readian, so much so
at times that no one but Reade could take them seriously, much
less consider them the foundations of Wisdom. The entries headed
"Sap Anglicana" and "Stultica Celtica" in the Notebook "Sapientia
Gentium" provide typical examples. Under the first heading Reade
undertakes a factual analysis of conditions in the French and
British Armies that reveals little more than his own sadistic-
humanitarian preoccupation with "spur . . . whip . . . lash," and
in the second his wisdom is still more uniquely Readian:

> Irish folly above wisdom in growing
> the potatoe [sic]. folly in cooking
> it with a raw indigestible bit in the
> middle

> The Irish in their conduct of the potatoe [sic]
> resemble that lunatic who got out of
> asylum. with many ingenious processes.
> and being outside threw up his cap
> and hurrahed. till the keepers woke
> with the noise, dressed, came out and
> recaptured the noisy jubilant
> Photograph two potatoes: the
> Club potatoe and one boiled by me. Send
> them to Dr. A. S. Taylor. for judgement [sic]
> proportions of water and farina.

In boiling potatoes, as in matters of copyright, it is once again
Reade versus a nation, for it is to be noted that the potato is
not to be boiled by an Englishman but "by me." That Reade could
go on so about a boiled potato, in the name of science and "The
Wisdom of Nations," shows how pathologically direct was the
connection between his ego and his sense of values. And this
connection in large measure determines the form and substance
of the entries more explicitly devoted to fiction and fictional
projects. Reade's plans for the nineteenth century short story,
for instance, are almost as vast as his plans for "The Wisdom

of Nations," and he certainly states them ("Digest," p. 59) with equal naïvete and grandiloquence:

> Good hard stories. The short story of the nineteenth century is one of the blunders of the age: it is a flabby anecdote generally without a true anecdote's backbone. It is impossible to write a story in a short compass containing character as well as plot. Dip into what repertory you will of short stories & substitute consonants for the characters, the story would [not] lose. There are one act farces containing famous characters. To this there is no parallel in the novel. The figures in Boccaccio's stories have some little distinctive character: but about as much as the peas in a pod. . . . This gap in fiction I mean to try and fill; with the aid of others: and I shall use the aid of others: for I hope to stir up an original writer in this kind, for I have hardly time or fertility to fill so large a gulf.[28]

This is again Reade the literary engineer surveying a project; and when he becomes more specific ("Digest," p. 1), the mechanical aspects of his approach stand out all the more clearly:

> Good Stories, or corpus fictorum
> Might use 1st my power of discerning the immortal element
> 2. My knowledge of what is to be done by excision
> 3. Power of translating
> 4. of turning good plays into stories by interstitial scenes.
> 5. Research into old repertories
> 6. Critical remarks on each.
>
> 1. *Leviathan.* 2. Good Fight 3. de Bernard[29]

Points one to six, like so many of Reade's technical memoranda, are but repetitions or systematized extensions of the plagiaristic techniques he had been using since he first started to adapt French plays. As for the three "good stories" the first, "Leviathan," he elsewhere identifies as *Moby Dick,* the second is his own "Good Fight," and the third is presumably a work (or works) by Charles de Bernard. A strange assortment certainly, and one which shows that, no matter how much he systematized his plagiaristic techniques, he still remained blind to any but the Sensation qualities of the works to be plagiarized, e.g., in his further references to *Moby Dick* he treats the novel as merely another "whaling story"— to be turned into an immortal work by the discreet application of his six points.

Nor is this a unique example. Everything Reade looked upon, from *Moby Dick* to boiled potatoes, was so much grist for his Baconian mill—to be stored and classified in his Notebooks under headings so various that he eventually felt obliged to work out an alphabetical index—a printed pamphlet in double columns entitled "List of Subjects entered as headings in my various guard books and solid digests." Typical are the headings listed under "C.", "H.", "L.", "N.", and "S.":

C. Calamities/Calibani et Calibanae, or human brutes/California/Cancer/Canine/Cant/Captures/Cat, the/Caractera vera/ Caractera ficta/Carrier Pigeon/Caveat emptor/Caves/Cave-dwellings/Celebrities/Cetacea/Characters, Scripture/Characters, Servants/Chaces/Children/Childery/Children, terrible/Child murder/ Child stripping/Child stealing/Chinaman, John/Churches/Church incidents/ Church, story of/Chloral/Chloroform/Citabilia/Circumstantial evidence/Classificanda/Claimants/Classificanda Miscellanea /Clearing out the Serpentine/Clergyman/Coal Mine/Coffins/Coiners/Coincidences/Colors, mixtures of; philosophy of/Commissioner/Royal and Parliamentary Commissions, Newspaper Commissioners/Collisions, Land and Sea/Common-place books/Comic/Copyright/Conjugalia/Conspiracies/Cornish/Cornwall v. Barry/Corpses /Costermongers/Costume/Country, scenes, characters, books. See Rus/Court/Crime, everywhere/The Criticaster/Cruelty/CURIALIA, or Man as revealed in Courts of Law: a vast heading/ Curiosities, of Mind, Nature, human nature, Law, Crime, Religion, Medicine, the Blue Books/

H. Hair dyes/Hallucinations/Hard labor. Heads, in Pict. lib./ HEROES AND MARTYRS/HEROINES/Hicks, career and execution (Giant Folio 2.)/High Feluten/Highwaymen/Hoaxes/Hoax, slain by/Houses, fall of Homœopathy/Honesty is the best policy/ Hopley Mrs. Foem. Vera/Horses/Hospital/Hotels/Housekeepers/ Housemaids/Household Management/Humbug/HUMORES DIEI, or Humors of the Day, a heading to embrace all the singular features, the dead hair, the blood-drinking by delicate women, the rinking, the Ritualism, Vegetarianism, Cremation, dust to dust. The gay party to inspect the basket coffins. The humors of medicine, religion, etc., etc. The baby shows, barmaid shows. Everything shows. Celibacy of the English clergy, Confession, Vestments, etc. etc./Hugo, Victor, fine trait/Husbands/Husband levanting/

L. Lacing tight/Ladies/Land Sharks and Sea Gulls/Launch/ Lauriana or Seymoriana/Law cases/Law costs/Law's delay/"LAW GIVER WANTED" Heading for the defects and inconsistencies of

existing law/Leaps/Leading Ideas/Legal errors in fiction/Legisla-
ture, comments on by the Judges/Letters/Libri et Libelli. The best
books on various topics/Libri emendi sive legendi/Life-boats/Life-
saving (at sea) service/Lighthouse/Links, for plots/Liquefaction
in writing/Little lady/Literary Zoology/ Locked up/Lodging-
houses/London sketches/Lost Heirs/Love/Love making/Love combined with Hate/Luck/Lunatica/Lust hard by hate/Lynch/Lynch,
Madam/

N. Names/Needle-woman/Newgate, sketches of/Nightshade/
Night of terror/NIGRI LOCI, or the dark places of the land. This
is a heading of vast extent, comprising cruelties and iniquities in
Prisons, Police cells, Asyla, Ships, Emigrant Ships especially, Mines,
Secret or demi-secret tribunals, like the Committee of Privileges,
House of Lords, Public Schools, Work-houses, Convents, Factories,
violent exclusion of females, China Painters, female robbed of the
maul stick, milliners' work rooms, etc/Nobleman, honest. Lord
Chandos/Novelizanda, all matter fit to be turned into fictitious nar-
rative/Noverca/NOVAE SCIENTIAE, new sciences proposed to be
created as Criticism, Education, Juriscription/Nunnery/Nurses/

S. Sabbatarian/Sacred drama/Sad story/Sad career of a girl/
Sailors. Jack ashore/Salt mine/SAP. GENT., or the wisdom and
folly of various nations/Sea, disasters and sufferings at/Scalped
by machinery/Scenes/Science/SCIENCE DETECTING CRIME/
Scientific women/Scripture-characters/Seduction/Self-denial/Sepul-
chre/Sera nunquam, or never too late to mend—examples/Servants/
Sharpers/Sham deaths, or doubtful/Ships, wilful destruction of, etc./
Shipwrecks/Shocking incidents/Sic vos non vobis/Short Stories/
Situations/Skeletons/Slang/Society, its humors/Spiritualism/Statis-
tics/Statute Fair/Steeple Jack/Stepmother/Street/Arabs/Strikes/
Subjects/Suburbs, brutality of the London/Suggestive/Suicides/
Suicide, advantages of attempted/Sunken treasure/Swindlers/
Swinging adventure/[30]

These indexed headings are the outward signs of Baconian
order with which Reade endeavored to give a show of systematic
objectivity to his *Instauratio*. But it is only a show, and at times
not a very good one. For a considerable number of the headings—
from "Ambidexterity" to "Words Invented by Reade"—are direct
reflections of his egomania; and the remainder, with few exceptions,
serve to rationalize the aberrational passions and beliefs he could
not express openly—including, of course, his lust for blood and
violence. Just by exploiting the numerous subheadings listed under
"Nigri Loci" he was able to record the grossest cruelties *ad*

nauseam—in the name of Art and Humanity and Truth. Furthermore there was, for less morally purposeful violence, the heading "Humores Diei," which provided him with an excuse for the inclusion of everything from "Cremation" to "blood-drinking by delicate women." [31] And when this heading was not applicable, he could fall back on "Calibani," "lust hard by hate," or any number of related headings.

Nor was Reade limited to specific headings. His Sensation theories fully justified his use of technical headings, such as "Plots," to record all sorts of harrowing accounts—one of which concludes: "She did so and they found her husband half in the window half out and the dog worrying him by the throat. He was fearfully torn and quite dead." [32] Also under "Plots" is a clipping "How Talma Won his Wife," a detailed factual account which explains how Talma, who had admired an actress for some eight years, finally won her from her husband—by sucking her wound when it would not bleed. To which Reade added, by way of professional comment: "Let the unhappy lover have tried everything in vain. Till this makes a good climax." [33]

Read in connection with the clipping, Reade's comment seems to have interesting sexual as well as literary implications. But there is no need for subtlety of interpretation when Reade's sadism is writ large on almost every page of these early Notebooks—not only under headings which in one way or another seem to justify it but under those which might be expected to preclude it. A clipping headed "Voces ex populo," for instance, explains how cannon might be made safer for sailors, three of whom had lost thumbs saluting the Prince of Wales.[34] And on the same page, under the heading "Self Government," Reade devotes a column labelled "con" to arguments that center around a newspaper clipping entitled "Terrible Railway Collision," and a column labelled "Pro" to an article by one Henry Allen, "the prosecuting officer to the Associate Institution for Promoting & Enforcing the Laws for the Protection of Women." On the "Pro" side Reade concludes his commentary thus: "See the excuse made by certain neighbors for not interfering with Mrs. Allens cruelty Aug x 60. See sneer at me in Sat Rev. for defending in Fletcher v. Fletcher. The same cause for which Hampden bled.—our liberty. Small minds cannot generalize." Then, on the very next page, as if to demonstrate once again his own Solomonian powers of generalization, he discusses "Arabian Wisdom," to conclude that the Arabians "make the horse a friend. We make him a brute. Humble and kick. . . . See Leader in Times about German dragoons kinder to their horses than English."

For the most part, however, Reade did not rely upon his powers of generalization—superior as he believed them to be. In discussing the shortcomings of English law (under "Legal") he observes: "The oath made more solemn in Scotland and France by lifting the hand. . . . Your Kephalomants would say the mode would never make the difference. I have studied human nature and believe that in many cases it would. But happily we are not at the mercy of Mr. Reade's or any other man's intelligent conjectures. Ecce Factum!" [35] Hence the inclusion of detailed articles and pictures having to do with pigeon shooting, cock fighting, horse beating, and man beating. This last category Reade found especially interesting when the beater was a muscular woman, as in the case of the woman doctor in Dewitt, Iowa, who whipped a male doctor.[36] Under the heading "Heroes" in this Notebook *(Viri feminaeque juventes)* Reade listed or recorded the feats of many such Amazons, usually with their addresses, or a notation as to where he might secure further information. And when he learned about the heroism of a local maid servant he resolved to carry out his researches in person:

HEROES

A *Maid servant at Twickenham*
not far from the church. fought with a
burglar for several minutes in
defense of her mistress, got him
down and bound him by sheer
strength and pluck he being
armed and she unarmed.

Mem.   *try and find her!*
Measure her throat. waist.
wrist   biceps and arm   Foot
Height.[37]

While there is no evidence that Reade actually tried to measure the Maid of Twickenham, he did act upon the similar notations that appear so frequently in the Notebook variously labelled "Digest 3," "Woman," and "Foemina Vera." Though ostensibly devoted to all phases and aspects of woman, more than half the entries in this Notebook are directly concerned with androgynism.

Typical of the briefer entries are those on page three in Reade's hand:

WOMAN PLAYING AT MAN

Pope Joan

The Dialogue between a Protestant and a Papist (Alex Cooke) Harleian Misc vol 4 p 63 cites Nuns that passed their lives as monks un discovered. . .

ELISABETH ANNE HOLMAN

A D 1858

aetat 23 a woman who says "she will wear man's clothes and do man's work though she should be transported for it" said this I think before the Mayor at Exeter. has two bastards Mayor, instead of punishing her, gave her money from poor box Mem. find date!

1859

late in Aug or early Sept a woman who has long served as a sailor: her excuse that she has a sickly husband. Mem! find out whether she supported him.

on opposite page, facing the above entry:

"Mem! Find the female sailor this year and 2 female navvy last year: X 59"

Pathetic story in "Monthly Mirror" woman hung for it in old times

Voyages de Montaigne. Search Annual Register

Female bricklayer at Liverpool married for years to another woman.   Collusion nummi causa

Of these and the numerous other examples of androgynism which Reade clipped, summarized, or discussed the one he investigated most thoroughly it would seem was that of Fred, a young married woman who, with her husband's consent, posed as his

[195]

son—and so successfully that, again with her husband's consent, she courted and became engaged to a young girl, one Miss Smith. For undisclosed reasons Fred and her husband then took Miss Smith to Moulton, where the three of them posed as father, son, and daughter, until Miss Smith's father arrived on the scene and exposed Fred for the woman she was—much to his daughter's surprise and dismay. All this plus a great deal more is included in a clipping of some one thousand words from "Loyd's Sept. 9, 1860" which Reade (following his own underlinings and markings: "a b c" and "1 2 3 4") annotated as follows:

> *The victim of hoax lives at Bedford. Fred & her husband*
> *at present, but probably not for long at Moulton*
> *Northamptonshire. For further information enquire*
> > *H.O. Nethercote Esq.*
> > *Moulton Grange*
> > > *Northamptonshire*
> *and look back to journals for the story has*
> *escaped me.   "observer"   Sept 9 X 60*

> *Queries suggested by the meagre account on this page.*

> *1st   Why did Miss Smith lend herself to the*
> *lie   a, and, if she did, why?*

2. *Was plunder intended or what by the husband?*

3. *Is it not possible that Miss Smith supplied*
   a certain want to this childless woman's
   heart. In short that she wanted something
   inferior to love and cherish, and look
   down on; to her husband she probably
   looked up as he is a blackguard, and
   she a woman age of Fred 25 of Miss
   Smith 17   The ring B   looks ugly

4. *What are the sentiments of a woman*
   who finds the man she is deep in love
   in is only a woman

c   *can the bare discovery cure*
    in one moment a passion that
    has become a habit, or is the
    discovery like the death of
    a beloved object.

[196]

These annotations fill the margins of page 1. On the page opposite
Reade wrote the single word "Rosalind," and on page 2 he continued his commentary:

c *What was the first origin of all*
   this mischief the injustice of man. Woman's
   labor is ridiculously underpaid. Fred
   saw this, and, to get fair wages, donned
   the breeches: that she was not found out by her
   inferior work shows it was a real injustice
   she baffled. This cause has operated [as?]
   above hundreds of times before Frederica
   *   Since writing all this a horrible solution*
   has been suggested. viz that Coombe and
   his wife intended to set up a brothel
   somewhere, and Miss Smith was to be at
   once a victim and bait. This to me in conversation
   the editor of "Globe," but citing "the observer"
   origin some Birmingham paper If true
   this nowise affects observation c but only
   queries 1, 2, 3, for Fred assumed male
   disguise before she knew Miss Smith.
   *   "Disguise I see thou art a counterfeit*
   *   In which the pregnant enemy does much"*
   *   Twelfth Night*
   Mem.   *Write Mr. Nethercote*   *Query a & 3*

On pages 5, 6 and 7 Reade pasted in a much longer and more
detailed clipping (presumably from a later issue of Lloyd's) which
gives still further details on the case, including a number of Fred's
love letters quoted in full. In the margin of page 7 Reade noted:

I have Mr. Nethercote's own word that Fred did not weep.
Only once when old Smith
detailed his paternal sufferings, his
eye went moist, no more
Mr. Nethercote is an accurate observer,
whom one can trust.

---

on visiting Moulton and after a long
talk with Mrs. Whiting, whom the two
lodged with, I am convinced the brothel
solution is all bosh. Fred is in figure
and in mind an eccentric woman, does
not care much for her husband, and had

a sort of passion for the girl. Nor is
this so very uncommon a thing. She
was jealous of the girl.
Mem. to write down that good
creature Whitings story
of it all before I forget her.[38]

In this last comment, as in his earlier query concerning Miss
Smith's sentiments, Reade shows a remarkable understanding of
Lesbian love. Possibly the understanding was really Mrs. Whiting's,
or Mr. Nethercote's, or perhaps the plight of the two girls aroused
his sympathies without challenging his feelings of emotional
security, thus permitting him to fuse his experimental and theatrical sophistication with his literary knowledge (e.g., "Rosalind")
to arrive at what, for a Victorian novelist, would seem to be a
uniquely sympathetic and perceptive estimate of Fred's Lesbianism.

In any event, the understanding he shows in this one instance
does not carry over to his other entries, which he almost invariably
dismisses with one or another of his usual over-simplifications, e.g.,
"nummi causa" or "Calibanae." In fact there is no indication that
he recognized the relationship between Fred's Lesbianism and that
of the Amazonian ladies whose feats he clipped and recorded
throughout the rest of the Notebook. As for the connection between
the muscular strength of these Amazons ("especially under excitement") and his own sadomasochistic interests and needs, that he
could not possibly see—despite the fact that nearly all his factual
Amazons are man-savers or man-beaters, usually after the manner
of his own Christie Johnstone but often going much further, as in
the clipping on page 44, which describes and illustrates "Fantee
Women stimulating Masculine Courage" by whipping a hapless
male.

VIII

Reade's systematized Notebooks thus duplicate the general
pattern of his earlier Baconian notes and jottings—though, for all
his fuss about "hard labor and severe system," the Notebooks are
less systematic, more idiosyncratic. In his earlier researches, conducted with a view to filling out the outlines of a given work or
works, he had perforce been obliged to follow the order and limits
imposed by his immediate fictional aims. And while those aims
had oftentimes encouraged him in one or another of his aberra-

tional propensities—witness the "black facts" of Birmingham Gaol—
he had still felt obliged to justify his factualism in relation to
that of great writers from Homer to Mrs. Stowe.

In the Notebooks, on the other hand, his sole responsibility
was to his Baconian machinery, which, as he conceived and
applied it, served to grind every recalcitrant fact to the consistency
of his boiled potato, and thus to justify the self-image that is
apparent on every page of the Notebooks, most clearly, perhaps,
on page 33 of *Viri feminique juventes:*

> *Owen Lovejoy of Illinois*
> *A Demosthenes: see his speeches*
> *against slavery Weekly Tribune*
> *(chez moi) the steady temper and*
> *resolution with which he persisted*
> *with the other party insulting him like*
> *terriers jumping at a Newfoundland*
> *dog is a lesson to you Mr. C.R.*
> *Grand Simile. Iceberg Query*
> *whether borrowed a little from*
> *Victor Hugo.*
>
> *Napoleon the little*

Reade's simile shows how great was his Narcissistic need for the
Notebooks. They provided him with the only theatre in which
he could play C. R. to his entire satisfaction, i.e., as a Newfound-
land dog amongst terriers. In the theatre of fiction as in that of
life, the terriers (led by the Criticasters, Anonymuncules, and
Kephalomants) could band together to challenge or deny his pre-
eminence; by devious means they could even send him down to
defeat. But in the Notebooks, since he was at once author, hero,
and audience, there could be no challenge, no defeat. He was
free to act out and justify and applaud his every whim, notion,
and passion in the name of Art and Baconian truth. And that, the
entries themselves reveal, is exactly what he did, to put together
a series of Notebooks true to nothing save his Solomonian and
sadistic fantasies.

But Reade of course remained blissfully unaware of any deficiencies in "the system." To him these early Notebooks represented the beginnings of an *Instauratio* that would eventually
rival Bacon's, and that, in the meantime, would provide him
with the machinery he needed to duplicate the greatness of his
prison epic.

CHAPTER IX

Hard Cash:

"Uncomparably My Best Production"

He plunged from the seaside novel into the sea of fiction. He rechristened that joyous art feckshin, and lashed its living professors, "You devour their three volumes greedily," said he, "but after your meal you feel as empty as a drrum; there is no leading idea in 'um; now, there always is—in Molière: and *he* comprehended the midicine of his age. But what fundamental truth d'our novelists iver convey? All they can do is pile incidents. Their customers dictate th' article; unideaed melodrams for unideaed girls. . . .

—*Hard Cash*

✐   ✐   ✐

How are hits made? By filling gaps. Comment: Hence the imitator of a hit maker fails; he does not in fact imitate: for he throws his duplicate on a mound; whereas the original threw No 1 into a gulf.

RECIPE

How to write such a story as Romola No 1 Fit a pump handle to your common place book: and hire a metaphysical bastard to work it or and let a bastard metaphysician work it.

To base a novel upon novels is to paint the shadows of shades. Novels ought always to be built on hard fact.

GOOD FOR PREFACE
TRUTH IN FICTION

What shall I but invent colorless lies, when Truth comes to me with her apron full of melodramatic truths, and charges me nothing for them.

—Charles Reade—Notecard headed Arundiniana

✐   ✐   ✐

The ordinary novel, which deals, however ably, with shadows only, is one kind of property, a story that cuts deep into realities of the day, and has already set hundreds discussing it as history and law, is a different thing; it finds buyers as well as readers, and that amongst a class that does not buy novels as a rule.

—Charles Reade (in a letter to Edward Marston)

✐   ✐   ✐

The "idea" for *Hard Cash*, like the "idea" for *Never Too Late To Mend*, Reade attributed to *The Times* (in a Letter to the Editor, August 26, 1871): "You put forth an able and eloquent leader on private asylums, and detailed the sufferings there inflicted on persons known to you. This took root in me, and brought forth its fruit in the second volume of 'Hard Cash.'"[1] While there is some truth in this statement it is nevertheless misleading: another strategic oversimplification designed to stress the topicality and respectability of his thematic purpose. The intellectual substance of Parson Eden's sermon on cruelty indicates that Reade was fully aware of asylums by the time he wrote on prisons. Indeed, given his interests and outlook, it could hardly have been otherwise, for both the Evangelicals and Benthamites were much concerned with asylums, going so far as to maintain that the insane and the feeble-minded were even worse off than prisoners; that they, like "slaves" and "factory children" were helpless victims, not free agents; that consequently their confinement should be strictly regulated by law to ensure their receiving sympathetic and intelligent care.[2]

These principles Reade shared with his fellow reformers, though in expressing them he went to extremes which betray a concern more personal than religious or philosophical. And quite understandably so. For, as Professor Sutcliffe has pointed out, "The *Memoir* makes plain that Reade was the occasional victim of deep and prolonged nervous exhaustion and depression of the kind that sometimes seizes his male characters, who have brain-fever and fall into fits, sometimes epileptic."[3] And what the *Memoir* does not make plain, Reade himself does, not only in his Notebooks but also in his published writings—nowhere more obviously than in his factual account of the Fletcher Case, in which he carries his defensiveness so far as to have the doctor who examines Fletcher testify to his, Charles Reade's, sanity. In this and other attempts at self vindication he was refuting without acknowledging the charges of madness that had been levelled at him since his undergraduate days—charges that he not only hated but feared; for, "urged by that terror of a madhouse, which is natural to a sane man, and in England is fed by occasional disclosures, and the general suspicion they exert,"[4] he apparently felt that such charges, coupled with his known crotchets and fits of depression, might be sufficient to secure his own incarceration under the statute *de Lunatico*.

[201]

During his earlier years of *Sturm und Drang,* when only Mrs. Reade stood between him and his father's wrath, he may possibly have had some basis for his "terror of a madhouse." By this time, however, his fears were entirely groundless—if for no other reason, because his fame as a novelist had in point of fact placed him beyond the reach of the Lunacy Laws. But such feelings are seldom if ever reasonable. And in Reade's case there is evidence that his fears went deeper: that he was not so much afraid of the law as he was of lunacy itself. While he could never admit this fear, he was nevertheless obliged, beginning at Oxford, to recognize that in many ways he did not and could not feel and thnk as his fellows did; that for this reason he was considered "eccentric" (or even "mad") and, still more intolerable, "inferior." Yet he could not change or conform without surrendering his own and his mother's ideals. To meet the charges of inferiority and madness he therefore had to believe and prove and maintain his superiority—especially in those areas in which inferiority was linked with madness. Hence his stress on the paraphernalia of systematic thought, particularly logic, which he invoked at every opportunity to prove the soundness of his mind as well as his arguments— never realizing that his Baconian ingenuity, applied to his whims and passions, magnified the eccentricity of his mind, and thus provoked still further jibes and attacks, punctuated with veiled charges of simplemindedness or insanity.

To all such attacks Reade invariably retorted in kind. No charge, no slight, however insignificant, was beneath his notice. He answered them all—in court, in print, in the Notebooks—as if his very life depended on it. As indeed it did, in a very real sense. His predicament may be compared with that of the harassed animal in Kafka's *The Burrow* who could not feel secure so long as there was a possible opening through which his enemies, real and imagined, might penetrate his protective maze. The one major difference is that Reade's Baconian rationalizations, particularly as embodied in his Notebooks, provided him with a burrow more nearly adequate to his psychic needs, one through which he could translate his deepest fears and passions, first into humanitarian facts, then into the fearless heroics of humanitarian fiction.

II

In keeping with his Sensation theories, however, the facts had to be "warm." Although he had been collecting data on "Asyla" since perhaps as early as 1851, it was not until May 21, 1858, that his matter-of-fact muse presented him with "the astonishing case of the Reverend Mr. Leech who, having gained by his father's will the absolute reversion of thirty thousand pounds, had forthwith announced that he would marry his housekeeper. Interested relatives had him committed at once to a private madhouse." [5] This case and others, as exposed and journalistically castigated in *The Times,* provided Reade with a humanitarian theme directly expressive of his own thoughts and feelings, plus atrocities almost as black and as fresh as those on which he had based "the immortal part" of his prison epic. And within a few months he himself became an actor in a real life drama that provided him with what he considered the ultimate in factual documentation. On August 6, 1858, he somehow learned that "a sane prisoner [one Fletcher] had escaped from a private madhouse, had just baffled an attempt to recapture him by violent entry into a dwelling house, and was now hiding in the suburbs." [6] Upon receiving this information, Reade took it upon himself not only to examine the prisoner but also to secure medical testimony certifying his sanity. Then, armed with these and other facts, he undertook to defend Fletcher "against the prompt and daring men . . . hunting him." Acting with the acumen and despatch of his own Resourceful Heroes, he hid Fletcher, placed him under guard, balked every attempt to recapture him by force, and then set about securing a fair trial. At this point Fletcher's accusers resorted to legal trickery and deception in an effort to prevent the case from being tried—and for a time they succeeded. But in the long run Reade was more than equal to their machinations. Wielding "the lash of Publicity" with the zeal of his own Parson Eden he publicized the case in a series of articles to the Press that eventually forced the accusers into open court, where, on July 8, 1859, Fletcher was not only declared unequivocally sane but granted damages "compounded for an annuity of £100 a year, £50 cash, and costs."

Reade's own account of the case (reprinted in *Readiana* under the title "Our Dark Places") leaves no doubt that he was primarily interested in validating his self-image. Indeed, if one can credit Compton Reade's testimony in the *Memoir,* Reade was so engrossed in his experiential heroics that he could not see what to nearly everyone else was perfectly plain: that "his orphan," as he called Fletcher, was a dangerously excitable if not an insane young man given to brandishing "his knife in order to point a moral and adorn a tale." Perhaps—but Compton Reade was not above heightening Fletcher's antics to adorn his own tale, or above distorting Reade's statements—presumably made "after it was over"—to point his own moral. Possibly Reade did remark, "No more Law suits. . . . No more Fletchers," but his words cannot be taken to mean that he seriously regretted his actions. For on July 10, just two days after the case had been decided, he wrote (in a letter "To the Editor of *The Daily Telegraph*"):

While thanking you as an enlightened Englishman and an individual, for your remarks on E. P. Fletcher's case, permit me to correct an error. He derived no help whatever from the Alleged Lunatics' Friend Society. He went to them, indeed, on his escape, but they did nothing for him, except let his address leak out. On this a ruffian-like attempt was instantly made to recapture him, with *the aid of the police, which was illegal*. He was saved wholly and solely by two women—Mrs. Carrat and Miss Church. These ladies had what your humbugging commissioners and societies have not—pluck. Mrs. Carrat threatened, very properly, to split the amateur policeman's scull, and demanded his warrant for forcing her bedroom door. She had the poker ready, as I hope we shall all have it when our castles are broken into without a magistrates warrant, and our liberties invaded. The other lady worked by wit, and, finally, "le petit Fletcher" got to the top of the house, jumped, at the risk of his life, to another house, and walked past Dr. Wood's policeman, in crinoline and black mustache. Then it was that another woman referred him to me, as to a man likely to kick at oppression. . . . The result you know. But the difficulties, the postponements, the torturing delays, the heartlessness of all whom the country is paying to have hearts, and the brainlessness of many it is paying to have brains—this, Sir, I defy you to conceive . . .

III

This final challenge looks directly forward to *Hard Cash*, and completes the Readian cycle of Heroism. The factual skirmishes won (by Reade and Mrs. Carrat and other men and women of action), and journalistically chronicled (by Reade and the editor of the *Daily Telegraph* and other humane reformers), it was up to Reade, in his role as novelist, to express what he conceived to be the ultimate significance of the facts: "to make you ladies and gentlemen *realize* things, what the chronicler presents to you in his dim, and cold, and shadowy way . . ." i.e., to do for private asylums what he had already done for prisons. And since his white hot experiential facts (combined with those from *The Times*) provided the ultimate in documentation, he was anxious to get started on the novel as soon as possible. But, as his letters to Fields make clear, there were difficulties, one of which was for the moment insuperable. "From a line in your letter," he wrote on Nov. 15, 1860, "I fear you think I am working for you [on *Hard Cash*]. Alas! I ought to be and should be much happier if I was: but you know this miserable good Fight was to be got rid of first; and my poor little head could never do two things at once. Jan 1 I hope to have finished the thing and then will take care of you at once."

That Reade actually believed he could finish "the thing" by Jan. 1 appears doubtful. "Do not," he warned Fields a few days later (Nov. 20, 1860) "be too precise in your announcements." And he continued to hedge, until in May Ticknor and Fields invoked the exigencies of the Civil War to cancel their contract for the novel. To this Reade consented (May 31, 1861), though he went on to explain that the delays were no fault of his own: "My medieval story has been interrupted by cruel lawsuits in defense of my copyrights, which have laid me on a sick bed, and hindered my work." While this may be true enough, his medieval researches were also causing him no end of trouble, and were primarily responsible for keeping him penned up at Oxford, hard at work on the novel, throughout the summer and into the fall of 1861. In almost every letter he wrote Mrs. Seymour during this period he bemoaned the difficulties engendered by his medieval theme, and even when the end of the novel was definitely in sight, and he had come to believe it might be a success, he constantly reiterated his earlier resolution: "I will never attempt an old world story again. . . . Henceforth I shall remember the advice, *soyez de votre siècle*. I am convinced that learning and research should be applied to passing, not to past, events. In the same sense alone is Dickens a learned man, and mark the results!" [7]

This statement once again looks forward to *Hard Cash*. In fact it would seem that Reade looked forward to *Hard Cash* throughout the time he was writing *The Cloister and the Hearth*. Yet that novel once completed he was apparently too exhausted to do anything but follow the advice he had earlier offered Wilkie Collins: "I highly approve your prudence in laying down the pen entirely after producing 'the woman in white': and if you will take my advice on a subject I have studied, give an hour or two more to bed than usual for the next fortnight. Of course I mean go to bed earlier. Sleep is *our* grand renovator." [8] And within a few weeks he began to experience what for him was even more renovating than sleep, viz., success. "How is it," he wrote Mrs. Fields (Jan. 20, 1862), "that your people can read a medieval story in the middle of a civil war. I thought we should sell two copies of the Cloister. . . . But my friend Cornwallis reports a success. If true I can't believe it." Yet Cornwallis' report was soon borne out by sales figures, and in England the novel was if anything an even greater success, not only with the public, but with the critics, who for once accorded him the praise he felt his work merited.

By way of celebrating his triumph he broke open a new Notebook in which he pasted in and commented on reviews. But he did not permit this pastime to interfere with practical considerations. His triumph had given his waning reputation a tremendous boost, and he took full advantage of this fact in negotiating terms for the as yet unwritten *Hard Cash.* "The success of 'The Cloister and the Hearth' here," he wrote Harper & Brothers (Jan. 17, 1862) "leads to various offers from the periodicals. Before I select my channel I should be glad to know whether you still wish to treat for the early sheets . . . some time ago Ticknor & Co. offered me £3 per page Atlantic M. and the usual percentage on book afterwards. This I think equal to £5 per page. . . . Considering my popularity in the U.S. I think you need not regret it. . . ." [9] Meanwhile he was driving an equally hard bargain with Dickens and Wills for serial rights in *All the Year Round,* and could look forward to realizing more than £5000 on the novel.

Nevertheless he was still smarting from the treatment he had received at the hands of Ticknor and Fields, and when Fields personally enquired about "that novel," presumably with the intention of reopening negotiations for it and succeeding works, Reade kindly but firmly set the record straight (May 30, 1862):

The History of that novel is as follows. I agreed to work on it as soon as ever I should finish "the Cloister" Meantime Dickens proposed to me to bring the said novel out first in "All the Year Round." I said I thought it could not be done without virtually depriving you of the early sheets. . . . You decided it was impossible and I threw Dickens over as I was bound in honor to do. Some months after this, the Cloister having held me longer than either you or I expected I received a letter from your firm, ignoring the little episode of Dickens, and throwing *me* over, at which I was surprised, but set it down to what I believe was the case, the then unhappy state of the US engaged in a Civil War, the duration of which seemed at that time indefinite. However, being thus liberated by my Boston publisher, I thought it only polite to let Dickens know: and he and Wills retaining their desire to be connected with me made me directly a very liberal offer. I accepted it; and the long talked of novel will commence if I live, next Nov or Dec in All the Year R. This arrangement is in its turn fatal to the Atlantic M as a vehicle of the early sheets; and indeed Messrs. Harper have always the refusal of the leading story in "All the Year Round" and they seem disposed to come to terms. I am sorry Ticknor & Co. had not some patience. Que Diable Great works of Fiction cannot be produced *quickly* like little shoes I cannot help thinking the story "All the Year Round" is going to publish would have done considerable good to the Atlantic. But it is not my fault. If you want anything from my pen you have only to tell me so. . . . *I will always give you the preference.* You know I recommended "the Cloister" to you: but you thought Harpers an obstacle I found him none. I just bought his dead stock of "Good Fight" and he was disarmed, nay friendly. And Messrs. Rudd & Carleton have done famously with it, as you would.

The other day a courageous firm made me a gigantic offer for a novel to be completed March 1864.

But there were conditions as to bulk etc. which gave me a sense of uneasiness: and I declined the golden bait. Had I accepted, you would have been locked out again. For the proposal included the American & European markets. I mention this only by way of showing I am for the present free . . . & have no engagement after the forthcoming one.

Considering the subject, and the fact that he had been rather shabbily treated, this letter is, for Reade, amazingly restrained. In part this was due to his genuine fondness for Mr. and Mrs. Fields, but not entirely, for other letters he wrote at this time—to Harper & Brothers, and to Dickens, Wills, Cornwallis, and Mrs. Seymour— also evince the same characteristics. The megalomania is still there, of course, but in a more controlled form which bespeaks greater confidence in his system and his powers.

IV

It was in this mood that, on May 30, he spoke of "going down to Oxford to write hard." From the beginning, his later remarks testify, he envisaged *Hard Cash* as his masterpiece. *The Cloister and the Hearth* was well enough in its way, but he felt confident that by "applying the same diligence and research to the subject of our own day" he could, in the words of the *Memoir,* "rival, if not cap, his glorious 'Sera Nunquam,'" and thus create a far greater novel than his medieval one.

His first concern was therefore to bring together the facts he had gathered earlier; then, since these facts were by his standards incomplete and in certain instances somewhat dated, to supplement them through further study and research. As a first step he drew up in one of his Notebooks ("No. 9 Folio") a list of books having to do with the main subjects he proposed to treat in the novel, including such titles as "Bartlett's dict Americanisms . . . Gilbert's logic of Banking . . . Young's Nautical Dictionary . . . Kitt's daily Bible illustrated . . . Manual of psychological Medicine. . . ." [10] Following many of these titles he included the name of the publisher, together with notes or comments indicating that he intended to purchase those items not available in the Radcliffe Library, where, as his letters to Mrs. Seymour and Mrs. Fields reveal, he read during the summer and fall: "The Radcliffe Library," he wrote Mrs. Seymour, "is fitted up like the British Museum. A good stock of books are within your reach in the building, and they communicate with the Bodleian, and get you any book you want. . . ." [11] And in describing the Radcliffe to Mrs. Fields (Sept. 3, 1862) he also noted that it had "lately been made a reading room for students . . . and unlike all other public libraries in this country it is well lighted and kept open till ten at night."

In the meantime, following his practice in writing *Never Too Late To Mend,* he had enlisted outside aid. For some time his brother, William Barrington Reade, had been contributing odd facts and observations to which Reade devoted a special notebook labelled "W. B. Reade." In this instance, however, he wanted special information, first about a character whom William knew in real life, one Mattingley, secondly about William's own experiences as a sailor, particularly his voyage from China—all of which William duly provided.[12] For help in his work on "asyla" he called upon Dr. Samuel Dickson, the eccentric doctor who had rendered such sterling service in connection with the Fletcher case, and who had for years been collecting facts relating to insanity and the treatment of the insane. Some of these facts Dickson had already embodied in his printed books, but the greater part of his materials, including the "manuscript narratives" Reade mentions in the preface to *Hard Cash*, were apparently in the form of rough notes and jottings which Dickson turned over to Reade *in toto*, to do with what he would.[13]

In addition Reade may have employed a secretary, plus various hacks, according to the plan he outlined in "Digest." He had hired a secretary in 1859, George Henry Guest, who for a short time kept Notebooks referred to as "Collectanea Guest"; and the secretary who succeeded him, J. G. Saunders, likewise helped with the Notebooks and the Notecards. Also there is a note on one of the Notecards ("See Courtly, on Asylums, & Langley's extracts") which suggests that a certain S. Langley, who devilled for Reade so extensively in the seventies, may have done some work for Reade at this time, along with "Bloxam and the University hacks" whom Elwin mentions.

With so much help Reade was in danger of being overwhelmed by the facts he so lusted after, and to handle them resorted to the special procedures he later described on the inside front cover of No. 9 Folio:

Hard Cash.
a few of my notes for:
I took notes for this work in various ways.

(1) I covered eight or ten large double folio cards. Some of these still survive.

(2) I pasted extracts from journals and Dickson's works on a screen, where I could see them in one view.

(3) I devoted a double sheet each to some of the characters.

(4) I took notes on the ordinary system in books.

(5) I worked on materials furnished by my brother William, whereof Mattingleiana, the basis of Maxley, and his voyage from China survive, I believe.

Altogether I bestowed the labor and my usual research that go to two or three *soi-disant* learned works.

The pleadings are from Fletcher v. Fletcher which case I had worked from first to last.

I have been accused of inaccuracy in all that relates to asyla, but I offered public inspection of my proofs and my detractors one and all shrunk from the test.

My materials are now somewhat scattered, but I shall endeavor to point out where several of my authorities can be found.

With regard to certain characters, I put them on separate double sheets of paper. I never did this before or since.[14]

In most essentials this description is borne out by extant manuscripts. The one exception is item four, which is correct, up to a
point, but nevertheless misleading—if the word books be taken
to mean Notebooks, as Reade evidently intended it should be.
Of course he did take notes in books, but not with the thoroughness his system demanded. Except for a few entries scattered
through a half-dozen Notebooks, the only materials of consequence are those in "No. 9 Folio," and they consist of only a
single page of "Libri" followed by nine pages of summary notes
on various characters (interspersed with scraps of dialogue and
a few technical notations). The truth would seem to be that
Reade's difficulties with *The Cloister and the Hearth* prevented
him from keeping up his Notebooks as he planned, that consequently when he entered upon the actual writing of *Hard Cash*
he transferred nearly all his materials directly to the large double-
folio cards mentioned in item one.

Fifteen of these giant cards still survive, along with twenty-
five slightly smaller ones, later copied by Saunders, Reade's secretary, from the original fifteen, making a grand total of forty
Notecards. The sheer bulk of this material can hardly be credited
until one has actually seen the cards themselves. Malcolm Elwin,
who was unable to consult the cards, justifiably stresses the variety
and extent of the facts recorded in the Notebooks, especially the
"appalling list of technical, medical, and statistical works read and
annotated for 'materials.'" Yet these materials comprise but a frac-
tion of those included on the Notecards. In his unpublished
doctoral dissertation, *Charles Reade's Manuscript Notecards for
"Hard Cash,"* Douglas Bankson has edited all forty of the Notecards, and in his commentary has observed that the cards "contain about 107,000 words which divide into 70,000 words in clippings and 37,000 words in notes." [15] Included in these figures are
614 separate bibliographical entries, which, together with the
credited materials on the cards, swell the total number of bibliographical references to almost a thousand.

These materials Reade brought together on the Notecards under
such main headings as "Dickeybirdiana," "Saulian System," "Medicine, Clippings," "Lunaticum A," "Insanity," "Madness," "Asylums
and Lunacy Law," "Harpers Weekly," "The Horrible Story," and
"Arundiniana." And under these headings he employed various
sub-headings. But to no avail. Although he intended the Notecards to be a means of bringing "notes and extracts . . . from all

his repertories into something like a focus for a present purpose," he simply could not maintain the desired focus in any but the Notecards devoted to clippings. For example, one of the cards headed "Dicksoniana" (a variation on "Dickeybirdiana"), begins systematically enough, with dicta characteristic of Dr. Dickson, then moves into passages of dialogue between Dickson and other characters, and from these, quoting Bankson, veers off into "an incident which characterizes Jane Hardie, some notes on, and bibliographical references to, insanity and asylums, a passage on the use of cosmetics, some remarks by Mrs. Dodd on the comfort of religion, a clipping containing an example of Yankee humor, the address of Reade's printer with a memorandum about marking proofs, a comment on the stock exchange and, finally, a clipping containing a bookseller's advertisement of 'Small Books on Great Subjects.'" [16] Furthermore Reade compounded the confusion with memoranda, references, and cross references as vague and complicated as those in the Notebooks.

As a consequence the Notecards did little to ease his writing difficulties. In the opening chapters, devoted to the introduction of the Dodd and Hardie families, he was able to draw upon his earlier *Love Me Little Love Me Long*, and so completed the first three numbers for *All The Year Round* without a hitch. But once he introduced Dr. Sampson, the fictional counterpart of the real Dr. Dickson, and was obliged to resort to the "Dickeybirdiana" of the Notecards, he again found himself mired in his materials. "So behold me in anxiety and despondency about a forthcoming production," he wrote Mrs. Fields on Sept. 3, 1862; and in his letters to Mrs. Seymour, written at about the same time, he continued in the same vein, though he attributed his difficulties, not to "the system" in general and the Notecards in particular, but to Dickson: "Never was there a writer so inconsecutive and ill-arranged. . . . I have pasted a whole screen over with his lines and topics, arranging them in something like order." And a few days later: "I have papered one side of a screen with classified extracts from his works, and now I am at others." [17]

Although Reade's attempted classifications are in themselves confusing he nevertheless managed to fight his way through Dickson's "ill written, inarticulate compositions," and after that, it would seem, everything went much easier and much faster, despite his continued reliance on factual materials. The explanation would seem to be that these materials lent themselves more readily to his time-tried plagiaristic techniques. Certainly this was true of W. B. Reade's contribution: Mattingleiana (recorded in "No 9 Folio" and on the Notecards)[18] he followed quite closely in his novelistic account of Maxley, and in a prefatory note to his short story *Rus* he later acknowledged "the manœuvres of the square-rigged vessel attacked by the schooner" to be his brother's contribution to *Hard Cash*. In other areas too, most notably in his treatment of religion and insanity, the Notecards reveal that he relied heavily on what he was pleased to label "plagiandum." Jane Hardie, the virgin martyr of the novel who serves as an Evangelical foil to the more truly Christian Julia Dodd, he derived primarily from two books—*The Life of Adelaide Newton* and Bonar's *A Stranger Here*. Similarly he derived the greater portion of his notes on insanity from the writings of Dr. Forbes Winslow, then introduced the Doctor himself (along with his writings) directly into the novel, renamed him Dr. Wycherley, and used him as a Scholastic butt for his own and the Saulian Dr. Sampson's Baconian wisdom.[19]

Whatever the artistic justification for these tactics they negate the *raison d'être* of the Notecards. Nor are these the only instances in which Reade, after gathering reams of material, drew his fictional facts from a few choice bits of plagiandum. According to Bankson, Reade used less than twenty per cent of the material on the Notecards in writing *Hard Cash,* and this twenty per cent constitutes in bulk little more than ten per cent of the novel. In part this was because the Notecards were so ill arranged and so unwieldly that on at least one occasion he actually lost sight of an article (having to do with fire-dogs) from which he had extracted the following verses:

> Stop me not, but let me jog,
> For I am Harmsworth's fire-dog.

These lines he had emended on the Notecard by replacing "Harmsworth's" with "the bold"—preparatory to including them in the novel. But when he came to write up the fire-scenes he completely overlooked the couplet (as well he might, since it appears under "Dickeybirdiana") and did not rediscover it until later, when he wrote "Forgot to use this—like an ass."

The fatuity of this notation is further emphasized by its appearance on the Notecard, amidst the masses of factual material he had failed to use—not because he had forgotten them, but because he had been unable to order and apply them. Designed to provide a "focus" the Notecards provided but another Baconian reflection of his inner confusion. The more facts he collected, the more confused he became; and the more confused he became, the more he was obliged to single out and follow works which lent themselves to his plagiaristic techniques. In fact his evasions of "the system" were so gross, and so clearly recorded on the Notecards, that Reade himself was hard put to maintain his Baconian pretensions. His most obvious tactic was to write "Used" (or some more elaborate notation) beside or through every entry that had provided him with the slightest suggestion for the novel. Complementing this tactic was his practice, in the novel itself, of inserting factual parentheses, and even footnotes, at every opportunity—a practice that gave the novel a more documented air at the same time it multiplied the number of entries on the Notecards beside which he could write "Used."

That Reade should go to such lengths to rig his own system was, for Reade, a necessity—every bit as much of a necessity as his earlier defense against the charge of plagiarism (in *The Eighth Commandment*). He had abjured "invention" in favor of "the system," and the system simply had to work—or his art would stand revealed as a plagiaristic lie, and he himself would be naked, and therefore defenseless—not only against the charges of his contemporaries but also in the eyes of posterity, for he laid the Notebooks and Notecards open to public inspection while he lived, and arranged that they should be preserved after his death.

v

The main value of the Notebooks and Notecards was therefore a self-justificatory one. With so elaborate a theoretical façade he was free, in practice, to duplicate the pattern he had followed in writing his prison epic; and that, the novel itself shows, is what he did—not only in his documentation of the purpose or "idea" of the novel but in his reliance on the *croix de ma mère* of Sensation fiction for the expression of that "idea."

The plot of *Hard Cash* is somewhat neater than that of *Never Too Late To Mend*—though constructed along similar lines. David Dodd (a ship-captain transplanted from *Love Me Little Love Me Long*) survives storms, attacks by pirates on the China Sea, a shipwreck on the coast of France, and ambush by desperate highwaymen to bring his savings (£14,000 in "hard cash") safely home to England, only to have Richard Hardie (a banker who had also appeared in *Love Me Little Love Me Long*) attempt to misappropriate the entire sum—an action which throws David Dodd into an apoplectic fit and eventually renders him insane—thus leaving Richard Hardie in possession of the cash. In the meantime, however, Alfred Hardie (Richard Hardie's son) has fallen in love with Julia, David Dodd's daughter, and threatens to expose his father's suspected dishonesty; whereupon Hardie Sr. secretly arranges to have Alfred incarcerated in a private madhouse, and, as a consequence of his mysterious disappearance (just before he is to be married) everyone but Julia comes to believe that he has deserted her to run off with some other woman.

While Alfred Hardie, the prime Resourceful Hero, is confined behind asylum walls, Edward Dodd (Julia's brother) replaces him in the outside world. Although Edward is not in time to save the life of the girl he loves (Jane Hardie, Alfred's sister) he is equal to all the other problems with which he is confronted—largely because, in the words of his sister Julia, "he has been all these years cutting up the *Morning Advertiser*, and arranging the slips with wonderful skill and method. He calls it "digesting the 'Tiser'! and you can't ask for any *modern* information great or small, but he'll find something about it in this digest." [20] Applying this Readian information in true Readian fashion ("He has written 'SOYEZ DE VOTRE SIÈCLE' in great large letters," Julia reports, "and has pasted it on all our three bedroom-doors.") [21] Edward develops into a true Readian hero. When the need arises and he must help out with the household expenses he therefore casts aside all foolish notions of gentility to become a fireman—and in this capacity rescues his father and Alfred Hardie from the burning asylum in which they have been confined.

Following their rescue both Alfred Hardie and David Dodd escape to the coast, where David, still insane, ships as a common sailor, and while trying to save the life of a fellow seaman presumably sacrifices his own. Yet at the moment when he is about to be buried at sea, his cousin, who commands the vessel, recognizes him through a tattoo on his arm and orders him embalmed—which is quite providential, for just as they are preparing to embalm him, a fly bites the presumed corpse, draws blood, and thus proves that he is not dead but in a state of suspended animation. From this state he quickly recovers, a sane man, and hastens back to England—to rescue the hard cash.

Meanwhile Alfred returns to London, finds Julia, fights off thugs hired to recapture him and, with the aid of the eccentric Dr. Sampson, brings suit for illegal confinement. During this time he also completes his studies at Oxford, taking a first-class degree in time to rush back to London and into court, where, pitted against the best legal minds present, he again carries off the honors of the day to prove not merely his sanity but his unexampled brilliance. Nevertheless he is still under a moral cloud because Mrs. Dodd, Julia's mother, quite unreasonably considers him responsible for her husband's escape to sea. But that difficulty quickly disappears when David Dodd returns sane, grasps the all important receipt for the £ 14,000 from the crackling fingers of a mummified corpse, and in due time returns happily to his wife and family—which soon is enlarged by Julia's marriage to Alfred, and the appearance of numerous offspring, including one that was rather unexpected, for "as so often happens after a long separation, Heaven bestowed on Captain and Mrs. Dodd another infant." [22]

For this final infant, as for the most unlikely and impossible happenings through which he manipulates the plot, Reade could cite all kinds of factual precedent. As in *Never Too Late To Mend* he feigned probabilities, recorded improbabilities. And the more improbable the facts, the more highly he regarded them—a typical example being David Dodd's suspended animation, which is no more essential to the plot than Krook's spontaneous combustion is essential to the plot of *Bleak House*. Reade, like Dickens, went out of his way to introduce the episode because it was new, and novel, and hair-raising—because, in a word, it was Sensational. The difference is that Reade was content to score a sensational *coup,* whereas Dickens went much further, to use his episode atmospherically and symbolically as well as sensationally. But this is a qualitative, not a conceptual distinction. Reade's overt aims were much the same as Dickens'—to express the Ideal through the Real by infusing Sensation with matter-of-fact Purpose and Philosophy.

To this end Reade filled out the framework of his plot with factual characters and scenes and descriptions much like those he had used in his first matter-of-fact masterpiece. Vespasian, the comical but heroic and high-minded Negro of *Hard Cash,* is an African variation on the Australian Jacky in everything from his antics to his mental characteristics. Moreover he is the ward of Joshua Fullalove, an eccentric yet ingenious Yankee preacher, who, like Jacky's master, Fielding, encounters innumerable set-backs in his efforts to turn a savage into a proper white man. Whatever Reade's factual warrant—Vespasian is not documented on the Notecards or in the Notebooks—it would appear that he merely transposed Jacky (who in any case is more of a stage darkie than an aborigine) to the pages of *Hard Cash*, altered his speech a bit, and called him Vespasian—with the deliberate intention of duplicating a character who had made a hit before, and might again. In most instances, however, Reade did not repeat entire characters, merely traits of character, which he then used to duplicate key motifs of his earlier epic. Most repetitive in their primary traits are the Resourceful Heroes of the novel, who not only feel and think and act like their predecessors but like one another. Almost equally repetitive are such minor characters as "poor little despised Noah Skinner" (the bank teller in Hardie's bank) whose passion for keeping accurate books duplicates the passion of Fry, the prison turnkey of *Never Too Late To Mend*, for keeping an honest record of punishments—and with remark-ably similar consequences, since in both cases the honest records lead to the exposure of dishonesty and injustice.

Repetitions of a similar nature occur throughout the novel, most frequently in the chapters devoted to asylums and insanity. For Reade still considered his prison chapters the immortal part of *Never Too Late To Mend*, and did not see how he could do better than to duplicate their art and purpose in treating private asylums. After all, the facts he had collected pointed to even less excusable atrocities, practiced against far more helpless and inno-cent victims, by asylum-keepers presumably aware of their respon-sibilities. Furthermore these men were, like Warden Hawes, sup-ported in their inhuman practices by "the heartlessness of all whom the country is paying to have hearts, and the brainlessness of many it is paying to have brains. . . ." And so Reade once again drama-tized his outrages in terms of the new vs. the old system, public vs. private madhouses, visiting justices vs. government inspectors, once again to demonstrate that "Justice is the daughter of Pub-licity"—so long as there are writer-heroes to confute the Carlyleans and publicize the facts.

Within the limits of Reade's narrowly reformist aims there was perhaps no reason why he should not repeat this old formula—save that it did not fit his new facts, which for all their similarities to his prison facts were in certain essentials quite distinct. For one thing they did not prove so bloody or so brutal and therefore did not lend themselves so readily to his harrowing process. Nor did they provide him with a ready made Carlylean villain whom he could nail to the cross of public opinion in the name of God and Justice and Humanity. Although the asylum-keepers may have been "soul-murderers," as Reade charged, few if any of them had, like Hawes, committed atrocities in clear defiance of the letter and spirit of the Lunacy Laws. Their most reprehensible atrocities were those that they committed with full medical and legal sanction, often in the belief that they were helping their patients.

Against these atrocities the legalistic concept of responsibility Reade had applied to Hawes was no longer relevant. Yet he could not abandon it without venturing into inner consciousness—and that he steadfastly refused to do, even when his Resourceful Hero was "chained sane amongst the mad; on his wedding-day; expecting with tied hands the sinister acts of the soul-murderers who had the power to make their lie a truth!" [23] At this point, following his usual practice, Reade draws upon his rhetorical powers to observe that "Hours of mortal anguish . . . rolled over that young head . . . that no tongue of man can utter, nor pen can shadow. . . . We can paint the body writhing vainly against its unjust bonds; but who can paint the loathing, agonized soul in a mental situation so ghastly? For my part I feel it in my heart of hearts; but am impotent to convey it to others; impotent, impotent." This final cry of "impotent, impotent" suggests the possibility that, for a moment at least, Reade was on the verge of self-recognition. But if so, he quickly drew back, to take refuge in the standard Victorian practice of shifting the imaginative burden from writer to reader: "Pray think of it for yourselves, men and women, if you have not *sworn* never to think over a novel. Think of it for your own sakes; Alfred's turn today, it may be yours tomorrow."

The creative demands of his theme thus disposed of, Reade proceeded to treat asylums exactly as he had treated prisons. But from first to last he encountered difficulties, primarily in his efforts to fit his new facts to his old formulas. Most disastrous perhaps was the effect of his legalistic concept of responsibility, which obliged him to center his exposé around those instances in which unscrupulous relatives or asylum keepers availed themselves of weaknesses in the Lunacy Laws to incarcerate the sane or physically maltreat the insane—instances so rare, and in comparison with his prison facts so bloodless, that despite the thoroughness of his researches he could not duplicate the harrowing effects of the Birmingham atrocities. Nor could he, as in his treatment of those atrocities, intensify their effects by setting his dramatic action in a single institution. The best he could do was to expose his hero, picaresque fashion, to the rigors of not one but three asylums, then supplement the hero's experiences and observations with his own—often interjected directly into the novel in the form of bald commentaries such as the following, tacked onto an account of "how lunatics' ribs get broken" that is itself tacked onto one of the hero's experiences: "Thus died Mr. Sizer in 1854, and two others quite recently. And how many more God only knows; we can't count the stones at the bottom of a deep well." [24]

VI

To enhance the appeal of his purpose (and incidentally to work out the complications of his picaresque plot) Reade drew upon his Notebooks to introduce another form of passion into the novel. Alfred Hardie, incarcerated on his wedding day, spends his wedding night strapped to a bed of torture rather than in a bed of married bliss with the incomparable Julia, whose budding passions Reade had already presented with a Thackeray-like archness bordering on the pornographic—most obviously in snatches of Julia's diary such as the following, written in his intimately avuncular style, and representing, not Julia's thoughts and feelings, but wish-fulfillments of the Victorian male: "Ah, love is a sweet, a dreadful passion. . . . Marriage! what a word to put down! It makes me tingle; it thrills me; it frightens me deliciously." [25]

Because she expresses her love in this way Julia is intended to represent pure and legitimate human love, in contrast to the immoral and illegitimate passion of the woman who next falls in love with Alfred—Mrs. Archbold, the headmistress of the first asylum ("Silverton House") in which Alfred is confined. Mrs. Archbold, ". . . a tall, well-formed woman of thirty, with dark-gray eyes, and straightish eyebrows, massive and black as jet . . ." has a mind and emotions that Reade, contrary to his usual practice, attempts to explain:

> The mind of Edith Archbold corresponded with her powerful frame, and bushy brows. Inside this woman all was vigor; strong passions, strong good-sense to check or hide them; strong will to carry them out. And between these mental forces a powerful

struggle was raging. She was almost impenetrable to mere personal beauty, and inclined to despise early youth in the other sex; and six months spent with Alfred in a quiet country house would probably have left her reasonably indifferent to him. But the first day she saw him in Silverton House, he broke through her guard, and pierced at once to her depths; first he terrified her by darting through the window to escape: and terror is a passion. So is pity; and never in her life had she overflowed with it as when she saw him drawn out of the tank and laid on the grass. If, after all, he was as sane as he looked, that brave, high-spirited young creature, who preferred death to the touch of coarse confining hands!

No sooner had he filled her with dismay and pity, than he bounded from the ground before her eyes and fled: she screamed, and hoped he would escape; she could not help it. Next she saw him fighting alone against seven or eight, and with unheard-of prowess almost beating them. She sat at the window panting, with clenched teeth and hands, and wished him to beat, and admired him, wondered at him. He yielded, but not to them: to her. All the compliments she had ever received were tame compared with this one. It thrilled her vanity. He was like the men she had read of, and never seen; the young knights of chivalry. She glowed all over at him, and detecting herself in time was frightened. Her strong good-sense warned her to beware of this youth, who was nine years her junior, yet had stirred her to all her depths in an hour; and not to see him nor think of him too much.[26]

Reade's language—particularly his manner of invoking such terms as "terror, pity, heroism"—testifies to the seriousness of his analysis, which harks back to Desdemona's response to Othello's dangers, and seems designed to present Mrs. Archbold's growing passion with a Shakespearean brevity and grandeur at once more true and more telling than George Eliot's vaunted psychologizing.

Reade firmly believed that he was emulating Shakespeare (as well as Scott and Mrs. Stowe) in every phase of his writing, that Shakespeare, like every other great writer, owed his greatness not to his imagination but to his facts. In a letter "to the editor of the 'Daily Globe,' Toronto" (in answer to "malicious and defamatory" charges levelled against his writings by Goldwin Smith) Reade wrote:

He now carries the same system, the criticaster's, into a matter of more general importance. He says that I found my fictions on fact, and so tell lies; and that the chiefs of Fiction did not found fictions on fact and so told only truths.

Now, where does he discover that the chiefs of Fiction did not found their figments upon facts? Where?—why, in that little asylum of idiots, the depths of his inner consciousness! It could be proved in a court of law that Shakespeare founded his fictions on fact, wherever he could get hold of fact. Fact is that writer's idol. It was his misfortune to live in an age when the supplies of fact were miserably meagre. . . . Living in that barren age, he did his best. He ransacked Belleforest, Baker, Hollinshed. . . .

Could Shakespeare be resuscitated, Reade concludes, "and a copy of the *Toronto Globe* handed him on the edge of the grave, he would fall on his knees, and thank God for that marvel, a newspaper, and for the rich vein of ore, whose value to the theatre he would soon show us, to our utter amazement." [27]

It was therefore as a modern follower of Shakespeare that Reade transformed Mrs. Archbold from a passionate woman into "a female rake"; then, to add further spice to her importunings, drew upon the Notebooks to provide her with an Amazonian rival, Baby-face Biceps. Together and apart the two women fondle Alfred, kiss him, tickle his feet, and in general subject him to sensuous trials more appropriate to a harem than an asylum— all of which Reade justifies on the ground that the love-making of the two women is true to nature and contributes to an understanding of his primary moral distinction. For Baby-face Biceps, in tickling Alfred's feet, is guilty only of innocent infatuation, corresponding to Julia's innocent love, whereas Mrs. Archbold is guilty of lust: "By and by, when she saw him getting thinner and paler . . . she shared his misery; ay, shed scalding tears for him; yet could not give him up; for her will was strong as the rest of her was supple; and hers was hot love, but not true love like Julia's." [28]

For Reade, as for Tennyson in "Lancelot and Elaine," it is true vs. sinful or hot love—though Reade, deviating from Tennyson (and Malory), presents his hero as a moral lover spurning the advances of a lustful and therefore sinful temptress:

With one grand serpentine movement she came suddenly close to him . . . and poured burning love in his ear. . . ."Let me be your housekeeper, your servant, your slave. . . . O Alfred, my heart burns for you, bleeds for you, yearns for you, sickens for you, dies for you."

"Oh, hush! hush! Mrs. Archbold. You are saying things you will blush for the next moment."

"I blush now, but cannot hush; I have gone too far. And your happiness as well as mine is at stake. . . . Say you the word, dearest, and I will bribe the servants, and get the keys, and sacrifice my profession forever to give you liberty . . . and all I ask is a little, little of your heart in return. Give me a chance to make you mine forever; and, if I fail, treat me as I shall deserve; desert me at once; and then I'll never reproach you; I'll only die for you; as I have lived for you ever since I first saw your heavenly face."

The passionate woman paused at last, but her hot cheek and heaving bosom and tender, convulsive hand prolonged the pleading.

I am afraid few men of her own age would have resisted her; for voice and speech and all were burning, melting, and winning: and then so reasonable, lads; she did not stipulate for constancy.[29]

Reade's forced *bonhomie* in these last remarks is intended to flatter the egos of his more sophisticated male readers, preparatory to confronting them with the youthful purity of Alfred's response—which might otherwise be mistaken for priggishness:

Alfred turned round to her blushing and sorrowful. "For shame!" he said; "this is not love: you abuse that sacred word. Indeed, if you had ever really loved, you would have pitied me and Julia long ago, and respected our love; and saved us by giving me my freedom long ago. . . ."

"You cruel, ungrateful!" she sobbed.

"No; I am not ungrateful either," said he, more gently. "You have always come between me and that kind of torture which most terrifies vulgar souls; and I thank you for it. Only, if you had also pitied the deeper anguish of my heart, I should thank you more still. As it is, I forgive you for the share you have had in blasting my happiness for life; and nobody shall ever know what you have been mad enough in an unguarded moment to say; but for pity' sake talk no more of love, to mock my misery."

Mrs. Archbold was white with ire long before he had done this sentence. "You insolent creature!" said she; "you spurn my love; you shall feel my hate."

"So I conclude," said he, coldly: "such love as yours is hard by hate." [30]

Were it not for Alfred's final words of denunciation, which echo the Notebook heading, "Lust Hard by Hate," this climactic scene between Alfred and Mrs. Archbold might be dismissed as nothing more than what it certainly is in part: a moralistic attempt to justify his pornographic presentation of female lust. For Reade, it has been shown, was astonishingly sophisticated in certain of his attitudes towards sex—so sophisticated, in fact, that much of the material he collected in the Notebooks and on the Notecards was far too shocking for inclusion in a respectable work of fiction. A typical example is the following bit of painfully risqué dialogue between Dr. Dickson (here identified as Saul) and Julia:

> *Saul to Julia.* Yon's a Jinny-us.
> *Julia.* Oh, Jenny ass! Don't rob him of his sex, Dr., or I shall not be able to marry him, at least I suppose not; though really I don't quite know why.
>
> . . . .
>
> *Julia.* Mamma, why do girls never by any chance marry girls?
> "It is not the custom," said Mrs. D., without moving a muscle.[31]

Although the exclusion of this and like "gems," as Reade called them, hardly weakens the novel, he was also obliged to exclude other and more promising materials on the Notecards, such as the entry concerning one of Mrs. Archbold's charges:

> In her lucid intervals she used to go about complaining of Dr. Wolfe, for seducing her, taking advantage of her occasional aberrations to seduce her.
> Lucid intervals reversed. The lady who, when lucid, complains Dr. Wolfe had seduced her, with the wonderful memory of her sex for occurrences of that kind. . . .
> "Seduction of calves and sheep," said the Archbold contemptuously. "You don't know my sex; and what fine words they use."

And in another and related entry—a personal notation under the heading "Arundiniana"—Reade went still further, to challenge one of the most sacred of all the Victorian sexual concepts: "The use of extravagant terms leads to fatal and unhappy results. The application of such big words as 'ruin' and 'destruction' to copulation before marriage, has a fatal effect on silly girls—they turn reckless; when in reality there was no harm done, but for the notion." In this form the notation anticipates Thomas Hardy, in his preface to *Tess of the D'Urbervilles.* Later Reade qualified his original phrasing, perhaps with a view to fictional application, by writing in "a single act of" before the word "copulation" and replacing the "no" before "harm" with "little." But the forces of Grundyism were not to be placated by shuffling concessions of this nature. The whole concept had to die on the Notecards, along with Mrs. Archbold's remarks on seduction and other such entries in the Notebooks and on the Notecards.

VII

Considered apart from their context, these entries may seem to indicate that in matters sexual Reade, like Thackeray, fell victim to Mrs. Grundy, that, given the freedom to develop his notations, he might conceivably have realized the artistic potential of his materials—perhaps by creating a mid-Victorian Tess, in contrast to George Eliot's conventionally moralistic treatment of Hetty Sorrel in *Adam Bede*. But the novel itself shows that Reade's difficulties were not quite so simple. For in Jane Hardie, the "Virgin Martyr" of the novel, he tried to create a character who may, with qualifications, be described as a sexual Dinah Morris— only to fall back upon moralistic props every bit as conventional as those George Eliot invokes in her treatment of Hetty.

Nor can Reade's conventionality in this instance be attributed to the forces of Victorian "Humbug," even though, as in his treatment of Mrs. Archbold, certain of his entries had to remain on the Notecards—notably the following "Materials for Dialogue":

> *Jane Hardie.* Oh when a new-born soul goes back to that weary round of dress, meals, visits, and amusements, all without a purpose but to murder time.
> *Dr. Saul.* And to catch a husband, if you please, Miss Newborn.
> Rebuked by Mrs. Dodd, he says, "Science to be gull-hub bub boo. Am I to let her think she can delude me, a priori at Sciences, the threadbare little humbug. She couldn't dance into a wedding-ring (husband) as quick as she wanted, so now she is going to preach into one."

In the long run Reade's forced abandonment of these materials (presumably dictated by his fear that Dr. Saul's directness might offend religious as well as moral susceptibilities) had little effect on his characterization—except perhaps to strengthen it, by obliging him to present Jane's sexuality through the self-revelations of her "Diary," a mode of presentation at once less offensive and more telling than Saulian commentary, and furthermore a mode admirably suited to his documentary techniques. For the religious material he had collected on the Notecards (primarily from *The Life of Adelaide Newton* and Bonar's *A Stranger Here*) breathed the spirit of the very Evangelicalism he was trying to reproduce in Jane: all he had to do was select and vary the passages to bring out their underlying sexuality. And this he did with remarkable delicacy and perception. On the Notecards, for instance, the following lines are tritely Evangelical: "Oh how closely he walked with God! His mind so exactly suits mine." Yet as modified in Jane's "Diary," and applied to Mr. Plummer, the handsome parson whom she so much admires, the lines take on a more personal note: "Got this idea from Mr. Plummer. How closely he walks! His mind so exactly *suits* mine." Thus, in the words of Dr. Bankson, "Plummer replaces God beside the girl and the new juxtaposition makes a significant comment on the relation of flesh and spirit." [32] Moreover a number of other passages are, if less subtle, equally revealing—particularly those in which Jane speaks of Plummer, who for the good of her soul not only held her hand and prayed with her but also showed a strong interest in her transcription of the *Book of the Songs of Solomon*—apropos of which interest Jane noted in her "Diary": "Poor man, his wife leads him a cat and dog life, I hear, with her jealousy." [33]

Jane's sexuality once revealed, however, Reade immediately set about denying its implications—as if he felt he had gone too far, and had to vindicate his ironical epithet, virgin martyr, by sending Jane to a bloody, virginal, and saint-like death. For she is attacked (some two-thirds of the way through the novel) by a crazed victim of her father's villainies who beats "her about the head and shoulders with his heavy stick," until Edward Dodd, her true love, arrives on the scene and "deals her assailant . . . a murderous stroke with the bludgeon . . . that laid him senseless, motionless and mute in a pool of his own blood." [34] In this manner sex is replaced with blood, according to the approved moral pattern of Sensation fiction; and in the ensuing scenes in which Jane succumbs to her blows everything is made right—again according to the approved Sensation pattern—by having Jane rise to "celestial bliss." [35] Her words, as in the "Diary," are the words of Bonar and Newton, but Reade here intends them to be taken literally, and to ensure their effect wreathes them in just about every death-bed piety known to stage and romance:

> One hour of pain, another of delirium, and now the clouds that darken this mortal life seemed to part and pass, and heaven to open full upon her. She spoke of her coming change no longer with resignation; it was with rapture. "Oh!" she cried, "to think that from this very day I shall never sin again, shall never again offend Him by unholy temper, by un-Christlike behavior!"

The strong and healthy wept and groaned aloud; but she they

sorrowed for was all celestial bliss. In her lifetime she had her ups and downs of religious fervor; was not without feverish heats, and cold misgivings and depression; but all these fled at that dread hour when the wicked are a prey to dark misgivings, or escape into apathy. This timid girl, that would have screamed at a scratch, met the King of Terrors with smiles and triumph. For her the grave was Jordan, and death was but the iron gate of life everlasting. *Mors janua vitae.* Yet once or twice she took herself to task: but only to show she knew what the All-Pure had forgiven her. "I often was wanting in humility," she said: "I almost think that if I were to be sent back again into this world of sin and sorrow I am leaving behind, I should grow a little in humility; for I know the ripe Christian is like the ripe corn, holds his head lower than when he was green; and the grave it seems to be ripening *me.* But what does it matter? since He who died for me is content to take me as I am. Come quickly, Lord Jesus, oh come quickly! Relieve Thy servant from the burden of the flesh, and of the sins and foibles that cling to it and keep her these many years from Thee."

This prayer was granted; the body failed more and more; she could not swallow even a drop of wine; she could not even praise her Redeemer: that is to say, she could not speak. Yet she lay and triumphed. With hands put together in prayer, and eyes full of praise and joy unspeakable, she climbed fast to God. While she so mounted in the spirit, her breath came at intervals unusually long, and all were sent for to see death conquer the body and be conquered by the soul.

At last, after an unnaturally long interval, she drew a breath like a sigh. They waited for another: waited, waited in vain.

She had calmly ceased to live.

The old doctor laid down her hand reverently, and said, "She is with us no more." Then with many tears, "Oh, may we all meet where she is now, and may I go to her the first!" . . .

Immediately after death all the disfiguring effect of pain retired, and the happy soul seemed to have stamped its own celestial rapture on the countenance at the moment of leaving it; a rapture so wonderful, so divine, so more than mortal calm, irradiated the dead face. The good Christians she left behind her looked on and feared to weep, lest they should offend Him who had taken her to Himself, and set a visible seal upon the house of clay that had held her. "O mamma," cried Julia with fervor, "Look! look! Can we, dare we, wish that angel back to this world of misery and sin?" And it was some hours before she cooled, and began to hang on Edward's neck and weep his loss and hers, as weep we mortals must, though the angels of heaven are rejoicing.

Thus died in the flower of her youth, and by what we call a

violent death, the one child Richard Hardie loved; member of a religious party whose diction now and then offends one to the soul: but the root of the matter is in them; allowance made for those passions, foibles, and infirmities of the flesh, even you and I are not entirely free from, they live fearing God; and die loving Him.[36]

In thus making his peace with Evangelicalism and reducing Jane's sexuality to "the infirmities of the flesh" Reade may well have been motivated by personal as well as strategic reasons. His Evangelically pious mother had just recently died, at the age of ninety; then too there was the memory of his saint-like sister Julia—in fact the death scene may in part be intended as a tribute to her memory. While these reasons do not in any sense redeem the writing itself, which reads like the death of Little Nell as it might have been recounted by Chadband, they do help to account for the discrepancy between the Jane of the Notecards and "Diary" and the Jane of the death-bed scenes—a discrepancy as extreme as that between the Mrs. Archbold and Baby-face Biceps of the Notecards and their nymphomaniacal counterparts in the novel. In treating sex as in treating madness Reade could give full artistic expression to his insights only so long as they were compatible with his ideal self-image; the moment they proved incompatible he retreated into his matter-of-fact rationalizations, and through them to the pietistic and heroic beliefs he shared with his readers. Hence his debasement of the sex and madness in the novel to the level of the heroic quest for "Hard Cash"—a quest he finally resolves (by sublimating the sex and madness to the cash) in a finale that George Orwell aptly characterized in *Dickens, Dali, And Others*. "If you are 'good,' and also self-supporting," Orwell remarks, in speaking of Dickens' *Nicholas Nickleby*, "there is no reason why you should not spend fifty years in simply drawing your dividends. Home life is always enough. . . . The 'genteel sufficiency,' the 'competence,' the 'gentleman of independent means' (or 'in easy circumstances')—the very phrases tell one all about the strange, empty dream of the eighteenth- and nineteenth-century middle bourgeoisie. It was a dream of *complete idleness*." [37] The spirit of this dream, Orwell observes, "Charles Reade conveys . . perfectly in the ending of *Hard Cash*. Alfred Hardie . . . is the typical nineteenth-century novel-hero (public-school style). . . . He is an old Etonian and a scholar of Oxford, he knows most of the Greek and Latin classics by heart, he can box with prize-fighters and win the Diamond Sculls at Henley. He goes through incredible adventures in which, of course, he behaves with fault-less heroism. . . ." Then, Orwell concludes, ". . . at the age of twenty-five, he inherits a fortune, marries his Julia Dodd and settles down in the suburbs of Liverpool, in the same house as his parents-in-law: 'They all lived together at Albion Villa, thanks to Alfred. . . . Oh, you happy little villa! You were as like Paradise as any mortal dwelling can be. A day came, however, when your walls could no longer hold all the happy inmates. Julia presented Alfred with a lovely boy; enter two nurses and the villa showed symptoms of bursting. Two months more, and Alfred and his wife overflowed into the next villa. It was but twenty yards off . . . etc. etc. etc.' This is the type of the Victorian happy ending—a vision of a huge, loving family of three or four generations, all crammed together in the same house and constantly multiplying, like a bed of oysters." [38]

VIII

As might be expected Reade's contemporaries—from Dickens and Wilkie Collins to Swinburne—praised *Hard Cash* for the very qualities that Orwell found objectionable, and their encomiums have been echoed by more recent commentators from W. T. Young to Malcolm Elwin. Of these sympathetic critics the most original and thorough is Swinburne, whose defense of the novel extends from its purpose, to its heroics, to the "snowy white villa" and its idealized inmates. "I am not so certain," he declares, in comparing Reade's characters with George Eliot's, "that her more laboured and finished characters have really more life in them than Reade's; that Caleb Garth, as an able and ardent advocate maintains, is a more actual and genuine person, a figure more distinct and posi-tive, more worthy to be remembered 'as a personal friend,' than David Dodd. . . ." [39] But what does this argument prove—except that David Dodd compares favorably with another idealized type whose presence in *Middlemarch* seriously weakens that novel. To Swinburne and the Victorians, Caleb Garth might be the fictional measure of a man, as Dobbin was the measure of a gentleman, and as Amelia and Agnes and Romola were, in their different ways, the measures of women. But the value structure on which these ideals of manhood and womanhood were posited has long since collapsed, revealing the emptiness of the ideals themselves, which in the light of modern psychology can be recognized as personifications of wish fulfillments the writers shared with their readers.

More acceptable by modern standards, but likewise dependent on Victorian values, is Swinburne's defense of Reade's epic structure and purpose. The madhouse scenes in the novel, he argues, are more restrained and therefore "more lifelike" than the corresponding scenes in *Never Too Late To Mend:* "In *Hard Cash* the crusade against the villainous lunacy of the law regarding lunatics was conducted with more literary tact and skill—with nobler energy and ardour it could not be conducted—than this previous onslaught on the system which made homicide by torture a practical part of such prison discipline as well deserved the disgrace of approbation from the magnanimous worshipper of portable gallows and beneficent whip: the harsher and the humaner agents of an insane law who figure on the stage of the narrative which attacks it are more lifelike as well as less horrible than the infernal little disciples of Carlyle who infest and impede the progress of the earlier tale." [40] In this comparison "the more lifelike" equals "the less horrible," a questionable assumption in itself and one which caused Swinburne to overlook the fact that, given Reade's purpose, "literary tact and skill" could not compensate for the absence of more primary virtues. Reade's first aim was to harrow his readers, just as he had harrowed them in his prison epic, and in making his asylum scenes "less horrible" and, in Swinburne's sense, "more lifelike," he vitiated his purpose, and by modern standards, his art. For it was through his castigation of "the infernal little disciples of Carlyle"—a castigation unchecked by "literary tact"—that he now and again approximated the art of Carlyle and Dickens.

In Swinburne's judgment, however, Reade's more conventional heroics represented the pinnacle of his art: "All other defects or infirmities of his genius disappear or become transfigured when it suddenly takes fire and spreads wing for heights far beyond the reach of the finest painter of social manners, the most faithful and trustworthy spokesman or showman of commonplace event and character. There is a vivid force in his best and highest examples of narrative which informs even prose with something of the effect of epic rather than dramatic poetry. There is more romantic beauty, more passionate depth of moral impression, in the penultimate chapter of *Westward Ho!* than in any chapter of Reade's; but it hardly attains the actual and direct force of convincing as well as exciting effect which we recognize in the narrative of the Agra's last voyage homeward. That magnificent if not matchless narrative is the crowning evidence of its author's genius: if it should not live as long as the language, so much the worse for all students of the language who shall overlook so noble an example of its powers." [41] While Swinburne's superlatives may seem a bit strained, they actually do little more than justice to the qualities he has singled out for praise. Reade is a master of exciting narrative, perhaps one of the greatest masters in fiction, and the narrative of the Agra's last voyage homeward is every bit as forceful and exciting as he maintains. Yet it does not follow that the narrative achieves the effect of epic poetry. Indeed the effect of Reade's epic techniques, as applied to the homeward voyage of the Agra, is closer to that of a drugstore thriller, since the force and excitement of the narrative attaches to nothing more meaningful than the safety of David Dodd and the "hard cash."

Reade's voyage is therefore as counterfeit in its pretensions as the dramatic efforts Henry James described in his review of M. E. Braddon's *Aurora Floyd*. "With the old poets," James pointed out, "dramatic interest lay in the fact that it [crime] compromised the criminal's moral repose. . . . With Mr. Collins and Miss Braddon (our Euripedes and Shakespeare) the interest of crime is in the fact that it compromises the criminal's personal safety . . . the nearer the criminal and detective are brought home to the reader, the more lively his 'sensation.' . . ." [42] And the voyage of the Agra is but a variation on this formula, with Reade, the modern Homer, using David Dodd's perils, not to express the symbolic meaning of the voyage (which is perfectly obvious), but to permit the reader to revel in the blood and excitement, in a word, the Sensation, of storm and battle.

IX

James's distinction between the genuine and the counterfeit thus exposes the underlying fallacy of Swinburne's criticism: its dependence on the illusory Victorian ideals so ably characterized by Orwell. Considered apart from these ideals, *Hard Cash* is little more than another version of *Never Too Late to Mend:* better plotted, and written with more literary tact and skill, yet lacking the sadistic power that in part at least serves to redeem the thematic purpose of the earlier novel.

The passages of sexual passion Reade derived from the Notebooks and Notecards mark his one significant artistic advance in *Hard Cash*. In these passages he ventured onto sanctified moral grounds that in his previous novels—*The Cloister and the Hearth* excepted—he had either evaded or skirted; and if in most instances he failed to do justice to his facts and insights, reverting to conventionalized evasions when on the verge of genuine artistic discovery, he now and again, as in his treatment of Jane's self-revelations, demonstrated the ability to go much further. What he needed, seemingly, in order to give significant expression to his insights, was a modern sexual theme comparable to that of his medieval romance—in other words a theme vital enough in its implications to rouse his latent sensibilities yet not so daring or so aberrant as to offer a direct challenge to his fears and ideals.

CHAPTER X

Griffith Gaunt:

"The Great Passions That Poets Have Sung"

THIS STORY *[Griffith Gaunt, or Jealousy]* has, ever since December, 1865, floated *The Argosy,* an English periodical, and has been eagerly read in the pages of *The Atlantic Monthly.* In this tale I have to deal, as an artist and a scholar, with the very period Henry Fielding has described—to the satisfaction of Prurient Prudes; a period in which manners and speech were somewhat blunter than now-a-days; and I have to portray a great and terrible passion, Jealousy, and show its manifold consequences, of which even Bigamy (in my story) is one, and that without any violation of probability. Then I proceed to show the misery inflicted on three persons by Bigamy, which I denounce as a crime. In my double character of moralist and artist, I present, not the delusive shadow of Bigamy, but its substance. The consequence is, that instead of shedding a mild lustre over Bigamy, I fill my readers with a horror of Bigamy, and a wholesome indignation against my principal male character, so far as I have shown him. Of course "Griffith Gaunt," like "Hard Cash," is not a child's book, nor a little girl's book: it is an ambitious story, in which I present the great passions that poets have sung with applause in all ages; it is not a boatful of pap; but I am not paid the price of pap. By the very nature of my theme I have been compelled now and then to tread on delicate ground; but I have trodden lightly and passed on swiftly, and so will all the pure-minded men and women who read me. No really modest woman will ever suffer any taint by reading "Griffith Gaunt," unless, indeed, she returns to its perusal, unsexed, and filled with prurient curiosity, by the foul interpretations of the "Prurient Prudes."

—CHARLES READE—"The Prurient Prude" [1]

✓   ✓   ✓

Hard Cash was Reade's most ambitious novel—his first thorough-going application of his newly systematized "Great System"—and he was consequently much chagrined when (in its serial run in *All The Year Round)* his self-styled "masterpiece" proved something less than a "hit." The fault, he believed, lay not in "The

System," but in the minds of the readers who, misled by attacks on the veracity of the madhouse scenes, had failed to appreciate the thoroughness of his researches. To vindicate "The System" and his humanitarian motives he therefore prefaced the novel in book form with a statement that is at once a defense and a challenge:

> "Hard Cash," like "The Cloister and the Hearth," is a matter-of-fact romance; that is, a fiction built on truths; and these truths have been gathered by long, severe, systematic labor from a multitude of volumes, pamphlets, journals, reports, blue-books, manuscript narratives, letters, and living people, whom I have sought out, examined, and cross-examined, to get at the truth on each main topic I have striven to handle.
>
> The madhouse scenes have been picked out by certain disinterested gentlemen who keep private asylums, and periodicals to puff them; and have been met with bold denials of public facts and with timid personalities, and a little easy cant about Sensation Novelists; but in reality those passages have been written on the same system as the nautical, legal, and other scenes; the best evidence has been ransacked; and a large portion of this evidence I shall be happy to show at my house to any brother writer who is disinterested, and really cares enough for truth and humanity to walk or ride a mile in pursuit of them.
>
> —CHARLES READE
>
> 6 Bolton Row, Mayfair,
> December 5, 1863

When no one accepted this invitation Reade became even more embittered, and in later editions of the novel included some fifteen pages of "Correspondence Elicited by The First Edition of 'Hard Cash,'" consisting first and foremost of his letter "To the Editor of the *Daily News*," in answer to the charges of an asylum keeper, one J. S. Bushnan, M.D. The tone as well as the substance of Bushnan's charges justified Reade in pouring forth the indignation (recorded in "suppressed passages from *Hard Cash*")[2] that he had been unable to express in the novel, and he made the most of his opportunity, annihilating Bushnan with fact and logic and humanitarian passion in passages of rhetoric more eloquent and sustained than in the novel itself. To substantiate further his "sincerity, and . . . patient, laborious industry" he then added his letter to the *Pall Mall Gazette* on "How Lunatics' Ribs Get Broken," concluding with his "Notice, 1863," in which, after inviting fresh communications concerning abuses in private asylums, he declared: "This great question did not begin with me in the pages of a novel, neither shall it end there, for where justice and humanity are both concerned, there—

> Dict sans faict
> A Dieu deplait"

Following this notice Reade was deluged with appeals—those discussed in the Notebooks, *A Terrible Temptation*, and *Readiana*, along with others he apparently felt obliged to treat as confidential, such as the letter from Rosina Bulwer Lytton which was later copied (through no fault of Reade's) and used as the basis for *A Blighted Life* by the Right Hon. Lady Lytton (London Publishing Office, 1880). The letter itself, described by Michael Sadleir (in his *Edward and Rosina*) as a "painful farrago of crude insults, hysterical inconsequences, and a spiritual anguish, none the less terrible for being largely self-inflicted. . . ."[3] Reade seemingly accepted at face value: "The narrative you have sent me," he wrote (Feb. 28, 1864),[4] "is indeed a romance. I cannot however but think that the idea of incarcerating you first occurred *seriously* to Sir E L after your appearance on the Hustings at Hertford. You then terrified as well as provoked him; and I think I could almost divine who it was that whispered into his ear what facilities the lunacy law affords for disposing of inconvenient wives. . . ." Reade then goes on to give a clinical yet sympathetic analysis of Rosina's narrative, concluding thus:

> I could have wished to have parts of your M.S. copied out To wit. The first visit of the doctors at Taunton . . . & the whole business at clarges St. (I say that rather takes the shine out of the parallel scenes in *Hard Cash*—I forgive you): but I could not, indeed had no right to submit the M.S. to another eye. Would you think me unreasonable were I to ask for a copy at your perfect leisure of these two parts, so curious in themselves, and so simply yet admirably told?—I must not conclude without thanking you for your good opinion of my book Go one step farther and believe that I and a few other writers mean what we say when the theme is justice and humanity.
>
> I don't mean to say that I for one am an universal philanthropist. I am not. Nine tenths of the woes of man don't come home to me, and so I don't feel them habitually. But when my limited intelligence does show me a great wrong, & enables me to

realize it, as Dei gratia I do realize the incarceration of the sane on medical certificates, then I burn with as true a fire as if I had never penned a line in my life

> Yrs very truly
> *Charles Reade*

This letter leaves no doubt that Reade was taken in by Rosina. And if she had petitioned his active aid, instead of his moral support, there can be little doubt that he would have championed her as he championed so many others. For much as he enjoyed writing out his own heroic vision of himself he enjoyed acting it out even more, and the notoriety consequent upon the publication of *Hard Cash* gave him his opportunity. In the years following he carried out so many heroic rescues that he actually did achieve, in life, the reputation he later sought to immortalize through the character of Rolfe (his acknowledged self-portrait) in *A Terrible Temptation*.

II

Along with his heroics Reade also found time to indulge his penchant for the theatre. While still negotiating with Dickens for the serial rights to *Hard Cash* he had promised Mrs. Seymour "a little dramatic spec."—apparently with his dramatization of *Never Too Late To Mend* in mind. Having peddled this play "seven mortal years"—only to have it rejected by the very managers who had been willing to produce it in pirated versions—he had come to believe that he was being black-balled for his lawsuits over dramatic copyright. Unless he was to surrender to what he considered a theatrical cabal his only alternative was therefore to produce the play himself. And this he did, using the sum he realized from *Hard Cash* to secure the services of John Coleman, at this time a theatrical manager of the Crummles stamp, who first produced the play at Leeds (in March, 1865), then took it on a provincial tour which began at Manchester on April 6.

Although the tour itself was not a success, according to Coleman, Mrs. Seymour nevertheless prevailed upon George Vining to produce the play in London at the Princess's Theatre, where, on the first night (October 4, 1865), the prison scene in which the boy Josephs is tortured to death proved so brutal that Frederick Guest Tomlins, a dramatic critic, rose in his seat and protested against its realism. The fault, if fault there was by melodramatic

standards, was seemingly not so much attributable to Reade or
Vining as to the actress who played Josephs; for (as Vining later
explained in the *Era*) she entered so thoroughly into the spirit of
the part that "the gaoler seemed to throw the boy down with . . .
a smack similar to a cod's tail slapped on the marble slab of a
fishmonger's shop. . . ."[5] But whatever the rights or wrongs of
the matter Reade was incensed beyond measure at what he conceived to be a "trades' union" attempt to drive his work off the
London stage. In *Reade's Luck* he declared:

> If you want a grain of humanity, or honor, or justice, or manly
> feeling of any kind, don't you go to a trades' union; for you won't
> find it there. The playwright critics concerted the destruction of
> the drama on the first night. They were seen to egg on Mr. Tomlins,
> the critic of *The Morning Advertiser*, to howl down the prison
> scenes by brute clamor. Tomlins, being drunk, 'his custom ever in
> the afternoon,' lent himself to this with inebriate zeal, and got up a
> disturbance, which with a feeble manager would infallibly have
> ended in the curtain being let down and the play withdrawn for-
> ever. But, for once, the clique ran their heads against a man. George
> Vining defied the cabal on stage; and, at last, some fellows in the
> gallery, shaking off their amazement at the misconduct below,
> called down, "Turn the blackguards out." Now when the dishonest
> blackguards in the stalls found the honest blackguards in the gallery
> had spotted them, they shut up, and prepared their articles for next
> morning in dead silence.
>
> Next day, of course, they wrote the piece down unanimously.
> But they had overrated their power. The public got scent of the
> swindle, rushed to the theatre, and carried the drama triumphantly
> for 148 nights. The profits were about £8000, of which £2000
> came to me on shares. The drama has outlived all the plays that
> were lauded to the skies that year by the venal clique. It was
> played in six houses this year, 1873.[6]

This was some eight years after the event. At the time Reade
was even more passionate in his bitterness. On Oct. 13, 1865, he
wrote, in a letter to Fields: "I have just brought out my great
drama 'Never too late.' . . . It plays four hours and constitutes
the whole performance. The London Press combined as one to
crush it; and the public has put its foot on them without ceremony.
The play is a grand success. . . ." And on Nov. 24 he once again
wrote Fields, not only in the same vein but in almost the same
words—as if the violence suggested by his metaphors had become,

in his own mind, a physical reality: "I have just atchieved [sic] a great dramatic success. The whole London Press caballed to crush it; and the public put its foot on them with a decision they will not forget in a hurry. d——n them."

III

In the midst of this turmoil Reade still managed to keep up his Notebooks, and to start work on a new novel, although, duplicating the practice he had followed after completing his prison epic, he did not immediately attempt another matter-of-fact romance. After *Hard Cash* and *The Cloister* that would have been too strenuous. Instead he essayed another and to his way of thinking less demanding type of novel. "It is a tale of the heart," he wrote Fields (Oct. 13, 1865), "and does not straggle into any eccentric topics. Need I say I shall make it as exciting and interesting as I can."

The outlines of this tale Reade seems to have drawn primarily from the two sources first identified in *The Round Table* (Dec. 1, 1867): 1) a fifty page story in Wilkie Collins' *Queen of Hearts* (1859) entitled "Brother Griffith's Story of a Plot in Private Life," and 2) "The Frenchman of Two Wives," an article in *Household Words* (Dec. 6, 1856) that was seemingly Collins' own immediate source for "Brother Griffith's Story. . . ." And behind this source was still another, a story called "Le Mort-vivant" which C. L. Connelly (*The Overland Monthly*, October, 1873) declared the source of both *Griffith Gaunt* and "Brother Griffith's Story"— although it would seem, on the basis of the evidence adduced by Edmund Morrison (in his *Charles Reade and his Novels*, 1940), that "Le Mort-vivant" was the source, not of Reade's novel or Collins' story, but of the "Frenchman of Two Wives."[7]

But there is no need to rehearse Morrison's arguments. Intelligent and restrained as they are they still tend to equate "source" with "conception," and in doing so necessarily oversimplify the creative process. Reade did not write *Griffith Gaunt* because he quite by chance stumbled onto a source or sources for its plot; he searched out these sources because he wanted to write such a "tale of the heart." The Notebooks are filled with "Plots" and "Plagianda" having to do with jealousy, priests, celibacy, bigamy, and the like. And these entries in turn reflect his autobiographical interests and experiences from the time of his first meeting with his Scotch wife, to his unhappy love affairs with Mrs. Stirling, to his more settled life (dating from 1853) with Mrs. Seymour. In all these love relationships Reade saw himself as the victim, not of his mother and his own Oedipal feelings, but of the rule of celibacy imposed by his Magdalen Fellowship. As late as 1876 he wrote in one of his Notebooks: "In my medieval romance *The Cloister and the Hearth* I use this expression celibacy of the clergy, an invention truly devilish. . . . The opinion I uttered in 1860 was even then twenty years old in me; it is now thirty-six." [8]

Cherishing these feelings, which he had been able to express only in *The Cloister and the Hearth,* and then not fully, owing to the limits of its historical framework, Reade was, the Notebooks indicate, constantly on the lookout for "Plagianda" that might enable him to write a modern variation on his medieval theme. And in Collins' story, and its even more lurid original, he found just the sources he needed. For "The Frenchman of Two Wives" is a circumstantial account of a late seventeenth century Frenchman who first becomes convinced that his wife is having an adulterous relationship with a priest, then commits bigamy himself—the whole affair ending in a confusion of wives and husbands and violence and murder trials. Given Reade's aims and interests these materials were invaluable in themselves, and to have them combined within a Sensation plot ideally suited to his needs and techniques (as in Collins' version) was, for Reade, to discover the basic form and substance of another masterpiece.

IV

The prime virtue of Collins' plot, considered as "Plagianda" or "Bon. Fab.," was that it lent itself to his time tried techniques of adaptation. To expand Collins' fifty page story of crime and detection into a five hundred page tale of the heart he needed, on the structural level, only a sufficient number of "generative incidents," and these he apparently found ready to hand in the Notebooks.[9] In any event he completely disregards plot in his notes for the novel (on the reverse side of the Notecard labelled "Notes for Griffith Gaunt"), taking the structure of his action for granted and concentrating on aspects of theme and character not to be found in his sources:

A Young Priest—A contradiction and clearly not intended. . . .
If the priest is to direct families he ought to have had one. . . .

A Bachelor Conducting married people.

The Angelic life. The confessor of a young wife is the jealous, secret enemy of her husband. His whole business is to insulate her and he does it conscientiously. It is the duty of him who leads her on the way of salvation to disengage her gradually from all earthly ties. modus operandi to discover of what threads each tie is composed and to separate and gnaw them away thread by thread.

Priest holds the key of the world to come. N.B. Avoid general statements.

Substitute the individual instance.

Fenelon according to Michelet Noble & shrewd, subtle, eloquent, close, very devout, and very intriguing. He bewitched souls, and filled them with transport. cf his letters. Yet in these fragments seduction is still omnipotent. besides a nobleness of manner, and an animative and refined turn of thought there is also a feminine delicacy that by no means excludes strength, and even in his subtlety an indescribable tenderness.

The confessional has corrupted many a soul by indelicate or injudicious probing Madame de Chantal really passed her life in a tempest of passion. Spiritual power must be purchased by the suicide of the body. He is my King. Really to reign is to reign over a soul. A soul that courts the sway

Compared with this what is physical dominion over the bodies of an unknown mob. [Prophet?] my Priest and my King

Father X A blunt, matter of fact priest Love, a magic word: and Leonard always talks of love. Love divine: love angelic. But the great substantive was always there; & its adjectives matter but little. Besides Love divine can be spoken of in accents that at once convey mortal love. And this one snare has caught a million hearts. Leonard passionately fond of Catherine's little girl as the Jesuits are of children.

Have him dragged through the horse-pond.

How [wild?] is imagination when let loose, and not trimmed by a little knowledge of the world.

About this time a certain cynical sentence from a famous pen was current in society

> I take her person   you her mind
> Which has the better bargain

Signs of love detected in Cathennâ [Casstinâ?]

Climax
     Her hand in leaving Leonard's shoulder; So he stoops a little
as he goes. She walked like a serpent when I first came; now she
goes a [hanging?] her head.
Any woman can see that she is become a part of him. Multiply
details
She uses the very words that I have heard in his mouth.
The great thirsty heart of woman that married or single, pines
for eternal Courtship,

See — the Simple Tale, and Father Clement for the English term
     applicable to a Director

Mrs. G./ I have given my husband just offense. He punishes me
     severly. I must be patient.

Griffith goes to the parish Church a Sunday with his new wife.
     Descants on this. —

How Griffith's new wife fascinated him. Habit

     Michelet—121. No violent attachment as for Kate but a soft
     seducing stealthy complacent habit. see Michelet. 121
                                                  good Dram.
Habit, gentle slope.
                         The religious orders for monks[10]

     In form as well as substance these notes, loosely strung out on
one side of one Notecard, appear incomplete and tentative—as if
Reade had in mind further additions and developments that for
some reason he failed to carry through. As the notes appear on
the Notecard, those having to do with Father Leonard and the
Church are by far the most fully developed—not only because
they involve Reade's deepest personal interests but also, it would
seem, because they mark a radical departure from his sources. In
Collins' story, for instance, the parson's character is summarized,
Dickensian fashion, in his name (Mr. Meek), and in any but a
Victorian story he would be a comic figure. Nor is there the
slightest hint, either in Collins' story or "The Frenchman of Two
Wives," that the priest's actions have any serious moral or religious
implications. The thematic development Reade suggests is entirely
his own, and seems designed to present the conflict between the
young priest and the young wife as another conflict between the

[239]

cloister and the hearth—with Father Leonard representing an authoritarian religious system that imposes the evils of enforced celibacy on its priests, then endows them, through the confessional, with the power to inflict the consequences of these evils on all true believers.

Working from this conception, with a personal as well as philosophical animus against the Church, Reade was no doubt tempted to cast Father Leonard in the role of melodramatic villain and "have him dragged through the horse-pond." But that would have meant sacrificing character to purpose in a manner incompatible with his thematic intention, which demanded that the priest be the physical embodiment of the young wife's religious ideals. Hence the notes from Michelet, which seemingly deepened his conception of the character, and encouraged him to treat Leonard (and his predicament) with the sympathy and understanding implicit in the notes on angelic lovemaking.

The notes on the young wife, Kate Gaunt, are equally original. Collins' heroine has none but the sterling qualities appropriate to a fictional heroine, and is consequently as pure as the driven snow, her sole interest in Mr. Meek being a musical one, based on her enjoyment of their daily duets. The young wife of Reade's notes, on the other hand, is a woman of spirit and sensibility who "pines for eternal courtship," and when she fails to find it in matrimony, turns to Father Leonard, stopping short only when her emotional response to his love ("Any woman can see that she is become a part of him") threatens to lead to physical consummation. Yet if Reade intended Kate's experiences and feelings to be titillating—and despite his published denials he most certainly did—he did not intend them to be merely that. Even in the notes under "Climax," which prefigure the Sensation climax of the novel, his references to Kate's indiscretions (e.g., "Her hand in leaving Leonard's shoulder") represent a serious attempt to dramatize the impulses of the female heart that his contemporaries (as well as his sources) had overlooked or denied.

In contrast the few notes on "Griffith's new wife" indicate that he was content to draw her basic character and function almost entirely from "The Frenchman of Two Wives," filling out the details with bits of *Foemina Vera* from Michelet and other such auxiliary sources. His aim, it would seem, was first to create a convincing variation on the saintly-submissive-domestic type for which he, along with the other Victorians, had such an inordinate fondness, then to subject her to a bigamous situation in a manner calculated to make the reader an enthusiastic, yet moral, "participant in the event."

As for the notes on the titular hero, they are so meagre as to suggest that Reade, following his sources, conceived Griffith as a conventional melodramatic type—a man of strong body and little mind whose impulses are sound and healthy except for his one great mania or foible, his Othello-like "Jealousy." The great merit of such a type, considered from Reade's point of view, was that it provided a convenient embodiment of the abstraction "jealousy" around which he could center his action, and so achieve a measure of dramatic unity not provided by his sources. In these notes, however, Griffith's foible does not loom so large as his simple-minded manliness, which Reade could at any given moment fill with stock responses appropriate to the action. Thus the note on "How Griffith's new wife fascinated him," followed by the word "Habit" and the reference to Michelet, which implies that Reade considered Michelet's distinction between "habit" and "violent attachment" striking as well as dramatic, and therefore applicable to Griffith's bigamous situation—the test being its appropriateness, not to Griffith as an individual man, but to Griffith's predicament, conceived in the most general terms.

The only other character mentioned in these notes Reade also conceived as a melodramatic type. Indeed he apparently had the type so well in mind that he merely identified him, playbill fashion, as "Father X, a blunt, matter-of-fact priest." Further characterization was hardly necessary because he had already cast him in a role common to nearly all his novels: that of elderly counselor to the hero and heroine. This role, ordinarily an autobiographical one, provided Reade with a dramatic platform, outside the main action, from which he could point, direct, comment and on occasion act as his own *deus ex machina*. In addition the role often provided a means of dramatic contrast, which in this instance he envisaged as the contrast between a common-sense priest and an heroic one.

And this, with the exception of a few odd references, would seem to be the extent and meaning of Reade's "Notes." That he did not even bother to mention any of the other major characters or aspects of the novel shows how little concerned he was about the writing of what amounted, in bulk, to something like eighty per cent of the novel. His prime interest was in that section of the novel centering around Kate and Father Leonard; the rest he considered a matter of extending and filling out his sources, and for this he apparently felt very little special preparation was required.

The remaining Notecards devoted wholly or in part to the novel are singularly bare, and the few entries they do contain are of no great significance, except as they indicate how cursory were his preparations, even in matters relating to the historical setting of the novel. Indeed there is but one entry on one Notecard to indicate that he was at all concerned with historical accuracy—an entry (on the otherwise blank Notecard headed "Notes for Griffith Gaunt") which seems to be a collection of eighteenth century words, idioms, and turns of speech:

Has been the ruin of one woman
already who was wife to his bosom friend.
I am out of countenance. P. for ashamed
Pray present my humble duty to my Mama
Made me some amends for what I had suff.
I stick close to my spinnet. daughter for God daughter
[One word illegible] excuse to me was bad tenants and a cheeky
    steward
Run mad for gone mad. He designs to enter himself.
Eternally yours, Lansdowne We had pure sport. [Thin?] of company
to what it used to be. We were twelve in company; and
it was proposed we should sit a man and a woman.
The loss you have made. The company—were free [libertine?] people
Old harridan   mother in law
French ladies   their faces and persons are so hid
he does not know what to make of them.
Foemina Vera That morning I was entertained with [Cuzzoni?]
Oh how charming! How did I wish for all I love and
like to be with me at that instant of time
The Babe is to be made a Ztian next Sunday
Mrs. Badge nor I could not rightly understand about
the Bohea tea. [pondering?] gown Sweetheart. applied to children
frighted hackneys for h. coaches Harpsichord
Upon my permission up comes the gentleman so spruce and finical.

Except for these rather desultory notes Reade showed less concern for historical accuracy than in his very first novel, *Peg Woffington*, written before he had developed his elaborate Baconian theories and techniques. The reason for this apparent inconsistency, it seems clear, is that for all his emphasis on "the very period Henry

Fielding has described" he did not really intend *Griffith Gaunt* to be an historical novel. His first interest was not "history" but "the heart," and he chose to set his tale in the period of Fielding, not because, like Thackeray, he understood the period, and found it spiritually congenial, but because its manners and morals and speech "were somewhat blunter than now-a-days" and in consequence lent themselves more readily to the expression of "the great passions that poets have sung."

v

The heart of Reade's tale, as set forth in these Notes, is also the heart of the novel. And if he had not felt obliged to be tri-voluminous he might conceivably have been content to write a one-volume novel entitled *Kate Gaunt* or *Father Leonard*. As it was, having committed himself to three volumes, he had no choice but to lengthen his tale with an introduction and a long drawn-out bigamous conclusion. In consequence *Griffith Gaunt* falls into three parts or dramatic sequences (corresponding roughly to the acts of a three-act play) which may be designated 1) courtship (Chs. 1-13, pp. 3-151); 2) temptation (Chs. 14-25, pp. 152-251); 3) bigamy (Chs. 26-46, pp. 252-489).

In the first or courtship sequence Reade (following Collins) sets his scene, introduces his leading characters, and establishes his theme, introducing Griffith's foible as early as page thirteen, and developing it through such commentaries as the following: "The mind as well as the body has its self-protecting instincts. This of Griffith's was after all an instinct of that class, and under certain circumstances, is true wisdom. But Griffith, I think, carried the instinct to excess; and that is why I call it his foible." [11] Here and elsewhere Reade's psychological analyses and commentaries are remarkably acute—though in his efforts to dramatize Griffith's excess he invariably falls back upon the language and techniques of *The Actors' Hand-Book:* "Hitherto she had but beheld the feeling of jealousy, but now she witnessed the livid passion of jealousy writhing in every lineament of a human face. That terrible passion had transfigured its victim in a moment: the ruddy, genial, kindly Griffith, with his soft brown eye, was gone; and in his place lowered a face older and discolored and convulsed, and almost demoniacal." [12]

But if Griffith's melodramatic duality is not convincing in itself it does provide a means of exploring Kate's responses, more especially her sexual responses, and Reade makes the most of it to introduce her as "a dreamy virgin" who for all her girlish enthusiasm and Catholic piety is yet a woman. The opening scene of the novel, in which Kate rides to the hounds, calls to mind the early scenes of *Daniel Deronda*. And the succeeding scenes, though more theatrical than Eliot's, are at times equally revealing, particularly those in which Reade shows Kate responding to both her suitors (Griffith and his rival, George Neville) not merely by turns but at the same time, on one occasion with both lovers in full view. While she watched Griffith ride away, "the inflammable George made hot love to her again"—and not without effect, despite her conscious efforts to repulse him:

> Fire and water were in his eyes, passion in every tone; his manly hand grasped hers and trembled, and drew her gently towards him.
> Her bosom heaved; his passionate male voice and manner electrified her, and made her flutter. "Spare me this pain," she faltered; and she looked through the window and thought, "Poor Griffith was right after all, and I was wrong. He had cause for jealousy, and CAUSE FOR FEAR."
> And then she pitied him who panted at her side, and then was sorry for him who rode away disconsolate, still lessening to her eye; and what with this conflict, and the emotion her quarrel with Griffith had already caused her, she leaned her head back against the shutter, and began to sob low, but almost hysterically.

Although the language is tritely theatrical, Kate's thoughts and actions are certainly not those of the stock Victorian heroine. For even as she sobs, "almost hysterically," she is aware of her duplicity, and when she seeks to justify it falls into still further confusion:

> Catherine turned her dreamy eyes on him [Neville].
> "You have had a good master. Why did you not come to me sooner?"
> She was thinking more of him than of herself, and in fact paying too little heed to her words. But she had no sooner uttered this inadvertent speech than she felt she had said too much.

Thus Reade, by the technically simple device of playing off Kate's words against her thoughts and impulses, probes the depths of her confusion. She does not know her own mind because what she feels for Neville she wants to feel for Griffith—not only because his inferior position and prospects render him more worthy, in terms of her ideals, but because for all his physical prowess, his more tentative maleness, as expressed in his slavish devotion, poses less of a threat to her own personality. Married to Neville she would have to be merely his wife; married to Griffith she could continue to be herself, submitting physically but retaining her emotional and intellectual independence, and in fact treating Griffith as she had treated her father.

What Kate finally wanted, it seems clear, was marriage and sexual fulfillment without emotional submission to a husband. Yet her feelings for Neville were so strong that she could not choose Griffith until she had inadvertently caused him to be wounded in a duel and robbed of his inheritance. Then she could no longer resist him. On the very night he was disinherited in her favor, she called him to her bedroom window, knowing that he was drunk, to say that she would be his wife:

Griffith burst into raptures; Kate listened to them with a complacent smile; then delivered herself after this fashion: "You have very little to thank me for, dear Griffith. I don't exactly downright love you; but I could not rob you of those unlucky farms, and you refuse to take them back any way but this; so what can I do? And then, for all I don't love you, I find I am always unhappy if you are unhappy, and happy when you are happy; so it comes pretty much to the same thing. I declare I am sick of giving you pain, and a little sick of crying in consequence. There, I have cried more in the last fortnight than in all my life before, and you know nothing spoils one's beauty like crying; and then you are so good, and kind, and true, and brave; and everybody is so unjust, and so unkind to you; papa and all. You were quite in the right about the duel, dear; he *is* an impudent puppy; and I threw dust in your eyes, and made you own you were in the wrong; and it was a great shame of me; but it was because I liked you best. I could take liberties with *you,* dear. And you are wounded for me; and now I have disinherited you; oh, I can't bear it, and I won't. My heart yearns for you; bleeds for you. I would rather die than you should be unhappy; I would rather follow you in rags round the world than marry a prince and make you wretched. Yes, dear, I am yours. Make me your wife; and then some day I dare say I shall love you as I ought.

In these lines Kate reveals the full implications of her choice. She is consciously rejecting love, the love she had begun to feel for Neville, in favor of self-sacrifice and devotion. And if she is rather wistful, despite the bantering tone of her remarks on beauty, she is also pleased and proud. For in giving herself to Griffith she feels she is expressing a higher kind of love, the love that she feels for the Church, and that she on one occasion expresses in almost exactly the same words: "My heart bleeds for the Church . . . and when I see her present condition I long to be of service."

In the light of this and similar statements it seems clear that, to Kate, marriage to Griffith is the next best alternative to becoming a nun—her ultimate ideal. But before she can marry Griffith, she must overcome the opposition of her father, as well as the still more formidable opposition of Father Francis, who has already squelched her romantic notions about entering a nunnery and is urging her, for practical reasons, to marry Neville. To ensure her own steadfastness she therefore offers Griffith "a friend's advice": "Then," she said, "I'll do a downright brazen thing, now my hand is in. I declare I'll tell you how to secure me. You make me plight my troth with you this minute, and exchange rings with you, *whether I like or not;* engage my honor in this foolish business, and if you do that, I really do think you will have me in spite of them all." Having so bound herself she then uses her wit and charm to disarm her father and Father Francis, and when, in Father Francis' case, her stratagems prove ineffectual, she resorts to tears and supplications:

"Spare me!" muttered Kate, faintly.

"Then do you drop deceit and the silly cunning of your sex, and speak to me from your heart, or not at all." (Diapason.)

At this Kate began to whimper. "Father," she said, "show me some mercy," Then, suddenly clasping her hands: "HAVE PITY ON HIM, AND ON ME."

This time Nature herself seemed to speak, and the eloquent cry went clean through the priest's heart. "Ah!" said he; and his own voice trembled a little, "now you are as strong as your cunning was weak. Come, I see how it is with you; and I am human, and have been young, and a lover into the bargain, before I was a priest. There, dry thy eyes, child, and go to thy room; he thou couldst not trust shall bear the brunt for thee; this once."

Then Kate bowed her fair head and kissed the horrid paw of him that had administered so severe but salutary a pat. She huried away up-stairs, right joyful at the unexpected turn things had taken.

While this scene is patently of the usual Reade construction—with Father Francis, the priestly embodiment of the elderly Readian adviser, evincing the manly emotions demanded by the plot—Kate's theatricality is in part redeemed by the dramatic context. If she speaks and acts like an actress it is because she is acting. She has learned the feminine appeals that touch the hearts of men, whether they be elderly priests or young suitors, and has no scruples about using them to serve her own ends, since, as she sees these ends, they are wholly unselfish and noble. It is only after she has completed her conquest of the male opposition by securing her father's consent to the marriage that she feels any compunction, and then her primary concern is to justify herself to Neville, whose forgiveness she entreats in a note so disarming in its seeming honesty that it leaves him no choice but to suffer nobly.

In these latter phases of the courtship Kate may be compared with the young Dorothea of *Middlemarch*. And while Reade's characterization lacks the Tolstoyan depth and finish of Eliot's, it is almost equally perceptive in its grasp of feminine psychology, and more daring, if not more perceptive, in its treatment of disguised sexual motivation. It shows that Kate, "the dreamy young virgin," is not so dreamy after all, that in sacrificing herself to Griffith she is seeking to fulfill her personal as well as her religious ideals. For Griffith, in contrast to Neville, does not demand emotional submission; he is rather the object of her charity and compassion—a man for whom she can bleed without staining the pristine purity of her virginal self-image.

VI

The second or temptation sequence of the novel Reade opens with a summary and a challenge:

> Mr. and Mrs. Gaunt lived happily together—as times went. A fine girl and boy were born to them; and need I say how their hearts expanded and exulted; and seemed to grow twice as large?
>
> The little boy was taken from them at three years old: and how can I convey to any but a parent the anguish of that first bereavement?
>
> Well, they suffered it together, and that poignant grief was one tie more between them.
>
> For many years they did not furnish any exciting or even interesting matter to this narrator. . . . In the absence of striking incidents, it may be well to notice the progress of character, and note the tiny seeds of events to come.

This is rather bold, even for Reade, since in thus reiterating his Sensation theories and relegating character analysis to the secondary position he feels it deserves, he is, in effect, challenging the Eliotians on their own ground. He is promising to delineate, within the space of a few pages, psychological developments that, in a George Eliot novel, might be analyzed through an entire volume.

Yet if the challenge itself is quixotic, and based on a misconception of Eliot's aims and techniques, there is no denying the validity of his own performance. The incisiveness of his commentary shows how inevitable was Kate's frustration, as Griffith, following the accepted pattern of the time, developed into a boozy country squire. Finding it impossible to bleed for such a husband, she again decided to bleed for the Church, only to be once again held in check by her spiritual director, Father Francis, whose common sense had by this time become so irksome to her that she felt relieved when he was ordered to another part of the country: "His mind," said she, "is set on earthly things. Instead of helping the angels to raise my thoughts to heaven and heavenly things, he drags me down to earth. Oh, that man's soul was born without wings. . . . There are plenty of honest men in the world," said she; "but in one's spiritual director, one needs something more than that, and I have pined for it like a thirsty soul in the desert all these years."

The something more Kate pined for remained undefined until she met Father Francis' successor: "His skin was dark and his eyes coal black; yet his ample but symmetrical forehead was singularly white and delicate. Very tall and spare, and both face and figure were of that exalted kind which make ordinary beauty seem dross. . . . This Brother Leonard looked and moved like a being who had come down from some higher sphere to pay the world a very little visit, and be very kind and patient with it all the time." None of these features were lost upon Kate, who "almost started at first sight . . . of a man so remarkable." He seemed to her "Religion embodied," and in her innocence she set about winning his approval in the same way she had won that of every other man she had encountered—with flutters, and blushes, and displays of feminine charm. But to no avail. Only when she began talking about "the prospects of the Church" did Leonard show the slightest interest, and then he dismissed her remarks with a "cold, lofty look of polite but grave disapproval."

The "look" is no more convincing than Leonard himself, who throughout this scene remains, in his stately aloofness, a clerical counterpart of Jane Austen's Darcy. But Kate's reactions to his rebuffs are convincing enough, particularly as they reveal her almost masochistic delight in having at long last discovered a man who could make her feel inferior. Even while she continued to resist his domination, out of wounded pride, she secretly hoped in "her woman's nature" that he would overcome her resistance—as he eventually did, to her entire satisfaction, through the over-whelming strength of his eloquence: "His first sermon was an era in her life. After twenty years of pulpit prosers, there suddenly rose before her a sacred orator . . . in the exercise of this great gift the whole man seemed transfigured; abroad, he was a languid, rather slouching priest, who crept about, a picture of delicate humility, but with a shade of meanness; for, religious prejudice apart, it is ignoble to sweep the wall in passing as he did, and eye the ground; but, once in the pulpit, his figure rose and swelled majestically, and seemed to fly over them all like a guardian angel's; his sallow cheek burned, his great Italian eye shot black lightning at the impenitent, and melted ineffably when he soothed the sorrowful."

In so far as this rhetorical portrait represents Kate's view of Leonard's preaching—and that is how it is primarily intended—its theatricalities are to some extent justified. In her state of mind she was prepared to see his figure rise and swell majestically and to respond accordingly:

> Mrs. Gaunt sat thrilled, enraptured, melted. She hung upon his words; and, when they ceased, she still sat motionless, spell-bound; loath to believe that accents so divine could really come to an end.
>
> Even whilst all the rest were dispersing, she sat quite still, and closed her eyes. For her soul was too high-strung now to endure the chit-chat she knew would attack her on the road home—chit-chat that had been welcome enough, coming home from other preachers.
>
> And by this means she came hot and undiluted to her husband; she laid her white hand on his shoulder, and said, "Oh, Griffith, I have heard the voice of God."

The sexual connotations of "hot and undiluted," clear enough in themselves and substantiated by Reade's entries on the Note-cards, serve to emphasize the sexual implications of Kate's words and actions, as she, in her "enthusiastic admiration," identified

[249]

Leonard first with St. Paul, then with Christ. Nor was she much sobered by Griffith's disapproval, or his impatience at having to delay Sunday dinner because of Leonard's eloquence. That Griffith could even mention dinner at such a time seemed to her incredibly gross, an impression that was deepened on the following Sunday by his refusal to accompany her to chapel, on the ground that it would look as if he were tied "to his wife's apron" and in any case would offend his own Anglican parson. To Kate these arguments seemed at best "stupid," and when, on the following Sunday, he once again fell to complaining about her being late for dinner, pointing out that the delay might upset the servants and spoil their Sunday, she expressed her sense of outrage in a speech that is all the more dramatically effective for being a direct answer to his bumbling attempts to equate Sunday dinner with the sanctity of the home: "Dinner! dinner! What! shall I starve my soul, by hurrying away from the oracles of God to a sirloin? Oh, these gross appetites! how they deaden the immortal half, and wall out heaven's music! For my part, I wish there was no such thing as eating and drinking; 'tis like falling from heaven down into the mud, to come back from such divine discourse and be greeted with 'dinner! dinner! dinner!'" These sentiments Kate presumably derived from the Sermon on the Mount (Matthew 6, 25), but the words, and more particularly the images, were of her own devising. And their crudity, not to say cruelty, reveals that her rejection of Sunday dinner was also a symbolic rejection of her husband and his animal appetites.

Having thus freed herself Kate became ever more devoted to her heavenly oracle, who had finally begun to succumb to her presence: "She was always there whenever he preached, and her rapt attention never flagged. Her gray eyes never left his face, and, being upturned, the full orbs came out in all their grandeur, and seemed an angel's come down from heaven to hear him. . . ." After leaving the pulpit, "and cooling," Leonard invariably remembered that Kate "was no angel but a woman of the world." The illusion, however, had become so necessary to him that, to avoid dispelling it through personal contact, he commissioned his assistant to visit her and receive her confessions. While this explanation of Leonard's motives may seem rather arbitrary, and certainly involves Reade in some rather arbitrary plotting, it provides just about the only possible circumstances in which such an ethereal love could take root and grow. So long as Leonard saw Kate only from the pulpit he felt no obligation to censor his feelings; after all, she was his inspiring angel. And so he made love to her, never realizing that he had in effect substituted the pulpit for the divan, holy words and looks for more conventional forms of endearment. And she, equally innocent in her idealism, met his words and looks with adoring looks of her own.

In consequence Leonard found it increasingly difficult to maintain the purity of his angelic image. More and more he tended to transform the ideal image into the real woman. And she, in her womanliness, hastened the transformation, when, stopping to chat with Mrs. Gough, the housekeeper of the parsonage and an old servant of hers, she discovered that Leonard's saintliness, as manifested in his obliviousness to food and comfort, caused him to experience periods of melancholy. Deeply moved by this information, she not only bribed Mrs. Gough to adulterate Leonard's food with meat but also arranged, again with Mrs. Gough's connivance, to have his study "filled with geraniums and jessamine. . . ." Then, having permitted Mrs. Gough to sweep aside her one doubt— that it might "be a sin, and a sacrilege to boot . . . for us to play the woman so, and delude a saint for his mere bodily weal"—she departed "with feelings strangely but sweetly composed of veneration and pity. In that Leonard was a great orator and a high-minded priest, she revered him; in that he was solitary and sad, she pitied him; in that he wanted common sense, she felt like a mother, and must take him under her wing. All true women love to protect; perhaps it is a part of the great maternal element; but to protect a man, and yet look up to him, this is delicious."

"Delicious," applied to a woman's feelings, nearly always carries sexual overtones in Reade's usage, and the present instance is no exception—though Reade, looking forward to the climactic action and the need for maintaining Kate's purity, stresses her maternal and reverential feelings (rather than the impulses that underlie them), and in manipulating the plot goes out of his way to absolve her of any real complicity in the matter of the flowers: "Now Mrs. Gaunt, after eight years of married life, was too sensible and dignified a woman to make a romantic mystery out of nothing. She concealed the gravy, because there secrecy was necessary; but she never dreamed of hiding that she had sent her spiritual adviser a load of flowers. She did not tell her neighbors, for she was not ostentatious; but she told her husband, who grunted, but did not object."

Although this bit of editorializing is not, in itself, wholly convincing, Kate's own words and actions substantiate the essential
innocence of her naïve high-mindedness. She could not know that
Leonard, already in love with his angelic image of her, would
cherish the flowers because they were "from her hand," or that
he would be even more delighted with two watering pots with
gold crosses on them because they not only were "from her hand"
but intended "for his hands." Nor could she know that "watering
the flowers that she had given him . . . with his own hands"
would become for Leonard a physical if ritualized act of love:
"He had a Madonna that cared for him in secret. She was human,
but good, beautiful, and wise. . . . And she knows me better
than myself. . . . Since I had these flowers from her hand, I am
another man."

Yet if these were not the reactions that Kate intended or
expected the fact remains that she was quick to recognize and
accept them:

> One evening Mrs. Gaunt rode by with Griffith, and saw him water-
> ing them. His tall figure, graceful, though inclined to stoop, bent
> over them with feminine delicacy, and the simple act, which
> would have been nothing in vulgar hands, seemed to Mrs. Gaunt
> so earnest, tender, and delicate in him, that her eyes filled, and
> she murmured, "Poor Brother Leonard!"
> "Why, what's wrong with him now?" asked Griffith, a little
> peevishly.
> "That was him watering his flowers."
> "Oh, is that all?" said Griffith carelessly.

These last few lines of dialogue are quite masterful, revealing as
they do the full extent of the psychic distance that separates the
naïve wife from the even more naïve husband. Griffith, having
taken refuge in peevish male jealousy could not possibly comprehend Kate's response, much less the more subtle evasiveness of
her reply, which suggests that she sensed more than she knew,
or at least more than she was willing to admit, even to herself.

In any event she was pleased and not at all surprised when, a
few days later, she heard that Brother Leonard had called on her
in person while she was out. What she did not know, however, was
that he had been directed to the grove (known as the "Dames
Haunt" because she so much frequented it) and that while there,
walking "to and fro, in religious meditation," his meditative eye
had "happened to fall on a terrestrial object that startled and

thrilled him . . . a lady's glove. . . . He stooped and picked it up. He opened the little fingers, and called up in fancy the white and tapering hand that glove could fit. He laid the glove softly on his own palm, and eyed it with dreamy tenderness. 'So this is the hand that hath solaced my loneliness,' said he: 'a hand fair as that angelical face, and sweet as the kind heart that doeth good by stealth. . . .' He put the little glove in his bosom, and paced thoughtfully home through the woods. . . ."

VII

This episode of the glove marks the end of Leonard's inno-cence—though not, of course, his self-deception. In Reade's words: "Love stole on him, masked with religious zeal, and robed in a garment of light that seemed celestial. When the mask fell, it was too late: the power to resist . . . was gone. The solitary man was too deep in love." And so he cherished the glove, and when he felt frustrated in his efforts "to sketch the inspired face he had learned to preach to," actually desecrated the pulpit by using it as an easel: "On his return home, he threw himself on his knees, and prayed forgiveness of God with many sighs and tears, and hid the sacrilegious drawing out of his own sight. Two days after, he was at work coloring it; and the hours flew by like minutes, as he laid the mellow, melting tints on with infinite care and delicacy. *Labor ipse voluptas.*"

Kate, on the other hand, remained innocent in her responsive-ness until, quite by chance, she discovered her glove and por-trait in Leonard's room. Then she too experienced feelings that brought her close to self-awareness—feelings that Reade describes imagistically in a passage that at once looks back to Bacon and anticipates Freud: "Her meditations were no longer so calm and speculative as heretofore. She found her mind constantly recurring to one person, and, above all, to the discovery she had made of her portrait in his possession. She had turned it off to Betty Gough; but here, in her calm solitude and umbrageous twilight, her mind crept out of its cave, like wild and timid things at dusk, and whispered to her heart that Leonard perhaps admired her more than was safe or prudent. Then this alarmed her, yet caused her a secret complacency: and that, her furtive satisfaction, alarmed her still more."

It was to such passages as this that Henry James was referring when he spoke of "those great sympathetic guesses with which a real master attacks the truth." [13] And in the dramatic passage that follows—the first personal meeting between Kate and Leonard— Reade does full justice to his insight by having Kate draw upon her suppressed awareness of Leonard's love to break down his reserves and to bring him to the point of sharing with her his hopes and ambitions for the Church.

After this meeting Kate departed from Leonard "like one in a dream . . . the world seemed dead to her forever." And in the weeks and months that followed, as she devoted herself wholly to Leonard and his religious activities, the world, including her husband, actually did come to mean less and less to her. She lived only for her meetings with Leonard—meetings that, for her as for Leonard, soon developed into disguised love trysts:

> Every syllable that passed between these two might have been published without scandal. But the heart does not speak by words alone: there are looks, and there are tones of voice that belong to Love, and are his signs, his weapons; and it was in these very tones the priest murmured to his gentle listener about "the angelic life" between spirits still lingering on earth, but purged from earthly dross; and even about other topics less captivating to the religious imagination. He had persuaded her to found a school in this dark parish, and in it he taught the poor with exemplary and touching patience. Well, when he spoke to her about this school, it was in words of practical good sense, but in tones of love; and she, being one of those feminine women who catch the tone they are addressed in, and instinctively answer in tune, and, moreover, seeing no ill but good in the *subject* of their conversation, replied sometimes, unguardedly enough, in accents almost as tender.
>
> In truth, if Love was really a personage, as the heathens feigned, he must have often perched on a tree, in that quiet grove, and chuckled and mocked when this man and woman sat and murmured together in the soft seducing twilight about the love of God.

This final paragraph underlines the fact that Kate was almost as deeply in love with Leonard as he with her, that, for all her innocence, she was well on the way to replacing her husband with her priest. But this, given his plot, theories, and techniques, Reade could not permit. To justify Kate's actions and to add sensational interest, he introduced Mrs. Ryder, a "female-rake" (patterned after Mrs. Archbold) who is also a "she-Machiavel," and therefore a fit instrument for working out the complications of the plot outlined on the Notecards. It is Mrs. Ryder who goads Griffith into

a jealous fury; it is she who foils as well as foments his scheme
to have Leonard dragged through the horse-pond; and it is she,
in her role of "she-Machiavel," who reveals to both Leonard and
Kate Griffith's part in the scheme—with a view to bringing the
wife and priest together and thereby securing the husband for her
rakish self.

Hopelessly melodramatic as they are in themselves these nefari-
ous machinations and threats of violence do enable Reade to
bring his pure heroine to the point of seduction without sacrificing
her innocence: "It was an evil hour when Griffith attacked her
saint with violence. The woman was too high-spirited, and too sure
of her own rectitude, to endure that; so, instead of crushing her,
it drove her to retaliation, and to imprudence." Since Leonard
could no longer come to her she would go to him:

One day, as he sat drooping and listless, there came a light foot
along the passage, a light tap at the door, and the next moment
she stood before him, a little paler than usual, but lovelier than
ever, for celestial pity softened her noble features

The priest started up with a cry of joy that ought to have
warned her; but it only brought a faint blush of pleasure to her
cheek, and the brimming tears to her eyes.

'Dear father and friend,' said she. 'What! have you missed me?
Think, then, how I have missed *you*. But 'twas best for us both to
let their vile passions cool first.'

Leonard could not immediately reply. The emotion of seeing her
again so suddenly almost choked him.

He needed all the self-possession he had been years acquiring,
not to throw himself at her knees and declare his passion to her.

Mrs. Gaunt saw his agitation, but did not interpret it aright.

She came eagerly and sat on a stool beside him. 'Dear father,'
she said, 'do not let their insolence grieve you. They have smarted
for it, and *shall* smart till they make their submission to you, and
beg and entreat you to come to us again. Meantime, since you
cannot visit me, I visit you. Confess me, father, and then direct
me with your counsels.'

. . . .

By this time Leonard had recovered his self-possession, and he
spent an hour of strange intoxication, confessing his idol, sentenc-
ing his idol to light penances, directing and advising his idol, and
all in the soft murmurs of a lover. . . .

Two days only elapsed, and she came again. Visit succeeded
to visit; and her affection seemed boundless.

Kate's "confess me, father" is so tantalizing, in context, as to be very nearly pornographic, and presumably she intensified her "tenderness" on her succeeding visits—though Reade dared not say as much. He had reached the end of his Victorian tether—as demonstrated by his frantic efforts to maintain Kate's innocence and purity, first by shifting the burden of moral responsibility wholly onto Leonard, then by interpolating moral platitudes to account for her seductive acts. So that, if one accepts Reade's commentary, rather than the full text, she is guilty of nothing more than indiscretion.

But Kate's actions and words speak for themselves, and they, together with Reade's hints and incidental revelations (e.g., that Kate had not been sleeping with Griffith since his threatened violence to Leonard) do much to redeem the otherwise stock melodramatic features of Leonard's attempted seduction and its aftermath. In fact Reade's treatment of Kate's reaction to the attempted seduction is in all essentials sound, and in certain of its touches remarkably perceptive:

> She went home straight to her husband . . . 'Griffith,' she said, 'will you grant your wife a favor? You once promised to take me abroad: I desire to go now: I long to see foreign countries: I am tired of this place. I want a change. Prithee, prithee, take me hence this very day.' . . .
> 'Well, but what a fancy to take all of a sudden!'
> 'Oh, Griffith, don't deny me what I ask you, with my arm around your neck, dearest. It is no fancy. I want to be alone with *you*, far from this place where coolness has come between us.' And with this she fell to crying and sobbing, and straining him tight to her bosom, as if she feared to lose him, or be taken from him.
> Griffith kissed her, and told her to cheer up, he was not the man to deny her anything. 'Just let me get my hay in,' said he, 'and I'll take you to Rome, if you like.' . . .
> Mrs. Gaunt had gradually sunk almost to her knees. She now started up with nostrils expanding and her blue eyes glittering. 'Your hay!' she cried, with bitter contempt; 'your hay before your wife? That is how *you* love me.'

The final "you," contrasting Griffith with Leonard, accounts for Kate's slipping on the stairs (just after the hay was in); also for her having an invalid's bed sent "by the doctor at her own request, and placed on a small bedstead," thus leaving Griffith once

again "as good as a widower." And to spell out the full implications
of Kate's illness, which would now be labelled psychosomatic,
Reade arranged for his "she-Machiavel" (now become a "female
Iago") to disillusion the sorrowful Griffith:

'It is nothing,' said she; then she paused and added, 'but my folly.
I can't bear to see you waste your feelings. She is not so ill as you
fancy.'

'Do you mean to say that my wife is pretending?'

'How can I say that? I wasn't there: *nobody saw her fall;* nor
heard her either; and the house full of people. No doubt there is
something the matter with her; but I do believe her heart is in
more trouble than her back.'

'And what troubles her heart? Tell me, and she shall not fret
long.'

'Well, sir: then just you send for Father Leonard: and she
will get up and walk as she used. . . . That man is the main of
her sickness, you take my word.'

Here as elsewhere Reade used his "female Iago" quite skillfully,
not only to further his plot but also to reveal aspects of his heroine's feelings that he, as Victorian author, could not treat directly.
For whatever Ryder's motives her words are true—as Griffith
discovers when he returns home unexpectedly to find his invalid
wife in the grove with Leonard, "springing along, elastic as a young
greyhound, and full of fire and animation."

Further than this, however, Reade dared not go. Indeed he
apparently felt that he had gone too far already, for in the climactic
scene that follows Kate has no sympathy whatsoever for Leonard,
even after he has been trampled by the maniacal Griffith. Her
sole concern is for her own dignity and honor, so cruelly be-
smirched by Griffith's curses, and she consequently dismisses
Leonard on the spot—in a manner appropriate to an Adelphi
heroine: "Mrs. Gaunt turned and flung her arm around so that
the palm of her hand, high raised, confronted Leonard. I am
thus particular, because it was a gesture grand and terrible as the
occasion that called it forth: a gesture that *spoke,* and said, 'Put
the whole earth and sea between us forever after this.'"

VIII

That Leonard should quail before Kate's meaninglessly theatrical gesture was as necessary to Reade's moral purpose as to his

melodramatic plot, and helps to explain why, following the episode of the glove, he presented Leonard as he did, drawing upon the Notecards to demonstrate that not Leonard but the Church itself must be held responsible for his actions: "Father Leonard was a pious, pure, and noble-minded man who had undertaken to defy nature with religious aid; and, after years of successful warfare, now sustained one of those defeats to which such warriors have always been liable." Moreover the Church provided the means as well as the justification for Leonard's attempted seduction. It was through the confessional that he gained the knowledge which finally brought him to the point of openly declaring his passion; and to gain this knowledge "Leonard . . . had only to follow precedents and ask questions his Church has printed for the use of confessors. . . ."

While these passages serve to enforce Reade's moral argument, their dramatic effect, most evident in the seduction scene, is to reduce Leonard to a weak-willed exemplar of the evils of celibacy. In consequence his cries of "jealous agony" and his torrents of "burning, melting words" have no personal or moral meaning whatever. At best they raise the question: "Will he or won't he manage to seduce our Kate?" And that soap-opera question lacks even the elementary quality of suspense, since the reader knows Kate will never give in, no matter how passionate his priestly importunings.

But Reade's failure with Leonard, serious as it is, does not weaken the later scenes of temptation nearly so much as might be expected, primarily because these scenes are so much Kate's. It is her temptation, not Leonard's, that is central and significant; and her temptation has little to do with Leonard. In fact she does not require or even want a lover: she wants only an embodiment of her romantic ideal and the more passive that embodiment the better. For she is still the same Kate who rejected Neville and married Griffith, and her feelings are still, in D. H. Lawrence's sense of the word, "masturbatory." She insists upon having the intimacy, the thrills, of a man-woman relationship without permitting the man in the case to be a man. He must remain her image of a man, i.e., a man who is not a man, but a priest (a man in skirts) who is besides effeminate in looks and manner. And when this, her ideal, violates itself by speaking hot words of physical love, she is both shocked and indignant.

IX

The third or final section of the novel, which presents the manifold consequences of Jealousy (". . . of which Bigamy is one . . ."), follows directly from the climactic scene in which Griffith confronts Kate and Leonard in the grove. After trampling "upon the poor priest with both feet" and damning the pair of them, he gallops away from Hearnshaw in a maniacal rage, never stopping until he reaches an obscure inn, some ninety miles away, where he experiences an attack of brain fever that might have proved fatal but for the efforts of the innkeeper's daughter, a dove-eyed milkmaid and Puritan named Mercy Vint. She nurses Griffith back to health, and innocently encourages his advances; whereupon he, in his bitterness and despair, courts and finally marries her—to settle down to a bigamous and happy life.

But not for long. Circumstances force him to return to Hearnshaw, where Kate completely vindicates herself, and he, too late, sees the crime he has committed. For he is now the husband of two wives (one with child, and the other, Kate, soon to be) and finds himself unable to desert either one or the other. So he temporizes until Kate, discovering his crime, threatens to stab him; then he leaves Hearnshaw, quite mysteriously, in circumstances that lead to Kate's being tried and very nearly convicted on charges of murder—despite her gallant and brilliant defense. At the last moment, however, Mercy Vint appears on the scene, having walked all the way from Lancashire with her child on her arm, to win Kate's love and to save her life—at the sacrifice of her own good name. For in proving that Griffith is still alive Mercy is forced to expose her own bigamous marriage. Nevertheless it all works out nicely in the end: with Henry Neville, Kate's old suitor, married to Mercy, and the Gaunts united as never before through the effects of a remarkable blood transfusion in which Griffith's "bright red blood" is sent "smoking hot into Kate Gaunt's veins." Henceforth the Gaunts are as happy as the Nevilles, and while the two families cannot appear in public together, because of the gossip, they remain close friends. In Reade's words:

> The wives . . . corresponded, and Lady Neville easily induced Mrs. Gaunt to co-operate with her in her benevolent acts, especially in saving young women who had been betrayed, from sinking deeper.

Living a good many miles apart, Lady Neville could send her stray sheep to service near Mrs. Gaunt, and *vice versa;* and so, merciful, but discriminating, they saved many a poor girl who had been weak, not wicked.

So, then, though they could not eat nor dance together in earthly mansions, they could do good together; and, methinks, in the eternal world, where years of social intercourse will prove less than cobwebs, these their joint acts of mercy will be links of a bright, strong chain, to bind their souls in everlasting amity.

In thus uniting the two wives in good sexual works that serve to remind them of their own inadvertent sexual transgressions Reade provides a fitting conclusion to this final section. The banality of his treatment derives in the first place from his efforts to combine so many wild and disparate actions within the confines of his borrowed plot—efforts so strained that he has little chance to develop or motivate even his leading characters, but must endow them with the stock responses necessitated by the action. On Griffith and the lesser melodramatic types carried over from the first two sections the effects of this treatment are hardly discernible. But on Kate they are disastrous. She degenerates from the complex woman of the first two sections to a female embodiment of conventional Victorian virtues, including many virtues ordinarily reserved for men: she bears her wrongs and sufferings "like a man"; she pleads her case in court with Portia-like charm and masculine logic; and in speaking to Neville of Mercy's plight she declares: "I wish I was a man: I'd cure her of Griffith before we reached the 'Packhorse.' And, now I think of it, you are a very happy man to travel eighty miles with an angel, a dove-eyed angel." Yet as Reade presents these traits they do not enhance or develop the androgynous side of Kate's make-up; they merely add piquancy to her bigamous predicament.

Nor is Reade's portrait of Mercy, who shares the feminine lead with Kate in this section, any more convincing or meaningful. Her piety is too patent, her mercy too strained, her womanliness too pure. Seemingly intended to combine the salient qualities of Dinah Morris and Hetty Sorrel she actually combines the stock features of these two characters—most obviously in the early scenes of pastoral courtship, in which she continually nurses and churns and sings and simpers, but also in the more crucial scenes of bigamous married life, in which she allegedly brings "our hero, now malefactor," a "sweet content" he had never enjoyed in his legitimate married life with Kate. Although the point of this intended contrast ("to clear away some vague conventional notions" about crime in general and bigamy in particular) may be legitimate enough, Reade's efforts to give it dramatic substance come to very little. Mercy is so theatrically obsequious in her wifely affection— what with tending the fire and tuning his viol da gambo—that the only significant effect of contrasting her love with Kate's is, once again, to heighten the piquancy of Griffith's bigamous situation.

And the scenes in which Mercy and Kate meet, glare, weep, embrace, examine Mercy's child, and then, quite literally, sleep together, have much the same effect, despite the purity of Reade's avowed intentions. Dickens, in politely refusing Wilkie Collins' invitation to defend the novel in court, discussed these scenes (along with others he found objectionable) in a letter that by implication defines the moral code to which all serious novelists were expected to adhere:

MY DEAR WILKIE,

I have read Charles Reade's book, and here follows my state of mind—*as a witness*—respecting it.

I have read it with the strongest interest and admiration. I regard it as the work of a highly accomplished writer and a good man; a writer with a brilliant fancy and a graceful and tender imagination. I could name no other living writer who could, in my opinion, write such a story nearly so well. As regards a so-called critic who should decry such a book as Holywell Street literature, and the like, I should have merely to say of him that I could desire no stronger proof of his incapacity in, and his unfitness for, the post to which he has elected himself.

Cross-examined, I should feel myself in danger of being put on unsafe ground, and should try to set my wits against the cross-examiner, to keep well off it. But if I were reminded (as I probably should be, supposing the evidence to be allowed at all) that I was the editor of a periodical of large circulation in which the Plaintiff himself had written, and if I had read to me in court those passages about Gaunt's going up to his wife's bed drunk and that last child's being conceived, and was asked whether, as Editor, I would have passed those passages, whether written by the Plaintiff or anybody else, I should be obliged to reply No. Asked why? I should say that what was pure to an artist might be impurely suggestive to inferior minds (of which there must necessarily be many among a large mass of readers) and that I should have called the writer's attention to the likelihood of those passages being perverted in such

quarters. Asked if I should have passed the passage where Kate
and Mercy have the illegitimate child upon their laps and look
over its little points together? I should again be obliged to reply
No, for the same reason. Asked whether, as author or Editor, I
should have passed Neville's marriage to Mercy, and should have
placed those four people, Gaunt, his wife, Mercy, and Neville, in
those relative situations towards one another, I should again be
obliged to reply No. Hard pressed upon this point, I must infallibly
say that I consider those relative situations extremely coarse and
disagreeable.[14]

The prime difficulty with this criticism, considered from a
modern point of view, is that it denies Reade his subject as well
as his treatment, and would apply with even greater force to such
a modern novel as Nabokov's *Lolita*. Nor is Dickens' attempt to
distinguish between the "artist" and "inferior minds" much more
helpful, confusing as it does moral with artistic values. The
passages in question are not "impurely suggestive to inferior
minds," they are purely (or merely) "suggestive" (or pornographic) to all perceptive minds, and for this reason tend to oversimplify or invalidate the sexual responses of the characters involved. No doubt Kate was curious about "every feature" of
Mercy's little boy, but in having the two women immediately set
about examining and kissing the boy's "limbs and extremities after
the manner of their sex" Reade endowed his heroine with "female
traits" that, in context, appear less characteristic than titillating.
To such a charge Reade would doubtless have replied by citing
various items in the Notebooks, among others the following (included in the Notebook entitled "Foemina Vera" under the heading "Traits"):

> Fonder of their own children than men,
> and kiss them ten times oftener
> fonder of children generally and [pillage them?]
> of their clothes in the
> street, which no male
> malefactor does.

A few pages further on, in the same Notebook, Reade includes a
clipping (Telegraph, April 7 X 64) illustrating the above observation, then on the next page repeats the observation itself—with
slight variations and additions:

> Women in connection
> with children
> Love children ten times more than
> men do; and kiss them thirty
> times more
> women are the child strippers
> See Theta 2
> woman throws a babe out of window
> Epsilon 12

But these factual traits do not in any sense justify those of Kate and Mercy—even if one accepts Reade's Baconian premises. For in adaptaing the facts to his characters he has oversimplified the facts (as well as the characters) by choosing to overlook or evade the sexual implications of the violence and child-stripping that render the facts meaningful. In other words the pornography is the result not of frankness but of evasiveness—an evasiveness that leads, first to the suppression of the full sexual responses of the two heroines, then to the presentation of their partial responses as conventionally pure manifestations of womanly curiosity.

And Reade bowdlerized nearly all the other sexual passages in much the same way to much the same effect—although the passages that most upset Dickens ("those . . . about Gaunts going up to his wife's bed drunk and that last child's being conceived") are perhaps more ludicrous than pornographic, since Reade's efforts to purify Griffith's actions (by attributing them to "habit") so closely parallel Tristram Shandy's explanation of his father's sex habits as to suggest the possibility that Reade was consciously drawing upon the well known fourth chapter of *Tristram Shandy*. Needless to say he was not, in fact could not, without compromising his work as well as his own moral position. If he was borrowing from anyone, the Notecards reveal, it was Michelet, whose observations on "habit" were entirely staid. Yet the Sternean parallels are still there—whether intended or not—and their effect is to render farcical Reade's strained efforts to purify Griffith's habit.

x

Also farcical are many of the passages Reade consciously intended to be Shakespearean—notably those in which Kate emulates Portia and Mrs. Ryder plays female Iago to Griffith's Othello. For by stressing these parallels and seeking to reinforce them with Shakespearean language Reade but calls attention to the discrepancy between his conventionally melodramatic characters and Shakespeare's—a discrepancy so great that it renders foolish passages that might otherwise be acceptable, such as those in which Kate pleads her own case. So long as she confines herself to reporting the bare facts or cross-examining witnesses her performance is genuinely moving, but when she resorts to the Shakespearean manner of Charles Kean in declaring her wrongs there is little to choose between her eloquence and that of her melodramatic predecessors.

The remaining passages in this section—in which Reade presents the scenes of blood, violence, and mistaken identity necessary to the resolution of his plot—are likewise conventionally melodramatic. Only in treating the blood transfusion, based directly on the Notebooks (*Red Digest*, p. 25),[15] does Reade manage to integrate his Sensation with his theme, and even then his efforts to develop the metaphoric and symbolic aspects of the transfusion hardly fulfill his intention—to render credible Kate's final submission to Griffith: "She wanted a good excuse for loving him as frankly as before, and now he had given her one. She used to throw it in his teeth in the prettiest way. Whenever she confessed a fault, she was sure to turn slyly round and say, 'But what could one expect of me? I have his blood in my veins.' . . . Once she told Father Francis, quite seriously, that she had never been quite the same woman since she lived by Griffith's blood; she was turned jealous; and, moreover, it had given him a fascinating power over her, and she could tell blindfold when he was in the room."

Reade's object in bringing Kate to such a point of abject love and submission is of course to qualify her for the concluding marital quadrille, in which, all passion presumably purified, the two heroines join hands with one another (as well as with their former husbands and lovers) to prove that Love and Charity can triumph over Jealousy and Bigamy. And while there is no doubting the sincerity of Reade's intention, the effect of this finalé (as might be expected) is to prove just the opposite, and in the process to carry the pornography and Sensation of the preceding scenes right down to the penultimate paragraph—in which Reade, in a final attempt at pietistic justification, actually stresses the carnal knowledge that the two heroines still share on earth and will presumably still share in heaven.

XI

In itself Reade's ending is perhaps no more banal than, say, the insipidly happy ending that Dickens, in deference to his readers and Bulwer-Lytton, tacked onto *Great Expectations*. But whereas the ending of *Great Expectations* merely provides a means for closing off the action, that of *Griffith Gaunt* represents the necessary fulfillment of the entire final section of the novel, which in turn represents the necessary fulfillment of the plot and ostensible theme that Reade formally announces as early as page thirteen in speaking of Griffith's foible.

Yet—and this is what saves the novel—Jealousy does not, accurately speaking, constitute the theme or even the subject of the novel; at most it provides the titular hero with a "humour" convenient for organizing the disparate elements of the action into a loose melodramatic plot. The subject of the novel, in Percy Lubbock's sense of "subject," is not Griffith but Kate; and the theme, in so far as it can be defined in a word, is not Jealousy but Adultery—the theme that Reade himself adumbrates on the Notecards and in the opening lines of the novel:

CHAPTER I

"THEN I say once for all, that priest shall never darken my doors again."

"Then I say they are my doors and not yours, and that holy man shall brighten them whenever he will."

The gentleman and lady, who faced each other, pale and furious, and interchanged this bitter defiance, were man and wife. And had loved each other well.

In this dialogue, repeated verbatim half-way through the novel (p. 210), Kate makes her choice: "The matrimonial throne for him till he resisted her priest; and then a stool at her feet and his." And in the following scenes Reade develops the implications of this choice, using Griffith's Jealousy and Mrs. Ryder's melodramatic machinations as a subordinate means of furthering and justifying his treatment of Kate. It is not until he has brought Kate to the point of seeming adultery, in the climactic grove scene, that he permits Griffith's *foible* to become dominant, and at this point he is obviously preparing to substitute Jealousy and its Bigamous consequences for the theme of Adultery.

Had Reade ended the novel here it might now be an acknowledged Victorian masterpiece; certainly if he had carried the theme of adultery to the ultimate conclusions prefigured in both his text and the Notecards its claims would be beyond dispute. But given Reade's theories and techniques and the moral demands of his readers he could neither conclude nor develop his adulterous theme. In fact he could not even abandon it: he had to replace it, then purify it. Hence the introduction (into this final bigamous section) of Kate's letters to Leonard proving that she had never really felt what, according to the dramatic text, she certainly had felt. Hence too the resourceful explanations of Father Francis, proving that her temptation had not been a temptation at all, but a series of misunderstandings brought about by her "imprudence"—not ordinary imprudence but imprudence derived from "Christian Charity . . . true and rare and exalted piety."

Taken at face value, these attempts at purification cancel out nearly the whole of the temptation sequence. But of course they cannot be taken at face value: their function—an accepted one in Sensation fiction—is akin to that of the last act in a "well-made" stage comedy, which consists, according to Shaw, "of clearing up the misunderstanding, and generally getting the audience out of the theatre as best you can." [16] One essential difference, however, is that Reade did not apply this conventional stratagem cynically: to him as to his readers it represented a moral necessity as well as a literary convention, and he saw no conflict between the two. The purification simply justified him in presenting aspects of his heroine's character that would otherwise have been morally reprehensible. And while the modern reader, acquainted with Zola, Hardy, Lawrence, *et al*, may consider this conception of morality in fiction to be naïve and contradictory, if not downright hypocritical, the fact remains that it was shared by nearly all the Victorian novelists, Dickens included, and therefore constitutes a necessary if limiting condition of their art.

Indeed it can be argued that the entire final section of the novel is of a piece with Reade's attempts at purification, and should be dismissed on similar grounds—as a conventional appendage corresponding in function to the closing chapters of so many other Sensational novels. But this argument, appealing as it may be to the modern reader, verges on the arbitrary when applied to a section that constitutes, in bulk, nearly half the novel, and that represents, on the plot level, the fulfillment of the announced theme of the novel. After all, the novel is entitled *Griffith Gaunt*, not *Kate Peyton,* and the melodramatic and pornographic aspects of the action that become dominant in the final bigamous section cannot be dismissed or rationalized away simply because they tend to mar and distort what is artistically valid in the first two sections.

The best if not the only critical alternative is to acknowledge that the novel, considered as a whole, is radically flawed—much as *Vanity Fair,* for instance, is radically flawed, with Mercy's bigamous purity corresponding to Amelia's widowed purity, Gaunt's insane Jealousy to Dobbins' insane devotion. As for pornography there is nothing more flagrant in *Griffith Gaunt* than the scene in *Vanity Fair* (already discussed) in which Thackeray descants on the charms of his sleeping heroine. And like parallels can be drawn from nearly all the other great Victorian novels—the point being, of course, that in Victorian fiction such blemishes are the necessary concomitants of creative expression, particularly in matters sexual. Thackeray could never have created Becky Sharp if he had not, in the very beginning of the novel, paired her off against Amelia; nor could he have developed her as he did, if he had not, towards the end of the novel, reduced her to a tawdry whore.

To apply the currently modish standards of Jamesian criticism to such fiction is therefore, as Percy Lubbock himself acknowledges, a bit ridiculous. Unless some of the greatest Victorian novels (including all of Dickens' novels, with the possible exception of *Great Expectations*) are to be rejected out of hand, the critic must recognize that the final test of a novel is not its perfection of Jamesian form but the intensity of expression it achieves in spite of or apart from its imperfections. By this test, which is James's own positive test, Thackeray's inanities are more than redeemed by what Lubbock has defined as its "richness of life." [17] And by the same token Reade's inanities are more than redeemed by the intensity he achieves in his dramatic portrait of Kate—an intensity, paraphrasing Reade's own words, that penetrates beneath the calm solitude and umbrageous twilight of Kate's idealism to reveal, with rare perceptiveness, the warped and twisted feelings that underlie it. And if James, in his encomiastic reference to "those great sympathetic guesses," overpraises Reade at George Eliot's expense, the fact remains that Reade's portrait (as it is developed in relation to the theme of adultery) will bear comparison, not only with the corresponding portraits of Eliot, but with those of the later Hardy—and that, in itself, should be sufficient to restore the novel to the first rank of Victorian fiction.

CHAPTER XI

Put Yourself in His Place:
Humanitarianism at the Point of a Bayonet

I HAVE DRAWN my pen against cowardly assassination and sordid tyranny: I have taken a few undeniable truths, out of many, and have labored to make my readers realize those appalling facts of the day, which most men know, but not one in a thousand comprehends, and not one in a hundred thousand *realizes,* until fiction—which, whatever you may have been told to the contrary, is the highest, widest, noblest, and greatest of all the arts— comes to his aid, studies, penetrates, digests, the hard facts of chronicles and blue-books, and makes their dry bones live.

—CHARLES READE—*Put Yourself in His Place*

✦ ✦ ✦

Griffith Gaunt was still being serialized in the *Argosy* and *The Atlantic Monthly* when (on Oct. 13, 1866) Reade wrote Fields: "I have a favor to ask you, which is to procure me two copies of a play in which Mrs. Wood has achieved a reputation. It is an adaptation of 'La Petite Fadette' by George Sand. I think the principal female character is called Fanchon. Shall be much obliged if you will send it me with speed."

Presumably Reade was already considering still another venture into stage production. Just at this moment, however, he learned about the charges that were being leveled against *Griffith Gaunt* in America, and he was off on another of his crusades—this time to rid the American Press, and later the Canadian and English Press as well, of the vermin he chose to designate "Prurient Prudes." Of these the most offensive, according to Reade, was "the editor of a New York weekly called *The Round Table,*" and it was primarily against this "assassin" that Reade directed his counter-charges in "The Prurient Prude" (a letter to the American Press reprinted in *Readiana*). "In all my experience," Reade declared, "I never knew the Press guilty of such a crime as the editor of *The Round Table* has committed. It is a deliberate attempt to assassinate the moral character of an author and a gentleman, and to stab the ladies of his own family to the heart, under the pretence of protecting the women of a nation from the demoralising influence of his pen." Reade continued to execrate the hapless editor through some five more pages; then, by way of close, threw down the gage of legal battle: "I shall only add that I mean to collar the editor of *The Round Table,* and drag him and his slanders before a jury of his countrymen. He thinks there is no law, justice, or humanity for an Englishman in the great United States. We shall see."

The letter itself, as these few lines indicate, is in many respects quite eloquent, as is the succeeding one directed against the editor of the *Toronto Globe* (reprinted in *Readiana* under the title "Second-Hand Libel"). But the eloquence is that of a barrister, not a philosopher, and its effect, accompanied as it is by direct threats of legal reprisal, is to reduce Reade's intended defense of his art to a melodramatic defense of his own person—a defense of a piece with his "Petition to the Lords of the Treasury" in connection with his fiddle trade.

At fifty-three, at the very height of his powers, Reade still viewed life as he had viewed it twenty or even thirty years earlier— as a melodramatic stage on which he could play the Resourceful Hero. The one difference was that, as he became more famous and more powerful, he could play the role more forcefully before an ever increasing international audience. And if he had been consistently able to act out his real life heroics the way his heroes did in his books he might well have abandoned his books to fulfill, at long last, the ideals of Christian service his mother had expressed in the manuscript "Dear Mother": "Immortal beings should not flutter among the trifles of literature. What a field for thought and action are the realities of life, and the certainty of a future state."

As yet, however, Reade could not act on this advice—at least not to the point of abandoning literature altogether. He was too dependent, emotionally, on the satisfactions he received from the Notebooks and the matter-of-fact heroics of his fictional alter-egos—satisfactions which his real life heroics still did not yield, for the very good reason that the forces he challenged still refused to conform to his Baconian preconceptions, his suit against *The*

Round Table, for instance, dragging on to a most unheroic finale in which the jury awarded him damages of six cents.[1] Although, as Elwin has pointed out, this particular verdict hurt Reade's pride more than his purse, it nevertheless served to strengthen his already acute awareness of the practical connection between his writing and his crusades. To play the Resourceful Hero in real life he knew that he had to have money and power and prestige; and he knew that, up to this point, his writing provided his only means to these ends. "My business is lying," he acknowledged in *A Terrible Temptation,* "and I drudge at it; so to escape now and then to the playground of Truth and Justice is a great amusement and recreation to poor me. Besides, it gives me fresh vigor to replunge into mendacity; and that's the thing that pays."

The ambivalence of this statement—in part defensive, in part ironic—helps to explain why, following his defense of *Griffith Gaunt,* he once again plunged into theatrical adaptation and speculation, and why, in the midst of this theatrical activity, he chose to write a novel, *Foul Play,* in collaboration with such an out-and-out commercial playwright as Boucicault. The novel itself can be considered later; as for the plays they hardly merit serious discussion, except as they serve to reveal Reade's continuing belief in the Keanian realism that he had attempted in *Gold* and his early adaptation. At that time, he believed, the greatness of his plays had gone unrecognized because of the vagaries of circumstance and the maliciousness of the critics who had formed a cabal to cry down his works. But he had defeated this cabal with *It's Never Too Late To Mend* (in 1865) and felt confident he could defeat it again. All he needed to do was to resuscitate some of his old adaptations, work out a few new ones, and then, if he could only find an actress who could carry his work, as he had wanted Mrs. Stirling to carry it earlier, success would be assured. The actress he had in mind was Kate Terry, and he did secure her for *Dora* (his dramatic version of Tennyson's "The Promise of May"). Nevertheless the play (Adelphi, June 1, 1867) proved a total failure, as did *The Double Marriage* (a revised version of his earlier adaptation of Maquet's *Le Château Grantier)* which starred Ellen Terry, Kate's then less well known younger sister (Queens, Oct. 25, 1867). And the stage version of *Griffith Gaunt* that Reade himself produced later in the year at Newcastle did not even appear on the London stage.

To complete the debacle the dramatic version of *Foul Play*

(which opened at Leeds in June, 1868) likewise failed, and in a manner which prompted F. C. Burnand to burlesque it at the Queens Theatre (June 20) under the title of *Foul Play, or a story of Chikken Hazard*. Then, while Reade was suffering from this "desecration," he was struck what he considered to be another foul blow by the reviewers of the novel, some of whom, following the lead of the reviewer in the *Mask*, declared the novel "a servile copy of an obscure French drama, called *Le Portefeuille Rouge*." For once, it would seem, Reade was guiltless, and he made the most of the fact in pillorying "the writer in the *Mask*" in "The Sham Sample Swindle" (*Once A Week*, August 22, 1868; also reprinted in *Readiana*). But the editors of the *Mask* had anticipated this rebuttal, and in a form which even he could not answer, by printing as a frontispiece to their August number a cartoon in which he is presented in the shape of "a hideous gorilla in knickerbockers."

II

The ultimate effect of these attacks—in which Reade, as always, saw the machinations of "a powerful cabal"—was to intensify the already paranoiac feelings of persecution that had led him to choose the evils of trades unionism as the subject for his next *magnum opus*. From boyhood, it has been shown, he had looked upon himself as a lone genius, fighting against cliques and cabals: at Oxford it was his fellow students who were caballing against him; in London, when he was struggling for recognition as a dramatist, it was the "playwright-critics" who banded themselves into "a little trades union" and "flew like hornets at every outsider who did not square them with champagne suppers or other douceurs, pecuniary bribes included. . . ." And so it went—until his feelings of persecution became so acute that when the early installments of *Griffith Gaunt* were received in England with what he described (in a letter to Fields, Feb. 26, 1866) as "a dead silence anything but encouraging" he immediately suspected a cabal. "I am sorry to say," he wrote Fields (May 6, 1866), "that in this country I must fight against a powerful cabal."

From cabals, real or imaginary, to trades unions was for Reade an easy transition, since from his laissez-faire point of view the employers were in exactly his own position. They were men of proved merit and ability subjected to the machinations of a conspiratorial oligarchy—an oligarchy, moreover, that was made up of lower-class men who were by nature and habit drunken and profligate beasts. Hence the significant words "dirty oligarchy" which appear beside every newspaper account of union activities that, beginning in 1862, he pasted into his Notebooks. But what finally inflamed Reade's hatred to frenzy, the clippings themselves reveal, was the fact that by his standards the unions were not only dirty and oligarchical but bloody—in the sense that it was they, not the employers, who resorted to overt physical violence.

Such were the attitudes with which Reade approached his subject. And when the Manchester and Sheffield outrages were made public in 1867 he apparently felt that his matter-of-fact muse had again provided him with the makings of a great epic. For these new facts were every bit as "warm" as those he had used in *Hard Cash* and *Never Too Late To Mend,* and they were causing even more of a stir—this time throughout the entire nation. Moreover they were as bloody as even the most rabid philanthropist could wish. Nearly every clipping in *pone te in loco,* the Notebook specifically devoted to *Put Yourself in His Place,* recounts the details of union rattenings, beatings, knifings, shootings, or explosions; and the Notecards include instances equally bloody that he took from the Bluebooks.

With such a plethora of fresh horrors to draw upon Reade was undoubtedly anxious to get started on the novel in 1867. But he was already occupied with *Foul Play,* and so it was not until June of 1868 that he actually set to work on the novel, and it was not until the spring of 1870 that he actually completed it.[2] These dates are important, for the Royal Commission investigating the Sheffield Unions acknowledged, after further enquiry, that the "savage crimes" they had first uncovered in June, 1867, were both isolated and unusual. In the words of Sidney and Beatrice Webb:

"For a short time [after June, 1867] it looked as if all the accusations hurled at Trade Unionism at large were about to be justified; but the examiners reported that four-fifths of the societies even of the Sheffield trades were free from outrages, and that these had been most prevalent from 1839 to 1861, and had since declined. The only other place in which the Commissioners thought it necessary to make inquiry into outrages was Manchester, where the Brickmakers' Union had committed many crimes, but where no complicity on the part of other trades was shown. It was made evident to all candid students that these criminal acts were not chargeable to Trade Unionism as a whole. They represented, in fact, the survival among such rough and isolated trades as the brickmakers and grinders of the barbarous usages of a time when working men felt themselves outside the law, and oppressed by tyranny." [3]

Such were the "facts," and these "facts," it must be stressed, were embodied in the "Reports of the Enquiry into the Sheffield and Manchester Outrages," three reports published in 1867-1868, before Reade began serious work on *Put Yourself in His Place*.

But Reade, who as usual was only a Baconian when it suited his purpose, dismissed these three reports as the work of "one-sided men," and when he himself was accused of being one-sided defended himself at length in a letter "To the Editor of the 'Daily Globe,' Toronto" (dated October, 1871, and reprinted in *Readiana* under the title "*A Terrible Temptation*"):

> I am not so sloppy-minded as to confound the Manchester district with the town of Manchester. That district numbers two million people, is infected with trade outrage, is losing its sympathy with the law even in face of murder, and is ceasing to be England. Nothing is more shallow than the frivolity with which Mr. Harrison and the other one-sided men dismiss this terrible phenomenon as exceptional. He, who has studied human nature, and the Bluebooks, so deeply as I have, and searched the provincial journals, knows that not two but forty trades have committed outrages, and that the exceptional ruffianism of certain Manchester trades is not a genuine exception, but only the uneducated workman's ruffianism carried fairly out. That the Sheffield outrages were stale when I wrote—is a lie. They have never intermitted. Bluebook exposure did not affect them for a moment. The town turned Roebuck out of Parliament, for not burking the exposure; and went on with their petards and other deadly practices; see the journals *passim*. Last year they knocked a whole row of non-union houses to pieces, and tried to slaughter the inmates. Were the miscreants at Thorncliffe cutlers? I thought they were this anonymuncule's pets, the miners. The fact is that the Union miners' hands, from John o'Groat's to Lizard Point, are red with the blood of non-union men. In the United States the trades are already steeped in human blood. Is America Sheffield, or Manchester? [4]

To anyone unacquainted with Reade and the Notebooks this defense might seem convincing. But when he refers to "the journals *passim*" he is, in fact, referring to the materials he had collected in his Notebooks and on his Notecards, and these materials prove nothing more, in the context of his argument, than his own sadistic reaction to violence.

III

To Reade, however, the facts in "the journals *passim*" represented, as always, "truth," and in writing the novel he treated these facts in his usual matter-of-fact manner—refurbishing them, then attaching them wholesale to the stock elements of his melodramatic plot. As for the plot itself it is but a standard variation on the usual Readian triangle that pits the Resourceful Hero against the unions as well as the villain in his quest for the gold and the girl—a conflict which Reade sought to strengthen, with Wilkie Collins' help, through the development of related contrasts between old Tories and new Benthamites, old rustics and new mechanics. On the final page of *pone te in loco* he noted:

> write the rustic up & the
> mechanic down
> Physical & moral contrasts
> Physical the snowy cottage & roses
> in garden   dismal

The moral contrasts included in this Notebook are equally banal, as are his first hand observations on life in the mills. At "Mr. Leakes Works," for instance, he was apparently so fascinated by the "burnished copper rollers" that he could not see the men, who seemed to him more "like students at college . . . than mechanics." Nor could he see "the young weaving girls" any more clearly. To him they seemed "like little ladies in their clean petticoats." And while he did observe that the rooms in which they worked were "abominably hot," even "stifling," this was of no consequence apparently, except for the fact that "the girls were said to ripen in these hot rooms before their time sexually"—a fact that reminded him of a passage in the *Germania* of Tacitus.

To Reade, as these myopically Baconian observations indicate, the lot of the workers was little short of idyllic. Did not the men at Mr. Leakes Works dress in broadcloth? Were they not seated at their work like students at college? Did they not receive from "£2 1s to £3 per week" for "57 hours or less?" Was not Greggs Cotton Mill situated in "a picturesque and wooded hollow?" How then could the workers condone such an act as that recounted in the "Evening Standard," 8 Oct. 1869:

"THE ALLEGED MURDER BY TRADES UNIONISTS."
Yesterday an inquest was opened at Saeford respecting the death of a mason named James Burns . . . Burns . . . was followed, over-taken, and in broad daylight, in the presence of a crowd of specta-tors, was knocked down, kicked, and finally killed by one of his [3] assailants, more brutal than the remainder, taking hold of the poor fellows hair and literally smashing his head upon the flags. . . .

From Reade's point of view, which was that of *The Evening Standard* carried to sadistic frenzy, such acts were many times repeated by many workers—and condoned by nearly all the others. In short the workers were not merely brutalized men; they were, literally, brutes. And that is how, in the novel itself, he endeavored to present them—though in the process of transcribing his journal-istic data he invariably adapted it to his earlier formulas. Grotait, a caricature of the real union leader, Broadhead, is merely another clever monster, cut after the pattern of Warden Hawes; and his subordinates, the ordinary workmen, are tabloid villains like Black Will, or at best a subhuman species with only one redeeming quality—that of loyalty to their fellows. To all other human feel-ings, even to feelings of paternity, they are dead. In decrying the brutality of working-class children Reade declared that "their parents, the lowest and most degraded set of brutes in England, teach them swearing and indecency at home, and rob them of all decent education, and drive them to their death, in order to squeeze a few shillings out of their young lives; for what?—to waste in drink and debauchery." [5] And when these brutes banded together to form unions, they constituted, in Reade's words: "A terrible confederacy, which, in England and in the Nineteenth Century, was Venice and the Middle Ages over again." [6]

As for the masters, they are, as Reade presents them, wholly unequal to the threat posed by the men and their unions; when hapless masters are not being shot, or blown up, which would seem to be their prime function in the novel, they are as ineffectual as Mr. Cheetham, whose commercial tactics in dealing with the unions are shown to be almost as despicable as the Venetian tactics of the unions.

To Reade as to Carlyle the great need was for masters who were heroes—though Reade of course wanted them to be Re-

sourceful Heroes. And since none of them were, he supplied one
of his own devising in the person of Henry Little, who embodies
every characteristic Bret Harte attributes to him in Chapter III
of his brilliant parody ("Handsome is as Handsome does" by
Ch-s R–de in *Condensed Novels):*

Young Little [Faraday Huxley Little] *was* clever. At seven he had
constructed a telescope; at nine, a flying-machine. At ten he saved
a valuable life.

Norwood Park was the adjacent estate,—a lordly domain dotted
with red deer and black trunks, but scrupulously kept with
gravelled roads as hard and blue as steel. There Little was strolling
one summer morning, meditating on a new top with concealed
springs. At a little distance before him he saw the flutter of lace
and ribbons. A young lady, a very young lady,—say of seven
summers,—tricked out in the crying abominations of the present
fashion, stood beside a low bush. Her nursery-maid was not present,
possibly owing to the fact that John the footman was also absent.

Suddenly Little came towards her. "Excuse me, but do you
know what those berries are?" He was pointing to the low bush
filled with dark clusters of shining—suspiciously shining—fruit.

"Certainly; they are blueberries."

"Pardon me; you are mistaken. They belong to quite another
family."

Miss Impudence drew herself up to her full height (exactly
three feet nine and a half inches), and, curling an eighth of an
inch of scarlet lip, said, scornfully, *"Your* family, perhaps."

Faraday Little smiled in the superiority of boyhood over girlhood.

"I allude to the classification. That plant is the belladonna, or
deadly nightshade. Its alkaloid is a narcotic poison."

Sauciness turned pale. "I—have—just—eaten—some!" And began
to whimper. "O dear, what shall I do?" Then did it, i.e. wrung
her small fingers and cried.

"Pardon me one moment." Little passed his arm around her
neck, and with his thumb opened widely the patrician-veined lids
of her sweet blue eyes. "Thank Heaven, there is yet no dilation of
the pupil; it is not too late!" He cast a rapid glance around. The
nozzle and about three feet of garden hose lay near him.

"Open your mouth, quick!"

It was a pretty, kissable mouth. But young Little meant business. He put the nozzle down her pink throat as far as it would go.

"Now, don't move."

He wrapped his handkerchief around a hoopstick. Then he
inserted both in the other end of the stiff hose. It fitted snugly.
He shoved it in and then drew it back.

Nature abhors a vacuum. The young patrician was as amenable to this law as the child of the lowest peasant.

She succumbed. It was all over in a minute. Then she burst into a small fury.

You nasty, bad—*ugly* boy."

Young Little winced, but smiled.

"Stimulants," he whispered to the frightened nursery-maid who approached; "good evening."

He was gone.[7]

Although in the novel Reade skips over the childhood of his hero, it had to be just as Bret Harte presents it. Otherwise there would be no accounting for Little's manly accomplishments and characteristics—which are those of Reade's first "Resourceful Hero," the Coventry of *Propria Quae Maribus*, adapted to the circumstances of a rising young workman. For Little the "Resourceful Hero" cannot remain a laborer: with his abilities he is bound to become a master—a great and powerful and humane master. The unions may thwart him for a time, the novel shows; they may even subject him to physical violence. But the tyrannies of Venice and the Middle Ages cannot long prevail in England and the Nineteenth Century. Little is bound to conquer, and does conquer, as Reade himself had conquered.

In the novel, therefore the conflict between Little and the Unions is but another idealized version of Reade's own conflicts, with Little showing the same courage and resourcefulness in his battle against the Unions that he shows in the climactic flood scenes—which are likewise matter-of-fact in the sense that Reade cribbed almost every detail of every scene from Samuel Harrison's *History of the Great Flood at Sheffield* (London, 1864).[8] In one scene, for instance, Little saves himself and the heroine from the water rising in his room (by making a hole in the roof with gun, axe, and saw)—a feat which duplicates that of Harrison's life-savers in all respects save one. Not being especially resourceful they had been obliged to make their holes with makeshift implements (e.g., "a pole off the bedstead") whereas Little was fully prepared: when the water began to rise in his room he had an axe, saw and rifle in his dresser drawers; later on, when the need arose, "he had his hatchet in his pocket." [9]

These heroic variations can hardly be considered improvements, and the few episodes on which Reade lavished more "imagination" are if anything even more ludicrous. Indeed the one scene which is almost entirely Reade's own is in most respects indistinguishable from Bret Harte's parody. As the scene opens the hero is trying to rescue the heroine (technically the villain's wife) as she is being swept past a window by the raging flood—all this in plain sight of the villain who is perched in a nearby tree:

> With a loud cry he seized her by her long floating hair, and tried to draw her in at the window; but the mighty water pulled her from him fiercely . . . [Needless to say, he eventually saves her "by an effort almost super-human"—and then!]
>
> He had her in his arms, and cried aloud, and sobbed over her, and kissed her wet cheeks, her lank hair, and her wet clothes, in a wild rapture. He went on kissing her and sobbing over her so wildly and so long, that Coventry [the villain], who had at first exulted with him at her rescue, began to rage with jealousy.
>
> "Please remember she is my wife," he shrieked: "don't take advantage of her condition, villain."
>
> "Your wife, you scoundrel! . . . Why didn't you save her?" . . . With this he kissed her again and held her to his bosom. "D'ye see that? liar! coward! villain!"

Having rescued the heroine several times, and scores of other *dramatis personae* at least once, a lesser hero might have been content to rest on his laurels. But not Little. He rescues all night and on into the next day; and when he is not saving lives, he is, with typical Readian avidity, peering at the corpses, which are far more numerous and naked than their factual counterparts. Whereas Harrison reported "two dead bodies . . . in the railway station—one that of a woman in a state of nudity," Little found twice that many "three of them . . . females in absolute nudity . . . the fourth . . . a male with one stocking on . . . who proved to be Hillsbro' Harry [Harrison's 'Sheffield Harry']." But the final sadistic touch in this sequence is wholly Reade's own: not content with reiterating (via Little) Harrison's sensational descriptions of the "cruelly gashed and mangled," he has one of his characters "tread on something soft . . . the body of a woman, embedded in the mud."

IV

That his Resourceful Hero should thus turn from fighting Unions to fighting a flood was for Reade a natural enough transition. For as he conceived of the Unions they threatened life in much the same way that the flood did, and had to be dealt with accordingly. In the words of Dr. Amboyne (who serves as Little's elderly mentor and speaks directly for Reade throughout the novel):

> Two thousand philosophers are writing us dead with "labor and capital." But I vary the bore. "Life, labor, and capital," is my chant: and, whereas life has hitherto been banished from the discussion, I put life in its true place, at the head of the trio. . . . Let pseudo-philosophy set the means above the end, and fix its short-sighted eyes on labor and capital, omitting life. (What does it profit a file-cutter if he gains his master's whole capital and loses his own life?) But you and I, Mr. Little, are true philosophers, and the work we are about to enter on is—saving cutlers' lives.[10]

And Little, needless to say, proves as adept at this type of philosophic life-saving as at any other. Despite the fact that he has had no formal schooling and seemingly no education of any kind (except through his mother's teachings and his own reading) he draws up a report that compares favorably with the real life report published by Dr. Hall—as well it might, since it is Dr. Hall's report (the Notecards reveal) presented in Readian form:

> A. What the masters might do.
>   1. Provide every forge with two small fires, eighteen inches from the ground. This would warm the lower limbs of the smiths. At the present their bodies suffer by uneven temperature; they perspire down to the waist, and then freeze to the toe.
>   2. For the wet-grinders they might supply fires in every wheel, abolish mud floors, and pave with a proper fall and drain.[11]

Even in extracted form this section of the report (included as an appendix to volume 1 of the novel) continues on for another page and a half, after which Little provides an even more complete body of suggestions headed "What the workmen might do." Of these number seven is perhaps most interesting:

> If files can only be cut on *bare* lead, the men ought to cut their hair close, and wear a light cap at work. They ought to have a canvas suit in the adjoining place (see above); don it when they come, and doff it when they go. They ought to leave off their insane habit of licking the thumb and finger of the left hand—which is the leaded hand—with their tongues. This beastly trick takes the poison direct to the stomach. . . . They might surely leave it to get there through the pores; it is slow, but sure. I have

also repeatedly seen a file-cutter eat his dinner with his filthy poisoned fingers, and so send the poison home by way of salt to a fool's bacon. Finally, they ought to wash off the poison every two hours at the taps.[12]

But why persist in farce. These are not the suggestions of a philosopher; they are the recommendations of a sanitary engineer— and what is worse, an engineer who cannot respect, much less sympathize with, the human beings whom he would render sanitary. Hence the reference to "this beastly trick . . . of licking the thumb and forefinger . . ."—a reference which echoes Reade's earlier applications of the word "beast." Hence too the tone and substance of the few entries in the report that endeavor to cope with moral as well as sanitary issues—as, for example, "2" under heading "B," which might have been written by Mrs. Pardiggle:

> 2. They [the workmen] might drink less, and wash their bodies with a small part of the money so saved: the price of a gill of gin and a hot bath are exactly the same; only the bath is health to a dry-grinder, or file-cutter; the gin is worse poison to him than to healthy men.[13]

That Reade could express such admonitions, and in fact use them as the moral basis for his dramatic action, shows how little he understood the works of the novelist he called master—particularly that passage in *Bleak House* in which the brickmaker answers Mrs. Pardiggle's moral charges:

> Now you're a-going to poll-pry and question according to custom— I know what you're a-going to be up to. Well! You haven't got no occasion to be up to it. I'll save you the trouble. Is my daughter a-washin? Yes, she *is* a-washin. Look at the water. Smell it! That's wot we drinks. How do you like it, and what do you think of gin, instead! An't my place dirty? Yes, it is dirty—it's nat'rally dirty, and it's nat'rally onwholesome; and we've had five dirty and onwholesome children, as is all dead infants, and so much the better for them, and for us besides. Have I read the little book wot you left? No, I an't read the little book wot you left. There an't nobody here as knows how to read it; and if there wos, it wouldn't be suitable to me. It's a book fit for a babby, and I'm not a babby. If you was to leave me a doll, I shouldn't nuss it. How have I been conducting of myself? Why, I've been drunk for three days; and I'd a been drunk four, if I'd a had the money. Don't I never mean for to go to church? No, I don't never mean for to go to church. I shouldn't be expected there, if I did; the

beadle's too gen-teel for me. And how did my wife get that black
eye? Why, I giv' it her; and if she says I didn't, she's a Lie! [14]

But Reade could no more understand this answer than Mrs.
Pardiggle herself. Nor could he accept (if he understood) any
other works, fictional or otherwise, which treated workmen sym-
pathetically. Indeed it would appear, on the basis of his entries
on the Notecards and in the Notebooks that the one book on the
working classes that he took seriously was a volume which he
identifies only by title: *Habits and Customs of the Working
Classes.* And what he derived from this book his own notes (Notecard 2B) make quite clear:

> Intelligent workmen exceptional. 9 out of 10
> blackguards & blasphemous. p. 6
> Want of courtesy. 7. Drunkenness, outside
> their trade. Credulity about the bloated
> Aristocracy. 50 per cent read and write
> like children. 80 per cent know nothing of
> literature. . . .

Moreover Reade used these facts, not as Carlyle or Arnold
("Wragg is in custody") or even Disraeli or Charles Kingsley
had used them, but as Mrs. Pardiggle used her "good book." For
he too was "a moral policeman," and as always in matters pertain-
ing to violence a relentless one—so relentless, in fact, that in the
concluding paragraph of *Put Yourself in His Place* he declared:
"The Executive is fast asleep in the matter [of union murders]—
or it would long ago have planted the Manchester district with a
hundred thousand special constables. . . ." And later, in "A Terrible
Temptation," he explained, in answer to Goldwin Smith's charges:

The masters are just as egotistical as the men: but, unlike the men,
they have never had recourse to violence. How long will that last?
Does this dreamer imagine that capital *cannot* buy fighting agents,
and ten thousand Colt revolvers, and a million grapeshot; and kill
lawless ruffians by the hundred, when they commit felony by the
hundred? When we come to this, and when the Unions have upset
the British Constitution through the servility of the Commons and
the blindness of the Peers, let it be remembered that a thinking
novelist, a lover of his kind, encouraged the workmen in lawful
combination, but wrote against their beastly ignorance and dirt,
and their bloody violence and foul play. In such a case it is either
books or bayonets. I have tried a book. Others will try bayonets. . . .

And when others did try bayonets (in America, in 1877) this "thinking novelist, a lover of his kind," exulted in the massacre. To the side of an illustrated newspaper clipping (see illustration No. 5) which shows unarmed unionists being shot down by well-trained militia Reade wrote: "The Dirty Oligarchy crushed by the Republic." [15]

These words (applied to this illustration) beautifully express the sadistic wish fulfillment that underlies the humanitarianism of the novel and give the lie to his moral protestations—which are like the protestations of all those lovers of mankind who preach humanitarianism at the point of a bayonet. Life, as Reade defined the word in his "Life, Labour and Capital," meant for the workers physical existence enriched by cleanliness, temperance, church attendance . . . all on the masters' terms. For it was only by accepting the masters' terms (morally and socially as well as economically) that they could approximate the good life, for workers, that rustic laborers had so long enjoyed—the good life exemplified in the novel by the Dences and the other rustic laborers and servants who are constantly pulling the forelock to Squire Raby.

Yet Reade, again like Carlyle, knew that his ideal Tory squire was a man of the past. The man of the future who was to succeed him was of course the Squire's nephew Henry Little, a man born a gentleman (like Reade) who was yet a self-made man (like Reade), and therefore a man who could (like Reade) embody the best of the old Tory and new Benthamitic values, and so lead masters and men to a new and better life—a life in which the masters and men would cease to be concerned with money and power and begin to put into practice his plans "for saving cutlers lives."

v

Thus it was that Reade, in the name of Life and Truth, reduced the complexities of his subject to the aberrational simplicities of his own intellectual and moral outlook—the same outlook, based on the same Horatio Alger and Jack the Giant Killer myths, that he had used to justify the humanitarianism of all his earlier Resourceful Heroes. Applied to prisons this outlook and these myths (or, more accurately, formulas) were not wholly inadequate, primarily because the abuses Reade was attacking through his Resourceful Hero were so clear-cut and so directly physical. But in *Put Yourself in His Place* Henry Little was not up against the simple iniquities and brutalities of a prison system administered by an English Simon Legree: the unions could hardly be equated with a prison system, even from Reade's point of view; neither could Broadhead be equated with Warden Hawes; and certainly the masters could not be equated with the prisoners. Yet for all Reade's editorial qualifications these are the equations that the dramatic action seeks to enforce.

In consequence the novel, as novel, is little more than a fictional prevision of Little Orphan Annie—a series of heroic, harrowing, and sentimental scenes in which a Resourceful Hero and his friends, dressed like masters and gentlemen, do violent battle with a hodge-podge of assorted stage villains dressed like workmen—all this so that the hero can patent his inventions, make his fortune, and marry the girl, who is sore beset by the prime villain, a renegade gentleman who has allied himself with the union murderers.

That Reade could, by way of postscript to the novel congratulate himself on having made these "dry bones live" shows only that his intentions were noble. The bones are still bones, and to the modern reader, or at least to this modern reader, their rattlings are so theatrical that they tend to defeat, and in fact invert, even the social purpose of the novel. A few chapters of Henry Little's priggish purity and one begins to sympathize with the poor bemuddled workmen in their efforts to blow him to bits. After all they are fighting for more than a hundred pounds with which to become a master and marry a silly woman.

But this is of course a modern response. At the time, the novel was a complete success with critics and public alike, for the very good reason that its blood and thunder as well as its purpose coincided with their own prejudices and propensities. In fact it coincided so completely that Reade met with very little censure, and that little was so mild that for once he did not feel obliged to launch into an immediate and elaborate defense.

CHAPTER XII

Last Efforts:

Repetitions and Variations

THROUGH MY WHOLE CAREER it has been so: a little faint, reluctant praise. Bushels of insolent vituperation.

But with the proceeds of a pen that never wrote a line till I was 35 years of age I have got me three freeholds in the Brompton Road, a leasehold in Albert Terrace, a house full of rich furniture and pictures and a few thousands floating, and so I can snap my fingers at a public I despise, and a Press I know and loathe. To God alone my thanks are due who gave me my good gifts and the sense to see that literature is a trade and that an author is a being secretly despised and who can only raise himself above contempt.

BY

RICHES

OR JE VISE AU SOLIDE

—CHARLES READE—8th June 1872[1]

✓ ✓ ✓

Put Yourself in His Place was Reade's last great effort—"the last book," in Elwin's words, "he was to write on his old idealised system." When, in 1878, William Collins urged Reade "to stir the public with a novel on the bank crash theme," Reade answered:

It is most proper that the pen should take up the cause in this case, should expose the iniquity and paint the misery of the sufferers so as to excite universal sympathy if possible. But I do not think fiction is the proper form. The reader of fiction is narrow and self-indulgent. He will read no story the basis of which is not sexual. I feel I could not write a good fiction or command readers on such a subject. Indeed, I have made a trifling experiment in that line already. Guided by the deaths and lunacies that followed the stoppage of the Leeds Bank, I endeavoured in my novel *Hard Cash* to impress upon the novel-reader that a fraudulent

Banker is a murderer as well as a thief. I even wrote a list of victims to prove it. It was wisdom wasted. Neither the novel-reading ass, nor the criticism ass received it. It was never commented on, and I believe everybody skipped it. Besides this there are other difficulties. A story—such as I write—can only be founded on a plot, and the distresses of several shareholders and depositors are not a plot. They are mere (-------) facts. To all this I must add something personal. I am old, and afflicted with a cruel cough, which subdues my energy so that for many months I have been obliged to decline all commissions of that serious kind.[2]

The cough was a serious affliction, and no doubt it was further aggravated by his concern for Mrs. Seymour, who was already suffering from the unknown ailment (cancer) that was to cause her death within a year.

But these personal afflictions of 1878 cannot account for the preceding eight years. In 1869, when he completed *Put Yourself in His Place*, Reade was fifty-five, and despite the quality of this one novel, at the very height of his powers. Moreover he had just recently moved into the new home he describes so proudly in *A Terrible Temptation*—the home that, with Mrs. Seymour established as housekeeper, at long last gave him a "hearth" he could call his own. Yet the years that followed, which he once described as the happiest years of his life, were not years of artistic fulfillment but of artistic decline. The writing of novels, it would seem, had become burdensome to him. His creative drive was gone, and seemingly he could not regain it—even with the help of his expanding collection of Notebooks, to which he devoted as much if not more time than in the 'sixties.

II

Most of the forty-five Notebooks in the Sadleir collection were compiled during the 'seventies, and a number of others were filled in, completed, or indexed during these years. In a Notebook labelled "gents mag vols 1,2,3,4" Reade noted: "Read pretty carefully . . . this vol 2 Gents Mag 20th November 1871. I am just now a good deal interrupted by watching the workmen in my room especially the carpenter planing my oak panels for varnish . . . and taking off 120 years paint. But for this could do a vol & a half & I think even 2 if I drank no wine. After all I think I must be a good one to attack the 120 vols Annual Register & [one word illegible]—what shall I say—180 vols Gents Mag at 57½ years of age. But Cato beat me if he really learned Greek at 70."

Why Reade was attacking these old journals is not clear, since only a few of the entries have even a remote connection with his eighteenth century novella, *The Wandering Heir*, and the few entries that relate to his projected novel on Voltaire seem to have no great significance.[3] But whatever his intentions his self-congratulations leave no doubt that he enjoyed this type of antiquarianism; and the entries themselves, which are for the most part eighteenth century duplications of his contemporary materials, leave no doubt as to the source of his enjoyment. Among the many gory entries in the Notebook labelled "31 Annual Register Twenty" (vols 4 and 5 AD 1761-2) is a clipping headed "Calibani. Lust hard by hate" that anticipates the celebrated rape in Faulkner's *Light in August:* "Bath, June 18. On Sunday last the most barbarous murder that has been heard of for many years was committed . . . on the body of Mary Allen, by several men, who are yet unknown. . . . A large quantity of blood. . . . Humanity obliges us to omit many particulars . . . lest the mention of them should make too great an impression. . . ." Yet even this clipping cannot match certain of those in "30 Annual Register vols 1,2,3, years 1758, 1759, 1760." Near the end of this Notebook Reade wrote (to the side of one clipping): "All the passions tend to murder." And the clippings on page thirty-one prompted him to summarize as well as comment:

> Distress at sea. Obliged to eat each other.
> Lot fell on . . . Ledane, the only son
> of a poor widow. He begged them not to
> kill him but cut off the calves of his
> legs and wait. This they did. He begged
> a morsel but was refused. In 30
> hours they killed him . . . they
> ate 4 bodies.
> Think of this in petty troubles ⎫
> But above all think of Christ ⎬ CR
> Crucifixion ⎭

That Reade should thus bring in the crucifixion in order to justify his interest in cannibalism may, to the modern reader, seem absurd, since the rationalization emphasizes exactly what it is intended to cover up. But Reade was of course less sophisticated, and in any case had to justify himself only to himself, since there is no indication that he intended to use any such entries directly in his writing. They were, as his admonitions suggest, intended solely for his own edification.

For if Reade could not acknowledge his own sadistic propensities he had learned from experience that, in fiction, he had to connect the blood with heroism or humanitarian purpose; that even then there were limits which had to be observed. In the notes he appended to the manuscript of *Put Yourself in His Place,* he wrote, following a description of "a man beaten to death's door" and other like horrors: "Query how much of these revolting materials would it be safe to use." [4] But these limits did not, of course, apply to his Notebooks, which he continued to fill with the same type of humanitarian and heroic horrors he had collected in the 'sixties—although here again his propensities overwhelmed his practical intentions, since with few exceptions his new horrors relate to specific subjects he had already treated in his earlier novels. Clippings having to do with prisons and asylums appear even in the Notebooks devoted to "Gents Mag" and "Annual Register," and in the topical Notebooks of this period they appear again and again, together with clippings having to do with union violence. In fact one Notebook, "Classificanda 1877," contains some ten pages of clippings headed "The Dirty Oligarchy."

For the most part, therefore, the humanitarian horrors in these Notebooks look backward rather than forward; and they look backward, it would seem, because Reade could not find any new humanitarian subjects big enough or wide enough or topical enough to provide him with themes comparable to those of his earlier epics of social purpose. The material on collieries suggests that he for a time considered the possibility of writing an epic of the collieries, but if so he did not carry his researches very far, perhaps because he found that his colliery facts were tending to duplicate those he had used in *Put Yourself in His Place.* As for the remaining humanitarian facts he collected—on everything from tight-lacing to "builders' blunders" to "baby-farming" to the adulteration of foods—he recognized that they were too limited and various to provide the basis for an entire novel, valuable as they might be for incidental passages or sections of novels.

III

In writing *A Terrible Temptation,* however, Reade was not much affected by these fears and doubts. Having just completed

Put Yourself in His Place, he was not, as yet, anxious to undertake another epic of purpose, but was content to follow his usual practice of turning from a "great" to a "lighter subject"—in this case a subject based on a clipping from the *Daily Telegraph* (February 4, 1870) that he had entered in "Solid Plot Lib. Magd. Coll." "I have lately signed with Cassell," he noted on October 30, 1870, "and am languidly working on a weekly serial. I have written one number. Rather smart, I think, but also rather loose. I fear it will offend the mothers of families. Indeed, query, will Cassell publish it? Yet, is it really wrong to tell the truth soberly—viz., that young men of fortune have all mistresses; and that these are not romantic creatures, but only low uneducated women bedizened in fashionable clothes?" [5] Reade was therefore aware, from the very first, that he was courting moral censure in *A Terrible Temptation,* and from the very first he took steps to forestall this criticism. So that when the attacks came he could, in all honesty, declare in *"A Letter to the Times"* (reprinted in *Readiana*): "The character of Rhoda Somerset I culled from your pages, and having observed with what firmness, yet coldness, you treated that character and topic I have kept your method in view, and, at all events, tried to imitate it. Whatever warmth I have shown is in the scenes of virtuous love; in the Somerset's scenes I am cold and sarcastic. Up to the period of her repentance how do I treat this character? Do I whitewash the hussy, or make her a well-bred, delicate-minded woman, as your refined and immoral writers would? I present her illiterate, coarse, vain, with good impulses, a bad temper, and a Billingsgate tongue. In close contrast to this unattractive photograph I am careful to place my portrait of an English virgin, drawn in the sweetest colours my rude art can command, that every honest reader may see on which side my sympathies lie, and be attracted to virtue by the road of comparison."

In so far as this moral defense is sound—and it is, for the most part—it points to the primary shortcoming of the novel. Reade does sacrifice Rhoda to his English virgin, and in the process necessarily sacrifices the perceptiveness he had shown in his earlier notebooks and novels to the Victorian ideal of virginity. For there is none of Mrs. Archbold's passion in Rhoda, none of the complexity of feeling that characterizes Jane Hardie in his English Virgin, Miss Arabella Bruce. She is as pure as even the *Times* could wish; and when she marries she becomes, in Reade's words, "a chaste woman passionately in love with her husband,"

and therefore a woman who could not, like Kate Gaunt, be tempted by another man, even though the other man, an Anglican counterpart of Father Leonard named Mr. Angelo, is himself much tempted. And the other characters are likewise conventionally pure—so much so that Reade was obliged to fill out the action with a melodramatic rehash of his unused and newly acquired materials on asylums, with himself, as Rolfe, playing the Resourceful Hero as he had played it in real life.

Except for the bowdlerized portrait of Rhoda Somerset, *A Terrible Temptation* is consequently no more than a pale and purified reflection of Reade's earlier and better work. Yet if the purification was as deliberate and intentional as it seems, an overt attempt on Reade's part to render his work conventionally acceptable, it was not so understood by his readers and critics, who, to his dismay, subjected the novel to even more virulent abuse than they had heaped on *Griffith Gaunt*. Elwin, after quoting Reade's letter to Harper's in which he asks whether or not "the comments of the Press on *A Terrible Temptation*" have affected their estimate of him, assumes that the New York firm "hastened to assure him of their continued appreciation of his financial value, enclosing as evidence the dazzling figures of sales which he vaingloriously paraded in his reply to *The Times*." Perhaps—but Reade asked J. R. Osgood and Co. the same question (Nov. 2, 1871), in offering them either one or both of his proposed new works (a one volume novel and a volume of short stories), and their reply (Nov. 18, 1871) is everything but conciliatory:

> As to terms; you ask us: "Have the comments of the press on 'Terrible Temptation' affected your estimate of me?"
> We must frankly say in reply to your question that the comments of the press on "Terrible Temptation" have affected our estimate of the commercial value of your books. In consequence we must propose an abatement in the rates of payment. We offer for these new works Three pounds sterling (£3) per Atlantic page instead of Five Pounds (£5) as heretofore. This payment to cover the Canadian copyright as well as the American market for both forms of publication.[6]

If, as Elwin rightly suggests, "there is despair as well as asperity in Reade's query," this answer was enough in itself to bring that despair to the point of complete embitterment. For if this was the response to his purified work what alternatives were left him (since he apparently could not write another epic of purpose) except to stop writing fiction altogether or turn out routine pot-boilers.

That he deliberately chose the latter alternative is borne out by his own statements at this time, the most direct, perhaps, being the memorandum (quoted, in part, as an epigraph to the present chapter) written beneath the cutting of a rabid American attack upon *A Terrible Temptation:* "I leave this," Reade wrote, "for the instruction of those who complain that authors work for money instead of contenting themselves with the meed of praise they receive. Was anything of mine ever praised as heartily as here an excellent and innocent story is abused. . . ." [7]

IV

A Terrible Temptation may then be said to mark the final turning point in Reade's career. The reception accorded this novel, itself a compromise, convinced him that he could no longer pursue the sexual themes that he had adumbrated in such novels as *Christie Johnstone, The Cloister and the Hearth, Hard Cash,* and brought to significant fulfillment in *Griffith Gaunt;* that if he were to treat such themes at all he would have to render them completely innocuous. And this he proceeded to do, first in *The Wandering Heir,* then in *A Simpleton,* and finally in *A Woman Hater* and the posthumous *A Perilous Secret.* Although *The Wandering Heir* includes material on female homosexuality from the Note-books that anticipates the *Well of Loneliness,* Reade's treatment is so tritely sentimental that the heroine's androgynism appears as nothing more than a charming manifestation of her pure love for the hero. Nor is this sentimentality much redeemed by the detective-story elements of the historical yet topical plot, in which Reade uses the eighteenth century Annesley Case to capitalize on the then nation-wide interest in the Tichborne Case.

Yet if *A Wandering Heir* is merely a good topical story, *A Simpleton* is not even that. It consists of a threadbare theatrical plot into which Reade introduces, as a central theme, the dangers of "tight-lacing." Seriously he does this. The heroine is dying; apparently she has consumption; presumably learned doctors are baffled by her case; then the hero, a young doctor who is also her sweetheart, takes over her case and discovers, with chagrin as well as blushes, that her illness is entirely attributable to "tight lacing." Whereupon she dismisses him for a time, then marries him, after which Reade ekes out the action, again from his Notebooks and Notecards, with the difficulties young householders are up against—because of "adulterated food," "builders blunders," dishonest auctioneers, etc. And when this vein is exhausted, Reade sends his hero to sea, to be ship-wrecked near South Africa, where he undergoes South African experiences taken almost verbatim from the Notebooks and Notecards. Then, by way of securing an appropriate finale, Reade draws upon the "Medicina Laici" of the Notebooks to effect a cure of the hero's insomnia that is indeed providential, since it enables him, in just the nick of time, to win his fortune and save his wife from the villain who is about to make off with her.

If *A Simpleton* is not Reade's worst novel it is his weakest, in the sense that it is a spiritless *tour de force*. And while *A Woman Hater* is a more ambitious novel, it is not, qualitatively, a much better one. For in writing this novel Reade completely abandoned the moral and artistic principles that he had compromised in *A Terrible Temptation* to grovel at the Grundyish feet of John Blackwood. In offering the projected novel to Blackwood, Reade wrote (to a friend, Langford, who was acting as an intermediary): "Mr. Blackwood, therefore, may be assured that I shall be most happy to submit to him a large portion of my MS. with a distinct statement as to the sexual incidents to follow, their nature and their treatment, and he does me no more than justice when he comments that I should not offer him a story for *Blackwood's Magazine*, if I hit upon a theme, and details, unfit for *Blackwood's Magazine*. But to provide for unforseen contingencies, of course, *if at any part of the tale* Mr. Blackwood finds lines in the MS. which it would give him pain to publish, they will be pointed out to me, and I shall excise them before the copy goes to the printer." [8] Yet Blackwood, even after seeing a good part of the novel, was still fearful, primarily, as he stated to Reade, because of "your love of plain-speaking and warm flesh tints." [9] Whereupon Reade became still more abject; and when Blackwood still hesitated, objecting that Reade's treatment of female doctors was revolutionary, Reade wrote:

> I am surprised you should think the sentence which has alarmed you equivocal or to use your words "that it may mean anything." . . . My meaning is that the young ladies did not lose

their virtue nor their modesty, but a certain bloom which lies on the surface of modesty in young ladies. If language can be found to convey that guarded meaning more precisely, you would only have to suggest it, and it should be employed. . . . But I am quite agreed with you that this subject carried out fully and forcibly would compromise both you and me.

I go further than you in this. It would not do to carry it out at all. Such a matter as this must not enter into the narrative. It is a mere part of the dialogue. . . .

Blackwood continued to object right up to the end of the serial run, and Reade continued to grovel. "I have been careful to save Zoe the future discredit of kissing and hugging with Severne," he wrote, "which is a piece of delicacy not one of our female writers would ever have thought of; nor even the discreet Mr. Trollope, who in *Ralph the Heir* makes his Clarissa kissed by one brother amorously, and married by the other. . . ." But Reade's most abject concessions are those he describes in an earlier letter: "I have struck out Rhoda's prayer [Rhoda is the doctress], and corrected the matter; also, with much pleasure, the word seduction, substituting a vague sentence that will convey no distinct idea to the reader. . . . Believe me, I make this sort of alteration for you with great pleasure, and as to the doctors I feel that on the whole your excisions have been improvements and that you deal with me in that liberal and friendly spirit, which has made the leading authors of the country your friends."

The novel itself reflects the abjectness of these letters—in everything from Reade's treatment of "the woman-hater," who is not a woman-hater at all, to his treatment of Rhoda Gale, the doctress, whose professional struggles and Lesbian attachments Reade either glosses over or treats with apologetic discretion. About the only character of any real vitality in the entire novel is the theatrical agent, Joseph Ashmead, whose addiction to advertising ("whilst I breathe I advertise")[10] at times proves even more powerful than his sentimental attachment to the opera star and heroine, Ina Klosking. For the most part, however, Ashmead merely serves as a crude foil to La Klosking's high-mindedness, which Reade, near the end of the novel, endeavors to justify on moral as well as artistic grounds: "Fiction has just as much right to select large female souls as biography or painting has; and to pick out a selfish, shallow, illiterate creature, with nothing but beauty, and bestow three enormous volumes on her, is to make a perverse selection, beauty being, after all, rarer in women than wit, sense, and goodness. It is as false and ignoble in art, as to marry a pretty face without heart and brains is silly in conduct. . . . Having all this in my mind, and remembering how many noble women have shone like stars in every age and every land, and feeling sure that, as civilization advances, such women will become far more common, I have tried to look ahead and paint La Klosking. But such portraiture is difficult. It is writing a statue." [11] And that, unfortunately, is what La Klosking remains—though even as statue she looks backward, since her nobility is indistinguishable from the Evangelicized purity which Reade imposed on his first actress-heroine in the final chapter of *Peg Woffington.*

v

The short stories that Reade wrote at this time (*Good Stories of Man and Other Animals,* first published in *Belgravia,* June 1876 to June 1877) also look backward to the 'fifties, and are without intrinsic significance. Nor can much more be said for his later short stories or his last short novel *Singleheart and Doubleface* (1883). As for his last full-length novel *A Perilous Secret* (published posthumously in 1884) it looks back to one of his earliest short stories, *Propria Quae Maribus* (as well as to Dickens' *Old Curiosity Shop*) and consists of stock melodramatic variations on the story of a gifted Baconian mechanic who, on his way to success, sacrifices, then regains, his daughter and her love. The melodramatic variations include the usual heroics and villainies, acted out in new settings, plus the climactic scenes (following an explosion in a coal mine) in which Reade introduces a number of new variants on his old sadistic horrors—including one instance in which a villainous miner, trapped in a mine and "maddened by thirst . . . had recourse to that last extremity better men have been driven to: he made a cut with his clasp-knife in the breast of the dead miner, and tried to swallow jellied blood." [12] But Reade's heart was not with this villain: it was with the "better men," as he himself explains in a last-paragraph defense of the novel: "For our part we will never place Fiction, which was the parent of History, below its child. Our hearts are with those superior men and women, who, whether in History or Fiction, make life beautiful, and raise the standard of Humanity. Such characters exist even in this plain tale, and it is these alone, and our kindly readers, we take leave of with regret." [13]

These lines—the last lines of fiction Reade wrote—recall those earlier lines in which he spoke of the characters he had seen in the plays of the 'thirties and 'forties as being the only friends of his youth; and the sad truth is that the characters he here invokes are but the fictional reincarnation of these earlier theatrical types—just as the episode of the blood-drinking is a fictional reincarnation (via the Notebooks) of his early experiences in the slaughterhouses and morgues of Paris.

VI

A Perilous Secret thus marks the final step in Reade's artistic decline. It is the work, not only of a dying man, but of a dying novelist. And he had been dying as a novelist, his work reveals, since as early as 1870, when, in writing *A Terrible Temptation*, he first set out to purify his art. In part, therefore, his unredeemed failure in this and succeeding novels can be attributed to the forces of Grundyism—but only in part, for these forces were not measurably stronger in the early 'seventies than a few years earlier. Nor was Reade more at the mercy of these forces than he had been in the 'sixties. If the attacks on *Griffith Gaunt* had enhanced his reputation for "plain-speaking and warm flesh-tints" they had also enhanced his artistic reputation, which never stood higher than in 1870. And while the attacks on *A Terrible Temptation* proved more serious, they were not, in themselves, sufficient to account for his complete and abject capitulation—which seems to be less the result of outward circumstances than of an inner failure of nerve.

Even before Reade wrote *A Terrible Temptation* he had begun to sense that he had written himself out; that he could merely repeat, with Notebook variations, the purpose and melodrama of his earlier novels. Furthermore he knew or sensed that, if he were to maintain his reputation, he would have to render these repetitious variations conventionally pure, and therefore acceptable, to his editors and critics and readers. This is why he was so bitter; why at times he pretended not to care; why at other times, as in his correspondence with Blackwood, he submitted to editorial dictation that, ten years earlier, he would not have tolerated for a moment. And this is also why, in an effort to escape from or deny his sterility, he turned more and more to the theatre, and to journalistic and real-life heroics.

VII

From 1867 onward it would seem that Reade devoted far more time and energy to the theatre than to his fiction. Long before *Put Yourself in His Place* had completed its serial run in the *Cornhill,* he had prepared a dramatic version (entitled *Free Labour)* which he himself produced at the Adelphi (on May 28, 1870) with his usual emphasis on factual realism, the star, Henry Neville, actually forging a real knife on the stage. Nevertheless the play proved "a comparative failure," and Reade's efforts to bolster it with an after-piece (a refurbished version of his earlier adaptation of Molière's *Malade Imaginaire)* had little if any effect at the box-office. Nevertheless Reade persevered: on May 1, when his lease on the Adelphi expired, he moved his entire company to The National Standard Theatre, and later, at the season's end, sent the company on tour. At this point, if Coleman is correct, "Mr. Charles Reade's London Company" already showed a deficit of five thousand pounds, and when the tour likewise began to prove unsuccessful, even Reade was obliged, in the words of his own "circular," to "suspend Theatrical Speculation for six months."

Although Reade's self-imposed suspension actually extended far beyond six months, his interest in the theatre and things theatrical remained as keen as ever. Mrs. John Wood produced his *An Actress of Daylight* (a refurbished version of his earlier *Art,* which was in turn an adaptation of Fournier's *Tiridate)* at the St. James's Theatre on April 8, 1871. And a year later, on April 1, 1872, at the Gaiety Theatre, John Hollingshead produced a play entitled "*Shilly-Shally,* or *Ralph The Heir* . . . By Anthony Trollope and Charles Reade Esq." [14]—despite the fact that Trollope did not even know that his novel was being adapted until the announcements of the play appeared. Trollope's indignation is therefore quite understandable, yet the ensuing quarrel, interesting and amusing as Bradford A. Booth has shown it to be (in his "Trollope, Reade and *Shilly-Shally,*" Parts One and Two, *The Trollopian,* March and June, 1947) ultimately drags on to a familiar conclusion, with Reade again taking refuge in his tradesman's view of authorship, the curiously defensive view that he had exercised in the early 'fifties, defined in *The Eighth Commandment,* and continued to apply on every occasion that suited his purpose—his letter to Hollingshead (February 1 [1872]), apropos of Hollingshead's production of *Shilly-Shally*, providing a typical instance:

Yours received old fox, and this is my reply.
1. Trade is trade. And in trade a bargain is a bargain.
2. Pigs will eat trash, but they don't confine themselves to it. Masks & Faces is not trash, and it is drawing more than [Tootles?]
3. There is room in an evening for "Shilly Shally," and also for Trash
4. I am ready to sue Scott, and call you and Toole as witnesses on your old proofs.
5. Should prefer another way, but can't afford to write masterpieces for waste paper and be libelled off the British stage. This is not trade, and

I'm a trader[15]

In this, as in the many other letters Reade addressed to Hollingshead in the years between 1870 and 1876, there is none of the discouragement or self pity that characterizes his references to his novels. He writes with his old vigour about everything from his own "masterpieces" to the laws of dramatic copyright, and even when he is obliged to peddle his players and scenery, after temporarily disbanding his touring company, his letters are still as optimistic as they are businesslike.[16]

And the same vigor is apparent in every aspect of his theatrical work during these years, especially after the success of his dramatic version of *A Wandering Heir*, first with Mrs. John Wood as his leading lady, then (beginning February 28, 1874) with Ellen Terry, whom he had lured out of retirement. At long last he had an actress who could carry his work, and who was willing to do so; and if she had arrived too late for him to fulfill his most grandiose theatrical ambitions, there was still time for him to exploit her capabilities in revivals of his earlier adaptations, such as *Rachel the Reaper*, *Our Seamen*, and *Griffith Gaunt*. Indeed it would seem, on the basis of his letters to Ellen Terry (which read like those he had written some thirty years earlier to Mrs. Stirling), that she at once enabled him to relive and in some measure fulfill the dreams of his youth. [17]

For in addition to his enjoyment of the theatre itself, there was the excitement of theatrical speculation, and, perhaps most important of all, the illusion that the adaptations (old and new) that he wrote or refurbished during these years were dramatic master-pieces—an illusion that his few successes and his one really great hit enabled him to maintain. The one great hit was *Drink* (an adaptation of the French dramatic adaptation of Zola's *L'Assomoir*), and the remarks Reade included in the acting copies of this play and *Jealousy* (his adaptation of Sardou's *Andréa*) show that his notions of dramatic authorship had neither changed nor developed since the early 'fifties, when he declared *Gold* a masterpiece. The notes he included in *Drink* end thus: "This drama is a play of giants—the product of many superior minds—if the artists will only shun the fatal snare of monotony, and study the real and distinct meaning of every line instead of overlarding heterogeneous lines with one tone, and delivering them at one pace of delivery. . . . This example may show how much can be done with the part of Gervaise [the heroine] if actresses will only bestow the same rev-erent study on her lines which they do upon *the comparatively small female creations of immortal poets.*"[18] And his Preface to "The Countess and the Dancer or High Life in Vienna" (his printed version of the play he adapted from Sardou's *Andréa)* reads as follows:

Now and then benevolent Fate offers the English dramatist a nugget of fine gold embedded in quartz and clay.

Then, if he has an eye for gold and an eye for rubbish, he separates the two boldly, and retains the ore; and the English theatre gets the treasure.

Example—Four French writers produced a drama, "L'Assomoir," with a broad human subject, fine situations, and many admirable scenes, but clogged with useless characters, irrelevant passages, weak buffoonery, uninteresting vice, and some downright poor stuff.

I preserved all the beauties of this drama with religious reverence, hacked away the superfluous characters and all the rubbish, not with a pruning-knife, but a bill-hook, wrote one new character in tune with the best scenes—and there was a great drama, "Drink."

The value of the process was shown at once by the punishment inflicted on the work. "Drink" has been stolen in various forms by at least forty scoundrels. No other contemporary drama has been stolen by ten. Now, an ephemeral drama is often praised up to the skies, but it is never greatly stolen. Wholesale theft is the one sure test of immortality.

Example II Victorien Sardou, the greatest dramatist of the age, wrote a comedy for an American actress, containing a character she could look—for she was beautiful—but could no more play than she could fly to heaven with a ballet-dancer's back fins. In this hasty production were twenty-two characters and several useless scenes, but the central plot good, the leading character a pearl of womanhood, and some scenes and situations gems of the purest water. Indeed, in parts of this loose and unequal composition that great master surpassed himself. I have applied to this compound the same process I applied to "L'Assomoir." I have cut away no less than nine superfluous characters and several useless scenes, added one original character, who tightens the plot, and preserved with utmost care and reverence every one of the inventor's jewels.

The result of my process is before you.

The work remains "High Comedy," and does not deal with life on a broad scale; but within its limits it paints faithfully. Young male aristocrats are generally vicious; female aristocrats, except in French fiction, are generally virtuous. This play shows the rule instead of the stale exception. It presents masculine vice fearlessly— Genius was never yet a coward—but it sides with virtue honestly, nobly, eloquently. As to the leading character, I pity the Anglo-Saxon dunces, wherever found, who have had the opportunity, but not the brains, to see the variety and beauty of this exquisite creation. Here are beauty, grace, breeding, love, jealousy, fire, tenderness, passion, virtue—everything. The author has given her a hundred fine things to say and to do, both in play and dumb-play.*

Happy the great actress, into whose hands she shall fall, and happy the public should the jealousy of the male actor permit it to see so multiform a character played by a great artist suited to the part.

May 1st, 1883   Charles Reade

---

* The dumb-play alone of the Countess in Stella's dressing-room is worth two months' study.[19]

And so Reade ended as he began, proclaiming his dramatic adaptations masterpieces, himself a dramatic genius—in defiance of all critics, including those who had just damned his last play, "Love and Money" (which he had written in collaboration with Henry Pettitt and produced at the Adelphi, November 18, 1882).[20] Writing of her life on tour with Reade a few years earlier, Ellen Terry remarked: "He had entirely succumbed to the magic of the 'irresistible theatre,' and it used to strike me as rather pathetic to see a man of his power and originality working the stage sea at nights. . . ." [21] And his playwriting is even more pathetic, viewed in relation to the Shakespearean heights to which he aspired. Yet he maintained his belief in his dramatic achievements to the very end, describing himself in his epitaph, "Dramatist, Novelist, and Journalist."

VIII

The word "Journalist," as Reade uses it in his epitaph, is intended to complete the outlines of his idealized self-portrait—in which he appears as a nineteenth century Voltaire, his writings for newspapers and journals as practical applications of the Baconian philosophy that he preached and lived. Earlier, in sketching his plans for "a Nova Scientia" (in the Notebook labelled "Digest") he had noted: "better be done in numbers"; and now, moderating his ambitions, he considered the possibility of working out a journalistic variation on these plans by founding and editing a popular magazine devoted to "truth, justice, and European wisdom." In fact he even went so far as to set down a statement of editorial policy (quoted in full in the *Memoir)* in which he explains that his ultimate aim is to make the magazine a published extension of the Notebooks—in everything from its attacks on "great defects and errors" to its "impalpable wisdom":

> But to tell the truth, our immediate danger is from what I call A DIRTY OLIGARCHY, i.e., a set of associated mechanics, who regulate their own numbers by terrorism, and so secure a monopoly, and then abuse that monopoly. . . .
> This dirty oligarchy, and not a republic, is England's rock ahead. . . .
> But a greater and harder lesson remains to be taught systematically. The wisdom of the mind is also distributed among nations as equally as mechanical skill: no nation realizes this: yet it is so; and would be seen in an hour if the wisest laws and the wisest customs of each nation could only be brought into one building, and presented to the senses. That unfortunately cannot be. This impalpable wisdom can only be shown on paper, and not vividly like the national products of industry. Yet, here a periodical will rise above all books, and be a small Crystal Palace of ideas; if lovers of mankind will co-operate with me, and striving nobly against blinding prejudices, will rise to the occasion, weigh the bits of superior wisdom they have seen in Europe, Asia, Africa,

and America, and bring them to a focus in these pages. My own reading in this kind has been long and large; but no man's private stores can build so great a work—a work which, if it prospers, will promote the interchange of that wisdom which is above rubies; will tend towards that world-wide, blessed uniformity of laws in civilized nations, and that great, but, alas, too distant good, the unity of nations.

Reade's titular metaphor ("a small Crystal Palace of ideas") is well chosen, as the illustrations he included in his initial discussion of this Solomonian plan (in "Digest") make quite clear. Had he carried through his projected magazine, the first number might well have included one article, corresponding to one exhibit, in which Reade himself demonstrated how to boil a potato; another article, corresponding to another exhibit, in which one of his "lovers of mankind" discussed "blood drinking in Boston"; still another in which another humanitarian discussed the question "why the lash in English Army, and not in French"; plus another in which an exponent of "Arabian Wisdom," demonstrated that "they comprehended the horse centuries before us"; or perhaps, in place of this last, an article on "animal life in Australasia" embodying Reade's own comments in "9 Notes and Press Cuttings on Various Subjects":

> In Australia Oxleys party killed a native dog and threw his body
> in a bush.
> Returning three days after they found the
> body removed three or four yards and a
> poor emaciated female of the species
> sitting helplessly beside it. She could
> not move. "It was deemed mercy
> to despatch her." The tender mercies . . .
> are cruel. "I should have
> given her a little milk with a
> teaspoon of wine in it.
>
> What a man respects in man, why despise
> it in a creature he calls his inferior.

Such bits of wisdom as these, Reade believed, would raise his periodical "above all books," and make it a "small Crystal Palace of ideas." And if someone had pointed out, as well they might, that his wisdom seemed remarkably like that of *The Daily Telegraph*, Reade would no doubt have agreed, and gone on to point out that such journals constituted, for nineteenth century man, the prime source of all printed wisdom. In fact he did point this out to M. E. Braddon, when he advised her (*Memoir,* p. 396) that she "should read the papers, and leave books alone," his justification being that nearly all books were, from his point of view, like poorly stuffed puddings, with far more filler and fewer plums per line than newspapers and journals. He constantly spoke of facts and knowledge and art in this plum-pudding sense, equating facts with gems, or pearls, or cream, or gold, and measuring the quality of a work by the number of pure gems or pearls or the amount of pure cream or gold it contained. Hence his ultimate assumption that, if lovers of mankind would cooperate with him, and would supply him with bits of wisdom to supplement those in his Notebooks, he could create a new and still richer type of magazine— one that would be chock full of plums, with only enough filler to hold them together, and therefore one that would "rise above all books."

The commercial (as distinct from the intellectual) possibilities of the projected magazine may be gauged by the extent to which it anticipates the essential features of *The Reader's Digest.* Yet nothing came of Reade's editorial plans. With his temperament nothing could. Nor could anything come of his related if more overtly commercial schemes, of which the one he outlined in a letter to Harper's (September 14, 1873) is perhaps the most interesting:

By resisting international copyright you play a small game when there is a gigantic game:

THE   BIG   GAME

Pass a measure of international copyright.

Be ready to set up a branch in London, you shall publish my work in both countries, on commission if you like or on terms yielding a sure remuneration in this country, to say nothing of the States. I will secure you Wilkie Collins too, or Miss Braddon, or anybody you like. Your MONTHLY with a fair proportion of European matter will knock the *Cornhill* and all the monthlies to the devil. Your WEEKLY, not being so superior to the English weeklies . . . will still hold its ground . . . besides being a handle to secure some good European matter at first hand, for your American issue.

The kindly co-operation of the English publishing trade and the wholesale houses could be secured by stipulation. . . . In a word this is your programme:

1. Pass International Copyright.
2. Set up a London Shop.
3. Form a little nucleus of authors in which I will be one and draw others.
4. Set up an English paper mill. They all pay. Yours would pay better than most, because you would be a large customer to yourself.

Sell American works in the United States and Great Britain, British works in Great Britain and the United States.

A publisher's shop in London is not an expensive thing: you do not retail anything, you only sell to the trade. The expense of delivery is also small.

The binders will warehouse your new books and deliver them to the trade for you and printers will hold for you and deliver in sheets to order.

If you will start a penny weekly the size of the Athenæum with news and cheap illustrations, done upon the plan of *Figaro*, they do not cost above five shillings apiece, I will edit it for you, as part of the whole scheme, but that is not worth thinking of.[22]

How the "penny weekly" fit into the remainder of Reade's Napoleonic scheme is not clear—unless he viewed such a "weekly" as a commercial substitute for his projected magazine. In any event Harper's negative response marks the end of his editorial plans— though not of his belief in the "impalpable wisdom" underlying those plans. Some of that wisdom he had already expressed in the *Pall Mall Gazette*, in four letters entitled "Builders' Blunders" (reprinted in *Readiana*) in which he discusses, with Baconian omniscience, every phase of house building, devoting over two full pages, for instance, to "the rational roof," for which he specifies under point seven an improvement reminiscent of Wemmick's Castle:

On each roof a little flag staff and streamer to light the gloom with sparks of colour, and tell the world is the master at home or not. This would be of little use now; but, when once the rational roof becomes common many a friend could learn from his own roof whether a friend was at home, and so men's eyes might save their legs.

Also rational, in much the same sense, are the letters and articles he wrote on various other subjects, ranging from "How Lunatics Ribs Get Broken" (a letter to the *Pall Mall Gazette,* January 17, 1870, now reprinted at the beginning of *Hard Cash*) to

"Cremona Fiddles" *(Pall Mall Gazette,* August 19-31, reprinted in *Readiana)* to "Dogs' Homes" (a letter to *The Daily Telegraph,* presumably published some time in 1875).[23] With few exceptions these miscellaneous letters and articles represent obvious variations on themes and notions he had carried over in his Notebooks from the 'fifties and 'sixties. Even *A Hero and A Martyr (Pall Mall Gazette,* November 25, 26, 28, and 30, 1874), Reade's account of one Lambert, a Glasgow workman who had set some sort of record for saving the lives of people drowning in the Clyde, dates from the late 'fifties, when, as Elwin explains, "he was collecting biographies as the best foundation for characters in fiction." It is as if Reade, having failed to establish his own "Crystal Palace of Ideas," felt obliged to scatter his long cherished gems of wisdom and truth and justice broadside, in any journal that would publish them.

Among the purest of these gems, he believed, were those he had begun to polish in 1873, and some three years later offered to Blackwood (December 8, 1876):

> I send you . . . by book post the preliminary flourish to the work on Trade's Unions I once projected. I find on reading it that the preface was written by my friend Edwin Arnold of the *Telegraph.* I remember now that I said to myself, "They dare not print this in the *Telegraph,*" and so tossed it aside, and it has been kicking about the house these three years.
>
> My materials are pretty careful notes on the eleven bluebooks, and a few years of the *Manchester Guardian.* I employed a Myrmidon to search the files and he found that not the bricklayers and the brickmakers only, as Mr. Harrison and others pretend, but a dozen other trades had been guilty of brutal violence. For this he has cited chapter and verse.
>
> But in my present state of health I feel little able to attack it, and I don't think the public wants to hear common sense or prophecy from me. Nevertheless, whoever does point out to the public that these gentry are not Republicans but Oligarchs will probably make some sensation.[24]

How Reade expected to create a sensation by appending new footnotes to old arguments against "the dirty oligarchy" that he himself had twice repeated is difficult to understand. Yet Reade's succeeding letter (December 20, 1876) suggests that Blackwood was not wholly unreceptive:

I have omitted to answer a query of yours about "the dirty oligarchy." I have not written a line more of it, and most likely never shall. These things don't pay. The public does not want wisdom, foresight, and public policy from *me*. . . .

The only thing that might tempt me would be your taking a positive fancy to the subject. . . . But I own I dread the labour. My cough takes my wonted energy clean out of me.[25]

With a little more encouragement from Blackwood there can be little doubt that Reade would have undertaken the work, no matter how much he dreaded the labor. For he continued to grind out similar gems of wisdom, including a work on ambidexterity (entitled *The Coming Man*) so unintentionally fantastic that it makes his "rational roof" seem rational indeed.

Yet even when his journalistic work created something of a sensation, as *The Coming Man* apparently did, he still felt that his wisdom was being wasted; that to be truly effective, it had to be mass produced for mass consumption. And since he could not have a magazine of his own for this purpose, he decided to do the next best thing, which in the words of the *Memoir,* was "to adopt, as a vehicle for his great ideas, some journal with a colossal circulation. . . ." On January 1, 1878, Reade himself wrote:

The plan I propose is, to make the most of my interest—a journal; to make and shake the nation, and *make it* write to me; for I have discovered that the only creature who knows *much* and various things is the public.

I open the year with these designs, but none of that certainty I shall accomplish any one of them which marks our sanguine youth. My contemporaries, and even my juniors, fall daily around, and I observe that nobody calls their deaths untimely. I therefore am due. . . . The time is certainly come when I ought not to write foolish or wicked or frivolous things for the public; but should I die in the middle of a sentence warning the good not to be uncharitable, the wicked not to despair, then, methinks, I should die well—better perhaps than if I died repeating prayers like a parrot in St. Paul's Church.

My first topic will be, I think,
"THE DARK PLACES OF THE LAND"
"('The dark places of the land are full of cruelty.'—Ps. xx)"
And if that does not sicken,
"THE WISDOM AND FOLLY OF NATIONS."

On this latter topic Reade wrote a four-page essay or preface (reprinted in full in the *Memoir*) in which he once again declares: "The Crystal Palaces point to the only way. There must be many contributors from every nation, and there must be a grand receptacle . . . the columns of a great journal might be the Crystal Palace to receive sifted contributions, and leave the world wiser than they found it." Seemingly, however, no great journal wished to become "a grand receptacle" or a "Crystal Palace," at least not with Reade acting as doge of the said palace.

Nevertheless the *Daily Telegraph* had expressed urgent interest in his first topic, "The Dark Places of the Land," and on December 31, 1878, he wrote Harpers to announce that he was about to begin work on this project:

You were good enough to express a desire that I would write letters again on some public matter.

I am about to do so—viz., to write upon "dark places" and the iniquities that are practiced in them. The subject is large and various embracing prisons, workhouses, Asyla, ships, schools, secret tribunals etc. And as I am "a citizen of the World" I have no aim to make it exclusively English. I would rather work for all Anglosaxony.

There is only one Man that knows more about anything

My Method therefore will be to elicit revelations, and make populations speak.

Will you kindly aid my preliminary researches as follows:

Will you cause the files of Harper's Weekly to be searched and every copy sent me that contains a case of manslaughter in a prison, or an asylum or a workhouse, or of cruelties in any such places: or, if you prefer it, ship me a complete set of Harper's Weekly, and I will set on my myrmidons to search the file. I fear there is no such thing as an Index to H.W.

Is there in the U.S. any Index to current events as there is here an Index to the *Times* newspaper?

May I request your kind and prompt attention to these items? as on the one hand the Editor of *Daily Telegraph* is urgent, and on the other I wish to start fair with all the information possible

My first topic will be Prisons, and the subtle systems of slaughter there pursued by contriving various causes that all depress vitality, instead of balancing the punishment—with numerous examples.[26]

In this letter, which harks back to the letters he wrote Mrs. Fields in the 'fifties, Reade can be seen trying to whip up facts and enthusiasm for still another attack on the same old abuses.

In his ideas as in his art time had, for him, stood still. The only changes he could recognize were the changes in his own and his friends' and acquaintances' physical make-up. He was older and less well; Mrs. Seymour was seriously ill; Dickens and many others had died. Yet life itself was still the same as in the 'fifties and 'sixties: the old abuses were still there and his old formulas, the formulas he had worked out in his passionate youth, were still valid—if only his myrmidons could provide him with the fresh warm facts he needed to give these old formulas new life.

IX

But he had no sooner begun to work on "The Dark Places of the Land" than he began to experience, in Mrs. Seymour's last illness, another kind of darkness that could not be dispelled by the old formulas. And when she died, on September 27, 1879, the darkness was, for Reade, complete. "So terrible was his state," as Elwin describes it, "that those about him seemed to have had fears of his sanity and the possibility of suicide." Nor did he ever fully recover: from this time until his death five years later he was a broken, dispirited man, the prey of the inner fears and doubts that he had for so long denied or rationalized, and that he now, with the help of the Reverend Charles Graham, sought to deny or rationalize by religious means.

Reade's emotional struggles during the weeks and months that followed are truly pitiable. During the time that he lived with his brother, Compton, he made a daily pilgrimage to Knightsbridge, where for three or four hours he tried to work in the mirror-lined study. But without Mrs. Seymour it was "silent as the grave, though in the heart of London. The great simple fireplace she planned to heat this cold north room does its work nobly; but, ah me! ah me! her seat by that fireplace is empty forever." And on March 16, 1880, he wrote:

Alone in the world this six months, after pining to a skeleton for the loss of my darling, and two or three ineffectual attempts to live in the house where she made me happy. I come over this day from Coningham Road to try and spend a night here. My heart is like lead. I no longer ignore God, as I used. On the contrary, I pray hard, and give money to poor people, and try to be God's servant. . . . Oh, to think that for five-and-twenty years I was blessed with Laura Seymour, and that now for the rest of my pilgrimage she is quite, quite gone. . . . Oh, my heart! my heart! I am wretched. I have lost my love of the world. I have not acquired the love of God. And I have no companion. . . . My dogs, and the portrait of my lost darling—they are all I have. Ah, would to God I could add that I have my Saviour. I believe he is here, and pities me, but from want of faith, I cannot feel his presence. O God, increase my faith!

A few months later Reade was further wounded by an article entitled "The Conversion of Charles Reade," in which one Stanton, a clergyman, made copy of the Reverend Graham's boasted "conversion" to represent "Reade as a life-long sinner, regardless of the spirit in thinking only of the flesh, who had foisted his rationalistic views upon Mrs. Seymour and consequently suffered remorse for his conduct at her death." To correct Stanton's errors ("that wound me cruelly and can edify nobody") Reade called upon Joseph Hatton, a journalist, who answered Stanton in a letter to *The New York Times* (June 17, 1880) that includes a personal letter from Reade in which he explains: "My grief for her is selfish. You know what I have lost—a peerless creature, wise, just, and full of genius, yet devoted to me. She alone sustained me in the hard battle of my life, and now, old and broken, I must totter on without her, sick, sad, and lonely."

By August Reade had once again returned to Knightsbridge: "I am now making another attempt to live here, my fourth or fifth. . . ." Yet the attempt was still too much for him. The mirrors were still there, and the Notebooks, but without Mrs. Seymour, his one true mirror, they no longer reflected the heroic self-image that had sustained him through the years. It was she who had lent human warmth and credibility to his rationalizations, and now that she was gone the rationalizations were no longer adequate. And so he had to devise new ones, by turning to religion, and finding support for his self-image in the Bible—for him not an impossible task, since with his powers of self-justification it was a simple matter to demonstrate (as he did in his posthumously published *Bible Characters*, 1889) that the characters of the Bible were much like the characters in his own novels, and therefore not only believable but factual, and therefore true.

But Reade himself was not wholly convinced—or, if he was, the faith in God that he achieved could not wholly compensate for the loss of Mrs. Seymour. Finally what he wanted from religion, and from God, was what Thackeray had expressed outright in his letters to Mrs. Brookfield—assurance that heaven was where he would find her again, together with his first love, his idealized image of his mother. Rose Eytinge, in her "Personal Reminiscences" of Reade, recalls finding him (during the last "year or two" of his life) seated "at his mother's desk . . . now laughing heartily at some little article, or scrap of paper, which reminded him of some childish escapade, now moved to tears, when some word she had written or trinket she had worn, reminded him of his mother. . . . Old man as he was, he was attached to the memory of his mother with the passionate tenderness of a child or a woman."[27]

That Reade should become as a child again, invoking his mother's image, may seem like, and in some respects is, a sad end to a sad life. Yet the fact remains that he was able to maintain his heroic self-image to the very end. He died, his letters show, believing that he was a great novelist, a great dramatist, and a true if misunderstood and unrecognized prophet. Moreover he died believing that in years to come, when the peoples of the world had become ambidextrous and London had become a city of rational roofs, his Notebooks would provide the final vindication for his "great ideas" as well as for his "great art." And since he had never doubted that, in practice, he was a resourceful and heroic humanitarian (one who had taken "a good many alleged lunatics out of confinement"), he died convinced that future ages would come to recognize him, not only as a great writer and a great thinker, but also as a great man—the Voltaire of the Nineteenth Century. And so it may be said that his defeat, which is all inclusive save for his better novels, is an artistic but not a personal defeat.

Sex, Sadism, and *The Cloister and the Hearth*

SINCE CHARLES READE's books are published in cheap editions, one can assume that he still has his following, but it is unusual to meet anyone who has voluntarily read him. In most people his name seems to evoke, at most, a vague memory of "doing" *The Cloister and the Hearth* as a school holiday task. It is his bad luck to be remembered by this particular book, rather as Mark Twain, thanks to the films, is chiefly remembered by *A Connecticut Yankee at King Arthur's Court*. Reade wrote several dull books, and *The Cloister and the Hearth* is one of them. But he also wrote three novels which I personally would back to outlive the entire works of Meredith and George Eliot. . . .

—GEORGE ORWELL

✓   ✓   ✓

The historical novel cannot help being what the French call *voulu*—a word that denotes both effort and artificiality. The storyteller who deals honestly with his own time achieves, without taking thought, a fidelity simply impossible to the story-teller who deals with the past, no matter how laboriously the latter may toil. . . . If we examine carefully the best of the stories usually classed under historical fiction we shall find those to be the most satisfactory in which the history is of least importance, in which it is present only as a background. . . .

Some think that fiction ought to be literature, and that "literature is a criticism of life." Some hold that fiction is mere story-telling—the stringing together of adventure, the heaping up of excitement, with the wish of forgetting life as it is, of getting outside of the sorry narrowness of sordid and commonplace existence into a fairy-land of dreams. . . . It is to readers of this second class that the ordinary historical novel appeals with peculiar force; for it provides the drug they desire, while they can salve their conscience during this dissipation with the belief that they are, at the same time, improving their minds. The historical novel is aureoled with a pseudo-sanctity, in that it purports to be more instructive than a mere story: it claims—or at least the claim is made in its behalf—that it is teaching history. There are those who think that it thus adds hypocrisy to its other faults.

—BRANDER MATTHEWS—*The Historical Novel and Other Essays*

✓   ✓   ✓

The late George Orwell, in his reappraisal of Reade's work ("Books in General," *New Statesman*, August 17, 1940), first of all attempts to account for "the attraction of Reade." "At bottom," he declares, "it is the same charm as one finds in R. Austin Freeman's detective stories or Lieutenant Commander Gould's collection of curiosities—the charm of useless knowledge. . . . If you have the sort of mind that takes pleasure in dates, lists, categories, concrete details, descriptions of processes . . . the sort of mind that likes knowing exactly how a medieval catapult worked or just what objects a prison cell of the eighteen-forties contained you can hardly help enjoying Reade."

Orwell's own favorite among Reade's novels is *Foul Play*, which he discusses at some length:

> Like most nineteenth-century novels *Foul Play* is too complicated to be summarized, but its central story is that of a young clergyman, Robert Penfold, who is unjustly convicted of forgery, is transported to Australia, absconds in disguise, and is wrecked on a desert island together with the heroine. Here, of course Reade is in his element. Of all men who ever lived, he was the best fitted to write a desert-island story. Some desert-island stories, of course, are worse than others, but none is altogether bad when it sticks to the actual concrete details of the struggle to keep alive. A list of the objects in a shipwrecked man's possession is probably the surest winner in fiction, surer than a trial scene. . . . Even a dismal book like *Robinson Crusoe*, so unreadable as a whole that few people even know that the second part exists, becomes interesting when it describes Crusoe's efforts to make a table, glaze earthenware and grow a patch of wheat. Reade, however, was an expert on desert islands. . . . Moreover, he was the kind of man who would have been at home on a desert island himself. He would never, like Crusoe, have been stumped by such an easy problem as that of leavening bread, and unlike Ballantyne he knew that civilized men cannot make fire by rubbing sticks together.
>
> The hero of *Foul Play*, like most of Reade's heroes, is a kind of superman. He is hero, saint, scholar, gentleman, athlete, pugilist, navigator, physiologist, botanist, blacksmith and carpenter all rolled into one. . . . Needless to say, it is only a month or two before this wonderful clergyman has got the desert island running like a West End hotel. . . .

That Orwell should like this sort of novel, and wish to declare it a superior example of a manifestly inferior type, is understandable enough. But he goes much further, by implication declaring its virtues and shortcomings (which are, of course, almost as much Boucicault's as Reade's) to be indistinguishable from those of *Hard Cash* and *Never Too Late To Mend*, the two novels that, with *Foul Play*, constitute "the three novels" that he "personally would back to outlive the entire works of Meredith and George Eliot. . . ."

Where this leaves poor Meredith and George Eliot it is impossible to surmise, since Orwell, having classified Reade's three novels as "desert-island stories," proceeds to dismiss them from serious literary consideration on much the same grounds that E. M Forster, in *Aspects of the Novel*, dismisses *The Antiquary*, along with the rest of Scott's fiction. "Reade was," Orwell concludes, "simply a middle-class gentleman with a little more conscience than most, a scholar who happened to prefer popular science to the classics. Just for that reason he is one of the best 'escape' novelists we have, *Foul Play* and *Hard Cash* would be good books to send to a soldier enduring the miseries of trench warfare, for instance. There are no problems in them, no genuine 'message,' merely the fascination of a gifted mind functioning within very narrow limits. . . . What he lacked was one notion that the early railway age, with the special scheme of values appropriate to it, was not going to last forever. . . . Of all the nineteenth-century novelists who have remained readable, he is perhaps the only one who is completely in tune with his own age. For all his unconventionality, his 'purpose,' his eagerness to expose abuses, he never makes a fundamental criticism. . . . He sees nothing wrong in an acquisitive society, with its equation of money and virtue, its pious millionaires and erastian clergymen."

Although there is no denying Orwell's percipience, granted his critical premises, his observations are, in part, simply mistaken. In matters sexual, the present study has demonstrated, no Victorian writer was more at odds with his age than Reade. Indeed it can be argued, as Elwin has in fact argued, that *Griffith Gaunt* (which Orwell apparently had not read) offers a more "fundamental criticism" of accepted Victorian values than any other novel of the time. And the sexual scenes and passages in a number of Reade's other novels can be defended on similar grounds—including, for example, these passages in *Hard Cash* in which "the virgin martyr" reveals the strength of her sexual propensities. Orwell's soldier in the trenches might well have found "escape" in the social purpose of *Hard Cash*, as Reade himself did, but the virgin martyr would surely have given him pause.

[311]

II

A number of the sadistically humanitarian passages in Reade's novels also go beyond the escapist blood and thunder that typifies Victorian sensation, notably those passages in *Never Too Late To Mend* (previously discussed) in which Reade carries his description to the point of sadistic frenzy. And if Reade could not, like Dickens, retain artistic control of his frenzy, and so achieve the depth and intensity of Dickens' *Chuzzlewit* or *Great Expectations*, his prison scenes will still bear comparison with the passages in Carlyle that they are intended to answer, or those in Marcus Clarke's *For The Term of His Natural Life* that they helped to inspire.

Moreover there are comparable passages in a half-dozen of Reade's other novels, not to mention the briefer touches that distinguish all his better novels—including *The Cloister and the Hearth*.[1] Near the beginning of this novel Gerard, the hero, clubs one of the villains who is hunting him down; and what had been, up to this point, a conventionally melodramatic man-hunt becomes considerably more complex. For when Gerard's companion, an old soldier named Martin, discovers that Gerard's blow has merely cracked the villain's skull, he expresses his disappointment with professional candor:

"Never strike your enemy but to slay him," said Martin gloomily.

Whereupon the tender Gerard, who has presumably never uttered a harsh word, much less struck a deadly blow, calls upon Heaven for another chance:

"I'll hit harder this time, if Heaven give me the chance," said Gerard.[2]

Melodramatically this answer may seem inconsistent; psychologically, however, it is so fully, even deeply, consistent that it breaks up the melodramatic pattern to reveal, for a moment, the human feelings that underlie it.

Another revealing touch in the novel is that in which Denys (the Burgundian soldier who accompanies Gerard on his journey to Rome) asks Gerard: "How would you bear to lie on the field of battle on a frosty night, as I did t'other day, stark naked, with nothing to keep me warm but the carcass of a fellow I had been

and helped kill?" To which Gerard answers: "Horrible! horrible!
Tell me all about it! Oh, but this is sweet." [3] And when, much
further on in the novel, Gerard sees the Princess Claelia beating
her maid, Floretta, he experiences sensations even more sweet and
horrible: "The antique toga left quite disengaged a bare arm,
that now seemed as powerful as it was beautiful; it rose and fell
like the piston of a modern steam engine, and heavy slaps sounded
one after another on Floretta's shoulders. . . ." Then, after expressing moral disapproval, Gerard, speaking as an artist, admits to the
Princess:

"I wish I could have drawn you as you were beating that poor lass.
You were awful, yet lovely." [4]

III

Yet these "moments of truth" have little effect on the novel as
a whole, which has been acclaimed "a great historical novel" on
the basis of characteristics much like those Orwell praised in *Foul
Play*. Whether or not Reade, "of all men who ever lived . . .
was the best fitted to write a desert-island story," he certainly was
among the best fitted to reproduce the outward features of life
in the Middle Ages. During his apprenticeship, it has been pointed
out, he studied the realistic theories and practices, not only of
novelists, but of painters, dramatists, and stage-managers, and in
his own plays and novels he adapted and developed their theories
and practices to such a point that he convinced even Henry James
that his picture of Australia, fabricated from some thirty miscellaneous books, was more real than that of Henry Kingsley. Moreover, in treating the Middle Ages, Reade enjoyed still another
advantage in that his Baconian and anti-Carlylean outlook encouraged him to apply his documentary techniques with passionate
purpose—to reproduce his medieval facts with the same Pre-
Raphaelite fidelity that characterizes his exposure of the abuses
in Birmingham Gaol.

In consequence his portrayal of the outward life of the Fifteenth
Century is marvellously full and accurate—in the same sense that
Frith's paintings, or Kean's stage settings, are marvellously full
and accurate. Indeed if one were living in the Fifteenth Century,
and planning to take a trip from Holland to Rome, he could hardly
find a more adequate guide to the various countries, cities, and
villages along the way than Reade's novel, which even provides

detailed information on the various inns in various countries—
their customs and prices, their dinner hours and tipping practices.
Nor does it matter, for readers who enjoy such matter-of-fact
details, that the details themselves are as useless as old railway
timetables. Their charm is the charm of Orwell's "useless knowledge," although, strictly speaking, Reade's Baedekerish information is not useless to those who find it charming, since it represents the kind of knowledge that they find real and comprehen-
sible, the kind of knowledge that they themselves accumulate on
their own European travels.

Moreover the charm of Reade's Baconian knowledge is
further enhanced, for such readers, by the Baconian and anti-
Carlylean use he makes of it—to show, as in his presentation of
the Princess Claelia, that "your true medieval" was as immoral and
as brutal as his inns were dirty and as he himself was ignorant;[5]
that, on the other hand, the true heroes and heroines of the Middle
Ages were so much "before their age" that they were, in all essentials, archetypal Victorians.

Yet, to do Reade justice, he did not work out this formula in
order to guarantee the success of the novel. Indeed, from his
Baconian and Macaulay-like point of view the formula was not a
formula at all; it was a philosophical statement of the facts of
nature and history that Carlyle had perverted, and that he himself had, from the first, been endeavoring to set straight. Both
Christie Johnstone and *It Is Never Too Late To Mend*, it has
been shown, are (in part) anti-Carlylean tracts, and in the late
'fifties he went so far as to project a book (to be entitled *Heroes
and Martyrs*) designed to "glorify obscure men and women who
performed noble deeds but were soon forgotten." It was while
Reade was studying for this work, Professor Albert Morton Turner
explains, that he happened upon the story of Erasmus' father, and
was "supremely attracted, for here was an obscure man who had
lived heroically and, moreover, a man who had suffered from the
same enforced celibacy as Reade." [6]

All this, and more, Reade himself acknowledges in the first few
paragraphs of *The Cloister and the Hearth*, in which he defines
his general purpose in the novel, specifies his subject and theme,
and acknowledges his primary source—in a manner and style
directly reminiscent of Chapter I, Book II, of *Past and Present*, in
which Carlyle states his purpose and theme, and introduces his
primary source, "The Chronicle . . . of Jocelin . . . the language

of it . . . Monk-Latin. . . ." Reade's own source he identifies as "a musty chronicle, written in tolerable Latin, and in it a chapter where every sentence holds a fact. Here is told, with harsh brevity, the strange history of a pair who lived untrumpeted, and died unsung, four hundred years ago; and lie now, as unpitied, in that stern page, as fossils in a rock. Thus, living or dead, Fate is still unjust to them. For if I can but show you what lies below that dry chronicler's words, methinks you will correct the indifference of centuries, and give those two sore-tried souls a place in your heart—for a day."

In context these lines suggest that Reade intended, at the very outset, to invite comparison with Carlyle; that, with due allowance for the difference in medium, he intended to do for Erasmus' *Compendium* what Carlyle had done for Jocelin's *Chronicle;* that, in short, he intended his novel to be a fictional answer to Book II of *Past and Present*.

Yet these intentions did not cause Reade to alter his usual matter-of-fact procedures, which, in this instance, were much simplified by the fact that the *Compendium* provided him with not only his theme and the germinal outlines of his leading characters, but also with a plot that anticipated the narrative pattern on which, with one exception, he based every single one of his novels: "the simple basic theme of lovers parted to be reunited." [7] And while Reade did vary this pattern, in line with the *Compendium,* by reuniting the two lovers in religion and good works rather than in marriage, this variation affects only the later chapters of the novel. Up to the time that Gerard returns as Father Clement "the essential narrative pattern is," as Professor Edmund Morrison has noted, "identical with that of *A Simpleton* . . . or practically any of Reade's works." [8]

Moreover Reade filled in, upholstered, and developed this pattern according to his usual formulas. Gerard's two villainous brothers, for instance, would have been completely at home on the Adelphi stage, as would Ghysbrecht, the villainous burgomaster— for the very good reason that they are refurbished versions of Reade's own stage villains, tricked out in elaborate medieval disʹ guises. Nor are the other supporting characters much more original, or effective. Although Reade does endow Gerard's mother with realistic traits (much like those of Gatty's mother in *Christie Johnstone*) these traits have no more effect on the dramatic action than the comparable traits of Martin, the old soldier, or those of

Denys, the Burgundian. Just as Gerard's mother is, dramatically, the loving but querulous mother, so Martin is "the old soldier," and Denys is "the true comrade," who, for all his addiction to women, wine, and profanity, is loyal, and good, and sweet.

The most effective of the minor characters are those whom Gerard encounters on the way to Rome and in Rome itself. The effect of these characters, who are really not so much characters as they are portraits or sketches, is something like that of the human figures in Breugel's paintings—an effect which may in part be accounted for by Reade's having used the plates in his medieval source books much as he used the illustrations in contemporary newspapers. "His account of a troop of Bohemians," Professor Turner has demonstrated, "is an exact description of a plate in Michel and Fournier . . . entitled 'Troupe de Bohemiens en Voyage' . . . after a print by the celebrated French artist Callot."[9] And his account of "the same group of Bohemians . . . this time encamped," Turner shows, "is but a description of a second plate after a print by Callot." [10]

The world of the novel is therefore the medieval world of Kean's melodramatic stage—a world of medieval props and stage settings filled with typed characters, lost wills, and forged letters designed to separate the hero from the heroine, and to subject him to the general evils of medieval life as well as those peculiar to the separation of true lovers. And since these general and specific evils were, as Reade conceived of them, much like those to which his contemporary Resourceful Heroes had been subjected, he apparently saw no reason why his medieval hero should not be much like his contemporary heroes, his heroine much like his contemporary heroines. In any case Margaret may be described as another Julia-type heroine, Gerard as another Resourceful Hero— a Readian superman whose anti-Carlylean heroics and romantic sufferings (throughout the first two-thirds of the novel) represent a medieval variation on those of his nineteenth century predecessor, Will Fielding.

And while Gerard must be acknowledged to be a more complex superman than Will, embodying more seemingly antithetical virtues (manly courage combined with feminine sensibility, religious faith with Baconian resourcefulness, Dutch practicality with Reade's own artistic percipience, moral purity with sexual passion) these extra virtues do not make him more convincing. If he is a more flexible puppet, with more heroic and romantic strings for Reade to pull, the pullings themselves are still obvious, still conventionally melodramatic in their effects—as, for instance, when Gerard, in the climactic passages following the false report of Margaret's death, first succumbs to brain fever, then becomes debauched, and finally attempts suicide—to be providentially rescued, reconverted, and transformed into Father Clement.

IV

Having effected the transformation, however, Reade was in an ideal position to develop his newly reborn and renamed hero along less conventional and more directly autobiographical lines. For he too had felt the cruel claw of celibacy, which by his own account had been tearing at his vitals since the death of his Scottish wife. As late as 1876 he wrote in one of his Notebooks: "In my medieval romance *The Cloister and the Hearth* I use this expression celibacy of the clergy, an invention truly devilish. A French critic is surprised at this violence in me since the rest of my work in general deals benevolently and benignly with Pope, Priests, Convents, and the unreformed Church in general. . . . The opinion I uttered in 1860 was even then twenty years old in me: it is now thirty-six." [11]

These are strong words, representing strong feelings, and it is these feelings, infused into Father Clement, which now and again give his outwardly melodramatic words and actions an intensity that is genuinely expressive. The sexual dreams and fantasies he experiences while in the hermit's cave, for example, are not merely convincing dramatically, but illuminating thematically, since they at least begin to reveal the unconscious sexual impulses that underlie Gerard's outward religiosity: "Awake he could pray and praise and worship God; he was master of his thoughts. But, if he closed his eyes in sleep, Margaret, or Satan in her shape, beset him a seeming angel of light . . . for she came glowing with two beauties never before united, an angel's radiance and a woman's blushes . . . awake he was Clement the hermit, risen from unearthly visions of the night, as dangerous as they were sweet; asleep he was Gerard Eliasson, the happy husband. . . ." [12]

Further than this, however, Reade could not go. Once Margaret herself appears in the flesh—to present Clement-Gerard with his child, and to restore him, as Vicar of Gouda, to his friends and family—Reade sets about dissolving the sexual conflict between the man and the priest into a conventionally pure conflict between the rigors of the cloister and the comfort of the hearth:

Their general tenor was now peace, piety, the mild content that lasts, not the fierce bliss ever on tiptoe to depart, and above all, Christian charity.

On this sacred ground these two true lovers met with an uniformity and a kindness of sentiment which went far to soothe the wound in their own hearts. To pity the same bereaved; to hunt in couples all the ills in Gouda, and contrive and scheme together to remedy all that were remediable; to use the rare insight into troubled hearts which their own troubles had given them, and use it to make others happier than themselves, this was their daily practice. And in this blessed cause their passion for one another cooled a little, but their affection increased. From the time Margaret entered heart and soul into Gerard's pious charities, that affection purged itself of all mortal dross. And as it had now long outlived scandal and misapprehension, one would have thought that so bright an example of pure self-denying affection was to remain long before the world to show men how nearly religious faith, even when not quite reasonable, and religious charity, which is always reasonable, could raise two true lovers' hearts to the loving hearts of the angels of heaven. But the great Disposer of events ordered otherwise.[13]

Yet if these efforts to purify Gerard and Margaret are sincere—as they seem to be—they are still somewhat ambivalent. And the succeeding passages—in which Reade shows their "loving hearts" to be filled with sexual passion, at the same time he declares them to be "angelic"—vaguely foreshadow Hardy's treatment of Tess in *Tess of the D'Urbervilles.* For while Clement insists on seeing Margaret as an angel, in order to avoid seeing her as a woman, she herself, with her dying breath, declares herself "no angel, but only a poor simple woman . . ."[14] and begs that he will continue to keep her eyes and lips before him after her death—whereupon he professes his love for her, not as a priest, but as a lover:

"So then the eyes that now can scarce see thee, they are so troubled by the pest, and the lips that shall not touch thee to taint thee, will still be before thee, as they were when we were young, and thou didst love me."

"When I did love thee, Margaret! Oh, never loved I thee as now."

"Hast not told me so of late."

"Alas! hath love no voice but words. I was a priest; I had charge of thy soul; the sweet offices of a pure love were lawful;

words of love imprudent at the least. But now the good fight is won, ah me! Oh, my love, if thou hast lived doubting of thy Gerard's heart, die not so: for never was woman loved so tenderly as thou this ten years past."

"Calm thyself, dear one," said the dying woman, with a heavenly smile. "I know it: only, being but a woman, I could not die happy till I had heard thee say so. Ah, I have pined ten years for those sweet words. Hast said them; and this is the happiest hour of my life. I had to die to get them; well, I grudge not the price."[15]

Seemingly there is no mistaking the implications of Margaret's words, or Gerard's. His "good fight" (the title of Reade's first version of the novel) is his fight against his sexual love for Margaret—a fight so all consuming that even after her death, when he thinks he has won, his actions belie his professions, although he insists on his own and Margaret's innocence to the end. When Father Jerome accuses him of "Dying for a woman" already dead, and declares that he had "better have yielded to it [earthly passion], and repented, than resist it while she lived, and succumb under it now, body and soul," [16] Gerard answers: "Passion there is none, but a deep affection, for which I will not blush here, since I shall not blush for it in heaven. . . . She was my good angel." [17] Nor does he blush in heaven when, following his death, the monks who undress him find "a horse-hair shirt . . . under his linen" and "under the horse-hair a long thick tress of auburn hair." [18]

Reade himself, however, comes very close to blushing—as if he knew or sensed that his efforts to transform Gerard's passion into pure affection were more titillating, not to say pornographic, than a straightforward dramatization of Gerard's "good fight." Perhaps too he somehow realized that, in purifying Gerard's fight, he had negated the deeper implications of his own struggles. In any event he did not consider *The Cloister and the Hearth* his masterpiece, and in *Griffith Gaunt* reworked the sexual aspects of the same theme, using the religiosity of his hero not to obscure but to reveal his sexual passions.

This is primarily why *Griffith Gaunt* is a good, very nearly a great novel, while *The Cloister and the Hearth,* for all its virtues and virtuosities, is little more than a Victorian bestseller—a series of picaresque adventures and anti-Carlylean heroics, plus authentic settings, combined with a romance that touches upon the evils of enforced celibacy, finally to dissolve them (via Christian charity) into a sentimental love story that, in its latter stages, is still titillating to modern readers—not merely because it throws priest and former lover together in tantalizing intimacy, but also because it reduces their sexual struggles to the pure and therefore accepted patterns of sexual renunciation symbolized by the "long thick tress of auburn hair" under "the hair-shirt."

v

Had Reade not imposed this pattern, had he not used the hairshirt to justify the tress of hair, and thus sentimentalized the connection between sex and sadism that he had begun to objectify in his treatment of Clement's hallucinations—then *The Cloister and the Hearth* would be a much better novel than it is, and the closing chapters might stand as a worthy prelude to *Griffith Gaunt*. But then—and this is perhaps the ultimate irony of Reade's career—the novel would never have achieved the popularity it did in his own time, nor would it still survive as a "classic." For the long drawn-out scenes of sexual renunciation and suffering conform in almost every particular to what Alex Comfort, in his "The Rape of Andromeda," has shown to be the archetypal pattern of modern erotic literature.

"Tatius rather than Longus," Comfort explains, "sets the key of the literary-erotic tradition of Christendom: it is with suffering, not women, that his readers are already expected to be in love. . . . The Alexandrian novel fuses the suffering hero and the suffering heroine into a combination new to literature, which is to dominate it from then on, the lovers who suffer together instead of sleeping together—for whom, in later writers, death will be the eventual orgasm. . . . By the end of the Nineteenth Century, the *motif* of shared bondage and death as a decent and more ecstatic form of coition has become completely explicit—in *Hassen*, or *Les Noyades*—and is even present in muffled form in improbable works like *The Last of the Mohicans*." [19]

Although, to Comfort, this *motif* represents attitudes which have "petrified the emotional development of an entire culture, to make Andromeda's chains more desirable than her person," he is nevertheless careful to acknowledge that a number of writers have still managed to use the *motif* creatively—among others, Shelley, whose *The Revolt of Islam* he cites as an example of a work "in which a compulsive fantasy has produced great literature." [20] **And** he might also have cited the work of Emily Bronte, whose treatment of "shared bondage and death" in *Wuthering Heights* stands in complete contrast to that of Reade in *The Cloister and the Hearth*. For Bronte, in E. M. Forster's words, uses the motif to raise "human love and hatred to such a power that their normal receptacles no longer contain them," [21] whereas Reade uses the *motif* to reduce human love and hatred to a glow of angelic affection and noble suffering commensurate with his readers' ideals—and his own.

Indeed the sufferings of Clement-Gerard, following Margaret's death, directly anticipate those of Reade, following Mrs. Seymour's death. As well they might. For Reade, it has been shown, had from the first been more in love with his celibate sufferings than with the persons of the women he loved or tried to love—his Scottish wife, Mrs. Stirling, the anonymous lady "beautiful as the dawn," and yes, even Mrs. Seymour, Reade was not looking for a flesh and blood woman, a physical wife, or at least that was not his prime desire. What he wanted, finally, was an angel on the hearth, someone who could give him the love and security he had felt as a child—at home with his mother and his sister Julia. And while no woman could fulfill these wants, Mrs. Seymour offered him a livable alternative—by giving him the love and affection and devotion of a wife while permitting him to remain emotionally celibate. That Reade lived platonically with Mrs. Seymour seems altogether unlikely, though by no means impossible; but whatever their physical relationship, he was still more in love with the sufferings he recorded in his Notebooks than with Mrs. Seymour's person.

Yet Reade's love of suffering, particularly violent suffering, was not so great but that he could at times recognize Andromeda's chains for what they were. And if it must be acknowledged that, in writing *The Cloister and the Hearth*, he sacrificed his perceptions to his ideals, to fashion a bestseller that has been mistaken for a great novel, [22] it must also be acknowledged that, in writing *Griffith Gaunt*, he remained true to his perceptions (at least throughout a major part of the work) to create a novel that has yet to achieve the recognition it deserves.

Notes

1. The Notebooks and Notecards I shall identify in Chapter VIII.
2. The late Morris L. Parrish was kind enough to permit me to consult the Reade manuscripts in his possession—the manuscripts that now form the basis of the Reade holdings in the Parrish Collection of the Princeton University Library. But I have not had an opportunity to consult the new acquisitions in the Parrish Collection, announced in Robert B. Martin's "Manuscripts and Correspondence of Charles Reade," *The Princeton University Library Chronicle* (Winter, 1959), pp. 102-103. Nor have I had an opportunity to consult the Reade manuscripts just recently acquired by the Pierpont Morgan Library. See below, pp. 347-349.
3. Thomas D. Clareson, Assistant Professor of English, The College of Wooster, Wooster, Ohio, has just recently written to inform me that members of the Reade family will make available to him family letters and papers (hitherto uncollected) for use in a new biography of Reade. Because of the critical nature of my own study I have not felt that I could, in good conscience, request aid from members of the Reade family.
4. Léone Rives's, ed., *Charles Reade, It's Never Too Late To Mend* (Toulouse, 1940), Introduction, pp. 13-14.

1. Clarence R. Decker, *The Victorian Conscience* (New York, 1952), p. 9.
2. Malcolm Elwin, *Victorian Wallflowers* (London, 1934), p. 223.
3. *Notes And Reviews By Henry James,* with a Preface by Pierre De Chaignon La Rose (Cambridge, Mass., 1921), p. 207.
4. Algernon Charles Swinburne, *Miscellanies* (London, 1886), p. 302.
5. Lewis Melville, *Victorian Novelists* (London, 1906), p. 163.
6. Rudyard Kipling, *Something of Myself For My Friends Known and Unknown* (New York, 1937), p. 245.
7. See Wayne Burns, "The Cloister and the Hearth: A Classic Reconsidered," *The Trollopian* A Journal of Victorian Fiction (Sept., 1947), pp. 71-81.
8. Hugh Walpole, "Novelists of the Seventies," in *The Eighteen Seventies,* ed. by Harley Granville-Barker (New York, 1939), pp. 34-35.
9. Malcolm Elwin, *Old Gods Falling* (New York, 1939), pp. 27-28.
10. Q. D. Leavis, *Fiction And The Reading Public* (London, 1939), pp. 156-157.

11. Julian Symons, *Thomas Carlyle The Life and Ideas of a Prophet* (London, 1952), pp. 103-104.

12. Julian Symons, *Charles Dickens* (London, 1951), p. 29 ff.

13. I am here quoting from James Wright's as yet unpublished essay: "On the Organic Relation Between Pecksniff and Chollop." Wright has developed his interpretation of *Martin Chuzzlewit* more fully in the final chapter of his unpublished doctoral thesis: "The Comic Imagination of the Young Dickens" (University of Washington, 1959).

14. William Carlos Williams, *A Beginning on the Short Story*, The Outcast Chapbooks, no. XVII (The Alicat Bookshop Press, Yonkers, New York), pp. 18-20.

15. I have criticized *Jane Eyre* more fully in my essay, "The Critical Relevance of Freudianism," *The Western Review*, (Summer, 1956), pp. 307-314.

16. See further my essay: "The Genuine and Counterfeit: A Study in Victorian and Modern Fiction," *College English* (December, 1956), pp. 143-150.

17. Charles Reade, *A Terrible Temptation*, pp. 220-221. Here and throughout the present study my references to Reade's works are to the "Grolier Edition"—unless some other edition is specified.

[NOTES TO CHAPTER I]

Emotional Development:
A Victorian Son and Lover

---

1. Goldwin Smith's remarks have been quoted and discussed by Malcolm Elwin, p. 56. To save time and space I shall not ordinarily give footnote references to well known materials contained in any of the four biographies of Reade. The present chapter is for the most part a reinterpretation of the biographical data contained in these books, due allowance of course being made for their shortcomings. The *Memoir* (1887) and John Coleman's *Charles Reade As I Knew Him* (1903) have been more or less accurately characterized by Elwin: "Coleman's elastic notions of a biographer's conscience allowed him to paraphrase Compton Reade's *Memoir* and call it Charles Reade's 'autobiography' as recounted to himself . . . Unfortunately for Coleman, the *Memoir*, whenever it strays from the quotation of documents, is itself a treacherous authority." Although Elwin's own biography (1931) is somewhat weakened by excessive distrust of the *Memoir*, his interpretation of Reade is, within its own limits, truly perceptive. Not so Rives's biography, which is mainly valuable for the new biographical data it includes. In short, the definitive biography has yet to be written.

2. W. B. Maxwell, *Time Gathered* (New York, 1938), pp. 23-27. Max-

well was the son of M. E. Braddon, to whom Reade dedicated *The Wandering Heir* as "a slight mark of respect for her private virtues and public talents." Certain passages from Maxwell's sketch reproduce his boyish reactions to Reade and the Reade household:

He wore very loose clothes by day, and they were nearly always grey in colour. During evening hours when in neat well-made dress suits of the orthodox black he seemed quite startlingly to have shrunk to half his customary size. He had a fine face, usually pale, an undeviatingly courteous manner, and a tranquil urbane voice. He did not become loud even when excited. Yet the excitement was sometimes intense. Although outwardly so quiet and undisturbed, he had roaring volcanic fires within. He burned with generous angers and indignations. Injustice was for him the unforgivable sin. He made himself the champion of the downtrodden, the eager fighter of protracted battles, no matter at what odds, on behalf of the weak if he believed they were suffering oppression at the hands of the powerful. Once he made a tremendous outcry, when he thought that he himself was going to be "put upon" by governmental authorities. His house at Knightsbridge was menaced with compulsory purchase and demolition in some local improvement scheme. "Never," said Charles Reade in a quiet but far-reaching voice, and he put up a great hoarding at the front of his house, calling public attention to it as "Naboth's Vineyard" . . . "The Home of Charles Reade," and so on. The scare passed, the house remained. Only now, so many years later, is it about to come down.

A plaque indicates its position, close to the hotel, one of the row of small residences backing upon Hyde Park. In the days of which I speak it offered many attractions to the young. A long narrow garden behind it ran to the very edge of the Park, and at the end had an erection that was summer-house below and platform or terrace above. Seated on this platform, we watched, round-eyed and admiring, as if in a large private box at a theatre, the pageant of Hyde Park in Fashion's brightest hour . . .

In the house, where Mr. Reade gave us a munificent high tea, we would always find things worthy of attention—delightful unexpected things sometimes, as for instance notably a small antelope or gazelle. I cannot remember the gazelle ever going into the garden, but it wandered freely from floor to floor and room to room indoors. It was a gentle tender-eyed creature that made one sorry for it . . .

As well as his crusades he had welfare movements, social innovation plans, and even fads, about which he would be quite hot and eager while their novelty lasted. One of these fads was ambidexterity . . . He begged us, for his sake, to attempt a restoration of skill in our left hands. We were so fond of him that we tried hard, and honestly pursued the exercise. But it was most wearisome. Moreover, the success we met with was small. I did as a supreme effort write a letter to him with my left hand, and he was highly gratified . . .

3. Compton Reade, "Charles Reade," *Contemporary Review*, XLV (1884), p. 707.

4. Quoted and identified by Rives, p. 35.

5. Cf. Elwin, p. 20. *The Diary* seems to have been lost or destroyed. When I refer to it I am actually speaking of the excerpts included in the *Memoir*.

6. George Orwell, "Such, Such Were the Joys," *Partisan Review* (September-October, 1952), pp. 505-545. Orwell's analysis of his own school-boy sufferings is in many ways a commentary on what Reade must have gone through at Rose Hill.

7. See *It Is Never Too Late To Mend* I, p. 362; *Memoir*, p. 42; Rives, pp. 29-34.

8. Ralph Straus, *Sala* (London, 1942), pp. 27-28.

9. Léone Rives (p. 20) describes the manuscript *Dear Mother* as follows:

> Nous avons pu nous faire de Mrs. Reade une idée plus juste que celle suggérée par Compton Reade, grâce à un manuscrit presque totalement inédit, intitulé *Dear Mother*, et qui a été conservé par la famille. Il renferme des fragments de lettres de Mrs. Reade, retranscrits avec un soin religieux par l'un de ses fils, nombre de ses mots saisis au vol et pieusement recueillis. La coloration générale de sa pensée, la substance intime de son moi réel sont comme cristallisées entre les feuillets de ce recueil. On y trouve des Poémes d'elle, ses Méditations sur la Grâce divine, la Foi, la Prédestination, la Prière, les Textes Bibliques; ses réflexions sur L'Inde, son mari, ses enfants, ses amis . . . Ce manuscrit est aujourd'hui en la possession de Mr. E. B. Reade, Streatham, Londres, qui a bien voulu nous le communiquer.

My own references are to Rives's excerpts from the manuscript.

10. The authors of the *Memoir* drew such a thick veil around the tension between Reade and his father that it is impossible to speak with certainty about their early relationships. Possibly the latent hostility was exacerbated and brought to the surface by Reade's long stay at home following his return from the schools of Mr. Slatter (1823-27) and Mr. Hearn (1827-29). The *D.N.B.* states that Reade was at home with his father from 1829 to 1831, during which time he "pursued unaided a systematic course of study."

11. J. W. Mackail, *The Life of William Morris* (Worlds Classics), p. 29. Mackail's wonderfully revealing description of Oxford in the early fifties (especially pp. 29-33) is directly applicable to Reade's Magdalen. Cf. Elwin, pp. 28-29; Goldwin Smith, *Reminescences* (New York, 1910), pp. 50-74.

12. Elwin disagrees with the present interpretation of Reade's career at Oxford. He says, ". . . Nobody who knew him [Reade] well disliked him. . . ;" that instead, Reade "was regarded with a mixture of curiosity and amusement." Elwin did not have all the facts. Reade was disliked by certain people (See Rives, p. 179). But even if one agrees that Reade was not disliked, that in reality he was usually dismissed as crazy, or at least eccentric—would that make his relationship to his college more pleasant? Cf. Elwin, pp. 58-60.

13. Reade apparently won the Vinerian in 1835 (rather than, as previously maintained, in 1842) though the Scholarship was not formally conferred upon him until February 17, 1842. In dating this and related events of Reade's college career I have followed Rives, whose account is in part based

on a manuscript "inédit et inachevé communiqué par Mr. E. B. Reade, Streatham, Londres: biographie de Charles Reade que Mr. Arthur Reade, Superintendant de l'Hôpital de Charing Cross à Londres, avait entrepris d'écrire, et qui, à peine commencée, fut interrompue par la mort."

14. Quoted by Rives, p. 41.

15. Reade also reveals his preoccupation with French violence, particularly whipping, in his letter to his mother (*Memoir*, pp. 123-4). In one passage he described a driver who indulged "in pantomimic gestures that ended in a flank all around him for his beasts." In another he noted that the French coachmen "drove horses just as Englishmen drive pigs, let the reins fall upon their backs, and laid the whip into them in forty different ways. The whip is everything with these fellows. It is never idle, always either cracking in the air or stinging the cattle."

16. Percy Allen, *The Stage Life of Mrs. Stirling* (New York: E. P. Dutton and Co.), p. 153. Some of the letters Allen quotes (pp. 128-155) are extremely interesting, particularly the undated letter (p. 136) from Reade to Mrs. Baylis in which Reade looks back on his lost love with complete detachment. The letter concludes: "Say! did I not love this woman? I am quite contented, dear Mrs. Baylis, and hope to be an artist of the pen before I die . . ."

17. Included with the Notebooks is a printed pamphlet entitled "List of Subjects Entered as headings in my various guard books and solid digests." Under "C" Reade lists "Calibani et Calibanae, or human brutes . . ." Emerson Grant Sutcliffe, in his invaluable "Charles Reade's Notebooks" (*Studies in Philology*, January, 1930) reprints the entire "List of Subjects."

[NOTES TO CHAPTER II]

Intellectual Development:
The One Road To Truth

1. Reade's biographers have had very little to say about his intellectual development, for the very good reason that little is positively known. Nevertheless it is possible, by drawing upon Reade's later writings and relating them to his "wasted youth," to reconstruct the main lines of his intellectual development. And that is what I have tried to do in the present chapter.

2. G. M. Young, "Portrait of an Age" in *Early Victorian England* vol. II (Oxford University Press, London, 1934), p. 413.

3. "The Bloomer," is included in *The Course of True Love Never Did Run Smooth*, p. 99. Though not published until 1857, "The Bloomer" was written much earlier. Elwin (pp. 88-89) suggests that it was completed as early as May, 1851.

4. See *Memoir*, pp. 313, 335.

5. See, for example, *Christie Johnstone*, pp. 127-128, 153, 178. A re-

viewer in the *North American Review* thought that Reade had "a disposition to elevate the 'lower orders' at the expense of the higher." See "Reade's Novels," *North American Review*, CXXXII (April, 1856), pp. 377-379.

6. *Memoir*, p. 2. Reade also gives a few of his own reasons in "The Bloomer," pp. 101-102.

7. Quoted by Elwin, pp. 63-64.

8. This petition is quoted at full length in the *Memoir*, pp. 148-149.

9. W. L. Courtney, "Charles Reade's Novels," *The Fortnightly Review*, 42 (1884), p. 465.

10. According to the *Memoir* (p. 85) Reade "cherished a sincere affection for Bernard Smith and . . . was positively chagrined when his friend elected to merge himself in the Church of Rome, and not only so, but to embrace Roman orders. He [Reade] always spoke of that gentleman as a brother whom he had lost by the sort of misadventure which he could neither comprehend nor quite tolerate."

11. See Elie Halévy, *The Triumph of Reform* 1830-1841 (London, 1950), p. 270-271. Halévy goes on to show how Marx parodied Ure in *The Communist Manifesto*.

12. *Christie Johnstone*, p. 75.

13. *Christie Johnstone*, pp. 74-76. Cf. James Anthony Froude, *Thomas Carlyle, A History of his life in London* (1910), I, pp. 242-248.

14. "The Rights and Wrongs of Authors," *Readiana*, pp. 232-234.

15. In *The Eighth Commandment* (p. 146) Reade defines "Cephalomant" and gives his reasons for using the word:

> To reason à priori is not in itself a disgrace to any man. It is our substitute for evidence, though a poor one. *The Cephalomant is he who opposes à priori reasoning, or mere assumption, to direct evidence, present or accessible.*
>
> I coin the word, not out of pedantry, but with a respectable motive. I have studied human nature, and observe it is as difficult to drive out a fallacy with no name in the dictionary, as it is to shovel away mephitic gas out of a mine. If, therefore, my readers will aid me to make that ugly, but useful and necessary word, current, they will be good friends to letters, and perhaps to the human mind.

16. In 1872 Augustus De Morgan (paraphrasing Hallam) observed that "Bacon has probably been more read in the last thirty years—now forty—than in the two hundred years which preceded. Augustus De Morgan, *A Budget of Paradoxes* (London, 1915), I, p. 89. See Thomas Fowler, *Bacon's Novum Organum* Oxford (1878), pp. 147-151, for a list of "the principal works of Bacon's philosophy." Fowler notes (p. 148) "how very rich the decade 1830-1840 is in works on Bacon." The Tractarian opposition to Bacon's philosophy is discussed in W. E. H. Lecky's *Rationalism in Europe* (London, 1946), I, pp. 147-148.

17. See J. A. Froude (I, 252) for a description of the intellectual climate of Oxford in the late 'thirties. Mill's influence at Oxford was at its height during the 'forties and 'fifties. See *Autobiography of John Stuart Mill* (Columbia University Press), p. 54; and Frederic Harrison, *Tennyson, Ruskin, Mill* (Macmillan, 1900), p. 297.

Reade may have encountered certain of Bentham's works in his law studies. See Mill's *Autobiography,* pp. 45-48, 80-82; cf. Charles Warren Everett, *The Education of Jeremy Bentham* (The Columbia University Press), pp. 32-50.

18. Lewis F. Haines, "Reade, Mill and Zola, a Study of the Character and Intention of Charles Reade's Realistic Method," *Studies in Philology,* XL (July, 1943), pp. 468-469.

19. *The Eighth Commandment* pp. 133-134. Reade adds a footnote "(a)" in which he explains: "Lord Bacon inculcated observation, but was a feeble observer. Solomon did not talk about it, but did it. And that is the man for my money."

20. *The Coming Man* (New York, 1878), pp. 77-79.

21. Quoted by George Henry Lewes, in *The Biographical History Of Philosophy* (New York, 1873) II, p. 431.

22. John Stuart Mill, *A System of Logic* (Longmans, Green, and Co., 1941), pp. 298, 578.

23. "Bacon's inductive philosophy," Fulton H. Anderson has explained, "can hardly be compared with that of Mill and his followers . . . Mill is an empiricist for whom the Universal is but a product of mental association. Bacon is a rationalist and a realist for whom the particulars are constituted of universal natures . . ." In defense of Bacon's method, Anderson further argues that the directions in the *Novum Organum* "include all and more than all that is to be found in Mill's five canons." But even if Anderson's comparisons are sound—and I, for one, am not convinced—there is no indication that Reade anticipated his arguments. See Fulton H. Anderson, *The Philosophy of Francis Bacon* (University of Chicago Press, 1948) pp. 300-301.

R. P. Anschutz, in his *The Philosophy of J. S. Mill* (Oxford, 1953), provides a more temperate, and to my mind, a more perspicacious treatment of the relationship between the two theories of induction.

24. A. V. Dicey, *Law and Opinion in England* (London, 1905), pp. 397-405. Dicey's analysis has been accepted and further developed by modern historians. See, for instance, G. M. Young, "Portrait of an Age," pp. 421-423.

25. These lines are from *The Advancement of Learning.* Fowler discusses Bacon's religious opinions in his *Bacon's Novum Organum,* pp. 43-53.

26. Reade's biographers have not discussed Reade's Benthamism, and literary historians have overlooked it altogether. See Granville Hicks, "The Literary Opposition to Utilitarianism," *Science and Society* (Summer, 1937). By Hicks's definition Reade was a full-fledged Benthamite, yet Hicks, failing to recognize this fact, declares (p. 454) that "Benthamism was almost without direct literary influence. Of the better known Victorian writers, Macaulay is the only one who, by any definition can be considered a Utilitarian, and Louis Cazamian, in *Le Roman Social en Angleterre,* can find only one *laissez-faire* novelist, Harriet Martineau."

Artistic Development 1835–1849:
"Fourteen Years a Student"

1. The first epigraph is from Wilkie Collins' "Dramatic Grub Street" in his *My Miscellanies* (New York, 1874), p. 360; the second is from W. H. Ainsworth's "Preface" to *Rockwood* (London, Richard Bentley, 1837).

2. Quoted by M. L. Parrish, *Wilkie Collins And Charles Reade* (London, 1940), p. 5.

3. Cf. *Peg Woffington*, p. 13.

4. Quoted by Matthew Josephson, *Victor Hugo* (New York, 1942), p. 119.

5. *The Eighth Commandment* (Boston, 1860), p. 148.

6. J. Brander Matthews, *French Dramatists of the Nineteenth Century* (New York, 1881), p. 37.

7. *The Eighth Commandment*, p. 51.

8. Allardyce Nicoll, *A History of Early Nineteenth Century Drama 1800-1850* (Cambridge, 1930), I, pp. 100-101.

9. Nicoll, *op. cit.*, I, p. 105.

10. See Ernest Bradlee Watson, *Sheridan to Robertson* (Cambridge, Massachusetts, 1926), pp. 97-134; William S. Dye, Jr. *A Study of Melodrama in England from 1800 to 1840* (State College, Pennsylvania, 1919), pp. 3-12; Ernest Reynolds, *Early Victorian Drama* (Cambridge, 1936), p. 46; and George Rowell *The Victorian Theatre A Survey* (Oxford, 1956), pp. 1-31.

11. Quoted by Nicoll, *op. cit.*, I, p. 49.

12. Gustave Garcia *The Actors' Art* (London, 1882), pp. 149, 113-114. For a revealing analysis of Nineteenth Century "Guides to the Stage" see Alan S. Downer, "Players and Painted Stage—Nineteenth Century Acting," *PMLA* (June, 1946), pp. 574-575.

13. Quoted by Nicoll, *op. cit.*, pp. 103-104. See also Augustin Filon, *The English Stage*, Translated by Frederic Whyte (New York, 1897), pp. 80-81.

14. Maurice Willson Disher, *Blood and Thunder* (London, 1949), p. 67.

15. Nicoll, *op. cit.*, I, p. 25.

16. *Ibid*, pp. 25-26.

17. Quoted by Charles E. Pearce, *Madame Vestris And Her Times* (London, n.d.), pp. 235-236.

18. Watson, *op. cit.*, p. 207. See also Clement Scott, *The Drama of Yesterday and Today* (London, 1899), I, pp. 35, 62, 119-120.

19. See Newell W. Sawyer, *The Comedy of Manners from Sheridan to Maugham* (University of Pennsylvania Press, 1931) pp. 36-63.

20. *The Eighth Commandment*, pp. 149-150.

21. Quoted by Watson, *op. cit.*, p. 274. See also Townsend Walsh, *The Career of Dion Boucicault* (New York, 1915), pp. 24-33.

22. Quoted by Nicoll, *op. cit.*, I, p. 171. See also L. H. Meeks, *Sheridan Knowles and the Theatre of His Time* (Bloomington, 1933), pp. 1-21.

23. *Notes and Reviews By Henry James*, with a Preface by Pierre De Chaignon La Rose (Cambridge, Mass., 1921), pp. 111-112.

24. Cf. William Bodham Donne, *Essays on the Drama* (London, 1858), pp. 120-155; and William Robson, *The Old Play Goer* (London, 1846), pp. 98-125.

25. Filon, *op. cit.*, p. 88.

26. *The Eighth Commandment*, p. 192.

27. *Bible Characters* (New York, 1889), pp. 6-7.

28. *Ibid*, pp. 76-78. See also Emerson Grant Sutcliffe, "Plotting in Reade's Novels," *PMLA* (September, 1932), pp. 834-836.

29. See *The Eighth Commandment*, pp. 274-275; and *Readiana*, p. 409.

30. *The Eighth Commandment*, p. 203.

31. *A Terrible Temptation*, p. 214. See also *Readiana*, p. 291, and Emerson Grant Sutcliffe, "Charles Reade's Notebooks," *SP* (January, 1930), pp. 102-103.

32. Edmund Ahlers, *Charles Reades Romane und ihr Verhältnis zu ihren literarischen Vorbildern* (Münster, 1914), pp. 24, 45, 87, and *passim*.

33. Walter C. Phillips, *Dickens, Reade, and Collins Sensation Novelists* (Columbia University Press, 1919), p. 136.

34. *The Journal of Sir Walter Scott 1825-1832* (Edinburgh, 1891), pp. 274-275.

35. *It Is Never Too Late To Mend* I, p. 283.

36. *Readiana*, p. 409.

37. *The Eighth Commandment*, pp. 155-156.

38. *Readiana*, p. 169.

39. *The Eighth Commandment*, p. 156.

40. Myron F. Brightfield, *Theodore Hook And His Novels* (Harvard University Press, 1928), p. 296.

41. Thomas Waters, *Recollections of a Policeman* (London, 1852), p. 3.

[NOTES TO CHAPTER IV]

Artistic Development 1849—1852:

Melodrama With a Difference

1. The first epigraph is from "The Rights and Wrongs of Authors" *Readiana*, pp. 217, 223-224; the second is from Watson's *Sheridan to Robertson*, p. 244.

2. "Reade's Luck" in *Memoir*, p. 320.

3. The play itself I have consulted in the copies described in M. L. Parrish, *op. cit.*, pp. 167-169. Donald Hutchens MacMahon summarizes the

play and discusses it at length in his *Charles Reade as a Dramatist.* (Unpublished doctoral thesis, Cornell University, 1935), pp. 26-37.

4. *The Lost Husband* (London, Thomas Hailes Lacy, n.d.), p. 36. This play too MacMahon discusses at length (pp. 48-57).

5. *Memoir,* p. 186.

6. Quoted by Percy Allen, *The Stage Life of Mrs. Stirling* (New York, n.d.), pp. 131-132.

7. MacMahon, *op. cit.,* p. 49.

8. This entry, and that of June 10, which follows, appear in the *Memoir,* pp. 188-191.

9. Arnold Taylor's account of the collaboration appears in the *Memoir,* pp. 190-193. See also Winton Tolles, *Tom Taylor and the Victorian Drama* (New York, 1940), pp. 82-113.

10. Coleman, *op. cit.,* pp. 94-95.

11. Quoted by Percy Allen, *op. cit.,* p. 142.

12. Quoted by Rives, *op. cit.,* p. 62.

13. Sir Philip Hendy, "Bourgeois Art" *Britain To-Day* (January, 1952), p. 14.

14. *Ibid,* pp. 11-14.

15. Quoted by Hendy, *op. cit.,* p. 11.

16. From Holman Hunt's conclusion to his *Pre-Raphaelitism and the Pre-Raphaelite Brotherhood,* included in D. S. R. Welland, *The Pre-Raphaelites in Literature and Art* (London, 1953), pp. 65-66.

17. *Ibid,* pp. 66-67.

18. William Gaunt, *The Pre-Raphaelite Tragedy* (New York, 1942), pp. 26-27. For a more complete and more fully documented study of this and other phases of Pre-Raphaelitism (as they relate to fiction) see my "Pre-Raphaelitism in Charles Reade's Early Fiction" *PMLA* (December, 1945), pp. 1149-1164.

19. D. S. R. Welland, *op. cit.,* p. 36.

20. These and the following lines of Dickens' criticism are from his "Old Lamps For New Ones," included in *Miscellaneous Papers Plays and Poems* (Gadshill Edition) I, pp. 255-259.

21. This and the following points having to do with Reade's criticism of the *PRB* I have documented and discussed in my "Pre-Raphaelitism in Charles Reade's Early Fiction."

22. This "Preface" is quoted in full by John William Cole, *The Life and Times of Charles Kean* (London, 1859) II, 184-188.

23. Cole, *op. cit.,* II, p. 65.

24. *Ibid,* II, p. 65.

25. *Ibid,* II, p. 224.

26. Maurice Willson Disher, *Blood and Thunder* (London, 1949), pp. 234-235.

27. Watson, *op. cit.,* p. 242.

28. *Christie Johnstone,* p. 180.

29. Edward Gordon Craig, *Ellen Terry And Her Secret Self* (London, 1931), p. 36.

30. *Christie Johnstone,* p. 55.

31. Coleman, *op. cit.,* pp. 118-119.

32. MacMahon, *op. cit.,* pp. 130-131.

33. *Gold* (Lacy's Acting Edition, No. 152) p. 12.

34. *Gold*, p. 35. Cf. William Howitt, *Land, Labour, and Gold* (Boston, 1855) I, p. 185.

35. *Gold*, p. 37. Cf. Godfrey Charles Mundy, *Our Antipodes* (London, 1852).

36. *Gold*, p. 33.

37. *Gold*, p. 33.

38. *Gold*, pp. 39-40.

39. *Gold*, p. 40. Cf. Newell W. Sawyer, *op. cit.*, p. 25.

40. William Bodham Donne, *Essays on the Drama* (London, 1858), p. 131.

[NOTES TO CHAPTER V]

Fictional Beginnings:
Peg Woffington and *Christie Johnstone*

---

1. See *Memoir*, p. 192 (Arnold Taylor's letter to Compton Reade).

2. Cf. *Peg Woffington*, pp. 39-40, with J. Fitzgerald Molloy, *Peg Woffington And The Period She Lived In* (New York, 1893) I, pp. 12-62, and Augustin Daly, *Woffington* (Troy, N.Y., 1891), p. 20.

3. Cf. *Peg Woffington*, p. 17, with Daly, *op. cit.*, p. 24.

4. In 1872 or thereabouts a biographer or would-be biographer of Peg Woffington apparently applied to Reade for help. Reade's answering letter, now in the Henry E. Huntington Library, reads as follows:

> 2 Albert Terrace
> Knightsbridge
> Jan 2

Dear Sir

"Peg Woffington"

1 A flimsy notice in "Galts lives of the players" without authorities—as usual with bad writers

2 Scattered notices of a mean, egotistical, and [word illegible] character in Tate Wilkinson's Memoirs, and George Ann Bellamy's

3 A facsimile letter published.

4 A word on her in Boswell's Life of Johnson

At Garrick Club, Pictures, some of which must [or "might?"] be false as the faces are so unlike each other

A reliable engraving of the actress in one of Shakespeare's characters, and I *think* her picture as Sir Harry Wildair.

At this distance of time I could not say how much of my story is imaginary. However I think it is true that she ended her days religious

She had certain good qualities Educated her Sister in a French convent and married her [word illegible] to Lord Cholmondeley I believe both she and her Sister Lady Cholmondeley [2 words illegible] at Twickenham. to which place I [recommend?] a pilgrimage

I believe these hints are all I can give you However by [following them?] up and [going?] a little into the play-bills, and the dramatic criticism of the day you may produce something less unworthy of the subject than false contemptible [libel?]

Yrs truly
Charles Reade

I forget the names of the [word illegible] dramatic censors at that early date. You can learn it at the British Museum.

The Gentleman's Magazine 1740-65
and the Annual Register 1750-65

may contain a hint or two. So may the numerous prints of that period which [now?] exist [only?] in the [Museum?] You should also look into old play-bills

[last eight or nine words illegible]

[With a little more study the words I have designated "illegible" might be deciphered.]

5. Cf. Janet Camden Lucey, *Lovely Peggy The Life and Times of Margaret Woffington* (London, 1952), pp. xi-xiii, and *passim*. According to Lucey, "Reade's novel is the finest piece of publicity Peg Woffington ever had after her death . . . But it is no more true of her than the 1760 *Memoires*."

6. Wilbur L. Cross *The Development of the English Novel* (New York, 1928), p. 213.

7. See further my "Pre-Raphaelitism in Charles Reade's Early Fiction" *PMLA* (December, 1945), pp. 1149-1164.

8. This "Auto-Criticism" is reproduced in full in the *Memoir*, pp. 228-233.

9. Emerson Grant Sutcliffe, "The Stage in Reade's Novels" *SP* (October, 1930), p. 655.

10. *Christie Johnstone*, p. 24.

11. *Ibid*, p. 29.

12. *Ibid*, p. 16.

13. *Ibid*, p. 181.

14. *Ibid*, pp. 60-62.

The Beginnings of the Great System:
Gold in Fictional Disguise

1. These and other references having to do with *Uncle Tom's Cabin* are fully documented in Wayne Burns and Emerson Grant Sutcliffe, "*Uncle Tom* and Charles Reade," *American Literature* (January, 1946), pp. 334-347.

2. Quoted by Grace Edith Maclean, *Uncle Tom's Cabin in Germany* (New York, 1910), p. 19

3. Winton Tolles, *Tom Taylor and the Victorian Drama* (New York, 1940), p. 95.

4. According to Michael Sadleir, "Reade replied to certain charges brought against the novel [*It Is Never Too Late To Mend*] in a pamphlet but I cannot determine the details of its title and appearance." Michael Sadleir, *Excursions in Victorian Bibliography* (London, 1922), p. 161. Although no copy of this pamphlet, or "Key," has yet been discovered, one of Reade's huge Notecards is labelled "Clavis ad sera nunquam," another "Key to Its Never Too Late To Mend." This latter card duplicates the first, and is apparently the work of a copyist.

Unfortunately this "Key," which would run to several pages in print, cannot be reproduced here. The most that can be said, at the moment, is that it does follow the general pattern of Mrs. Stowe's *Key*—although the great majority of the entries date from the late 'fifties or early 'sixties. (On this last point, as it relates to Mrs. Stowe's *Key*, cf. Wayne Burns and Emerson Grant Sutcliffe, *op. cit.*, p. 346.)

5. Quoted by Percy Allen, *op. cit.*, p. 154.

6. *It Is Never Too Late To Mend*, I, pp. 61-63.

7. The manuscript is the "Original Autograph Manuscript of 'Gold, a Drama'; 86 pp. . . .," as described in Catalogue 132 issued by the Carnegie Book Shop. The Carnegie Book Shop was good enough to permit me to consult this manuscript.

8. *It Is Never Too Late To Mend*, I, p. 45.

9. *Ibid*, I, p. 45.

10. *Ibid*, I, p. 64.

11. *Ibid*, I, p. 64.

12. *Ibid*, I, p. 66.

13. Montagn Frank Modder, *The Jew in the Literature of England* (Philadelphia, 1939), pp. 230-231. Cf. Rabbi David Philipson, *The Jew in English Fiction* (Cincinnati, 1903), pp. 18; 34-53; 77-78; 90-96; 108-124; 136-160.

14. *Our Antipodes* (London, 1852) 3 vols. I have given exact page references in the text in an effort to indicate the sequential pattern of the factual passages in Mundy.

15. *It Is Never Too Late To Mend,* I, pp. 463-465.
16. *Ibid,* II, pp. 309-310.
17. For a more thorough and more fully documented discussion of the works of these and other writers, as their works relate to Reade's "Jacky," see my unpublished doctoral thesis: Wayne Burns, *Charles Reade: The Making of a Social Novelist* (Cornell, 1947), pp. 184-199.
18. Quoted in *Memoir,* p. 326.
19. *It Is Never Too Late To Mend,* II, p. 136.
20. See Carl R. Woodring, "Charles Reade's Debt to William Howitt," *Nineteenth-Century Fiction* (June, 1950), pp. 39-46. In this article Professor Woodring demonstrates the full extent of Reade's indebtedness to Howitt.
21. Quoted by Woodring, *op. cit.,* pp. 41-42.
22. Cf. *It Is Never Too Late To Mend,* I, pp. 478-484, with Peter Cuningham, *Two Years in New South Wales* (London, 1827), I, pp. 253 ff.
23. This letter to Fields, and those that follow, in this and succeeding chapters, comprise the Reade-Fields correspondence now in The Henry E. Huntington Library. Annie Fields quoted from a number of these letters in her "An Acquaintance with Charles Reade," *The Century Magazine* (XXIX, 1884), pp. 72-77; and James C. Austin has reproduced a few others in his *Fields of "The Atlantic Monthly"* (The Huntington Library, San Marino, California, 1953), pp. 386-394. But since the great majority of the letters I have quoted are available only in manuscript, I shall not attempt to footnote individual letters. When the contents of a letter do not serve to identify it I shall specify dates or other distinguishing features.
24. *Notes and Reviews by Henry James, op. cit.,* pp. 62-63.
25. Susanne Howe, *Novels of Empire* (New York, 1949), p. 139.

[NOTES TO CHAPTER VII]

It Is Never Too Late To Mend:
"The Immortal Part of the Work"

1. The letters to Fields are in the Huntington Collection; the letter to an unidentified reader is reproduced in full in the *Memoir,* p. 244.
2. Quoted in "Facts Must Be Faced," *Readiana,* p. 437.
3. "A Terrible Temptation," in *Readiana,* p. 388.
4. For a more complete and more fully documented study of prisons and prisoners in relation to the genesis of Reade's chapters see my unpublished thesis, *op. cit.,* pp. 216-255.
5. See Hepworth Dixon, *The London Prisons* (London, 1850), pp. 391-412.
6. See "Extracts from various Notices of the Work," quoted on the last

page of Kingsmill. Joseph Kingsmill, *Chapters on Prisons and Prisoners* (London, 1852).

7. "The Autobiography of a Thief," p. 4, Reade's opening statement seems to derive from the following passage in Kingsley's *Yeast* (New York, 1885), pp. 20-21:

"Then let the reader believe, that whatsoever is commonplace in my story is my own invention. Whatsoever may seem extravagant or startling is most likely to be historic fact . . ."

8. *It Is Never Too Late To Mend*, II, pp. 75-78.

9. *It Is Never Too Late To Mend*, I, pp. 216-219.

10. *It Is Never Too Late To Mend*, I, pp. 537-538.

11. See the epigraph to the present chapter. This is one of the letters reproduced in Annie Fields, "Charles Reade," *The Century Magazine* (November, 1884), p. 70.

12. Algernon Charles Swinburne, *Miscellanies* (London, 1886), p. 273.

13. *Memoir*, p. 201.

14. "A Terrible Temptation," *Readiana*, pp. 388-389.

15. For a full and accurate description of the "Pennsylvania system" see William Parker Foulke, *Remarks on Cellular Separation* (Philadelphia, 1861). Foulke (pp. 108-112) reprints a letter in which William Peter endeavors to refute Dickens' charges against "the system."

16. Emerson Grant Sutcliffe, "Charles Reade's Notebooks," p. 82.

17. *It Is Never Too Late To Mend*, I, p. 307.

18. *Ibid*, I, p. 286.

19. Cf. Dixon, *op. cit.*, pp. 391-394 with *It Is Never Too Late To Mend*, I, pp. 128-131.

20. *It Is Never Too Late To Mend*, I, pp. 182-183.

21. *Ibid*, I, p. 240.

22. *Ibid*, I, pp. 242-243.

23. *Ibid*, I, p. 253.

24. This passage appears in *It Is Never Too Late To Mend* (Boston, Ticknor And Fields, 1856) II, pp. 421-422. Reade later deleted this passage, along with others in a similar vein (II, pp. 415-423). See *Memoir*, pp. 244 and 365.

25. Cf. Fitzjames Stephen, "The License of Modern Novelists" (*The Edinburgh Review*, CVI, 1857), pp. 136-143.

26. *It Is Never Too Late To Mend*, I, pp. 298-299.

27. In "Our Dark Places," for instance, Reade opened his second letter with the statement: "In England Justice is the daughter of Publicity." See *Readiana*, p. 155. Reade also repeated the statement in *Hard Cash*, III, p. 217, and on the Notecards, under the heading *Arundiniana*. See Douglas Bankson, "Charles Reade's Manuscript Notecards for *Hard Cash*" (unpublished doctoral thesis, University of Washington, 1954), p. 54.

28. *The Times*, September, 12, 1853.

29. See John Hollingshead, *My Lifetime* (London, 1895), I, p. 167; also Henry Morley, *The Journal of a London Playgoer* (London, 1866), pp. 380-381. For an informed and thorough analysis of "the connexion between spectacular realism and serious social purpose in Reade's work," see Sheila M.

Smith, "Realism in the Drama of Charles Reade," *English* (XII), pp. 94-100. In this article Sheila M. Smith discusses *It's Never Too Late To Mend* at some length, comparing its realism with that of Reade's later plays, including *Free Labour, Foul Play*, and *Love and Money*.

30. Samuel Warren, *Miscellanies, Critical, Imaginative, and Juridical* (Edinburgh and London, 1855), I, p. 413.

[NOTES TO CHAPTER VIII]

The System Systematized

1. See Stephen, *op. cit.*, pp. 136-143. Reade denied Stephen's charges in a letter (reprinted in *Readiana*, p. 423) to *The Saturday Review*, whose editor (or editors) had written a long article echoing Stephen's accusations in *The Edinburgh Review*. See also Goldwin Smith, "Polemical and Propagandist Novels," *Literature*, (February 9, 1889), p. 279.

2. Q. D. Leavis, *Fiction and the Reading Public* (London, 1939), p. 156.

3. See Nathaniel Hawthorne, *The English Notebooks*, ed. Randall Stewart (London, 1941), p. 646.

4. *Memories of Old Friends* ("being extracts from the Journals and Letters of Caroline Fox"), ed. Horace N. Pym (London, 1882), p. 310.

5. Apparently the novel went through five editions in England alone during the years 1856-1857, and it seems to have been equally popular in the United States. Cf. *Memoir*, p. 243; also Rives, *op. cit.*, p. 480.

6. See *Memoir*, pp. 250-253.

7. According to Wilkie Collins (*My Miscellanies, op. cit.*, p. 140) Reade was the first "English writer with a literary position to write for the 'Unknown Public' of 'The Penny Weeklies.'" In this statement Collins is referring to Reade's serialization of *White Lies* in *The London Journal*.

8. Elwin, p. 137.

9. Quoted by Elwin, p. 137.

10. See Elwin, pp. 123-126.

11. *The Eighth Commandment*, p. 247.

12. *Ibid*, p. 126.

13. *Ibid*, pp. 126-127.

14. *Ibid.*, p. 128.

15. *Ibid.*, p. 128.

16. *Ibid.*, p. 125.

17. *Ibid.*, p. 122.

18. Quoted in *Memoir*, p. 275.

19. This is the famous "Century List," reprinted by Annie Fields, *op. cit.*,

and reproduced by Albert Morton Turner, in his *The Making of "The Cloister and the Hearth"* (Chicago, 1938), pp. 5-6. Turner (p. 6) declares that his study of this list "forms the base of the present book."

20. Quoted in *Memoir*, p. 285. See also *Memoir*, p. 306. Turner (p. 4) declared that "The books and cards used in the preparation of *The Cloister and the Hearth* are not known to exist . . ." The Notecards Turner here refers to are now in my personal possession—as are all of Reade's other Notecards.

21. Reade had also applied, some ten days earlier, to Kinahan Cornwallis of the *New York Herald*. Reade's letter of July 14, 1860 to Cornwallis (quoted by Morrison, *op. cit.*, p. 84) reads in part:

> "I should take it very kindly if you would buy me any copies (I don't care if the collection should grow to a bushel or a sack) of any American papers containing characteristic matter—melodramas, trials, anything spicy and more fully reported than in the Weekly Tribune which I take in. Don't be afraid to lay out money for me in this way. . . ."

22. Quoted in my "More Reade Notebooks," *SP* (October, 1945), pp. 834-836. In this article I have reproduced other selections from this Notebook, along with selections from the three other Parrish Notebooks.

23. *Ibid.*, pp. 837-838.

24. Many of the Notebook entries I have quoted have been previously quoted, in other connections, by Sutcliffe, Elwin, or Rives. The present entry, for instance, Sutcliffe reproduces in part in his "Charles Reade's Notebooks," pp. 78-79.

The thirty-two Notebooks Professor Sutcliffe describes in his "Charles Reade's Notebooks" Elwin has labelled the "London Library Collection." The forty-five (actually forty-six) other Notebooks Michael Sadleir presented to the London Library in 1940 Elwin has labelled the Michael Sadleir Collection. This collection Elwin himself described in a "Schedule" now listed with the Notebooks in The London Library. In matters of numbering and nomenclature I have followed Elwin's "Schedule," since the discrepancy between his count of forty-five Notebooks and my count of forty-six is of no great consequence.

The seventy-seven (or seventy-eight) Notebooks now in the London Library, together with the four Parrish Notebooks (described in my "More Reade Notebooks") now in the Princeton Library, constitute the eighty-one (or eighty-two) Notebooks now available to scholars. Other Notebooks which Reade himself refers to have apparently been lost or destroyed. See below, pp. 346-349.

25. "Charles Reade's Notebooks," p. 77.

26. *Ibid.*, p. 77.

27. Quoted in part in "Charles Reade's Notebooks," p. 77.

28. "Charles Reade's Notebooks," p. 79.

29. *Ibid.*, p. 78.

30. These indexed headings, from "A" to "Z," are reproduced in Sutcliffe's "Charles Reade's Notebooks," pp. 106-109.

31. Pasted in at the end of the Notebook entitled "Humores Diei" is an

article describing how (in Boston) even ladies go to the stockyards to drink blood.

32. In the Notebook labelled "Digest 4 Materials for Fiction," p. 44.

33. In the Notebook labelled "Digest 4 Materials for Fiction," p. 43.

34. In the Notebook labelled "2 Sapientia Gentium," p. 126.

35. *Ibid.*, p. 69.

36. In the Notebook labelled "Viri feminaeque juventes," p. 17.

37. *Ibid.*, p. 50.

38. Reade continued to correspond with Nethercote (sometimes spelled "Nethercoat"). A letter in my own collection of *Readiana* reads (in part) as follows:

> 6 Bolton Row
> Mayfair
> Dec 12 [1860?]

Dear Nethercote

I am just profiting by your two missives, having returned last night from a visit to a sick relation . . . I am very glad to have your approbation of my book, as, I know, it is not so very easily obtained by works of Fiction. . . .

So Fred has disappeared from history. This is too bad. People should consider the writer of Fiction more than they do: and not go and close an interesting career at the first act. . . ."

[NOTES TO CHAPTER IX]

Hard Cash:
"Uncomparably My Best Production"

1. "Facts Must Be Faced," in *Readiana*, p. 437.

2. See A. V. Dicey, *Law And Public Opinion in England* (London, 1905), pp. 187-188.

3. Emerson Grant Sutcliffe, "*Foemina Vera* in Charles Reade's Novels," *PMLA* (December, 1931), p. 1269.

4. *Hard Cash*, II, p. 225. Goldwin Smith, apparently sensing Reade's "terror of a madhouse," suggested, in a violent critique of Reade's works that "Mr. Rolfe, previously identified with Mr. Reade, may perhaps end his days in a madhouse." See "A Terrible Temptation," in *Readiana*, p. 398.

5. I am here quoting Morrison, who shows that the case of Leech is the first of the two cases to which Reade is referring in his letter to *The Times* (August 26, 1871) entitled "Facts Must Be Faced" (reprinted in *Readiana*, p. 437). For a thorough and perceptive discussion of Reade's indebtedness to *The Times* in matters relating to asylums see Edmund Mor-

rison's unpublished thesis: *Charles Reade and His Novels* (University of California, 1940), pp. 190-197.

6. Here and throughout the remainder of this paragraph I am quoting from Reade's own account of the Fletcher Case, reprinted in *Readiana,* pp. 151-168, under the title "Our Dark Places."

7. Quoted in *Memoir,* pp. 287-288.

8. This advice is included in a letter in the Reade Collection of the Pierpont Morgan Library.

9. This letter is included in the Reade Collection of the Yale Library.

10. The Notebook labelled "No 9 Folio," p. 1b. See "Charles Reade's Notebooks," p. 81.

11. Quoted in *Memoir,* p. 309.

12. See Elwin, pp. 169-170.

13. The Reade Collection of the Yale Library includes a reprint of a paper by George Blumer, M.D., entitled "Notes On the Physicians of Fiction"

I: Doctor Sampson of Charles Reade's "Hard Cash"

According to a footnote on the title page of this paper it was "read before the Beaumont Medical Club, October 12, 1923."

The paper itself constitutes a summary of Dr. Samuel Dickson's medical theories and writings, together with a brief discussion of his reputation and influence.

Douglas Bankson's study of the Notecards for *Hard Cash* includes a most valuable discussion of the use Reade made of Dickson's words, notes, and published writings in presenting Dr. Sampson in *Hard Cash.* See Douglas Bankson, "Charles Reade's Manuscript Notecards for *Hard Cash,*" unpublished thesis (University of Washington, 1954), pp. 255-264.

14. Quoted by Elwin, pp. 168-169.

15. Douglas Bankson, *op. cit.,* p. iii.

16. *Ibid.,* p. iii.

17. Quoted in *Memoir,* pp. 309-310. A letter in my personal collection of *Readiana* indicates that Dickson, or Mrs. Dickson, or both Dickson and Mrs. Dickson, objected to certain features of Dr. Sampson. On May 5 [1863?] Reade wrote:

Dear Dickson,

The enclosed may go a little way to show you what a fool I should be to alter my work for any individual's peevish objections. What seems a blot to one is a gem to another. You see my caricature has won you an admirer in the depths of Wales, or at all events paved the way for you, who need no help from me when you can once *get a hearing;* which you CAN'T by fair means; so it must be done by foul. I can't afford to send William my copy of "Physic and its phases" having marked it all over. Will you kindly send him one if you can spare it I am [one word illegible] ashamed to ask it.

His address is

W B Reade Esq

Tenby

South Wales

I am

Yours Very Sincerely

Charles Reade

Please show this to Mrs. Dickson, who, if I know anything of human nature, is not much in love with me at present.

18. See Bankson, *op. cit.*, p. vii.
19. See Bankson, *op. cit.*, pp. 244-265.
20. *Hard Cash*, II, p. 152.
21. *Ibid.*, II, p. 152.
22. *Ibid.*, III, p. 328.
23. These and the following quoted lines in this paragraph are from *Hard Cash*, II, p. 232.
24. *Hard Cash*, II, p. 264.
25. *Ibid.*, II, pp. 162-163.
26. *Ibid.*, II, pp. 261-262.
27. "A Terrible Temptation," in *Readiana*, pp. 385-386.
28. *Hard Cash*, III, p. 112.
29. *Ibid.*, III, pp. 119-120.
30. *Ibid*, III, pp. 120-121.
31. Notecard 8H.2. This entry and others that follow from the Notecards on *Hard Cash* can be identified in Bankson's previously cited study, which includes a transcription of the forty Notecards having to do with *Hard Cash*. The Notecards themselves, like Reade's other Notecards, are in my personal library.
32. Bankson, *op. cit.*, p. 247.
33. *Hard Cash*, II, p. 169. See also R. H. Bowers, "'The Canceled Song of Solomon' Passage in Reade's 'Hard Cash,'" *Nineteenth-Century Fiction* (March, 1952), pp. 225-233. In this article R. H. Bowers reproduces and discusses "the canceled passage (from Morgan MS MA 360, vol. 18019), which . . . records a deleted wrangle prompted by Alfred's anger at Jane's interference with his courtship of Julia Dodd." Bower's critical analysis of "the toned-down 'Song of Solomon' passage" tends to confirm my own interpretation of Jane Hardie.
34. *Ibid.*, III, pp. 36-37.
35. See Bankson, *op. cit.*, p. 244.
36. *Hard Cash*, III, pp. 50-52.
37. George Orwell, *Dickens, Dali, And Others* (New York, 1946), p. 53.
38. *Ibid.*, pp. 53-54.
39. Algernon Charles Swinburne, *Miscellanies* (London, 1886), pp. 278-279.
40. *Ibid.*, pp. 274-275.
41. *Ibid.*, p. 300.
42. *Notes And Reviews By Henry James*, with a preface by Pierre De Chaignon La Rose, (Cambridge, Mass., 1921), p. 111.

Griffith Gaunt:
"The Great Passions That Poets Have Sung"

1. This epigraph from "The Prurient Prude" is reprinted in *Readiana*, pp. 426-427.

2. I am referring to the manuscript in the Pierpont Morgan Library entitled

"I Original Drafts of
various Passages
in
Hard Cash
afterwards suppressed
or re-written"
Bound with the above (I) is
"II Original Draft
of a Letter by Charles Reade
to the Editor of
"The Daily News"
replying to an attack on
"Hard Cash"
made by Dr. Bushman"

3. Michael Sadleir, *Bulwer: A Panorama I Edward and Rosina 1803-1836* (Boston, 1931), p. 396.

4. This letter is in the Henry E. Huntington Library.

5. Quoted by Elwin, p. 183.

6. Quoted in *Memoir*, pp. 324-325.

7. See Edmund Morrison, *op. cit.*, pp. 197-199.

8. Quoted in "Charles Reade's Notebooks," p. 103.

9. See "Charles Reade's Notebooks," *passim*.

10. This Notecard, like Reade's other Notecards, is in my personal possession. My transcription of the Notecard is, for the most part, complete, although I have not always reproduced Reade's exact format, and in a few instances I have not reproduced variant phrasings that Reade himself had crossed out or marked through.

11. *Griffith Gaunt*, p. 13.

12. *Ibid.*, p. 17. Since I shall be quoting from *Griffith Gaunt* often and at length (throughout the rest of this chapter) there seems to be little point in footnoting individual passages. Ordinarily my commentary will provide an identifiable context for these passages.

13. *Notes and Reviews By Henry James* with a preface by Pierre De Chaignon La Rose (Cambridge, Mass., 1921), p. 207.

14. Quoted by Elwin, pp. 188-189.

15. See "Charles Reade's Notebooks," p. 86.

16. George Bernard Shaw, "Preface" to *Three Plays By Brieux* (New York, 1911), p. xxiii.

17. See Percy Lubbock, *The Craft of Fiction* (New York, Charles Scribner's Sons, n.d.) p. 117.

[NOTES TO CHAPTER XI]

Put Yourself in His Place:

Humanitarianism at the Point of a Bayonet

---

1. Unfortunately I have not had an opportunity to consult the new acquisitions in the Parrish Collection of the Princeton University Library. According to Robert B. Martin [in his "Manuscripts and Correspondence of Charles Reade," *The Princeton University Library Chronicle* (Winter, 1958), pp. 102-103] these new acquisitions include "an interesting series of letters and documents related to the lawsuit which Reade instituted against *The London Review* for reprinting excerpts from a review of *Griffith Gaunt* in an American journal of dubious reputation, *The Round Table*. At the time *The Atlantic Monthly* was publishing Reade's novel, *The Round Table* claimed that the publishers of the *Atlantic* had 'no right to use their Magazine to insult young girls and virtuous women by thrusting upon them what no modest woman can read without a blush.' The whole story of how Reade achieved a full apology is given in the letters and papers now acquired; copies of most of the journals are included, among them the *New York Daily Transcript* of January 7, 1867, giving in full the documents of Reade's suit against *The Round Table*." See below, p. 349.

2. See Elwin, p. 362.

3. *The History of Trades Unionism* (New York, 1926), pp. 268-269.

4. In *Put Yourself In His Place*, II, pp. 365-368, Reade enlarges upon these statements. Cf. Frederic Harrison, *Autobiographic Memoirs* (London, 1911), I, pp. 315-327.

5. *Put Yourself In His Place*, I, Appendix, iv.

6. *Ibid.*, p. 308.

7. Bret Harte, *Condensed Novels* (Boston, 1871), pp. 3-6.

8. I established the nature and extent of Reade's indebtedness to this book in my article: "The Sheffield Flood: A Critical Study of Charles Reade's Fiction," *PMLA* (June, 1948), pp. 686-695. I have recently discovered much new evidence on the Notecards, and in the "Notes on 'The Great Flood'" (in Reade's own hand) that appear at the end of the "Original Autograph MS of *Put Yourself In His Place*" now in the Henry E. Huntington Library. But since this new evidence confirms what I had already argued in my earlier article I have not felt obliged to include any part of it here.

9. I have included detailed references to these and other comparisons (between Harrison's and Reade's treatment of the flood) in the article mentioned above.

10. *Put Yourself In His Place*, I, pp. 132-133.

11. *Ibid.*, I, Appendix, ii.

12. *Ibid.*, I, Appendix, iii-iv.

13. *Ibid.*, I, Appendix, iii.

14. Charles Dickens, *Bleak House* (Gadshill Edition), I, pp. 130-131.

15. This entry appears in the Notebook labelled "26 Classificanda 1876." Under this label Reade wrote:

"Reviewed Aug 1877
Skimmed & extracted
March 2"

[NOTES TO CHAPTER XII]

Last Efforts:
Repetitions and Variations

1. Quoted by Sutcliffe, "Charles Reade's Notebooks," p. 82 and reproduced by Elwin, p. 242.

2. Quoted by David Keir, *The House of Collins* (London, 1952), pp. 192-193.

3. See Emerson Grant Sutcliffe, "Charles Reade's Notebooks," *SP*, Jan., 1930, p. 96, for Reade's own commentary in another Notebook.

4. The notes I refer to are bound up with the "Original Autograph MS. of *Put Yourself In His Place*" in the Henry E. Huntington Library.

5. Quoted by Elwin, p. 216.

6. This letter is in the Yale Collection of Reade's letters and manuscripts.

7. Quoted by Elwin, p. 242.

8. Quoted by Elwin, p. 293.

9. This excerpt and those that follow I have taken from Elwin, who reproduces the correspondence between Reade and Blackwood at length (pp. 293-314).

10. *A Woman Hater*, II, p. 313.

11. *Ibid.*, p. 524.

12. *A Perilous Secret*, p. 299.

13. *Ibid.*, p. 362.

14. I am quoting from M. L. Parrish's reproduction of the title-page. The play itself was not published. See M. L. Parrish, *Wilkie Collins and Charles Reade* (London, 1940), p. 236.

15. This letter, which is in the Huntington Collection, has already been

quoted by Bradford A. Booth in his "Trollope, Reade, and *Shilly-Shally*" (*The Trollopian*, Part Two, June, 1947), p. 46.

16. These letters are in the Huntington Collection.

17. I am referring to the letters quoted in Ellen Terry, *The Story Of My Life* (London, 1908).

18. I am quoting from the "Author's Note" (pp. 70-71) in the copy of *Drink* (presumably an acting edition) now in the London Library.

19. I am quoting from the copy of this play now in the London Library.

20. The title page of the copy of "Love and Money" now in the London Library reads (in part) as follows:

London, 1883:

Printed by J. C. Durant, Clements House . . .

Strand, W.C.

But Not Published

21. Ellen Terry, *op. cit.*, p. 86.

22. This letter is in the Yale Collection.

23. This letter, now in the Henry E. Huntington Library, clarifies the reference that Elwin (p. 290) could not identify.

24. Quoted by Elwin, p. 315.

25. Also quoted by Elwin, p. 316.

26. This letter is in the Yale Collection.

27. I am quoting from a clipping in the Library of the University of California at Los Angeles. The clipping (from *The Theatre*, p. 271-273) is entitled:

Charles Reade

Some Personal Reminescences of the

Great English writer and

Humanitarian

by

Rose Eytinge

[NOTES TO CRITICAL POSTSCRIPT]

Sex, Sadism, and *The Cloister and the Hearth*

---

1. I have summarized the plot of *The Cloister and the Hearth* in *Colliers' Encyclopedia* (under the heading "Charles Reade"). For an excellent account of the earlier serial version of *The Cloister and the Hearth* see Royal A. Gettmann, "The Serialization of Reade's 'A Good Fight,'" *Nineteenth-Century Fiction* (June, 1951), pp. 21-32.

2. *The Cloister and the Hearth*, vol. I, p. 146.

3. *Ibid.*, p. 182.

4. *The Cloister and the Hearth*, vol. II, pp. 169-171.

5. *Ibid.*, vol. II, p. 204.

6. Albert Morton Turner, *The Making of "The Cloister and the Hearth,"* (The University of Chicago Press, Chicago, Illinois, 1938), p. 3.

7. Edmund Morrison, *Charles Reade and His Novels* (unpublished doctoral thesis, University of California, 1940), p. 104.

8. *Ibid.*, p. 105.

9. Turner, *op. cit.*, p. 102.

10. *Ibid.*, p. 103.

11. Quoted by Elwin, *op. cit.*, p. 44.

12. *The Cloister and the Hearth*, vol. II, p. 406.

13. *Ibid.*, vol. II, pp. 468-469.

14. *Ibid.*, vol. II, p. 478.

15. *Ibid.*, vol. II, p. 478.

16. *Ibid.*, vol. II, p. 483.

17. *Ibid.*, vol. II, pp. 483-484.

18. *Ibid.*, vol. II, pp. 486-487.

19. Alex Comfort, "The Rape of Andromeda," *Literature and Psychology* (The Quarterly News Letter, General Topics 10, Modern Language Association, Winter, 1960), pp. 17-19.

20. *Ibid.*, p. 19.

21. E. M. Forster, *Aspects of the Novel* (New York, 1926), p. 182.

22. Although I now consider my earlier criticism of *The Cloister and the Hearth* to be in part mistaken, it does include points (not reproduced here) that help to account for the reputation of the novel. See *"The Cloister and the Hearth,* A Classic Reconsidered," *The Trollopian* A Journal of Victorian Fiction (September, 1947), pp. 71-81.

Addendum to the Notes

SINCE COMPLETING THE PRESENT STUDY I have consulted the newly acquired letters and manuscripts in the Reade Collections of the Princeton and Pierpont Morgan Libraries, and I have been much relieved to discover that these materials seem to bear out my earlier findings and interpretations.

A typical case in point is provided by Reade's letter to the editor of *London Society* (apropos of the illustration of *A Simpleton*) in which Reade, taking up where he had left off some eighteen years earlier in his letters to Fields, sets down his final criteria for judging an illustraton:

> 4. Nothing is worthy of the name of an illustration that could not be transplanted to the theatre and make a tableau vivant interesting and striking.
> 5. Following the same [tests?], nothing is a fine illustration unless it presents a stage situation; that is to say, such a tableau as might bring the act drop down with effect in a theatre.

This excerpt is from one of more than two hundred letters in the Parrish Collection of the Princeton Library. Other letters in the Collection also relate directly to central phases of the present study, and, space permitting, these letters should be discussed individually—along with a number of the letters from the much smaller Harper's Collection now in the Pierpont Morgan Library. Indeed one letter in this latter collection (a letter from Reade to Harpers, dated Dec. 18, 1876) must be quoted at length, since it embodies one of Reade's severest criticisms of George Eliot and her fiction, and lends further substance to the charge (discussed by Morrison, *Charles Reade and His Novels*, pp. 118–121) that the article in appreciation of Reade published in *Once A Week*, January 20, 1872 (and reproduced in "Charles Reade's Opinion of Himself and His Opinion of George Eliot," *The Bookman*, Nov. 1903, pp. 252-260) actually was written by Charles Reade.

In the letter itself Reade launches his attack on Eliot by objecting to Harper's suggestion that the price of his "good stories" be fixed on the basis of what they had paid George Eliot for *Daniel Deronda:*

But really in regard to "the good stories plus engravings I wish you could suggest some other mode of fixing the prices than the bulk of so flabby a story as Daniel Deronda. In Daniel Deronda everything is sacrificed to bulk. It is parvum in multo: Now my stories are multum in parvo. You might as well estimate the precious metals by superficial area and pay what you pay for a bag of feathers. . . . The bulk of Daniel Deronda entails on the publisher a greater expense of paper that is all. The book will not sell any [2 words illegible] for all that verbosity. However with regard to the novel I submit cheerfully to the injustice, because I am much to blame for not discussing this matter with you months ago.

As to the stories I will ask you to consider what follows.

1. George Eliot has a fine mind, but is a novice in Fiction, and cannot tell a story well. I can,
thanks to
[2 words illegible] study of the art

2. She lives with an anonymous writer, and they have bought the English press. and humbugged the English public. But they cannot humbug the American public. She is not so popular in the U S as I am, and never will be

3. If by a cabal she can attain higher prices in England than I can, it is no reason why injustice should cross the Atlantic. The American public prefer me, and I expect to profit by the preference

4. Daniel Deronda is below her average: it is a wind bag To use the [words ?] of Milton it is "Bulk without spirit vast" It is a bungling, ill constructed story with an [ignoble?] heroine, an immoral hero, and a lot of romantic, greasy Jews the Anglosaxon despises . . .

There is no excitement, and no instruction That dreary waste of words leaves on the mind not one really [powerful ?] situation, not one new and salient idea, not one great lesson of virtue, [one word illegible], justice, or public policy. It is [purely ?] a [one word illegible] of a pretentious kind, and its verbosity will land it in the [one or two words illegible] shop in [two ?] years at farthest.

Now my good stories [whatever ?] they may be compared with the tales of Boccaccio, "The Arabian Nights," and the short tales of Edgar Poe, are models of art, construction, and above all *condensation* compared with anything that [poor ?] wordy woman can produce: and each has a solid idea in it.

The illustrations also add to the value of the property, and it's permanence.

As might be expected Reade's paranoiac defensiveness is also much in evidence in the papers and manuscripts in the Parrish Collection having to do with his personal affairs—including, of course, the suit he brought against the *London Review* for repeating the charges of *The Round Table* against *Griffith Gaunt*. Yet these materials, interesting and voluminous as they are, do not seem to offer any very significant revelations; in fact I should say, on the basis of my admittedly hasty survey, that the materials are primarily valuable for the added light they throw on already accepted features of Reade's character.

In a similar sense the notes and preliminary drafts of *It Is Never Too Late To Mend* (included in the Parrish Collection, along with the manuscript of the early portions of the novel) confirm and supplement the evidence on which I based chapters six and seven of the present study. Furthermore I should say, again on the basis of my hasty survey, that at least two of the five newly acquired Notebooks in the Parrish Collection (the Notebooks labelled "Notes for Hard Cash" and Old Notes, Cloister and the Hearth) likewise confirm and supplement the evidence that I drew upon in writing chapter nine and the "critical postscript" to the present study. And while the individual entries in the three remaining Notebooks (labelled "Picture book and dictionary," "Octavus Lex," and "Duodecimo Digest 2") do not seem to be of any great consequence in themselves, the latter two Notebooks are clearly among the very earliest Reade compiled, and the recurrence of entries dated "X59," under such headings as "A Simpleton la Niaise," "De Lunatico," and "Pone te in suo loco" not only tends to confirm my suggestion (chapter eight) that Reade had worked out the essential pattern of the Notebooks by the time he first began compiling them, but also suggests the possibility that he had worked out the ideas for certain of his later novels much earlier than has generally been assumed.

This last possibility actually calls into question a number of points in my discussion of Reade's artistic development, particularly in my discussion of his "last efforts" (chapter twelve), but the points have not seemed crucial enough to warrant revision—especially since, in other respects, the evidence of the two Notebooks seems fully as complementary as that of the other manuscripts in the Parrish and Harpers Collections.

Index*

Abraham (Bible), 138
Achilles, 159-60
Actors and the Art of Acting, On, 74
Actors' Art, The, 69
Actors' Hand-Book, The, 69-70, 74, 138, 243
Actress of Daylight, An, 295
Adam Bede, 127, 223
Agnes *(David Copperfield),* 227
Ahlers, Edmund, 77-78
Ainsworth, Harrison, 65, 78-79, 85, 117, 129
Albert, Prince, 94
Alexandrian, 320
Alien Vision of Victorian Poetry, The, 19
Allen, Mrs., 193
Allen, Henry, 193
Allen, Percy, 39
All the Year Round, 206-7, 211, 231
Amazon, 194, 198
Amazonian, 121, 198, 220
Amelia *(Vanity Fair),* 125, 227 267
America, 11, 16, 47-48, 54, 206-7, 211, 268, 273, 282, 302
American, 152, 175, 182-83, 185, 205, 207, 268, 289-90, 298, 301
Andréa, 297
Angelo (Hugo), 68, 89
Angelo (Reade), 89
Anglican, 250, 289
Annesley Case, 290
Anonymuncule, 199
anti-Carlylean, 17, 55, 129, 132, 159, 313-14, 316, 319. (See also "Carlylean")
Antiquary, The, 12, 311
Argosy, The, 231, 268
Argus, 58
Aristotle, 36
Arnold, Edwin, 303

Arnold, Matthew, 93, 169, 281
Arnold, Thomas, Dr., 28
Art, 295
"Arundiniana," 200, 210, 222
Aspects of the Novel, 311
L'Assomoir, 297
Athenaeum, The, 115-16, 173, 302
Atlantic Monthly, The, 206-7, 231, 268
Auberge des Adrets, 74
Auden, W. H., 16
Aurora Floyd, 73, 84
Austen, Jane, 26, 249
Austin, William, Lt., 164, 167, 170
Australia, 16, 104, 106-7, 130, 132, 134-35, 143-44, 146-49, 153, 310, 313
Autobiography of a Thief, The, 177
"Auto-criticism," 122
Awakened Conscience, The, 95, 97

Bacon, Francis, 45, 54, 57-59, 61, 128, 163, 169, 199
Baconian, 20, 22, 54, 57-63, 77, 79, 81, 85, 98, 100-2, 112, 116, 118, 120, 128, 132-33, 146, 163, 170, 182, 185, 187, 192, 198-99, 202, 212-13, 242, 263, 269, 273-74, 293, 299, 313-14, 316
Balzac, 65, 79
Bankson, Douglas, 210-12, 224
Bataille de Dames, 87
Baylis, Mrs., 39, 133
Becky Sharp *(Vanity Fair),* 142
Bede, Mrs. *(Adam Bede),* 127
Belgravia, 293
Bendigo, 163
Bentham, 45, 53, 61
Benthamism, 23, 27, 45-46, 49, 53-54, 57, 60-63, 169, 201, 274, 282
Bentley, Richard, 173-74, 176-77, 179

---

* This index has been compiled by Miss Harriet Thompson.